Jung

C. G. Jung

Jung

A BIOGRAPHY

Gerhard Wehr

Translated from the German
by David M. Weeks

SHAMBHALA
BOSTON & LONDON
1987

For Else, Gabriele, and Matthias

Shambhala Publications, Inc.
Horticultural Hall
300 Massachusetts Avenue
Boston, Massachusetts 02115

This is a translation of *Carl Gustav Jung: Leben, Werk, Wirkung*

9 8 7 6 5 4 3 2 1

FIRST EDITION

Printed in the United States of America
Distributed in the United States by Random House
and in Canada by Random House of Canada Ltd.

Library of Congress Cataloging-in-Publication Data
Wehr, Gerhard.
Jung, a biography.

Bibliography: p.
Includes index.
1. Jung, C. G. (Carl Gustav), 1875–1961.
2. Psychoanalysts—Switzerland—Biography. I. Title.
BF173.J85W44213 1987 150.19'54 87-9794
ISBN 0-87773-369-4

Thanks are extended to Pantheon Books, a division of Random House, for permission to quote from *Memories, Dreams, Reflections* by C. G. Jung, recorded and edited by Aniela Jaffé, translated by Richard and Clara Winston, ©1961, 1962, 1963 by Random House, Inc.

What we people in this world want most is to seek again what we have lost. But if we want to search for it, we need not seek outside ourselves. —JAKOB BÖHME

I don't want to prescribe a way to other people, because I know that my way has been prescribed to me by a hand far above my reach. . . . I am only trying to be a decent tool and don't feel grand at all.

—C. G. JUNG, 1948 (*Letters* I, p. 492)

Interesting as it is to follow a great spirit in his travels, I am willing to follow anyone only as far as he himself goes with me. —RUDOLF STEINER

Contents

1. "I Am on My Road and I Carry My Burden" 1
2. Origins and Genealogy 9
3. "Possession of a Secret": Early Experiences 22
4. Two Personalities: A Spiritual and Religious Awakening 42
5. Studies in Basel 54
6. Experiments in Parapsychology 68
7. Psychiatrist at Burghölzli 76
8. The Encounter with Emma Rauschenbach 86
9. Sigmund Freud: "The First Man of Real Importance" 96
10. The Inevitable Break 127
11. Transformation Begins Within 161
12. The "Night Sea Journey" and the Confrontation with the Unconscious 165
13. The Work 199
14. Traveling and Tower-Building 215
15. The Encounter with Alchemy 245
16. Eranos: A "Navel of the World" 262
17. The Remarkable Journey to India 278
18. Again and Again, the Religious Question 291
19. National Socialism: "Yes, I Slipped Up" 304
20. Night over Europe: The Second World War 331
21. After the War 346
22. The Codex Jung 365
23. The Signs of Age: Creativity and Growth 371

24. "Answer to Job" 381
25. *Mysterium Coniunctionis* 396
26. A Modern Myth 409
27. Late in Life 416
28. Under the Sign of Wholeness: The Last Days 452

Essays
Western Consciousness and Eastern Spirituality 459
C. G. Jung in Dialogue and Dispute 469
Prolegomena to a History of Jung's Influence 486

Bibliography 493
Chronology 501
Notes 507
Index of Names 539

1

"I Am on My Road and I Carry My Burden"

> I am afraid that my biography, or what occurs to me as such, is unlike other biographies in many regards. Without wishing to pass value judgments, it is quite impossible for me to remember all the myriad personal details, and afterward to overvalue them so that people even tell them over again in all seriousness. I know there are people who, even during their lifetime, live in their own biography and act as if they were already in a book. For me life has been something that had to be lived and not talked about. Besides, my interest has always been held by little but meaningful things that I could not speak about anyway, not at least before I had carried them around with me until the time was ripe to speak of them. Furthermore, I was so consistently not understood that I lost the desire to remember "meaningful conversations" at all. So help me, even Goethe struck me as a pompous turkey when I read Eckermann's *Conversations*! I am what I am—an ungrateful autobiographer![1]

These words of C. G. Jung at age eighty-three, addressed to a correspondent in the United States, characterize the problems faced by the biographer of this "ungrateful autobiographer." This difficulty is not alleviated by the fact that Jung was not at all the totally inner-directed man he described himself (albeit with good reason) to be. He did not live in reclusive retirement from the world, nor shun the company of men. Rather, his life—one rich in adventures both inner and outer, the life of neurologist and psychotherapist, writer and lecturer, and not least, world traveler—gained depth and density, as well as vitality and color, from meeting with people of all levels of society.

Still, no one who had a direct and more than passing acquaintance with C. G. Jung needed to wait for the actual written appearance of his autobiography, *Memories, Dreams, Reflections*, to be convinced of the validity of what was said in his letter. There is no question about it: the leading role in this life was played not by demonstrable external dates and events, but by that which normally escapes careful observation: inner, subjective experience, which can be communicated only to a very limited extent. This is one reason why Jung opposed any biographical or autobiographical presentation during his lifetime, yielding only reluctantly to the unrelenting urgings of his friends and students. Their persuasion succeeded. But was his secret revealed?

A first attempt was made by those students who wished to learn in their teacher's own words how he had arrived at the experience and exploration of the unconscious. The answer took the form of a seminar Jung gave, in English, in Zürich from March to July 1925, lengthy excerpts from which appeared in the later autobiography. But the impetus for *Memories, Dreams, Reflections* came from Kurt Wolff, the former Leipzig publisher living at the time in New York, while he was attending a session of the Eranos conference, of which Jung was a cofounder and long-time collaborator, at Ascona in 1956. Jung's personal assistant, Aniela Jaffé, eventually saw to the copying and editing of that work, which is indispensable for an intimate knowledge of analytical psychology.[2]

The problems I have mentioned naturally arose even as these *Memories* were being recorded. As Aniela Jaffé reports, "I often asked Jung for specific data on outward happenings, but I asked in vain. Only the spiritual essence of his life's experience remained in his memory, and this alone seemed to him worth the effort of telling."[3]

And as Jung had just begun partly to dictate autobiographical material for transcription and partly to remain reticent, he wrote a friend of his student days, Gustav Steiner, of the "impossibility of self-portrayal," because self-deceptions and ulterior motives constantly put in doubt the desired, albeit unattainable, objectivity. Here, too, the letter-writer had to maintain a fact that was decisive and therefore fateful for him, namely that in his life

> all the "outer" aspects [have been] accidental. Only what is interior has proved to have substance and a determining value. As a result, all memory of outer events has faded, and perhaps these "outer" experiences were never so very essential anyhow, or were so only in that they coincided with phases of my inner development. . . .[4]

But how is it that memories of "external phenomena" have for the most part vanished? Jung supposed that he had apparently "never really been with it," although he had taken part in the events of his time "with all my energies." He could also refer to his psychology, and in particular his notions of psychological types, in which this particular tendency of the psyche is called "introversion" ("turning within") and explained accordingly. In contrast with the extravert, the introvert's interests, in accordance with this tendency, are essentially concentrated upon the processes and contents of the inner life. Hence in the end he also arrives at a different evaluation of what he encounters in the course of his life, what he has done and experienced. Both biographer and reader would thus do well to make clear in their own minds, at least to begin with, which of these two attitude types are meaningful for them (setting other typological factors aside for the time being), if they wish to gain entry into the secret work of C. G. Jung.

In fact, to understand C. G. Jung means to be concerned not with the individual and personal alone, nor merely with the individual unconscious, to which Sigmund Freud first helped open up the way. In Jung, as in no other psychologist of his time, the superindividual was paramount. A decisive role was played by the transpersonal,[5] not only as a biologically and instinctually grounded driving force, but as an "archetype," a physical, mental, and spiritual motive power that points beyond man precisely by engaging him in a lifelong process of maturation. This is "individuation," the path to full humanness, which is the central theme of Jungian psychology.

With this we enter a wider space—in the strict sense in which Heraclitus, the Dark One of Ephesus, understood it two and a half millennia ago: "You cannot discover the bounds of the soul, even if you have walked off every step—so deep is its meaning (*logos*),"[6] a statement that has lately been confirmed in multiple ways by modern depth psychology.

This is not an arbitrary theme. Academic discussion is not enough; rather it always involves the questioner himself. It involves the whence and whither, the why and wherefore of human existence in general. It concerns the future and the concrete possibilities for self-realization. With this, dimensions of reality come into view that point beyond the realm of goals and things to the unconditioned—hence also Heraclitus' emphasis on the unboundedness of the human soul. But when it comes to the person who seems to be at home beyond things, this couplet from Goethe also needs to be taken seriously:

> If thou wouldst into the infinite stride,
> Explore the finite on every side.

Thus the various facets of a biography include place and time, environment and contemporaries, interests and goals, and the problems, fears, and longings of an entire century and of an era—in the end, to explore "on every side" means to inquire into the history and the concrete circumstances of a person's life. This in itself is already difficult, for it is hard to shut out the tangle of voices that have expressed themselves with considerable conviction, some for and some against, on the subject of C. G. Jung. On one hand, the circle of students and "adherents" grows steadily, ever since the fruitfulness of the influences and stimuli arising from Jungian psychology became clear. These extend to the formulation of natural and physical scientific and parapsychological questions, as well as religious and wider intellectual ones.

On the other hand, reservations and prejudices against Jung have been great from the beginning.[7] His first professional mentor, Eugen Bleuler, was sometimes skeptical about his young coworker, although he never doubted his outstanding talent. In his *Allgemeine Psychopathologie* (1913), Karl Jaspers expressed rejection in harsher terms. Sigmund Freud, who had chosen his nineteen-years-younger colleague as his "crown prince," attested shortly after their breakup to Jung's alarming "disregard for scientific logic." Since that time Jung's style has been reputed to be difficult and confused—an overgeneralization indeed. Some would see in him an "obscure" mystic, an eccentric esoteric, while failing to make clear what they understand, or misunderstand, by "mysticism" and "esoterism." Others do not hesitate to malign an analyst whom they find disagreeable. Prominent contemporaries, too, were not always very particular, even when it came to accusations involving the catchwords "racism," "anti-Semitism," or even "Nazism." Ernst Bloch, for example, managed to reduce Jung to a "fascistic, frothy psychoanalyst." Yet competent critics of the caliber of Viktor von Weizsäcker had to acknowledge that "Jung has done an extraordinary good for psychotherapy, in that he has humanized it and freed it from its psychoanalytical and scientific arrogance. Through him it has become clear what is really involved in the crisis of culture."[8]

As far as this criticism of Jung is concerned, it is not hard to concur with Marie-Louise von Franz: "The name Jung seldom leaves people cold; when one mentions him, one almost always runs into emotionally loaded rejection or enthusiasm, and only rarely objective judgment. But on closer inspection this generally turns out to be that god or demon, the unconscious, whose existence many modern people do not want to admit, and this is why they often raise the most niggling objections against analytical psychology, without realizing that they do so out of fear. Hence Jung's work lies as a stumbling-block in the midst of contemporary intellectual production."[9]

The creator of this work was intimately bound up in it, precisely because it presents the results of experiences that passed through the person of Jung himself—*personare* means literally "to sound through." Therefore a few preliminary remarks about his physical appearance and the effect he had on his contemporaries are in order.

Count Hermann Keyserling, the philosophical writer and founder of the Darmstadt "School of Wisdom"—where Jung often lectured in the twenties, though he did not identify himself with its intentions—was struck by a "mixture of archaic and modern" in the analyst, a "peculiar roughness, coupled with a very great diligence and flair." This "paradoxically affecting frame of mind . . . found a singularly faithful embodiment in his physical presence. Jung's body was that of a bear, lumbering and strong and agile all at once, without gracefulness; his movements matched his oddly unkempt, even uncouth style; but atop this shapeless mass was set a head with one of the finest noses I had ever seen, and the small eyes had an expression that was not only sharp but refined."[10]

The Berlin neurologist and psychiatrist J. H. Schultz, the originator of Autogenic training, vividly recalled Jung's "gigantic stature" when he met him as early as 1900 or so, and later: "This heavyset, powerful, broad-shouldered man with his immense head, his deep-set brown eyes, now pensive, now flashing, now suspiciously watchful behind keen spectacles, his high Olympian forehead and powerful mouth, radiates mentally, spiritually, and bodily—if we must use these dangerous terms—an unbounded primitivity, in which robust rusticality, childlike wisdom, and visionary fanaticism are all mixed together. A unique personality!"[11]

To the description of Jung's physical and bodily appearance let us add a word about his psychic disposition. Even though the fundamental essence of a person cannot be discerned by means of comparisons or typological classifications, characteristics of this kind can nevertheless help to throw a profile into sharper relief. Jung himself contributed to laying the groundwork for such an effort, both by distinguishing between introverted and extraverted personality types in his system of typology, and by describing the personality that forms part of the concrete life as "Number 1," and the one lying more in the background as "Number 2." But more of this later. Another distinction is also possible, depending on the predominance of either the thinking or the feeling function, of sensation or intuition. Key experiences of various kinds led him to combine the opposition and the interplay of psychic factors, full of tension yet pointing toward a harmonious completion, into a conceptual scheme that can also be applied to the psychologist himself.

In Jung's case, the functions of intuition and thinking played a determining role. By his own admission Jung classed himself primarily as an introverted thinking type. In an interview with the North American psychologist Richard I. Evans, he stressed the role of intuition, for here the subject was the possibility of spontaneous inspiration:

> Intuition provides us with perception and orientation in situations where sense, understanding, and feeling are completely useless to us. . . . This is an enormously important function if you live in more primitive circumstances or are faced with vital decisions that you cannot master with learned rules or logic.[12]

It is obvious how important it is for a psychotherapist not only to grasp human situations, such as those of the unconscious life, at a glance in this intuitive way, but then also to be able to elucidate them rationally and raise them to consciousness. This double functioning of though and intuition in Jung was also confirmed graphologically. In the handwriting studies that she executed on the occasion of his sixtieth birthday, the graphologist Gertraud Gilli did refer to a "predominantly systematic mode of thinking, whose direction is dictated by logic and a gift for synthesis." However, she said, the essential features of Jung's psychological type can only be grasped "if we consider also his auxiliary function. His thinking is deeply suffused with intuition, and hence is in a real sense creative."[13]

Those who were able to observe the subject of this description at closer range, such as his pupil and former analysand Gustav Richard Heyer, could say more precisely how this intuition worked. Heyer likened his teacher's psychic style to that of a medium; at any rate he attested to a "power of perception that could often be called mediumistic" in him.[14] Impressed by the accuracy of Jung's dream interpretations, Heyer wrote: "What appears after such interpretations to be a logically arrived-at certainty (and which he readily offered as 'substantiation' in such cases) was at bottom frequently the result of such a highly intuitive inspiration that one cannot help calling it 'mediumistic'."[15] Many of the reservations against this psychic researcher may rest in no small part on this charisma of his. Such things are held to be incredible or even sinister. Undoubtedly, intuition that extends beyond the normal level does give rise to both admiration and mistrust. But Jung did not allow himself to be particularly influenced by either of these reactions. With characteristic matter-of-factness he once noted:

> Nobody, as long as he moves about among the chaotic currents of life, is without trouble. . . . I am on my road and I carry my burden just as well as I can do. . . . There is no difficulty in my life that is not entirely myself. Nobody shall carry me as long as I can walk on my own feet.[16]

2

Origins and Genealogy

On 26 July 1875, Carl Gustav Jung was born in Kesswil, a small village near Romanshorn on Lake Constance, in the Swiss canton of Thurgau.[1] Carl Gustav was the second child of Johann Paul Achilles Jung, Ph.D. (1842–1896), a Reformed Protestant vicar, and his wife, Emilie, née Preiswerk (1848–1923). Because his father (and his mother as well) held citizenship by birth in the city of Basel, more than one hundred kilometers away, according to Swiss law their son too was a Basler. Their firstborn child, Paul, had died a few days after his birth two years earlier. Carl Gustav grew up for some time as an only child, as nine years were to pass before the birth of his only sister, Johanna Gertrud, nicknamed Trudi (1884–1935).

The little boy could not have preserved any childhood memories of his birthplace on Lake Constance, for only six months later his parents moved down the Rhine to Laufen in Canton Zürich. This small place lies across the border from Schaffhausen-Neuhausen, where the Rhine, some 150 meters wide, plunges over an outcropping of Jura limestone. The barely three-year-old boy's earliest islands of memory emerge here: "I recall the vicarage, the garden, the laundry house, the church, the castle, the Falls, the small castle of Worth [on the opposite bank of the river], and the sexton's farm." First impression of a warm summer day: "the sky blue, and golden sunlight darting through green leaves. . . . Everything is wholly wonderful, colorful, and splendid." And the child's deep sense of harmony: "a sense of indescribable well-being." Another time: "a lovely summer evening. An aunt said to me, 'Now I am going to show you something.' She took me out in front of the house, on the road to Dachsen. On the far horizon the chain of the Alps lay bathed in glowing sunset reds. The Alps could be seen very clearly that evening. 'Now look over there'—I can hear her saying to me in Swiss dialect—'the mountains are all red.' For the first time I consciously saw the Alps."[2]

Life in the idyllic setting of the Rhine Falls lasted only a scant four years. In 1879 Reverend Paul Jung was transferred for the last time, once again down the Rhine to Klein-Hüningen, on the right bank of the river across from Basel and incorporated since 1908 into the canton of Basel City. Here the father was to practice his ministerial calling until his early death in 1896. From the 1880s he was also required to act as pastor for the Friedmatt mental institution in Basel. It is notable that the motif of river and lake accompanied the growing youth from the very beginning. Because water can be considered an elementary symbolic vehicle of the unconscious and spirituality, it is not surprising that the future psychotherapist left his official residence in the urban clinic, soon after his marriage, in order to move with his family to his newly built home in Küsnacht on Lake Zürich. His later workplace and vacation retreat, in its rural setting in Bollingen, was also situated directly on the lake. Thus the secret of Jung's destiny seems to be foreshadowed very early in the proximity to water.

One decisive stamp on Jung's fate came from the fact that he was Swiss, and another is to be seen in the Jung family tree. Switzerland, as a pluralistic state with its three great ethnic groups and three principal languages (German, French, and Italian), embodies a general stability that is expressed in a rarely seen faithfulness to tradition, the cultivation of local customs and dialects, and the careful observance of democratic-federalist rules in the life of the community. Having looked widely around him at other countries, it meant a great deal to Jung to become distinctly aware of himself as a Swiss. Even at nearly eighty-three years of age, he still emphasized how in his youth, in order to visualize more accurately its geographical shape, he had "tackled" Switzerland from four different directions:

> From Germany, the Franche Comté, Vorarlberg, and the plain of Lombardy. From the heights of the Black Forest one looks away over the Rhine into the broad bowl between the Jura and the Alps; from France one hikes over softly climbing waves to the sudden drop into this same bowl. From Italy one climbs over the high ridge of the Alps, shaped something like the hinge of a mussel-shell, and from the east Lake Constance and the deep valleys of the Rhine and the Landquart complete the oval. The people who live in the mussel and around its edges are the Swiss, and I am one of them. The fact that some of them speak different languages depending on their neighborhood is only natural, and means very little compared with the overwhelming fact of the mussel-shell.[3]

A certain "primordial feeling," he said, struck the Swiss Carl Gustav Jung as the beginning of all things.[4] And as a psychologist who lowered the sounding line of research and analysis into the depths of a superpersonal and collective unconscious, he was not indifferent to the cosmic dimension as astrological tradition sought to comprehend it. In the same letter, Jung continued:

> Since we stay in the central mussel, we are "the sons of the mother." Hence the old astrological tradition says that our zodiacal sign is Virgo (the Virgin). To be sure, there is no unanimity in this, for the other version reads that our sign is Taurus (the Bull). This is a masculine, creative sign, but an earthly one like Virgo. This old psychological understanding expresses the fact that what is contained within the mother is a creative seed that will one day burst forth. . . .[5]

To this Jung attributed the unapproachability, stubbornness, and all other such things that might be seen as common peculiarities of the Swiss character. On the other hand, the psychologist saw in the combination of the masculine and feminine principles, expressed in the two zodiacal signs, "the *principium individuationis* as a supreme union of the opposites." In this way he closely connected structural elements of the Swiss mentality with those of his own therapeutic activity.

But fateful predispositions also turn up when one casts a glance at the Jung family tree. Both parents came from families rich in tradition; his mother, Emilie, was from the clerical Preiswerk family of Basel, and his father, Paul, was the son of the noted professor and physician Carl Gustav Jung, also of Basel. But his pedigree is informative not only from the usual genealogical point of view. In the foreword to *Symbols of Transformation*, the book that marked a milestone in Jung's career and signaled his break with Freudian psychoanalysis, the author explained how important it was for him to shed light on his own past. In this connection he pointed out:

> The psyche is not of today! Its age is measured in many millions of years. Individual consciousness is only the flower and fruit of a season, which grows up from the perennial rhizome under the earth, and it finds itself more in harmony with the truth if it takes the existence of the rhizome into account. For the root-network is the mother of all things.[6]

Here there is a dichotomy to be considered. On the one hand there exists in every person an unmistakable individuality, his intellectual shape, which can neither be explained by his bloodline nor grasped typologically. On the other hand there is something like an "ancestral life" that towers above the individual, a physical and psychic predisposition that is related to the individual mentality as a vessel is to its contents. When one considers Jung's life and work more closely, there is no question that his looking into the depths and secret motives of the psyche, with its share in the "ancestral life," was of much greater interest to him than the more Platonic study of the heights of mental individuality. And yet Jung was also Platonic. Part of the special insight he gained in the course of his psychoanalytical research was precisely that the stars had fallen from the sky of the spiritual world and that there was pulsating a "secret life in the unconscious."[7] Or, referring to himself: he, the Swiss citizen Carl Gustav Jung, could tap a yet deeper, hidden side of his nature, a "No. 2," as it were. Hence, recording only the external facts of someone's life by no means touches the secret of that person's being, and so Jung came to the realization that we must pay heed not only to the more outwardly directed threads of a person's life. Precisely because the individual himself is rooted in the past in so many ways, we must also come to grips with the "myth" that permeates and accompanies his outward life-course, engraving, ordering, and illustrating its growth:

> I suspected that myth had a meaning, which I was bound to miss if I lived apart from it in the haze of my own speculation. I was compelled to ask myself in all seriousness, "What is the myth you are living?" . . . I simply had to know what unconscious and preconscious myth was shaping me, that is, what kind of rhizome I arose from. This resolve led me to my years of exploration into the subjective contents produced by unconscious processes, to work out the methods that would partly make possibly, and partly assist in, the practical exploration of the manifestations of the unconscious.[8]

On his father's side Jung's ancestors came from Mainz. Aniela Jaffé, whose genealogical research goes back to the seventeenth century,[9] reports, among others, a Carl Jung, Dr. med. et jur., who held the post of university rector and died in 1654. Jung's great-grandfather Franz Ignaz (1759–1831) married a Sophie Ziegler. He too was a physician, who was in charge of a military hospital during the Napoleonic Wars and who moved to Mannheim with his family.

The best-known personality among Carl Gustav's forebears was his grandfather of the same name (1794–1864). Family tradition had it that C. G. Jung Sr. was the illegitimate son of Goethe. In his student days the grandson seems to have pointed out this supposed fact with some playfulness, or so at least it appears from the description by his former fellow student Gustav Steiner, who recalled: "It was not the legend itself that puzzled me, but the fact that he told us about it."[10] To his coworker Aniela Jaffé, though, the elderly C. G. Jung expressed himself with more reserve:

> The wife of my great-grandfather . . . , Sophie Ziegler, and her sister were associated with the Mannheim Theater and were friends of many writers. The story goes that Sophie Ziegler had an illegitimate child by Goethe, and that this child was my grandfather, Carl Gustav Jung. This was considered virtually an established fact. My grandfather says not a word about it in his diaries, however.[11] He mentions only that he once saw Goethe in Weimar, and then merely from behind! Sophie Ziegler Jung was later friendly with Lotte Kestner, a niece of Goethe's "Lottchen." This Lotte frequently came to see my grandfather—as, incidentally, did Franz Liszt. In later years Lotte Kestner settled in Basel, no doubt because of these close ties with the Jung family. My grandfather was also close to her brother, a diplomatic counsel who lived in Rome, and in whose home Goethe's son stayed just before his death.[12]

It is the way of family traditions to be not always free from considerable inaccuracies, and the same must also have been true of the Jungs'.[13] Apart from this, Aniela Jaffé reported that Jung occasionally spoke of the "annoying rumor" with a certain amusement; at any rate he put up with this inextinguishable story, in view of his high regard for Goethe's *Faust*, even in his old age. What is no less important is that the grandson held his grandfather, whom he never met, in high esteem. Like his father, the elder C. G. Jung had studied medicine in Heidelberg. Politically the era was one of national upheaval, the time before the "revolution" of 1848, in which the issue was not only one of throwing off the yoke of the French emperor Napoleon, but above all of joining together a multitude of rival territories into a united Germany. Culturally, the youth and student days of the elder C. G. Jung were the period of German romanticism. He was personally acquainted with famous writers and journalists of the time, and he also felt the movement of religious enlightenment, which greatly expanded denominational boundaries. No less than the renowned theologian and clergyman of Berlin, Friedrich Daniel Ernst Schleiermacher, converted him, a Catholic, to Protestantism. There were already kinship ties with the Schleiermacher family: Jung's great-grandfather's brother, later knighted as Sigismund von Jung (1745–1842), chancellor of Bavaria, was married to Schleiermacher's youngest sister.

In view of the time he lived in, it was only natural that Grandfather Jung should join the ranks of those students and faculty who demonstrated in favor of a united Germany at the Wartburg in 1817, to mark the occasion of the 300th anniversary of the Reformation. But at that point the reaction struck. As a sympathizer of this early student protest movement, the young man was arrested and imprisoned for thirteen months without proper legal proceedings. Jung became friends with Karl Ludwig Sand (b. 1795), who came from Wunsiedel in upper Franconia, and who had murdered the Russian councillor state August Kotzebue, despised as a reactionary writer. Emigrating to Paris, Jung met the geographer Alexander von Humboldt (1769–1859), who recommended him to the university at Basel. Thus Jung became Swiss. C. G. Jung the elder made a name for himself as a renovator of the medical faculty and was known as an excellent doctor. As a professor of medicine, the university chose him as its rector, and his portrait from the year 1848 still hangs in the old forecourt. As grand master he headed the Swiss society of Freemasons, an expression of his fundamentally humanitarian and philanthropic attitude, which was widely acknowledged. In 1885, the anatomist Wilhelm His of Leipzig wrote of his teacher, the elder C. G. Jung: "In Jung, Basel possessed an unusually full and rich human nature. Thanks to his spirit, Jung gladdened and refreshed his fellow men for many decades; his creative strength and his warm devotion bore fruit . . . that benefited the sick and the needy above all."[14] Here it is also remembered that he had the so-called citizens' hospital enlarged, and founded a home for feeble-minded children that he dubbed the "Institute of Hope." In this connection we find Jung's own assessment of his grandfather:

> He was a strong and striking personality. A great organizer, enormously active, brilliant, witty, and eloquent. I swam in his wake myself. "Oh, yes, Professor Jung, he was really something!" they used to say in Basel. He had a great influence on his children. They not only admired him, but they were afraid of him too, for he was something of a tyrannical father. After lunch he used regularly to take a nap for about a quarter of an hour, during which all his numerous family were sometimes required to remain seated at the table, quiet as mice.[15]

From C. G. Jung Sr.'s marriage (his third) to Sophie Frey, the daughter of a mayor of Basel, came Jung's father, Paul. He studied ancient languages in Göttingen, developing a particular fondness for Hebrew and Arabic. He took his Ph.D. with a work on an Arabic version of the Song of Songs, but rather than entering the scientific career that would have suited his philological talents, he became a simple village parson, being an inwardly directed man in contrast to his famous, strongly extraverted father. He was said to have a kind-heartedness and modesty admired by his rural parishioners; his colleagues sometimes thought him boring.[16] His famous son said of him:

> As a country parson he lapsed into a sort of sentimental idealism and into reminiscences of his golden student days, continued to smoke a long student's pipe, and discovered that his marriage was not all he had imagined it to be. He did a great deal of good—far too much—and as a result was usually irritable. Both parents made great efforts to lead devout lives, with the result that there were angry scenes

> between them only too frequently. These difficulties, understandably enough, later shattered my father's faith.[17]

Jung's maternal grandfather, Samuel Preiswerk (1799–1871), was also a striking personality who enjoyed great prestige in Basel. A preacher in the parish of Leonhard there, he had presided over the reformed clergy as the so-called Antistes, or head vicar. The grandson was able to say later with some satisfaction that, at least through the Preiswerk family, he had roots in the Swiss nation going back five centuries.[18] Samuel Preiswerk had qualified as a senior lecturer in Hebraic languages and was the author of a Hebrew grammar that was circulated as far as America. In the monthly journal *Morgenland*, which he edited, he expressed his interest in the resettlement of Palestine by the Jews—several decades before Theodor Herzl's Zionist movement, which convened its inaugural meeting in Basel in 1897, twenty-six years after Preiswerk's death. Calling attention specifically to his relationship to the supernatural, Jung said of Samuel Preiswerk:

> I did not know my maternal grandfather personally. But from all I have heard, his Old Testament name Samuel must have suited him well. He even believed that they spoke Hebrew in heaven, and therefore dedicated himself with the utmost diligence to the study of Hebrew. He was not only highly learned, but also had a pronouncedly poetical mind; indeed he was a rather peculiar man, and believed himself to be constantly surrounded by ghosts. My mother often told me how she had had to stand behind him while he wrote his sermons. He could not put up with ghosts getting behind his back and distracting him while he was trying to think! If a living person sat behind him, the ghosts would be scared off![19]

In any case, Preiswerk was, as Albert Oeri reports, "a visionary who experienced whole dramatic scenes, complete with conversations with spirits."[20] His second wife, Jung's maternal grandmother, was once comatose for thirty-six hours during an attack of scarlet fever in her youth, and to this was attributed the fact that she was endowed with "second sight." Phenomena of this sort show that Jung had a heritage from his maternal ancestors that allowed the other side of reality to appear more consciously and concretely than is normally the case. Hence Gustav Richard Heyer was justified in suggesting that his teacher possessed a "power of perception that could be called supernatural"—unquestionably an important prerequisite for the doctor and psychotherapist who ventures into the fringes of the human psyche.

This brings us to the psychic makeup of Jung's mother, Emilie. Paul Jung, the philologist, had met his wife in the home of the Hebraist Preiswerk when she was about seventeen. Her son described his mother much more impressively and intimately than his father, from whom he was alienated early on. He praised her as

> a very good mother to me. She had a hearty animal warmth, cooked wonderfully, and was most companionable and pleasant. She was very stout, and a ready listener. She also liked to talk, and her chatter was like the gay plashing of a fountain. She had a decided literary gift, as well as taste and depth. But this quality never properly emerged; it remained hidden beneath the semblance of a kindly, fat old woman, extremely hospitable, and possessor of a great sense of humor. She held all the conventional opinions a person was obliged to have, but then her unconscious personality would suddenly put in an appearance. That personality was unexpectedly powerful: a somber, imposing figure possessed of unassailable authority—and no bones about it. I was sure that she consisted of two personalities, one innocuous and human, the other uncanny. This other emerged only now and then, but each time it was unexpected and frightening. She would then speak as if talking to herself, but what she said was aimed at me and usually struck to the core of my being, so that I was stunned into silence.[21]

This inheritance from his mother's side clearly made a strong impression on the psychoanalyst's own inner experience as an adult. Time and again he pointed out that father and mother are to be taken not only according to their personal appearance, but that there is always a suprapersonal significance attached to them as well.[22] In an early study from his psychoanalytical period, Jung examined—in Freudian fashion—"The Significance of the Father in the Destiny of the Individual,"[23] referring directly to a "fateful demonic power." It goes without saying that Jung, too, cannot be understood solely by his own past; indeed his life's mission clearly consisted not only in arriving at an interpretation of genetically conditioned and early childhood influences, but in working out and thus transforming them with a view to the self-development of the adult. And though Jung always viewed the individual together with those "many centuries-old roots" that determine his lineage, he also stressed just as clearly: "Children do not belong to their parents, and they only appear to result from their parents. . . . The young generation has to start life from the beginning, and can burden itself with the past only where absolutely necessary."[24]

Of course the starting point of such a new beginning is always surrounded by fate-runes; thus Jung's parents were both "the last-born of large families, who belonged to a certain extent to the 'sacrificed generation,' for they had come into the world when their fathers had already been reduced to poverty."[25] Even as a "head vicar," Antistes Preiswerk fought a lifelong battle with financial troubles, trying to maintain his large family. His teaching post at the university was more an honor than an additional source of income. Things were not much different for Professor Jung the elder in Basel. To be sure, through his third marriage to the mayor's daughter, Sophie Frey, he came into "better society," but the prospect of a considerable inheritance came to nothing. In the entry for 20 March 1849 he wrote: "Today I was informed that Papa Frey has lost everything. Thus I have no hope of an inheritance." And because he (a university professor!) had been taken to task for occasionally having spent a great deal on the purchase of books, he accounted for this too, hinting at what he intended to leave to his sons, including Jung's father, Paul: "It is true that I have sometimes spent a lot on a book, but when one considers that I have sons and could have hoped that one would follow in my footsteps, . . . what I have earned goes toward their education. . . . And now, because misfortune has caught up with my father-in-law, because my sons are mediocre brains and cause me worry and anxiety . . . I must . . . provide more for their physical well-being after my death."[26]

Thus Paul Jung was able to finish his philological studies with a promotion to the doctorate, but the funds required for his official qualification in philology were lacking. "But then a relative died unexpectedly, leaving behind a sum of money to be used for the education of a family member who had the desire to become a minister."[27] The emergency seemed to be over. But did Paul Jung really have this desire? To judge from the description by his son, who hinted at the considerable tension in his parents' marriage and made clear his father's serious crisis of faith, it has to be doubted. Obviously Paul Jung was compelled by financial considerations to study theology and change over to the pastorate, without the requisite inner disposition to preaching and the ministry. But where was such a father to find the spiritual leadership that would be demanded when his son Carl Gustav, who was haunted by extraordinary experiences, turned to him for advice? In his memoirs this son drew the sobering conclusion:

> Theology had alienated my father and me from one another. . . . I had a dim premonition that he was inescapably succumbing to his fate. He was lonely and had no friend to talk with. At least I knew no one among our acquaintances whom I would have trusted to say the saving word. Once I heard him praying. He struggled desperately to keep his faith. I was shaken and outraged at once, because I saw how hopelessly he was entrapped by the Church and its theological thinking.[28]

It only remains to add that this unfortunate choice of profession led to anything but a comfortable life. Certainly, as

"Herr Vicar" in a small village, his father was the number one respectable figure, but later, when Carl attended the Gymnasium in Basel, he came to perceive that as a parson's son he lived in quite modest circumstances.

3

"Possession of a Secret": Early Experiences

"My entire youth can be understood in terms of [the] secret," Jung wrote in retrospect. In his old age he added significantly, "Today as then I am a solitary, because I know things and must hint at things which other people do not know, and usually do not even want to know."[1]

What secrets could there be for a child growing up in the sheltered atmosphere of a Swiss village parson's house near the end of the nineteenth century? Outwardly, the years in Laufen above the Rhine Falls, like his life in Klein-Hüningen near Basel, were defined by the everyday routine of farmers and fishermen. The arrhythmia and hectic pace of modern technology were still virtually excluded, and in what did take place there was nothing of the sensational or discordant. The peaceful life of nature in forest and field was reflected in the quiet waters of nearby Lake Constance, or in the river as it carved its channel over the Rhine Falls and away to the west and north. It was the world of the rocks, plants, and animals that attend the rustic life, and the still dream-enveloped play of a child, from year to year. A childhood paradise, it would seem. "Everything is wholly wonderful, colorful, and splendid," says the very early recollection already mentioned. And these early *Erinnerungen* may be taken quite literally as "internal experiences," even when they refer to things heard and seen externally. This is unquestionably the major difficulty in writing a biography of Jung. This inward-directedness was later termed "introversion," or "turning within," in the context of his studies of psychological types. In his old age the only events of his life that seemed worth reporting were those in which the "imperishable world irrupted into the transitory one," thereby presenting him with the raw material, the *prima materia*, for his life's work. Hence that which is perceived with the five senses has also a deeper dimension, one which belongs just as much to reality, and which therefore must not be neglected if one would not lose the fullness of being. Impressions leave their mark: a very small Carl hears some schoolchildren discussing an outing to the Uetliberg near Zürich. Of course, at the age of three or four, he wants to go along too. "From then on the Uetliberg and Zürich became an unattainable land of dreams, near to the glowing, snow-covered mountains."[2] The path of destiny was beginning to open.

When the boy traveled with his mother to visit friends on Lake Constance, he was mightily attracted to the water: "I could not be dragged away from the water. . . . The lake stretched away and away into the distance. This expanse of water was an inconceivable pleasure to me, an incomparable splendor. At that time the idea became fixed in my mind that I must live near a lake; without water, I thought, nobody could live at all."[3] His twofold wish for a life near Zürich and on the lake would be fulfilled—two decades later.

Other memories push their way up, fascinating, cryptic occurrences, like the Rhine fishermen dragging a dead body up on land beside the waterfall and carrying it to the washhouse near the parsonage. They tried to spare Carl, not yet four years old, the sight of the dead man, but he was able to find out what he wanted to know. What had happened to this man was of extraordinary interest to him. Looking back, Jung himself had to admit to "a fatal resistance against life in this world": once, a fall down the stairs caused a painful head injury, the scar from this was still visible until late in his secondary school years. Another time a maid was leading the child across the Rhine Falls bridge toward Neuhausen, when he fell and nearly slipped out under the railing. He was rescued at the last second. But it was not only the mightily roaring falls whose peculiar marginal experiences marked a danger zone, for the immediate vicinity of the parsonage, church, and cemetery also seemed to be included; at any rate this is how it seemed to the son of Reverend Paul Jung:

> In the cemetery nearby, the sexton would dig a hole—heaps of brown, upturned earth. Black, solemn men in long frock coats with unusually tall hats and shiny black boots would bring a black box. My father would be there in his clerical gown, speaking in a resounding voice. Women wept. I was told that someone was being buried in this hole in the ground. Certain persons who had been around previously would suddenly no longer be there. Then I would hear that they had been buried, and that Lord Jesus had taken them to himself. . . . I began to distrust Lord Jesus. He lost the aspect of a big, comforting, benevolent bird and became associated with the gloomy black men in frock coats, top hats and shiny black boots who busied themselves with the black box. These ruminations of mine led to my first conscious trauma.[4]

These as yet inarticulate fears were eased somewhat by the bedtime prayer that mother and child would say together: "Spread out thy wings, Lord Jesus mild,/And take to thee thy chick, thy child./'If Satan would devour it,/No harm shall overpower it,'/So let the angels sing!" The question was, what was this "Lord Jesus," who had a tendency toward darkness, and whom his own father served in his black frock coat, really like? Was he the Jesus of the reassuring evening prayer, or was he the one who called people away from life and took them to him deep in the grave? A world of enigmas and secrets had opened up, the night realm of the soul, and at the same time the sphere of dreams and imagination, which was to be a lifelong source from which Jung could draw the "raw material" for his scientific work.

His first remembered dream, which he had at the age of three or four when he and his parents still lived in Laufen on the Rhine, is already especially significant in this regard. It remained with the dreamer throughout his life, and more than six decades would pass before Jung, as a mature man of sixty-five, explained the content of his dream: the boy sees himself standing before a dark, rectangular, stone-lined hole which he finds in a large meadow (the one behind the sexton's farm), not far from his parents' house. What the child saw in the dream was unlike anything he had ever seen before. Jung reported:

> I ran forward curiously and peered down into it. Then I saw a stone stairway leading down. Hesitantly and fearfully, I descended. At the bottom was a doorway with a round arch, closed off by a green curtain. It was a big, heavy curtain of worked stuff like brocade, and it looked very sumptuous. Curious to see what might be hidden behind, I pushed it aside. I saw before me in the dim light a rectangular chamber about thirty feet long. The ceiling was arched and of hewn stone. The floor was laid with flagstones, and in the center a red carpet ran from the entrance to a low platform. On this platform stood a wonderfully rich golden throne. I am not certain, but perhaps a red cushion lay on the seat. It was a magnificent throne, a real king's throne in a fairy tale. Something was standing on it which I thought at first was a tree trunk twelve to fifteen feet high and about one and a half to two feet thick. It was a huge thing, reaching almost to the ceiling. But it was of a curious composition: it was made of skin and naked flesh, and on top there was something like a rounded head with no face and no hair. On the very top of the head was a single eye, gazing motionlessly upward. . . . The thing did not move, yet I had the feeling that it might at any moment crawl off the throne like a worm and creep toward me. I was paralyzed with terror. At that moment I heard from outside and above me my mother's voice. She called out, "Yes, just look at him. That is the

> man-eater!" That intensified my terror still more, and I awoke sweating and scared to death. For many nights afterward I was afraid to go to sleep, because I feared I might have another dream like that.[5]

This is an uncommonly richly differentiated, "grand" dream, even granting that the reporter may have discerned its individual details little by little, impressed by the urgent presence of this inner vision, as is true at least for the dimensions we are given. Certainly several decades went by until it was first recorded. And what of its content, its meaning? Here too, it was only after decades that Jung began to discover that this terrifying, numinously tinged event must involve a ritual phallus, a mystery object to be kept hidden, like those (of more limited dimensions, of course) that played a central role in the mystery places of antiquity. That it could not have come from a mere fragment of memory from within the child's experience is obvious. Hence what is seen in the dream picture goes beyond the memory, and as such is of a suprapersonal character. The depression in the meadow likely refers to a grave. "The grave itself was an underground temple whose green curtain symbolized the *meadow*, in other words the mystery of Earth with her covering of green vegetation. . . . At all events, the phallus of this dream seems to be a subterranean god 'not to be named,'" said Jung.[6] Is this alleged "man-eater" not the underground counterpart of the ambivalent "Lord Jesus"?

Jung's method of "amplification"—that is, accumulating related motifs from intellectual and religious history—comes to the fore here. Jung's long-time coworker Marie-Louise von Franz, an important exponent of analytical psychology, says correctly in this connection, "A whole book could be written about this deeply meaningful dream symbol,"[7] for the historical documentation collected in such a book would constitute just such amplifications, and would require psychological explanation and individual assimilation in its own right. One need only consider the powerful phallic deities—native to many religions, such as those of the Celts, the Germanic peoples and Greeks, in Egypt, the ancient Near and Middle East, and the religions of the Far East—who are the embodiment of creative, life-bestowing power. "For there is no temple," says a text from the sphere of early Christian gnosticism, "in which the hidden thing [the phallus] did not stand naked before the entrance, standing erect and wreathed with the fruits of all becoming. . . . And this mystical symbol the Greeks adopted from the Egyptians, and they preserve it to this day. Hence we see that the *hermae* are worshiped by them in this form. The Cyllenians, however, revere it especially as the *Logos*. That is, 'Hermes is the *Logos*.' . . . This is the many-named, thousand-named, ungraspable thing which every creature aspires after in ever-changing ways."[8]

In other words, the gnostic figure of the Anthropos, or original man, appears as a nature-fulfilling procreative spirit, a symbol of the "union of spiritually alive and physically dead matter,"[9] as Jung put it. This touches upon the great theme of the *mysterium coniunctionis*, the secret of the union of the opposites, which is discussed in depth in Jung's late work of the same title,[10] as well as under the heading of *Psychology and Alchemy*.[11] All these, and many other accumulated elements through which the meaningfulness of this first early childhood dream becomes clear, already suggest the physician and psychotherapist's mature work. But in the first place the dream motif itself indicates the birth of his spiritual life; more precisely, this dream of the majestic subterranean god is both a symbol of spiritual birth and an anticipatory image of the goal of the maturing human personality, and thus of what will be aimed for on the road to individuation.

Yet this life, taking root in secret, is complemented by a further aspect, that of death and the grave. Significantly, the dream locates this ritual phallus in the depths of a hole in the earth. And for this, too, numerous historical religious parallels can be adduced. Von Franz, pointing out expressly that Jung's childhood dream is constellated around a *grave*-phallus, continues: "The ancient Etruscans, Romans, and Greeks used to erect such things over a man's grave; they served as symbols of the dead person's continued spiritual existence and guarantors of his resurrection. In Jung's dream the deceased clearly becomes a king, who now awaits resurrection in the form of a grave-phallus. In the same way the dead sun-king in ancient Egypt, for example, was worshiped as Osiris and represented as a pillar of Djed. Setting up this pillar in the burial chamber signified the arising of the dead, or rather the god Osiris, the green or black god of the lower world who also embodied the spirit of vegetation."[12]

Finally, we must not overlook the time at which the childhood dream appeared to Jung. It was the moment when the cry "God is dead" was ringing out. If we can locate Jung's dream in the year 1879–80, then there is barely a year between it and this famous proclamation of Friedrich Nietzsche, recorded in his book of aphorisms, *Joyful Wisdom* (1881), conceived during his summer stay in Sils Maria (thus also in Switzerland). And it was not only the death of God that the great "soul-diviner"[13] had described—before Freud, Adler, or Jung. Did he not also already have an inkling, after the great eclipse and darkness of God, of the "next steps," that "almost indescribable kind of light, happiness, relief, cheerfulness, encouragement, dawn"?[14] Furthermore, Jung must have felt even within his own family—beginning, for instance, with his father's inability to believe—how fragile the traditional theology and religion of the dead god had become. But if the religious-historical amplification of the phallus's double aspect of death and life is correct, then C. G. Jung's childhood dream signals an experience of special importance. It is an announcement that in the midst of a time of God-is-dead consciousness, new life is stirring from the depths of the psyche, struggling toward the light of consciousness in the form of an obscure, yet-unbroken code. We may concur with Thorkil Vanggaard's assertion that the conscious understanding of phallic symbolism has been lost, its expressive function now mainly seen only in terms of masculine dominance and supposed feminine inferiority: "Not only has the symbolism of the phallus become foreign to us, but also many of its outward forms we no longer understand. Their disappearance from our everyday life is closely linked to the far-reaching social upheavals of our time."[15]

And yet this symbol can and should be interpreted beyond its social aspect, especially when we read Jung's childhood dream within the intellectual and historical context of Nietzsche's proclamation that "God is dead" and connect both with the modern experience, as well as nonexperience, of God. For even for Nietzsche, the preacher's son, new horizons were beginning to open amid the twilight of God. Jung for his part understood this dream for himself personally as an initiation "into the secrets of the earth":

> What happened then was a kind of burial in the earth, and many years were to pass before I came out again. Today I know that it happened in order to bring the greatest possible amount of light into the darkness. It was an initiation into the realm of darkness. My intellectual life had its unconscious beginning at that time.[16]

Further experiences of this kind appeared as time went on, even if not all caused such a shock as the first dream. Gradually, however, it was possible to classify them with it. For the growing child, whose daily life was spent in the village school in Klein-Hüningen, playing with farm children of his own age, a secret life had begun, which those around him suspected practically nothing of. What presented itself over the years to the outside observer was more the picture of a solitary child, a loner. Albert Oeri, his childhood friend and later editor of the Basler *Nachrichten*, who rose to a position in the Swiss National Council, relates: "I suppose I saw Jung for the first time in my life when we were still very small boys. My parents were visiting his, and they wanted their little sons to play together. But it was no use. Carl sat in the middle of a room, busying himself with a little game of ninepins and not taking the least notice of me. Why do I even remember this encounter after some fifty-five years? Probably because I had just never run across such an asocial monster. I was brought up in an exuberantly crowded nursery, where you either played together or got beaten up, but either way you constantly associated with people; he was all by himself—his sister had not yet been born at that time."[17]

The subject of this portrayal confirmed the description, attributing it to the great sensitivity and vulnerability of a child, and on the other hand to the great loneliness of his early youth:

> I played alone, and in my own way. Unfortunately I cannot remember what I played; I recall only that I did not want to be disturbed. I was deeply absorbed in my games and could not endure being watched or judged while I played them.[18]

Which even unacquainted observers were bound to do when one kept busy manipulating stones, or working on the large stone blocks of the old garden wall. The crevices between the blocks invited one to light a little fire, which had to be continually rekindled and fed. Helpers might need to be recruited for this who would collaborate with equal zeal. But these schoolmates also had their influence:

> I found that they alienated me from myself. When I was with them I became different from the way I was at home. I joined in their pranks, or invented ones which at home would never have occurred to me, so it seemed; although, as I knew only too well, I could hatch up all sorts of things when I was alone. It seemed to me that the change in myself was due to the influence of my schoolfellows, who somehow misled me or compelled me to be different from what I thought I was. The influence of this wider world, this world which contained others beside my parents, seemed to me dubious if not altogether suspect and, in some obscure way, hostile. . . . I became increasingly aware of the beauty of the bright daylight world where "golden sunlight filters through green leaves. . . .[19]

So there was on the one hand an emergence from the interior realm of childish self-absorption, and on the other a seduction into a kind of double life. One lived with others and yet was apart from them. The passion for solitude, the delight of being alone, predominated.[20] Close at hand, and reliable in a peculiar way, there was

> an inescapable world of shadows filled with frightening, unanswerable questions which had me at their mercy. My nightly prayer did, of course, grant me a ritual protection since it concluded the day properly and just as properly ushered in night and sleep. But the new peril lurked by day. It was as if I sensed a splitting of myself, and feared it. My inner security was threatened.[21]

But is it really possible to experience this "inescapable world of shadows" that is the dark side of nature and psyche, without some such split within the self, or without exposing oneself to symptoms of neurosis? Behind this childhood neurosis of C. G. Jung we see a "psychically conditioned disturbance of health whose symptoms are the indirect consequence and symbolic expression of an unhealthy psychic conflict which remains unconscious."[22] Jung himself regarded neurosis as a part of the individual's struggle to reconcile the seemingly contradictory, opposing aspects of the self. One who is neurotic, however, does not succeed especially well in this.[23] Hence the tension between the child's everyday world and just that dimension that exists beyond the everyday cannot be ignored. This other side of reality was already present in the person of his own mother. Jung himself described what the nighttime atmosphere felt like to him in his childhood.

As a child he slept in his father's room. But from the door to his mother's room he thought he could feel "frightening influences"—the perceptions of an extraordinarily sensitive and intuitive person. "At night Mother was strange and mysterious."[24] It was this side of his mother's nature, her mysteriousness and the immeasurable depths of the maternal principle in general, that put an ineluctable stamp on her son. Frightening dreams began to appear, in which, for example, objects would grow into gigantic shapes and roll toward the sleeping child. At about seven years of age he suffered from a

▲ Jung's mother, Emilie Jung-Preiswerk (1848–1923).

◀ (*Above*) Jung's father, Johann Paul Achilles Jung (1842–1896).

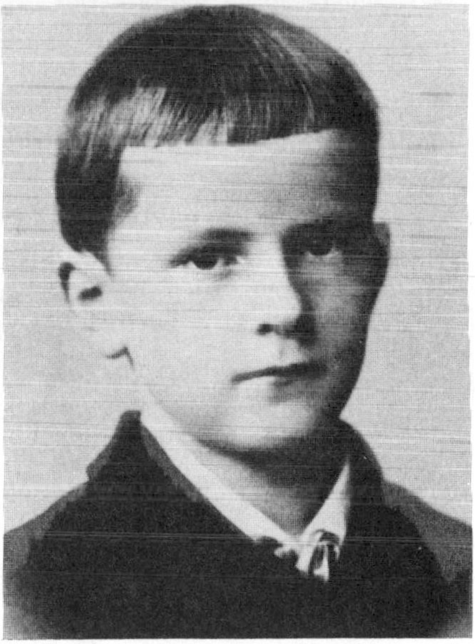

Carl Gustav Jung at age six. ▶

◀ Nineteenth-century drawing of the parsonage in Klein-Hüningen, near Basel (rear view).

so-called pseudo-croup, a childhood disease accompanied by choking fits, which can occur in nervous children with a tendency to hypersensitivity.

So how could the child, from the age of eight to around ten, protect himself against the ominous, primally dark, and confusing influences of the "other side"? The nighttime prayer often failed to provide enough "ritual protection." The religious life of church and parsonage proved of little help. It was not the first time that a preacher's child confessed how reluctantly he went to church. Moreover, in C. G. Jung's case it was the Reformed church, which had divested itself of all sacred trappings. The congregation, as they sang, prayed, and listened to the Word, had to content themselves with a pictureless space. But there was an exception:

> The one exception was Christmas Day. The Christmas carol "This Is the Day That God Has Made" pleased me enormously. And then in the evening, of course, came the Christmas tree. Christmas was the only Christian festival I could celebrate with fervor.[25]

As the traditional religion neither satisfied his need for insight and experience nor had any therapeutic help to offer, instinct and intuition had to take effect in the child's games—his familiarity with rocks, plants, and animals and his play with fire have already been mentioned. Special stones fascinated Carl, such as the smooth, blackish pebble from the Rhine that the boy painted colorfully with watercolors so that an upper and a lower part were clearly contrasted with each other. In this way the everyday stone took on a special, individual quality, and so the ten-year-old pondered over what kind of container he should fashion for it.

> I had in those days a yellow, varnished pencil case of the kind commonly used by primary-school pupils, with a little lock and the customary ruler. At the end of this ruler I now carved a little manikin, about two inches long, with frock coat, top hat, and shiny black boots. I colored him black with ink, sawed him off the ruler, and put him in the pencil

> case, where I made him a little bed. I even made a coat for him out of a bit of wool.[26]

Next to this figure Carl laid the carefully prepared stone, and the mystery object was finished. Now it only remained to find a suitable secret place for it, where no one could discover it.

> Secretly I took the case to the forbidden attic at the top of the house (forbidden because the floorboards were worm-eaten and rotten) and hid it with great satisfaction on one of the beams under the roof—for no one must ever see it! I knew that not a soul would ever find it there. No one could discover my secret and destroy it. I felt safe, and the tormenting sense of being at odds with myself was gone.[27]

Obviously this story refers to much more than simply a meaningless childish game—insofar as childhood fantasies and games can ever be called meaningless. The fire-play, the encounter with the great phallic stone, and the hand-whittled little man with its blackish pebble were signatures and landmarks of an inner development. The ritual actions connected with them imparted a sense of self to the child, shored up by the elemental, primitive feeling that played such a remarkable role for C. G. Jung. The Catholic theologian Johannes Tenzler notes on this point: "This instinctive act of dissociation on the part of a ten-year-old, without lapsing into old familiar—and therefore intelligible—escapist tendencies, is plainly admirable, but such courage and independence are characteristic of Jung."[28]

If we wish to penetrate the basic structure of the Jungian mentality, this assertion still needs further clarification. If, in connection with his initiation-dream (his "initiation into the realm of darkness"), Jung spoke of the beginning of his spiritual life, what was meant by "spirit" is not the Logos of the heights of the ideal, but the Eros of the chthonic and primitive depths; not the paternal, but the maternal principle. This anthropological situation was duplicated and symbolized in his actual relationship to his father and mother. The son loved both, at least as far as his conscious attitude was concerned.

But in his father, contact with the life-bearing powers of the depths seemed to have been lost; the original powers of the religious tradition had evaporated. For him, the theologian, "God" was dead. This could not help but lead to tension between father and son. His relationship to his mother, with her inherited astral and extrasensory talents, turned out to be much more positive. And yet one would be misinterpreting Jung if one tried to assign him exclusively to the world of the "mothers." Though a "thoroughly chthonic man" (J. Tenzler), he was no prisoner of those depths. The importance of C. G. Jung lies precisely in the fact that he recognized the threat from the chthonic, maternal side and—at first for himself, later, as therapist, for others—sought to open a way *through* the world of the mothers. In the end, what matters is to escape the danger of being devoured by the powers of the unconscious and to set out on the road to light and consciousness. This is where the motif of the hero comes in, to which Jung gave particular attention in his works (*Symbols of Transformation*, among others). On one hand, the hero is expressed in innumerable mythical examples as well as in striking fairy-tale characters (such as the brave little tailor, among others), and on the other he simply personifies the prototype of humankind:

> The hero represents man's unconscious self. This appears empirically as the sum total and the quintessence of all archetypes, and thus it also includes the type of the "father," that is, the wise old man. In this sense the hero is his own father, and begets himself.[29]

This individuation or self-becoming—as Jung's psychology shows—requires a special amount of courage. So one will not go wrong in viewing even the early experiences of the child in this light; indeed it involves growing through the frightening, numinous events, to awaken step by step to one's own personality. Thus Jung's autobiographical description of the dawning of his ego-consciousness is characteristic. Of himself at about twelve he wrote:

> I was taking the long road to school from Klein-Hüningen, where we lived, to Basel, when suddenly for a single moment I had the overwhelming impression of having just emerged from a dense cloud. I knew all at once: now I am *myself!* It was as if a wall of mist were at my back, and behind that wall there was not yet an "I." But at this moment *I came upon myself.* Previously I had existed, too, but everything had merely happened to me. Now I happened to myself. Now I knew: I am myself now, now I exist. Previously I had been willed to do this and that; now *I* willed. This experience seemed to me tremendously important and new: there was "authority" in me.[30]

This first experience of ego-existence, rising up as it were "out of a dense cloud," stands in sharp contrast to those—such as that of Jean Paul—in which the ego-consciousness is abruptly there like a lightning flash; lighting up the entire surrounding world all at once, the sense of being-in-the-world becomes conscious for the first time.[31] In both cases it is a birth of ego- or self-consciousness, although the individual nature of both the experience and its description in each should not be overlooked. Whereas the poet (who belonged to Jung's grandfather's generation) compared his experience with a natural phenomenon from above, the psychologist's report still bears a thoroughly chthonic stamp; the event is not there like a flash, but develops like an organism.[32]

This growing consciousness of an inner development was also matched by an external step in Jung's life, the move from the country to the city, the separation from his rural playmates, and his encounter with the "great world": after preparing him with instruction in Latin, Paul Jung sent his son to the more advanced Upper Gymnasium school in Basel. The year was 1886. This city on the Rhine numbered some fifty thousand inhabitants, and for the parson's son it was indeed the epitome of a world "where powerful personages, far more powerful than my father, lived in big, splendid houses, drove about in expensive carriages drawn by magnificent horses, and talked a refined German and French. Their sons, well dressed, equipped with fine manners and plenty of pocket money, were now my classmates."[33]

Here the boy encountered much that was unfamiliar. Unlike most of his schoolmates, he could not boast of weeks-long holidays at the sea or in the mountains. His simple outfit could not stand up to a comparison with their smart school suits. The long walk to school every day soon wore out the soles of his shoes, and it was no secret to anyone that Carl Jung was showing up in socks that had been darned over and over again. It became clear to him how poor his family was, and from then on he began to look at his parents with new eyes, and to understand them better. He realized that they had worries and lived with conflicts that actually cast their shadow even over him, for because of his unusual sensitivity he suffered from the discord in his parents' marriage. That there were only three children born to the Jung family must be surprising, considering the large numbers of children that were common at the time, and also the fact that Paul and Emilie Jung were each the thirteenth child in a family. It goes without saying that today's methods of family planning could not have been discussed between them—both were from clerical families, after all! In short, the incompatibility between father and mother must have been considerable. Moreover, we know of a temporary separation of his parents, to which the child reacted with an attack of eczema. Soon neurotic disturbances arose that overshadowed Carl's childhood life.

As far as school was concerned, other problems were arising. To a boy wholly taken up in his games, classroom lessons were pure tedium. Religion class struck the parson's son as "unspeakably dull." Mathematics produced "downright fear" in him:

> The teacher pretended that algebra was a perfectly natural affair, to be taken for granted, while I didn't even know

> what numbers really were. They were not flowers, not animals, not fossils; they were nothing that could be imagined, mere quantities that resulted from counting. . . . To my horror I found that no one understood my difficulty.[34]

Again the youngster was left to his own devices. He was excused from drawing class, as the teacher put it, on grounds of utter incapacity. But, unknown to him, his pupil was perfectly capable in this regard, so long as what he drew was allowed to take shape out of his imagination. But such a thing was apparently not asked, for what was required, according to the custom of the time, was the rendering of naturalistic likenesses—the more "natural" the better.

Then an escape route out of the misery of school seemed to open to the barely twelve-year-old youth. As he was waiting for a friend in the cathedral square in Basel on an early summer day in 1887, the fairly robust boy received a shove from some boisterous schoolmates. He fell, unluckily striking his head on the curb of the sidewalk, and was dazed for a short time. And as soon as he felt the blow, the thought flashed through his mind: "Now you won't have to go to school anymore!" The thought became fixed in his mind, and from then on fainting spells began to appear, curiously enough, whenever scholastic duties summoned. So there was nothing left for his parents but to withdraw their son from the Gymnasium for half a year. At last Carl had the time he wanted to immerse himself completely back in his world of games and fantasy, to draw caricatures, and to make his first forays into his father's library. "I frittered away my time with loafing, collecting, reading, and playing. But I did not feel any happier for it; I had the obscure feeling that I was fleeing from myself."[35] The doctors they consulted had no answers; the possibility of epilepsy was suggested. No one could foresee what would come next. Then it happened that his father unburdened his heart to a visitor. He didn't know what would happen to Carl in case it was epilepsy, for then he would not be able to earn a living for himself, and they had no fortune—all the thoughts of anxious parents for the future. Their son remembers:

> I was thunderstruck. This was the collision with reality. "Why, then, I must get to work!" I thought suddenly.
>
> From that moment on I became a serious child. I crept away, went to my father's study, took out my Latin grammar, and began to cram with intense concentration. After ten minutes of this I had the finest of fainting fits. I almost fell off the chair, but after a few minutes I felt better and went on working. "Devil take it, I'm not going to faint," I told myself, and persisted in my purpose. This time it took about fifteen minutes before the second attack came. That, too, passed like the first. "And now you must really get to work!" I stuck it out, and after an hour came the third attack. Still I did not give up, and worked for another hour, until I had the feeling that I had overcome the attacks. Suddenly I felt better than I had in all the months before. And in fact the attacks did not recur. From that day on I worked over my grammar and other schoolbooks every day. A few weeks later I returned to school, and never suffered another attack, even there. The whole bag of tricks was over and done with! That was when I learned what a neurosis is.[36]

But even this represented a state of secrecy, in which he had been able to indulge his "passion for solitude, away from the human world." But what had at first been staged as an escape from the unpleasantness of school, and an evasive maneuver from his troublesome contemporaries, presently led the young dropout back into reality—the neurosis and overcoming it were a chance to gain experience on an inner path and receive a push toward maturity. For the dissolution of neurotic symptoms can lead to a sense-making, life-affirming new orientation. Of his childhood neurosis Jung reported:

> . . . it induced in me a studied punctiliousness and an unusual diligence. Those days saw the beginnings of my conscientiousness, practiced not for the sake of appear-

> ances, so that I would amount to something, but for my own sake.[37]

Regularly the Gymnasium student was up by five in the morning, and sometimes even earlier, to prepare himself for school before setting out on the road to Basel. His commitment to school, however, evidently remained on the whole marginal. Whereas his effort and performance—apart from mathematics—were evaluated as good to very good, his teachers said that the boy, who was given to all kinds of practical jokes, did leave something to be desired in terms of conduct. Thus his second-quarter report for 1894 remarked explicitly: "He was reprimanded because of his willful behavior and his participation in disrupting the school outing."[38] And Albert Oeri attests to the fact that even as a boy his school friend had distinguished himself by his loud peals of laughter, particularly when some boyish prank succeeded.

4

Two Personalities: A Spiritual and Religious Awakening

Be it sudden or gradual, the development of the awareness "I am I" marks the beginning of the vital question "But who *am* I, then?" This first conscious self-awareness, though it bestows the certainty of one's own existence, is just the beginning, and above all the foundation that makes possible the search for one's own identity. In Jung's case this ego-experience, emerging as it were out of a cloud, was accompanied by another experience, this time immediate and sudden.

One day the young man looked out of the parsonage at Klein-Hüningen to see a coach from the Black Forest driving by: "A primitive carriage, like something from the eighteenth century." But strange and surprising as this odd vehicle seemed to him, he could not help saying to himself, "This wagon really isn't all that unfamiliar." Indeed, the certain feeling arose:

> "That's it! Sure enough, that comes from *my* times!" It was as though I had recognized it because it was the same type as the one I had driven in myself. . . . I cannot describe what was happening in me or what it was that affected me so strongly; a longing, a nostalgia, or a recognition that kept saying, "Yes, that's how it was! Yes, that's how it was!"[1]

Longing and nostalgia, for what? Rather—these at best in his later life—than considering the notion of reincarnation and taking this present life as a reembodiment of a previous one, another, more perplexing thought took hold of him, namely that this "I am I" was so to speak only one side of himself, as it were only the "No. 1," which was unable to express his whole personality. And this No. 1 was just the village parson's son, the schoolboy from Basel who didn't understand math and who also had so many other sorts of weaknesses. Quite different was the "No. 2" of his personality, for that one commanded respect, as one acts respectfully toward an old, powerful, and influential man. And the boy also formed specific notions of this rather august figure. He wore a white wig, for example, had shoes with buckles on his feet, and rode in that old-fashioned carriage. And something like this was how old Dr. Stückelberger, a famous physician and citizen of Basel who had also lived in the eighteenth century, had looked, as he could be seen in the form of a brightly colored terra-cotta figurine. One of Carl's aunts owned this memorable statuette, which was always an occasion for the boy to wonder about himself—that is, his "No. 2"—when he looked at it. How strongly this feeling of homesickness and nostalgia affected him could be seen in a slip he often made, when instead of writing the date correctly as 1886, the eleven-year-old would repeatedly jot down "1786." He was also fascinated by his grandfather Carl Gustav, who, much like Dr. Stückelberger, had also been a well-known doctor and respected citizen of Basel. Relatives and acquaintances spoke of him time and again, often mentioning the "annoying tradition" that the elder Carl Gustav Jung was an illegitimate son of Goethe.

Eventually the autobiographer became used to the notion that he was really living in two times and embodied two personalities, now the little parson's son Carl, now the respected figure from long ago, who was incidentally not so much a clearly identifiable person as someone who had already lived and died and who somehow had something to do with human nature as such. Hence No. 1 soon found himself more and more attracted to the world of the Middle Ages, as it had been expressed in literary form in Goethe's mystery-enshrouded *Faust*. Is it any wonder that the representative of this No. 2 was entranced with the tale of Faust, having already found this entrance into the world of the late Middle Ages in his early youth?

And in fact, following a suggestion from his mother, Carl did immerse himself in *Faust*, which he now "had" to read. It soon began to have so great an influence on him that he bent every effort to find an interpretation of the Faust legend in an essay. Thus in looking back he declared, "My godfather and authority was the great Goethe himself."[2] Undoubtedly it was the underlying No. 2 in his personality, long since passed away and yet timelessly present, that kept the maturing student on the lookout for more intellectual nourishment than the lesson plan of a grammar school—then as now—could provide. But there was still another existential reason why Carl had to look about for spiritual allies, for the two personalities, No. 1 and No. 2, were constantly at loggerheads. The contradictions demanded to be cleared up. The Church, as would have been obvious, had no help to offer. The time spent in his instruction for confirmation, given by his own father, once again produced only boredom. The consecration itself, and the first communion of the newly confirmed, which was touted as extraordinarily meaningful, left the young man disappointed. Although the Reformed concept of communion—as opposed to the Catholic and even the Lutheran sacramental doctrine—had abandoned the notion of the living presence of Christ, even here it still remained a central article of Christian faith and life. All the greater the disillusionment for a young man who had cherished a special religious expectation that simply refused to materialize when he received the sacrament. The majesty of God (*maiestas dei*), with his grace and mercy as well as his punishing wrath—which was especially emphasized in Calvinistic theology—left the questioner with no answers. Was the God who gets angry with sinners not the same one who had created them, along with the world that had sunk into spiritual death? Is this God himself not jointly responsible for the evil in the world, indeed for the act of sin itself?

For Carl these and similar questions were by no means simply figments of his speculation and curiosity. They had troubled him for a long time. He drew the bold conclusion: "Then it was God's intention that they [Adam and Eve] had to sin." This totally unorthodox idea began to free the young thinker from his worst torments. Now he gathered up all his courage to consider an unheard-of blasphemy, as if it meant jumping into the abyss of hellfire and thereby forfeiting his soul's eternal salvation. In his imagination he saw before him the cathedral in Basel on a bright summer day,

> . . . the cathedral, the blue sky. God sits on His golden throne, high above the world—and from under the throne an enormous turd falls upon the sparkling new roof, shatters it, and breaks the walls of the cathedral asunder.
>
> So that was it![3]

The young man who imagined this scene was naturally not the slightest bit aware of its ramifications, that in the last analysis it has to do with the fact that evil, with its otherworldly potency, can by no means be separated from God and made into the devil, but rather belongs as it were to the image of God, as its dark aspect. And what if this God himself destroys the temporal structure of his Church, from on high and not at all through "evil people or powers"?

In any case, the blasphemous thoughts and the "sinful" image were followed not by the feeling that now God had damned him forever, but rather quite the contrary, a sensation of grace, happiness, and gratitude. Instead of being punished, which the parson's son would have had to expect on the basis of his religious training, the certainty arose in him that he had experienced an enlightenment. What had before been unclear became understandable. In a word, what the young man underwent as he wrestled with the ultimate questions became for him a deep experience of God. It had an entirely different quality from the familiar wisdom of pulpit and catechism, as

The cathedral of Basel, city of Jung's student days.

he had gotten it in school and at home, not least through his father's instruction. And it was this very certainty of God's acceptance of him that stood in sharp contrast to what Paul Jung had to pass on to his son—what for him as a theologian had long since become an existential problem with which he did not seem to have come to terms. Jung devoted a thorough discussion to this opposition between father and son in his *Memories*.

As an initiate into the secrets of the earth from his early childhood, whose interest in natural phenomena, plants, and animals had only increased during his time in school, he was unable to achieve any affinity for all the dogmatic side of religion. Everything ecclesiastical and dogmatic, as it had been presented to him for years, produced in him the same discomfort as the "Lord Jesus" who had aroused mistrust in his early years. Above all, it was the form of religiosity that the youth objected to. The quite different world of mysteries which he lived in, but which he could not speak of to anyone for lack of understanding, was utterly foreign to both his father and his uncles, who also served in the Church. It was his mother who was most apt to have an instinctive access to the domain her son inhabited. Jung recalls:

> At that time, too, there arose in me profound doubts about everything my father said. When I heard him preaching about grace, I always thought of my own experience. What he said sounded stale and hollow, like a tale told by someone who knows it only by hearsay and cannot quite believe it himself.[4]

Since two uncles and six of his mother's relatives were also Reformed clergymen, Carl witnessed many religious conversations and theological discussions, to say nothing of the uncounted compulsory sermons he had to undergo Sunday after Sunday. But it was not in or through these, talking about "Lord Jesus," that he gained the realization of God that he identified in retrospect as "one of the most certain and immediate of experiences."[5] For these representatives of theology—Paul Jung included—would hear nothing of critical debate; they would allow only unconditional belief. All this taken together could only strengthen skepticism and doubt still further, doubt about the credibility of those who demanded "faith," yet who were not themselves moved by the certainty of their own conviction and devotion to Jesus. This at any rate was the young man's impression. For he had seen that his father not only had no access to his son's inner religious experience, but could not reconcile himself to his own faith as a Christian and minister of the gospel, and that he suffered from this precisely because he strove, together with his family, to lead a life as faithful to his creed as possible. The son thought his father had never experienced the miracle of grace. He had taken the Commandments of the Bible as his guide and more or less blindly believed in its contents, as the tradition of his fathers demanded.

> But he did not know the immediate living God who stands, omnipotent and free, above His Bible and His Church, who calls upon man to partake of His freedom, and can force him to renounce his own views and convictions in order to fulfill without reserve the command of God.[6]

In this crisis Carl sought to help his father—the minister's son helping the minister! Vainly he tried to share something of his own experiences, particularly later when he reached eighteen and had many discussions with his father. Resignedly he had to report: "Our discussions invariably came to an unsatisfactory end." The final outcome we already know:

> Theology had alienated my father and me from one another. . . . I was shaken and outraged at once, because I saw how hopelessly he was entrapped by the Church and its theological thinking. They had blocked off all avenues by which he might have reached God directly, and then faithlessly abandoned him.[7]

This sight was bound to remain with C. G. Jung throughout his life. A few years before recording his autobiography, he attempted once again to make clear, to the Protestant theologian Walter Bernet, the point of departure to which the opposition between knowledge and experience we have mentioned, on the one hand, and on the other the materialistic notions with which he had had to come to terms later as a doctor decisively contributed. His letter of 13 June 1955 reads:

> The tragedy of my youth was that I saw my father, before my eyes, so to speak, break to pieces against the problem of his faith and come to an early death. This was the objective, external event that opened my eyes to the significance of religion. Subjective, inner experiences prevented me from drawing from my father's fate negative conclusions with regard to faith that would otherwise have been obvious. I grew up, after all, in the heyday of scientific materialism. . . . I had to rely on experience alone. Paul's experience in Damascus was always before me. . . .[8]

Thus the maturing youth found himself confronted with realities that were of the deepest concern to him, and which he wished he could discuss with someone who knew and had experienced them. But he was left to himself. It was fate itself that made him, in the full sense of the word, an esoteric: that is, a person who draws upon inner experiences and attains insights that render him alone among his contemporaries. Here let us recall an early paper (1909) in which the thirty-four-year-old physician and analyst C. G. Jung discussed "The Significance of the Father in the Destiny of the Individual." He remarked, among other things:

> If ever we wish to see the workings of a demonic power of fate, we see them here, in these dark, silent tragedies that are played out slowly and painfully in the diseased psyches of our neurotics. . . . If we who are "normal" investigate our lives, we see how a powerful hand guides us unfailingly to our destinies, and this hand cannot always be called a kindly one. Often we call it the hand of God or the devil, thereby expressing more correctly than we know an extremely important psychological factor, namely the fact

> that the impulse that shapes the life of our souls has the nature of an autonomous personality, or at least is experienced in this way, so that from time immemorial, as still in modern idiom, the source of such fates appears as a demon, a good or evil spirit.[9]

Jung may have been thinking of his own childhood when he wrote these lines as a young psychoanalyst in Freud's camp, and of the difficulties that attended his fate and that of his father.

Still, Jung's father was anything but authoritarian—quite the contrary. In fact, his permissiveness quite precluded any youthful rebellion in his son. Thus Jung occasionally explained, for example to his student Barbara Hannah, likewise a clergyman's child, that he was in no way compelled to go to church—one simply went.[10] And when it became clear to him after his confirmation that in future he would have to forgo the feast of communion because nothing of religious importance happened for him there, Reverend Paul Jung accepted his son's decision without a word. The suspicion that he was under the influence of a personal complex because he was a minister's son was later always denied by Jung. At seventy-seven he wrote to the Swiss theologian Dorothee Hoch:

> Actually I had a good personal relationship with my father, and thus no "father complex" of the usual sort. To be sure I was not fond of theology, especially because it gave my father problems which he could not solve and which I felt were unjustified.[11]

In this context and elsewhere,[12] in contrast, he did admit to a personal mother complex, specifically with respect to his high regard for the religious life. For Jung, therefore, the opposition was formulated as Religion versus Theology and the Church.

Here, too, it was above all his own experience that made it possible for C. G. Jung to lift the mother complex out of the strict psychopathological framework and to determine more accurately the positive influences it produced in him. It entailed an exceptional wealth of religious sensibility, a wealth "which made the *ecclesia spiritualis* into a reality, and . . . a spiritual receptivity that is a willing vessel of the revelation"[13] To this same sphere of influence also belonged the differentiation of the Eros principle, somewhat in the sense of Plato's *Symposium*—a development of taste and aesthetics, educational qualities calling for feminine powers of intuition, plus a sense of comradeship and gregariousness as well as a historical mind, that is, an understanding of the value of the past which serves to preserve it. In sum, it was the inheritance of his mother's side of the family, of which Jung too received a not inconsiderable share. The outward picture he drew of his mother was that of a rustic matron who, from her physical appearance alone, would more likely be thought of as having a large family of many children, a good-natured, hospitable, merrily chattering, wholly lovable fat old lady.

Yet this characterizes only the everyday appearance, the No. 1 of her personality. Much more significant, as we have seen, was the background figure, which even as a little boy he had already felt to be so enigmatic and powerful, perceiving his mother's sometimes quite terrifying presence even when he slept in his father's room. With this also came the extrasensory talents of the Preiswerk family. Thus there was a considerable difference between her two personalities. The autobiographer traced bad childhood dreams back to this hidden side of his mother, for

> by day she was a loving mother, but at night she seemed uncanny. Then she was like one of those seers who is at the same time a strange animal, like a priestess in a bear's cave. Ancient and ruthless; ruthless as truth and nature.[14]

Jung was convinced that he himself had something of this dark side of his mother's nature in him. From it, for example, came the gift—be it instinctive or intuitive—of being able to see people and things with "eyes in the background": that is, prerationally and without any special deliberation—not always a very agreeable talent, as Jung attested. He said it often happened to him that he suddenly knew something that by rights he actually could not have known. Thus he could speak spontaneously about a situation, as one suddenly says whatever comes into his mind, and leave those present struck with the pinpoint accuracy, and even indiscretion, of what he said. But by the same token there were also sudden emotional outbursts, sarcasms, angry eruptions or curses that could be bewildering to unprepared bystanders—manifestations of the No. 2, just as the son in his turn had witnessed them in his mother. For there had also been "moments when her second personality burst forth, and what she said on those occasions was so true and to the point that I trembled before it." It was much the same with her son, who was compelled to enter into vigorous confrontation with the productions of the unconscious. But his mother was evidently not capable of this, for Jung added: "If my mother could then have been pinned down, I would have had a wonderful interlocutor."[15]

So for C. G. Jung, from his youth, there was a twofold isolation. On the one hand he was left alone with his inner experiences by his father, who lacked anything comparable, and on the other there was his aloneness vis-à-vis his mother, who, though she herself drew from ancient depths of the psyche, was not in a position to speak with her son about these matters and gives him the psychagogical guidance that is needed in youth. We shall not go far wrong in assuming that where the task lay for C. G. Jung, therefore, was in establishing the correspondence between the personality's No. 1 and No. 2, between consciousness and the unconscious, and thus leading the way to the integration of the human psyche, be it as doctor, andragogue, or spiritual leader whose duty it is to set human beings on the road to maturity.

This raises the question of how one becomes qualified for this work, the question of occupation. But is this enough, when it comes to a life's work that goes far beyond what can be learned through school and study, or through traditional professional training? Must one not actually tread the path into the depths in which this hidden side of man's nature, the personality's No. 2, is grounded?

Understandably, the problem of finding a vocation stood in the foreground, especially for his parents, who already by the time he was about fifteen years old sought to discover what profession Carl would settle on. The study of theology and the goal of becoming a minister of the gospel were out of the question; Carl was certain of that from the beginning. One relative or another must surely have suggested it, though—for example, his uncle, who officiated as vicar at Saint Alban's in Basel and who had not failed to notice Carl's interest in the theological table-talk. On this point Paul Jung, though probably for other reasons, was on his son's side, for his opinion was that Carl could choose any field of study he liked, except that he should not become a theologian. "By this time there was a tacit agreement between us that certain things could be said or done without comment. . . . the farther away I was from church, the better I felt," the autobiographer remarked, looking back on this period.[16] His parents supported their Gymnasium student's naturalistic inclination, allowing him to subscribe to a journal of natural science. He reported a "passionate interest" in everything that was discussed in it. Carl began to collect Jura fossils and all the minerals, insects, and mammal and human bones, such as those from the gravel pits on the Rhine plains, that he could possibly get his hands on. And once again the *Memories* indicate that the young scholar was very much more concerned with living entities, such as plants and flowers, than with the scientific analysis of them, which took no account of the hidden, secret meaning of these growing, blossoming forms. But could a vocation be found that would allow the necessary free play for this way of thinking, while at the same time making a living for the one who took it up? To make things more difficult, both of the souls within him, No. 1 and No. 2, laid claims that had to be brought together under a single common denominator. For No. 1 was the student, who was interested in the subjects of natural history, while No. 2 felt himself drawn to the rather far-removed field of the history of religion. While on one hand the young man's interests lay in zoology and biology, on the other it was the questions of biology and paleontology that fascinated him, those disciplines that sought to penetrate into the early reaches of the history of the earth and nature. His particular areas of interest in the framework of comparative religion lay in the Greek and Roman periods; ultimately they went back still further into prehistoric archeology. Only much later did it become clear to Jung how the two divergent interests were connected with the dual nature of his character:

> What appealed to me in science were the concrete facts and their historical background, and in comparative religion the spiritual problems, into which philosophy also entered. In science I missed the factor of meaning, and in religion, that of empiricism. Science met, to a very large extent, the needs of No. 1 personality, whereas the humane or historical studies provided beneficial instruction for No. 2.
>
> Torn between these two poles, I was for a long time unable to settle on anything.[17]

It was in this mood, in the spring of 1895, at the age of nineteen, that C. G. Jung sat at the Upper Gymnasium in Basel for his final examination for university entrance, passing—once again, apart from mathematics—with generally good marks.

5

Studies in Basel

The die was now cast; the road to further study was open. On 18 April 1895, Carl Gustav Jung enrolled in the medical curriculum at the University of Basel. Five years of study, beginning with the summer semester of 1895 and ending with the winter semester of 1900–1901, lay before him. It was the same course taken by his grandfather Carl Gustav—as well as by Paracelsus, who managed to cause a considerable sensation in the sixteenth century. Jakob Burckhardt (1818–1897), the creator and unrivaled master of the modern style of cultural history, was still alive, as was the explorer of the so-called maternal genealogy, Johann Jakob Bachofen (1815–1897), a professor at the university.[1]

Jung's intellectual kinship with a significant nonnative of Basel must not go unmentioned at this point, namely Friedrich Nietzsche, professor of classical philology at Basel from 1869 to 1879, who was also still living at the time of Jung's matriculation, though he was mentally deranged. The year Jung died, he still recalled Nietzsche's extremely strong influence on him as a young student in Basel, and later as a psychiatrist:

> Living in the same town where Nietzsche spent his life as a professor of philosophy, I grew up in an atmosphere still vibrating from the impact of his teachings, although it was chiefly resistance which met his onslaught. I could not help

> being deeply impressed by his indubitable inspiration ("Ergriffenheit"). He was sincere, which cannot be said of so many academic teachers to whom career and vanity mean infinitely more than the truth.[2]

What had particularly impressed Jung, besides *Thus Spake Zarathustra*, were the eye-opening *Thoughts Out of Season*: "All in all Nietzsche was for me the only man of that time who gave me some adequate answers to certain urgent questions which then were more felt than thought," he said in a letter to an American theologian. Two ministers' sons who found the crucial answers for their lives far from home and church!

As he had done in his Gymnasium days, Jung made the daily journey to his lectures and seminars on foot. Taking up lodgings by the individual semester at the home of relatives in Basel was apparently not considered, apart from an occasional visit. And renting a room was out of the question for financial reasons. Not once, when it came time to pay the regular student fees, was there enough money. A stipend for which his father applied to the university was granted, to the beginning student's humiliation.

> I was ashamed, not so much because our poverty was laid bare for all the world to see, but because I had secretly been convinced that all the "top" people, the people who "counted," were ill disposed toward me. I had never expected any such kindness from them. I had obviously profited by the reputation of my father, who was a good and uncomplicated person. Yet I felt myself totally different from him.[3]

In fact Paul Jung had great difficulty in financing his only son's professional education. Apart from the modest sources of income of a village parson, which consisted largely of the produce of his rural community, this problem went back to his ineptitude in handling cash—a trait also acknowledged in his wife, Emilie. There was all the more cause for frugality in that not only were his father's "depressive moods" growing worse, but serious physical complaints were also beginning to appear, as he suffered from what seemed to be "stones in his belly," presumably a cancer that was diagnosed much too late and much too inexactly. Soon Paul Jung could no longer carry out his duties as pastor. Late in the autumn of 1895 he was confined to what quickly turned out to be his final sickbed. On 28 January 1896, Paul Achilles Jung died, not yet fifty-four years old. The studies that had begun threatened to come to a halt for financial reasons. The Jung family had no savings to speak of, and a regular pension in today's sense for widows of clergymen was still unknown. Further, the family was forced to vacate the parsonage in Klein-Hüningen for their successors in the position. With her relatives in the nearby Bottminger Mill in Binningen, Emilie Jung, with her twenty-year-old son and her daughter, Gertrud, only eleven, found a new residence in the spring of 1896. The ancient house, an Alsatian frame structure surrounded by a long-neglected parklike garden, was also reputed to be haunted. The members of the large Preiswerk clan had reported supernatural happenings there; in view of the family tradition already mentioned, such things were nothing out of the ordinary. So in the end it was quite natural that the beginning medical student would be able to extend his extraordinary stock of experience deep into parapsychology. Whereas some of the relatives advised Carl to take up a profession he could make a living at as soon as possible and cancel his second semester, others provided for him to continue his training at the university through their financial support, with the help of loans. In his last year as a student his loan debt had grown to some three thousand francs, a considerable sum for the time, around 1900. "I would not have missed that time of poverty," say the *Memories*.

Despite the economic difficulties and problems at home, C. G. Jung was anything but a sad child. His life as a student, at any rate, included not only his eagerly pursued academic studies, but also social life with other students. As early as May 1895, a few weeks after matriculating, he joined the Zofingia, a Swiss student fraternity. Its Basel chapter, consisting of theologians, philosophers, jurists, and medical students, numbered around 120 members by the turn of the century, and the weekly meetings were attended as a rule by as many as eighty people.[4] Paul Jung himself had been an enthusiastic member of the Zofingia. The young "fox"—that is, freshman student member—got a vivid impression of this when he participated in the fraternity outing to the Markgrafen country along with his father, who—for the last time before his fatal illness—conjured up the old times in a lively speech, abetted by a quantity of wine:

> The words fell heavily on my soul. Once upon a time he too had been an enthusiastic student in his first year, as I was now; the world had opened out for him, as it was doing for me; the infinite treasures of knowledge had spread before him, as now before me. How can it have happened that everything was blighted for him, had turned to sourness and bitterness? I found no answer, or too many. The speech he delivered that summer evening over the wine was the last chance he had to live out his memories of the time when he was what he should have been.[5]

We must picture C. G. Jung, the medical student in Basel, as a tall, athletic-looking young man, although sports had certainly not been among his areas of achievement during his school days. But that only time of boredom in his long life was now finally past. This was not solely because of his student activities in the fraternity, but Jung's years in Basel are unthinkable without the social activity of the Zofingia. Many new friendships were formed. Albert Oeri was there again, his friend of the same age from their childhood days, a grandnephew of Jakob Burckhardt and now Jung's fraternity brother in the Zofingia. In his memoirs of his own youth[6] he described Jung—known in the club as "the Barrel"—as an exceedingly cheerful fellow who was always in a willing mood for any kind of fun. "He seldom got drunk, but when he did he was loud. In the beginning he did not think much of Zofingia dances, idling about with the girls, and such romantic stuff.

But then he discovered that he was really quite a good dancer. At a large party in Zofingen, dancing on the beautiful 'Heitern Platz,' he danced past and fell apparently hopelessly in love with a young French-speaking girl. The next morning he went into a shop, asked for two wedding rings, laid twenty centimes on the counter, said thank you very much, and was about to leave. But the owner stammered something about the rings costing so and so many francs. Then Jung gave them back, picked up his twenty centimes again and left the store, cursing the proprietor who had the nerve to keep him from getting engaged just because he happened to have no more than twenty centimes. The groom was very embarrassed, but he did not take up the subject again, and so 'the Barrel' went on for quite a few more years without getting engaged." Jung himself could give examples of his enforced frugality, such as the fact that a box of cigars that he got as a gift actually lasted almost an entire year because he only dared to allow himself a smoke on Sundays. Still, despite a shortage of luxuries, Jung seems to have enjoyed the obligatory evening drinking parties in the "Breo," the old Zofingia tavern in the suburb of Steinen, until late into the night. Then a considerable stretch of road still had to be walked to get back to the "Bottminger Mill." The road led through a wood with the romantic-sounding name of Nightingale Woods, where it was popularly rumored that weird things happened. Oeri recalls: "As we left the inn, he [Jung] would simply start telling one of us something especially interesting, and so you would go along with him, without noticing it, to his front door. On the way he would interrupt himself, pointing out, 'Right here is where Doctor Götz was murdered that time,' or something like that. Then when saying goodbye he would lend you a revolver for the trip home. I wasn't afraid of Doctor Götz's ghost or of living fiends, but I was of Jung's revolver in my coat pocket."[7]

Probably more significant is another story of Oeri's, according to which "Jung, the self-willed outsider, occasionally held everyone under his intellectual thumb." This alludes to Jung's ability to fascinate his colleagues in lectures of all sorts and discussions on the most controversial subjects possible. The minutes of these meetings give an insight into the young medical student's areas of interest. For example, at the age of about twenty-two or twenty-three he expressed his opinion "On the Limits of Exact Science," a favorite basic theme at the end of the nineteenth century. He also spoke on "The Value of Speculative Research"—psychology was already beginning to play a role, which is all the more remarkable as the 1890s, at least in official scholarship and teaching, were the time when scientific materialism was in the ascendancy. Hence anyone who seriously engaged in the rapidly growing spiritist and psychological literature, as Jung did with great eagerness, was risking his reputation as an educated man. Albert Oeri, who took notes on this early lecture on psychology, recorded no fewer than thirty comments in response to it. Also on the list of Jung's topics was "Reflections on Approaches to Christianity," with the subtitle "With Particular Consideration of Albrecht Ritschl." Ritschl (1822–1889), a Protestant theologian influential before and around 1900, wished to reject the old metaphysics and introduce a new, stronger relationship to faith, with reference to the historical influence of Jesus on one hand and insistently in accordance with Martin Luther on the other. Jung, who even when his father was alive had explored his small theological library, reading among other things Aloys Emanuel Biedermann's Hegelian-oriented dogmatics in order to gain some clarity on the question of God, afterward remained close to his father's former vicar and discussed with him questions of contemporary theology as well as the early church fathers and the history of dogma.

At the end of his second semester, Jung made a discovery that would be fraught with consequences for him, and which must have had a lasting influence on his activity as a student lecturer as well. In the collection of an art historian, the father of one of his colleagues, he found a small book on "psychic phenomena." It was an account of the beginnings of spiritism and came from the pen of a theologian. Since 1882, when the

Society for Psychical Research was founded, critical standards had begun to be applied widely to the evaluation of so-called occult phenomena. Thus it was hoped that headway could be made step by step in a field entailing innumerable possibilities for deception. At first Jung could not suppress doubts about what was described, but they were quickly dissipated,

> for I could not help seeing that the phenomena described in the book were in principle much the same as the stories I had heard again and again in the country since my earliest childhood. The material, without a doubt, was authentic. But the great question of whether these stories were physically true was not answered to my satisfaction. Nevertheless, it could be established that at all times and all over the world the same stories had been reported again and again. There must be come reason for this, and it could not possibly have been the predominance of the same religious conceptions everywhere, for that was obviously not the case. Rather it must be connected with the objective behavior of the human psyche. But with regard to this cardinal question—the objective nature of the psyche—I could find out absolutely nothing, except what the philosophers said.[8]

This was Jung's great concern. For what he learned in the courses in science and natural philosophy he took at the university surely extended his factual knowledge in unprecedented ways. This sort of scientific research, he had to admit, even guaranteed a high degree of precision and accuracy through measurement and experimental verification. But what this field provided in the way of real insight was in fact relatively scant, and as a rule of a quite specialized kind. Jung felt the lack of depth and comprehensiveness. And because he knew from his philosophical reading (Arthur Schopenhauer and Immanuel Kant, for example) that in the end it was the psyche that lay behind all this, the most comprehensive knowledge of the psyche possible seemed to him indispensable. Most of the time, however, it was tacitly taken for granted, for example by the great physician and psychologist of the romantic period, Carl Gustav Carus (1789–1869), or else one started from some more intuitive understanding of the soul, which could not, or could no longer, be regarded as a universal possession.

All these are among the reasons why, along with his required medical studies, Jung familiarized himself with all the occult-spiritist literature—that which today falls mainly under the rubric of parapsychology—that was available to him, such as the books of Johann K. Zöllner (for example, *Transcendental Physics and So-Called Philosophy* [Leipzig, 1879]) or the English chemist William Crookes, who had made a name for himself in the investigation of psychic phenomena as well as in his own area of specialization. Kant's *Dreams of a Spirit Seer* likewise belonged to this collection, as did the numerous works of the multifaceted Munich philosopher Carl du Prel (1839–1899), who had paced off the entire range of questions connected with the problem of the psyche and arrived at a "monistic doctrine of the soul." Jung himself also mentioned older works in his *Memories*, for example those of Justinus Kerner (*The Seeress of Prevorst* [Stuttgart and Tübingen, 1829]) and the Frankfurt physician Johann Carl Passavant (1790–1857), who went beyond his own discipline to demand, in his writings on natural philosophy and theology, spiritual qualities of the physician also. Mention is also made of the circle of Eschenmeyer and Joseph Görres, whose members included on the one hand the Swiss-born physician and hypnotist Franz Anton Mesmer, and on the other the French theosophist Louis-Claude de Saint-Martin,[9] Friedrich Oberlin,[10] and Heinrich Jung-Stilling, who was also on familiar terms with the "spirit realm." Special mention is made of "seven volumes of Swedenborg,"[11] the eighteenth-century Norwegian visionary who had made a lasting impression on the young Goethe.

Even if all these figures and their adherents marked only an intermediate stage in C. G. Jung's development, he did not underestimate their value to him at the beginning of his own reconnaissance in the no-man's-land of psychic and parapsychic phenomena:

> The observations of the spiritualists, weird and questionable as they seemed to me, were the first accounts I had seen of objective psychic phenomena. . . . For myself I found such possibilities extremely interesting and attractive. They added another dimension to my life; the world gained depth and background.[12]

The young man's questioning and searching is reflected in his diaries from the late nineties. Thus late in 1898 he complained of the "lifeless idol of science" that denied him precisely that which moved him. He described striking dreams with "foreboding glimpses of blooming landscapes, endless blue seas and sunny shores, but often with images of strange roads in the dark night, friends parting from me and hurrying away toward a sunnier destiny while I was alone on deserted paths facing an impenetrable darkness." That one living in provincial narrowness and economic straits should dream of "sunny shores" and "endless blue seas," of all things, is perfectly understandable. At the same time he kept in mind the records of his renowned grandfather of Basel. On this subject, too, the diary for 1898 gives an opinion:

> "Oh, plunge yourself into a positive belief," wrote my grandfather Jung. Yes, "plunge," gladly, if I could, if that depended only on my higher self. But an inexplicably difficult something, an immobility and torpor, exhaustion and weakness always prevents the decisive last step. I have already taken many steps, but nothing near the final one. The greater the certainty, the more superhuman the doubt, the disturbing infernal power.[13]

These reports of his inner grappling naturally took on another aspect when Jung spoke up before his Zofingia society brothers at their fraternity soirées. Here, too, the confessional tone was in evidence. But here, instead of the note of resignation, there was an optimistic, indeed Faustian motif. It was, he said, the person as a person that one had to get to know, "and not as an amiable social animal. In this way we guard against judging by appearance, superficially. In this way we build a relation of 'friendship' that will satisfy the 'Amicitia' of our motto. In this way we pave the way toward 'litteris' (knowledge), to the education which nowadays no university gives us anymore. . . ." And after these notes of criticism he appealed to the student alliance to raise itself to a higher level of common aspiration: "To further intellectual commerce is your task and mine. It is lofty, but not unattainable. It is our duty to further it. But we will always fulfill our duty, for morality does mean something after all—Nietzsche notwithstanding. This is 'my confession.'"[14] With this confession, he set himself a twofold task. On the one hand there was for him no alternative to the conscientious pursuit of the study of medicine, which would give him the practical and theoretical ideas for his later calling as a physician, and on the other hand was his resolve to break out of the narrow restrictions of the "lifeless idol of science" and to gain some free space, which could not yet be more precisely defined, for the investigation of the psyche and a widening of the knowledge of the human being.

Here again we see the two minds within him, the No. 1 and No. 2 of his personality, with the No. 1, devoted to his everyday obligations, coming fully into its own—in his studies themselves, in the fraternity, and not least in managing the household with his mother and sister. Here, for example, he was burdened with the less-than-easy task of limiting his mother to sensible use of their extremely scant finances, apportioning the available funds out to her a week at a time, because she was unable to do this herself.

Conscientious study was called for by the fact that during his very first semester, because of his particular interests, Jung was appointed a junior assistant in anatomy at Basel and was then entrusted with conducting the course in histology. His predilection for pathological anatomy and his ability prompted his teacher, Professor Friedrich von Müller, to consider Jung for an assistantship when he himself was called to Munich. In fact Jung was undecided for a time as to whether he should settle upon surgery or internal medicine. Then an event occurred that marked the decisive turning point of Jung's career, and with it the rest of his life. In preparing for the state examination in October 1899, he obtained a copy of the fourth edition (1890) of Richard von Krafft-Ebing's textbook on psychiatry. Up to then he had been unable to interest himself in the subject. Of course he had attended psychiatric lectures and worked out clinical exercises, but he could not remember a single one of the cases that had been demonstrated in the clinic, only the distaste and boredom that went with them. In his *Memories* the autobiographer coyly withheld the name of his teacher, Professor Ludwig Wille, who in 1873 had founded the St. Urban cantonal mental asylum, but who did not succeed in awakening an interest in the subject of psychiatry.

It was with some skepticism that the examination candidate opened Krafft-Ebing's textbook, for some rather depressing experiences his father had had as official pastor of the Friedmatt asylum in Basel still lingered in his memory. Furthermore, psychiatry did not enjoy very high standing in the curriculum at the time, as "mental illness" was regarded as a thoroughly fatal business, and the asylum a place of hopelessness in which neither patients nor guardians ought to harbor any illusions. Jung turned first to the preface, in order to familiarize himself with the author's point of departure. There he read: "It is probably due to the singularity of this field of knowledge and the incompleteness of its development that psychiatric textbooks bear a more or less subjective stamp." Krafft-Ebing referred to psychoses as "diseases of the persona." These very first lines, and eventually the entire book, began to have an effect on the reader that was at first unexplainable. Jung acknowledged:

> My heart suddenly began to pound. I had to stand up and draw a deep breath. My excitement was intense, for it had

> become clear to me, in a flash of illumination, that for me the only possible goal was psychiatry. Here alone the two currents of my interest could flow together and in a united stream dig their own bed. Here was the empirical field common to biological and spiritual facts, which I had everywhere sought and nowhere found. Here at last was the place where the collision of nature and spirit became a reality.[15]

The author's very expression of his "subjective stamp" must have become the keyword and the solution to the puzzle, for it was precisely at this point in his reading that the reader's strong emotions set in and made him aware that he was experiencing a fateful moment. The subject of the union of nature and spirit is indeed the central Jungian theme of the "reconciliation of the opposites," which is supposed to take place in individuation, the lifelong process of self-becoming. As a student he had never heard anything like this from his teachers; so he said at any rate. And yet he seemed to have been waiting for precisely this signal as if for the answer to a riddle. Thereupon his decision was made, like a flash. Neither a career in the field of internal medicine nor the prospective assistantship in Munich was of any further interest, only total concentration on his new task of learning and working as a psychiatrist. Friedrich von Müller was disappointed, and his colleagues were astonished. How could someone with such fine professional prospects fall into such a sidetrack? Jung spoke of the "confident feeling that I was a 'united double nature'"—a central motif in Goethe—that carried him "as if on a magical wave" through the state examination, which he passed with the highest marks. But what was this discipline to which the young doctor would henceforth devote himself? Jung's answer was:

> . . .psychiatry, in the broadest sense, is a dialogue between the sick psyche and the psyche of the doctor, which is presumed to be "normal." It is a coming to terms between the sick personality and that of the therapist, both in principle

> equally subjective. My aim was to show that delusions and hallucinations were not just specific symptoms of mental disease but also had a human meaning.[16]

With this, however, a brand-new start was indicated, the beginning of a path that would necessitate further stages in inner as well as outer progress. And as far as his sudden insight upon reading the psychiatric textbook is concerned, one should still not underestimate the importance of another factor that had played a considerable role since Jung's early childhood, namely the experience of the "outsider's" confrontation with extraordinary occurrences. Even life in the Bottminger Mill during his Basel school days had brought Jung into contact with experiences of the sort that could also, in their turn, be seen as elements of experience for his later calling, and it is to these that we shall turn next.

6

Experiments in Parapsychology

One of the early convictions that C. G. Jung maintained throughout his life was the insight that "our image of the world corresponds to reality only when the improbable also has its place in it."[1] But for him, an empirical investigator concerned with establishing precise facts, it was not enough merely to find the "improbable" attested to in the literature, separate from the science of the university, even if the occult and spiritist writings of his time in principle left no room for doubt about what they reported. His associates in the Zofingia, of course, found his opinions on this score difficult to accept, for at the turn of the century these were too far from the modernistic material-positivist scientific dogma.

At that time something remarkable occurred. It was during the summer vacation, presumably in 1898, at the time when Jung was still wondering whether to decide on surgery or internal medicine, and psychiatry as a professional goal had not yet come into the picture. The student was poring over his textbooks in his study in the Bottminger Mill. Nearby in the family dining room, where the round walnut dining table stood, his mother sat knitting in her armchair by the window, and the door was ajar. The only other person in the house was the maid, who was busy in the kitchen. His sister, Gertrud, was expected home from school momentarily. Suddenly a crack "like a pistol shot" rang out from the dining room. Jung jumped up and rushed into the next room.

> My mother was sitting flabbergasted in her armchair, the knitting fallen from her hands. She stammered out, "W-w-what's happened? It was right beside me!" and stared at the table. Following her eyes, I saw what had happened. The table top had split from the rim to beyond the center, and not along any joint; the split ran right through the solid wood.[2]

The two were speechless. How such a thing could happen of course has to do with the drying out of the wood in the seventy-year-old table (part of the dowry of his paternal grandmother). In view of the relatively high humidity at the time, for the wood to crack, and moreover with a bang like an explosion, was more than unusual. Jung called it a "coincidence." His mother, in contrast, said ominously, "Yes, yes, that means something." But what, indeed?

Less than a fortnight had passed when Jung came home one night to find the family in a state of great agitation:

> About an hour earlier there had been another deafening report. This time it was not the already damaged table; the noise had come from the direction of the sideboard, a heavy piece of furniture dating from the early nineteenth century. They had already looked all over it, but had found no trace of a split. I immediately began examining the sideboard and the entire surrounding area, but just as fruitlessly. Then I began on the interior of the sideboard. In the cupboard containing the bread basket I found a loaf of bread, and, beside it, the bread knife. The greater part of the blade had snapped off in several pieces. the handle lay in one corner of the rectangular basket, and in each of the other corners lay a piece of the blade. The knife had been used shortly before, at four o'clock tea, and afterward put away. Since then no one had gone to the sideboard.[3]

The next day Jung took the knife that had burst into four pieces with him to Basel, in order to have it examined under a magnifying glass by a cutler, who pronounced the steel to be completely normal. Only by the deliberate application of force, said the craftsman, could the knife have been shattered.[4] No one dared to assume yet another dubious "coincidence," and all were greatly perplexed. At the time, Jung does not seem to have considered the fact that such phenomena were occasionally known to occur in the vicinity of young people in puberty, without their outward complicity; Gertrud was about fourteen years old.

His suspicion fell instead on another young girl who was only a little older than his sister. His reasoning, of course, was different. Having already been prepared by his specialized reading, he had heard that spiritistic séances were being held among his relatives.[5] At the center of this circle was Helene Preiswerk, nicknamed "Helly" (1881–1911). She was his cousin on his mother's side; that is, Helene's and Carl Gustav's mutual grandfather was Samuel Preiswerk, the Antistes of Basel whose own psychic gifts have already been alluded to. It should not go unmentioned in this connection that Jung's paternal grandfather, Professor Carl Gustav Jung, for his part, must in his time have expressed his explicit dissociation from the ghosts that were then becoming fashionable. In his journal, for example, there is an entry for 11 April 1853, referring to spiritistic apparitions in Bremen, which he had learned of from the newspaper: "A chain is formed for this purpose. . . . Those participating are seated a foot apart from one another. Their clothes must not be touching. . . . Each one lays his hands loosely on the table . . . with his little finger touching his neighbor's." Grandfather Jung's trenchant comment reads: "So there is still nonsense in the world!"[6] Meanwhile, his grandson set about paying so much attention to this "nonsense" that he devoted his medical doctor's thesis to the psychology and pathology of "so-called occult phenomena," based, in fact, on the parapsychological experiments he carried out with his cousin Helene.

As a rule they gathered for sittings every Saturday evening, and at the beginning Carl was the only male participant.

Helly's mother, Celestine Preiswerk-Allensbach, was not pleased with the business. But in the end even she came to put up with the séances, since after all Jung's mother, Emilie Jung-Preiswerk, was present, whose own father, the long-deceased Reverend Samuel Preiswerk, appeared to speak through the voice of his beloved granddaughter as the "guide and guardian of the medium." In addition Jung's sister Gertrud, "Trudi," was also present later. In his dissertation Jung gave a description of the medium, but without mentioning that she was related to him or that through his own mother he had a share in the "hereditary burden" of a definite parapsychic talent, which he did appropriately attribute to the medium's family. Helly was the eleventh child of Jung's uncle Rudolf Preiswerk. To preserve some anonymity, Helene Preiswerk appears in the dissertation as "Miss S. W.," whom Jung depicted as follows:

> Miss S. W. is very well built, exhibiting slightly rachitic skull formation without pronounced hydrocephalus, somewhat pale facial color, and dark eyes of a peculiarly piercing brightness. . . . In school she was average, showed little interest, and was absent-minded. In general she showed rather reserved behavior, which could however suddenly give way to the most boisterous, excited glee. She is of ordinary intelligence, has no particular talents, and is rather unmusical. She is not fond of books, preferring handicrafts or sitting about daydreaming. . . . As a result her level of education is relatively low, and her interests of correspondingly restricted scope. The range of her knowledge of literature is similarly limited.[7]

In the dissertation Jung dates his experiments with "Miss S. W." in the years 1899 to 1900. That the first séances had clearly taken place as early as 1895, though, when Paul Jung was still alive and the family still lived in the parsonage at Klein-Hüningen, was left unmentioned in his report. Thus his statements about the events are somewhat inconsistent, including, to an extent, on matters of content. Possible lapses of memory aside, the doctoral candidate was obviously at pains to conceal his own role, and especially his close kinship relationship, thus forestalling from the start any further critical inquiry that might have thrown the scientific validity of the entire work into question.

And so we shall have to imagine the external proceedings. The participants sit down at a round table. (Contrary to Jung's statements, this evidently came from Samuel Preiswerk's household, and not from his paternal grandmother's dowry as suggested in the *Memories*.) On the table a glass full of water has been placed. Now the spiritistic "chain" is formed, with everyone touching each other lightly by the fingertips. Then they wait for "the spirit" to announce itself. Those present are convinced that it is none other than grandfather Preiswerk. Someone asks him a question, and his communication or instruction is understood as a message from the spirit world. In case it is still too bright outside in the early evening, the curtains are drawn in order to cut out any distraction or source of disturbance. Suddenly the glass in the middle of the table begins to vibrate. There is great astonishment. What will happen today? The girl—Helly—falls into a trance and begins to speak as a medium, that is, any imaginary forms that might be present speak through her. Another time a card on which the letters of the alphabet have been written might be used. The drinking glass is turned over, and again the chain is formed. All at once the glass begins to move, dancing as it were from letter to letter to form words. They must be written down immediately—this was Carl's job—in order to get the content of the message, which might be banal remarks or an announcement such as: "Be at peace, my beloved children, and do not be afraid. It is I, your grandfather. And someone else is with me—Carl's grandfather, Professor Jung. Together we shall watch over you."[8]

For the doctoral candidate it was a "case of somnambulism in a disturbed person."[9] What struck Carl as an experimenter was the great sensitivity with which the medium grasped his reading, including Nietzsche's *Thoughts Out of Season* as well as *Thus Spake Zarathustra*. The girl had likely been sitting nearby when he had spoken about Schopenhauer and Nietzsche among his friends; although she was unable to follow what she heard with her waking consciousness, she had unconsciously absorbed it and transformed it into a message that reflected the contemporary rejection of Nietzsche. In the trance state she would pronounce now solemnly, now with commanding authority what were meant to seem the admonitions of his pastoral grandfather: "Carl, Carl, believe your grandfather! Nietzsche's doctrine contains many errors with regard to God!" And Stefanie Zumstein-Preiswerk, another relative, commented at this point in her account, "She counseled him as if she were the Antistes, or rather as if the Antistes were speaking to the doubt-tormented grandson. Her empathetic abilities and her downright intellectual appreciation of C. G. Jung's problems at that time were unbelievable."[10]

Naturally the medium's utterances took various forms. Sometimes they were fancifully embellished stories from family gossip, sometimes romantic tales and spicy adventures, and sometimes the idea of reincarnation played a dominant role, where the girl speaking in a trance appeared as a prominent, multiply-incarnated personality, the "No. 2," as it were, of her real everyday ego. A definite highlight of these trance-expressions was the figure of a circle, which the medium claimed was revealed by the spirit powers of this world and the other side. Helly would dictate this pattern, or mandala, for the experimenter to write down, making use of exotic-sounding names like "Kara," "Hefa," "Nakus," "Magnesor," "Athialowi," and so on. These claims of "mystical science"[11] turn out not to be particularly original when we consider that Jung himself had given his cousin, on her fifteenth birthday in 1896, a copy of Justinus Kerner's then widely read book *The Seeress of Prevorst*, in which the sun-circles of Friederike Hauffe, among other things, were thoroughly discussed.[12]

Before long Helly's productive possibilities as a medium were exhausted. The experimenter recorded a gradual decrease in the vitality of her ecstasies, and her utterances became more colorless and trivial. Finally he caught her simply trying to produce any kind of phenomenon at all, obviously for her cousin's sake. Jung terminated the experiments, and indeed

> . . .very much to my regret, for I had learned from this example how a No. 2 personality is formed, how it enters into a child's consciousness and finally integrates it into itself. . . . All in all, this was the one great experience which wiped out all my earlier philosophy and made it possible for me to achieve a psychological point of view. I had discovered some objective facts about the human psyche. Yet the nature of the experience was such that once again I was unable to speak of it. I knew no one to whom I could have told the whole story.[13]

Nevertheless, he did make the attempt. Again, it was his friend Albert Oeri who acknowledged how much moral courage it must have taken for him, even as a young student, to advocate these extraordinary phenomena and the consequences they entailed for his outlook. Gustav Steiner, too, who also preserved memories of Jung's student days, confirmed in his own way the commitment with which Jung championed his views on marginal fields, including dream research, before his colleagues: "'Jung will make a great storyteller yet,' said one commentator with a laugh. But that was really what roused him to anger or even insults—when he was not taken seriously, not understood. The longer this went on, the more he fell out with the theologians."[14] On the other hand, Jung must nonetheless have found enough understanding of his early experiments in Eugen Bleuler, his later supervisor and teacher at the psychiatric clinic, to allow him to discuss the results of his séances with Helene Preiswerk in the text of his medical dissertation. The title page of his "Inaugural Dissertation on the Attainment of the Doctoral Degree in an Advanced Course of Medical Study at the University of Zürich," published in Leipzig in 1902, bore the legend "Approved at the request of Prof. E. Bleuler."[15] C. G. Jung was altogether aware that with his doctoral thesis he had produced neither a conclusive nor even a scientifically satisfactory result. The conclusion reads on this point:

> My effort has been aimed above all against public opinion, which has nothing but a disdainful smile for so-called occult phenomena, at presenting the numerous connections of these with the concerns of the physician and of psychology, and at drawing attention to the many important questions which this unexplored territory still holds in store for us. The beginning of this work has given me the conviction that a rich harvest for experimental psychology is ripening in this field. . . .[16]

7

Psychiatrist at Burghölzli

What Jung could not yet have suspected while he was still studying medicine—the horizons of knowledge that would open up to him through his eventual choice of profession—became ever clearer to him after his encounter with Krafft-Ebing's textbook. Psychiatry, he found, was an exceedingly interrelated discipline which reached out into a number of other fields of knowledge, such as neurology, psychology, sociology, psychotherapy, and ultimately even philosophy. Concerning its development, Henry F. Ellenberger said in his account of the discovery of the unconscious, "No branch of knowledge has gone through so many metamorphoses as has dynamic psychiatry: from primitive healing arts to magnetism, from magnetism to hypnotism, from hypnotism to psychoanalysis and the later dynamic schools. Furthermore, these various directions have repeatedly undergone waves of rejection and acceptance. Nevertheless, the newer dynamic schools have never been accepted as unanimously as the physical, chemical, or physiological discoveries. . . ."[1]

The psychiatrist's concern is with the person who is in some way estranged from reality, whose behavior appears bizarre or abnormally puzzling—which of course already raises the basic philosophical question of what ought to be regarded as the "norm" of humanness. Is not the very person who acts creatively as a scientist or artist already deviating considerably from those norms that are rashly declared to be the values of a "healthy cross-section"? And those of deep insights, who live with an expanded consciousness, those who are spiritually experienced, are they not all too often dismissed by the "normal" as "cranks"? From this standpoint Jung's early confrontation with his own inner nature, and with the parapsychic manifestations that were perceivable even outwardly, was of decisive importance, as he was completing his studies in Basel in July 1900 and beginning to look for a first professional position. The need to procure gainful employment as quickly as possible arose from his extremely straitened financial circumstances after his father's death. His mother and sister were virtually penniless. A loan obligation of around three thousand francs had to be repaid. On this point, we learn that Jung had already had himself appointed to various sorts of practical medical assignments and temporary substitutions in his later semesters. Given his decision to go into psychiatry, the obvious course was to begin as an intern in one of the cantonal sanatoria or nursing institutions. A motif from his childhood—the attraction of living near a river or lake—may have played a part in his decision, at the age of twenty-five, to apply for a volunteer position at the Burghölzli, the psychiatric clinic of the University of Zürich, and thus to take up residence not far from Lake Zürich. Before he could begin there in December, he had to fulfill the compulsory military service, the so-called recruit school, with the infantry at Aargau, which took a fairly short time since it involved nothing but military basic training. Like every Swiss, Jung also had to be available for further maneuvers at regular intervals; later, during the First World War, he served as an officer in a Swiss medical unit.

The move from Basel to Zürich meant first of all a painful separation from his mother and sister. In addition it was a change from a city with a rich intellectual tradition, but provincial narrowness, to one of commerce and cosmopolitanism.

I was glad to be in Zürich, for in the course of the years

> Basel had become too stuffy for me. For the Baslers no town exists but their own: only Basel is "civilized," and north of the river Birs the land of the barbarians begins. . . . In Basel I was stamped for all time as the son of the Reverend Paul Jung and the grandson of Professor Carl Gustav Jung. I was an intellectual and belonged to a definite social set. I felt resistances against this, for I could not and would not let myself be classified.[2]

As far as his professional life was concerned, Zürich marked the definitive switchpoint for the rest of Jung's career. Burghölzli, the university's psychiatric clinic since 1870, was known as the most significant institution of its kind at the time, both within Switzerland and beyond, for its size and facilities and its idyllic setting lying above the lake and—at least at that time—on the outskirts of the city, no less than for the exemplary care its patients received. Under the leadership of Eugen Bleuler (1857–1939), Professor of Psychiatry at the University of Zürich from 1898 to 1927, the model reputation that the clinic had already achieved under his predecessor Auguste Henri Forel (1848–1931)[3] grew even greater. Along with the German Emil Kraepelin in Munich, Bleuler could be considered the leading representative of his profession, renowned as a physician who showed humaneness and kindness to the sick and an inspiring master teacher of young doctors. In a time of fundamentally new directions in the humanistic disciplines, Bleuler sought to understand the mentally disturbed patient in all his abnormal forms of expression and to contact the essential nucleus of the individual, hidden behind his oddness. That he lived under the same roof with his patients and expected the same of his coworkers was not open to discussion. Thus Jung too was assigned a room; after his marriage he obtained a flat above that of his supervisor. The new worker from Basel submitted unconditionally to this strict regulation of work and life. Some called it a "secular monastery," while the view of others was expressed by Jung's colleague and follower for many years, Alphonse Maeder: "The Burghölzli was at that time a kind of factory, where one worked hard and was paid badly. Everyone, from the professor down to the youngest assistant, was completely absorbed in his work. Everyone was compelled to abstain from alcoholic beverages. . . . The patient was the focus of our interest, and the student learned how he was supposed to talk to him."[4] At 8:30 every morning there was the working conference, in which the residents were to report on their patients; hence their morning rounds had to be completed by this time. Several times a week there were additional general conferences, the so-called joint sessions, presided over by Director Bleuler. In these there was discussion of the case histories of new patients, for example, or coworkers' papers were introduced or recent professional literature discussed. One of the first works of this kind with which Jung was charged was a review of the newly appeared *Interpretation of Dreams* by Sigmund Freud. It was likely Bleuler, who as a student of Forel's had transplanted psychoanalysis to Switzerland, who made Jung aware of Freud's original work and with it his dream research,[5] since he had taken a predominantly positive attitude to the Freudian approach as early as the nineties. Thus psychoanalysis was the subject of daily discussion at the Burghölzli clinic, and this long before Freud could count on more general recognition among psychologists and psychiatrists. Here, however, it should not be overlooked that although Bleuler took up and expanded upon psychoanalytical concepts, he also maintained his own objections, some of which would reappear a few years later in the correspondence between Jung and Freud. This exchange of ideas between Vienna and Zürich, then, also reflected disagreements that had existed between Bleuler and Jung before the year 1910.

To begin with, though, Jung immersed himself entirely in his work. In order to form a general view of his new field of endeavor as quickly and thoroughly as possible and to familiarize himself with psychiatric thought from its beginnings, he read through the fifty volumes of the *Allgemeine Zeitschrift für Psychiatrie*.

> I wanted to know how the human mind reacted to the sight of its own destruction, for psychiatry seemed to me an articulate expression of that biological reaction which seizes upon the so-called healthy mind in the presence of mental illness. My professional colleagues seemed to me no less interesting than the patients. . . .
>
> Dominating my interests and research was the burning question: "What actually takes place inside the mentally ill?" . . . Psychiatry teachers were not interested in what the patient had to say, but rather in how to make a diagnosis or how to describe symptoms and to compile statistics. From the clinical point of view which then prevailed, the human personality of the patient, his individuality, did not matter at all. Rather, the doctor was confronted with Patient X, with a long list of cut-and-dried diagnoses and a detailing of symptoms. Patients were labeled, rubber-stamped with a diagnosis. . . .[6]

Jung's recollections here are interesting, inasmuch as it was precisely with Eugen Bleuler that he learned to maintain an emphatically humane relationship with the "mentally ill." Bleuler had specialized in the study and treatment of the disease that Kraepelin called "dementia praecox" and he himself termed "schizophrenia."

For half a year Jung practically locked himself behind the walls of this "secular monastery" and submitted to the prescribed "vows," including of course the prohibition against the use of alcohol, which had been required of the Burghölzli's doctors since Forel's time. Bleuler appreciated his young colleague's zeal and conscientiousness. And while Jung claimed that even at this time he was not well understood by his colleagues, it was nonetheless his chief who accepted the topic he had begun to discuss in his doctoral thesis, and in fact it was Bleuler who approved his dissertation. Or perhaps the explicit notice to this effect on the title page of *The Psychology and Pathology of So-Called Occult Phenomena* should simply be taken as an expression of his indebtedness to his doctoral advisor? But this is hardly likely. In fact, it is striking that in his autobiography he neglected to give due credit to the extraordinary qualities of his teacher. To speak of the famous Burghölzli around 1900 without emphasizing the part played by its director will not do! This suppression of Eugen Bleuler's name in the *Memories* is all the more remarkable in that at other opportunities he specifically did recall this man. When someone once tagged Jung—thirty years later, in 1933!—as a disciple of Freud, he called this a mistake. He had not come from the Freudian school at all, he said: "I am a student of Bleuler's, and through my investigations into experimental psychology I had already gotten a scientific reputation when I began supporting Freud and actually opened the discussion in earnest."[7] Or in a letter he wrote at seventy-five to Bleuler's son and follower, Manfred Bleuler: "The impressions and suggestions I received from your father are all the more vivid in my memory, for which I shall always be thankful to him. Not only am I most deeply committed to psychiatry, but have always remained inwardly very close to it."[8]

The year 1902 also saw a further step in Jung's military career; after the annual exercises he was able to add to his medical doctorate a commission as a lieutenant. The results of his first psychiatric studies were published in a series of articles, including "The Psychology of Dementia Praecox" (1906; published 1907), the fruit of three years of experimental research and clinical observations, as well as "The Content of the Psychoses" (1908), originally a lecture held in the Zürich city hall.[9] His many conversations with patients taught the young doctor how important it was, for them, that he become thoroughly familiar with their life histories, and above all understand their "stories" and take these no less seriously than the information given by a healthy person. He summed it up:

> Through my work with the patients I realized that paranoid ideas and hallucinations contain a germ of meaning. A personality, a life history, a pattern of hopes and desires lie behind the psychosis. The fault is ours if we do not under-

> stand them. It dawned upon me then for the first time that a general psychology of the personality lies concealed within psychosis, and that even here we come upon the old human conflicts. Although patients may appear dull and apathetic, or totally imbecilic, there is more going on in their minds, and more that is meaningful, than there seems to be. At bottom we discover nothing new and unknown in the mentally ill; rather, we encounter the substratum of our own natures.[10]

In order to be better fitted for his job and to learn about other methods of diagnosis and treatment, Jung enrolled in a semester abroad. Thanks to the obligingness of Eugen Bleuler, he was able to travel to Paris in late autumn of 1902, to spend the winter semester 1902–1903 studying with Pierre Janet (1859–1947), who was, in Ellenberger's estimation, the "first to establish a new system of dynamic psychiatry."[11] He taught at the famous Salpêtrière, at that time a psychiatric center of international reputation, which Sigmund Freud had attended as a student a scant decade and a half before Jung. When Jung arrived, this hospital with its unique style could already look back on a long and checkered history. It had undergone a fundamental renovation under Jean-Martin Charcot (1825–1893), the "greatest neurologist of his time" according to Ellenberger. In his own way Janet carried on the tradition Charcot had begun, thus becoming a link between the early dynamic psychiatry and the later systems and in many respects a forerunner and pioneer of psychoanalysis. In the works of Josef Breuer and Sigmund Freud, Janet saw the results of his own research confirmed, if not in fact plagiaristically reformulated in different terminology. Hence in view of his later work Jung could hardly have made a better "choice" of place, person, or time.[12]

Janet was of lasting significance for Jung especially because of his strong influence even on the later doctrine of psychological types. Where Janet, for example, started from the existence of two basic neuroses, hysteria and psychoasthenia, Jung later spoke of the extraversion of hysteria and the introversion of schizophrenia. In the first case the center of gravity of psychic activity lies within (introversion), and in the second, outside (extraversion). This established the two attitude-types around which Jung's typology revolved, along with the so-called functional types (thinking, feeling, sensation, and intuition).

Mention should also be made in this connection of the French psychologist Alfred Binet (1857–1911), whose book *The Experimental Study of Intelligence*, in which the key typological concepts of "introspection" and "externospection" were thoroughly discussed, appeared some time during Jung's stay in Paris.[13] Clearly these fundamental concepts, which have come to be commonly thought of as the specific contributions of Jungian research, were first coined and extensively developed by both Janet and Binet. Hence Jung's profit from his relatively short sojourn in Paris cannot be overestimated. Apart from this, though accustomed to strict discipline at work, he did leave himself enough time to enjoy the amenities of the international city on the Seine. We hear nothing more of financial straits. At any rate Jung was able to take lodgings in a passable hotel, and now and then there was enough money for a relatively opulent dinner party or attendance at the opera or theater.[14] C. G. Jung was even seen strolling along the Rue Royale to the Place de la Concorde in the company of a lady; this was his cousin Helene Preiswerk, who was active in the fashion business and who, as Jung now perceived to his surprise, gave quite a self-confident impression. Séances and such things were no longer of interest. How they both had changed! The little Helly who had seemed to be of rather below-average talents had become an able, even successful young woman in her profession as a hatter, and Carl was long since no longer the spiritistically inclined student from Basel, but a doctor with a great career before him.[15]

Returning from Paris, Jung devoted himself to a specific field of endeavor, the so-called association research, aimed at obtaining insight into the problems of neuroses and psychoses. To this end a laboratory for experimental psychopathology was constructed at the Burghölzli. Subjects were presented with a list containing certain stimulus words (such as *head*, *green*, *water*, *sing*, *death*, *long*, *ship*, etc.). As quickly as possible they were to respond to these associatively: that is, by saying whatever came into their minds. The reaction times were evaluated along with the answers. During the association experiment fluctuations in electrical resistance of the skin were measured by means of a galvanometer. These inquiries, conducted and recorded by Jung, led him to the discovery of the feeling-toned complexes—autonomous contents of the unconscious that acted as disturbances in the experiment. These experiments, analyzed in cooperation with his colleague Franz Riklin, proved to be of practical use, for example in criminal trials for indicating the credibility of testimony, so that the association experiment was later applied in the evaluation of legal cases.[16]

Recognition was not long in coming. In the clinic Jung was promoted to the senior staff, and after qualifying in psychiatry he became a recognized *Privatdozent* at the University of Zürich in 1905. With this his academic lecturing activity, which continued in this form until 1913, took its place beside his work at the clinic. In 1909, during his trip to the United States, as will be discussed later, Clark University in Worcester, Massachusetts, awarded him an honorary doctorate in law for his researches.

All these advances, which would not have been possible without the collaboration of the director and his colleagues at the Burghölzli clinic, could not prevent the dissensions that gradually arose between Jung and Director Bleuler as the years went on. At all events his departure could not have been caused by the size of the workload alone, as Jung suggests in his *Memories*. Hard words were exchanged, and strong criticism was voiced in correspondence. To Freud, there was once actually mention of the "Burghölzli swindle." Controversies over factual matters pertaining to psychoanalysis played a part in this, as did personal tendencies, such as the fact that the hitherto obediently antialcoholic Jung no longer felt compelled to adhere to the house's strict regulation. Jung later referred to his psychiatric work at the Burghölzli as the time of his learning years, which in itself suggests a definite break in continuity. This said, however, the real split—which would come in his middle life—was not yet at hand.

In the part of Jung's life that we have discussed so far there also occurred two further encounters that were extremely significant for him, and which demand separate treatment: his meeting with his wife, and that with Sigmund Freud. In fact Jung had his eyes on psychoanalytic thinking already from the year 1900, that is, from the time when he took up his position at the Burghölzli.

8

The Encounter with Emma Rauschenbach

The central theme in the work of C. G. Jung is that of individuation, the self-development of the human being through the process of unifying the opposites. And because every person is embodied as either man or woman, yet carries within a predisposition to be completed through the other sex, the polarity of masculine and feminine stands at the center of all human existence.

Rather than philosophizing about such things—Jung always rejected the mere philosophical discussion of a problem for its own sake—his psychoanalytical inquiries led him to assume the existence of an oppositely sexed soul-image within the person's unconscious: the anima in the case of a man, and the animus in a woman. In the productions of the unconscious, for example in dreams, such anima- or animus-images are manifested in characteristic ways, and Jungian dream analysis makes corresponding assertions about them.[1] In waking consciousness the soul-image of animus or anima that everyone carries within often tends to be projected onto other persons. Thus a woman can come to carry the projection of a man's own unconscious inner femininity—in other words, something that comes from within him, a specific complex of his own inner functions, confronts him from without, whether by fascinating him, awakening sympathy or erotic feelings, or in the form of some dark side or inferiority, which everyone likewise carries within but projects onto others if he is not consciously aware of it.

As far as the man's anima is concerned, even in folklore it is said that every man carries his Eve within him. Naturally the image of the mother, as the first woman in every man's life, is very closely bound up with this anima. Jung repeatedly mentioned the ambivalence of his own mother and her character, speaking of an explicit mother complex that was troublesome for him to overcome. This calls to mind especially the enigmatic No. 2, the side of her nature that was open to the supernatural. Other feminine figures, insofar as he mentions them, appear in contrast to have played no great part in his childhood and youth, though there is no lack of peculiar first encounters with the other sex. (He said, incidentally, that he had for a long time connected with femininity a feeling of "inherent untrustworthiness.") But there was one fleeting impression imparted to him—permanently—at the age of three or four, even though on the surface of it nothing spectacular had happened, which involved the Jung family's maid. The way the girl held little Carl on her arm as he laid his head trustingly on her shoulder engraved itself on the child's memory:

> She had black hair and an olive complexion, and was quite different from my mother. I can see, even now, her hairline, her throat, with its darkly pigmented skin, and her ear. All this seemed to me very strange and yet strangely familiar. It was as though she belonged not to my family but only to me, as though she were connected in some way with other mysterious things I could not understand. This type of girl later became a component of my anima. The feeling of strangeness which she conveyed, and yet of having known her always, was a characteristic of that figure which later came to symbolize for me the whole essence of womanhood.[2]

Around the same time, when his parents were separated for a short time, another young woman made her appearance. She

▲C. G. Jung and Emma Jung-Rauschenbach, 1903.

▲ Carl and Emma Jung at their home in Küsnacht, 1955.

◀ The family on holiday in Châteaux d'Oex, 1917: son Franz; Carl and Emma Jung; daughters Agathe, Marianne, and Gret.

had blond hair and blue eyes and was very amiable. And again the setting remained in the autobiographer's memory—a stroll beneath golden maple and chestnut trees on a blue autumn day "along the Rhine below the Falls, near Wörth castle. The sun is shining through the foliage, and yellow leaves lie on the ground." And, Jung added, twenty-one years later he would meet this woman again; she was his future mother-in-law, Bertha Rauschenbach-Schenk.

Many years later, Jung, as a student at the Gymnasium, was visiting his father, who was on leave in Sachseln, where the Swiss saint Brother Klaus (Niklaus von Flüe)[3] had lived. The youth had visited Klaus's hermitage, where he was deeply moved by the *genius loci*, the peculiar atmosphere of the place. He was just about to come back down from the hill to the valley, when suddenly there appeared the slender figure of a young lady, a friendly farm girl in native costume. The two made their way down together. Carl was unable to conceal his awkwardness in conversation; at the Gymnasium in Basel there were only boys, and the few girls he had ever met were his cousins. The boy sensed the "impenetrable wall" that stood between them.

> Sad at heart, I retreated into myself. . . . Outwardly this encounter was completely meaningless. But, seen from within, it was so weighty that it not only occupied my thoughts for days but has remained forever in my memory, like a shrine by the wayside. At that time I was still in that childlike state where life consists of single, unrelated experiences. For who could discover the threads of fate which led from Brother Klaus to the pretty girl?[4]

One day the time came to fasten upon, or perhaps pick up again, one very specific life-thread, to seize upon one out of the manifold facets of the feminine soul-image, the unique face of his own anima. The occasion itself was once again quite ordinary. Jung, still a student in Basel in about his second semester, was visiting a friend from Schaffhausen, quite near the place where he himself had spent his earliest childhood years. When his mother heard of this plan, she made a suggestion: "If you visit that friend in Schaffhausen, you go and see Mrs. [Bertha] Rauschenbach, too—we knew her as a young woman." He was supposed to convey greetings, and Carl, age twenty-one, looked forward to a reacquaintance after two decades. But when he entered the Rauschenbachs' home, he saw on the stairway a girl of about fourteen, in pigtails. And like a flash it was clear to him: This is my wife! Working on his memoirs with his secretary Aniela Jaffé, he added in his old age: "I was deeply shaken by this, for I had really only seen her for a brief instant, but I knew immediately with absolute certainty that she would be my wife."[5]

A friend in whom he confided laughed at him, especially as Jung had to admit that he had so far not exchanged a single word with the girl. Emma, the daughter of the Rauschenbach family, came from an extremely well-placed middle-class home. Her father was a well-to-do manufacturer in Schaffhausen. What chance was there for a destitute student who was incurring a debt of several thousand francs just getting through his studies? But Jung was certain of his quick intuition, and was comparable in this crucial situation with Sigmund Freud, who once stated his personal practice as follows to the psychoanalyst Theodor Reik: "When I had to make a decision that was not too important, I always found it advantageous to weigh all the pros and cons. In vitally important matters, however, such as the choice of a partner or an occupation, the decision has to come from the unconscious, from somewhere within us. In the most important decisions of our personal life we must, I think, let ourselves be guided by the deep inner needs of our being."[6] As we know, Jung's decision to go into psychiatry was also arrived at spontaneously.

Some six years after this first meeting, Carl Jung proposed to Emma Rauschenbach. After all, he was now officially a doctor with a position at a respected clinic. At first, though, she turned him down. The same thing had happened to his grandfather Carl Gustav, and only with the second attempt was he successful. Gerhard Adler, one of the few able to get a look at the two lovers' correspondence, which was still retained in the family archive, testified to the romantic beauty and sentimental charm that was expressed in their love letters. When Jung went to study with Janet in Paris in the fall of 1902, he was already engaged. Immediately after his return—only a short trip to London was planned—the wedding took place on 14 February 1903.

After a honeymoon at Madeira and the Canary Islands, the Jungs moved into a flat above Eugen Bleuler's lodgings, in the central wing of the Burghölzli clinic. The view westward soared out over the beautiful Lake Zürich. By taking up residence in the clinic, Jung was on one hand following the well-known rule according to which the doctor was expected to live under the same roof with his patients. But on the other hand it was an expression of how important the young husband's work was to him, then as ever. The new life-style he adopted, on account of his wife and also thanks to her dowry, was unmistakable. When purchases had to be made, for example, Emma was present to make sure of quality. The days of financial want were over.

His youthful wife was not lacking in self-confidence and quickly became accustomed to her new role. Emma Jung was known everywhere as a quiet, clever, and self-possessed personality. Her engaging manner made her well liked in her new surroundings, and Director Bleuler did not neglect to congratulate his colleague on his excellent choice of a mate. Aniela Jaffé, who had known Emma Jung-Rauschenbach since 1937, described her as a person who combined earnestness and spontaneous gaiety. "And she made an impression because of an inner calm, which beautifully compensated for C. G. Jung's often volcanic temper."[7]

After a year offspring began to appear. On 26 December 1904 Agathe was born; Gret followed in February 1906, and Franz in November 1908. At this point Jung's family determined to leave their residence in the Burghölzli and build their own house, especially as the necessary financial conditions had long since been met. From his cousin Ernst Fiechter's plans a stately country house was built in Küsnacht (at Seestrasse 1003; since 1915 Seestrasse 228) only a few kilometers distant from Zürich and situated—in fulfillment of Jung's childhood dream—directly on the lake. The three children up to that time were joined by Marianne in September 1910 and then Helene in March 1914. Above the entrance gate of the house Jung had an inscription carved in Latin, one that he had first seen at the age of nineteen in a text of Erasmus of Rotterdam (*Collectanea adagiorum*, 1563):

> *Vocatus atque non vocatus deus aderit.*
> "Invoked or not invoked, the god will be present."

Even in a letter from the last year of his life, the master of the house declared unmistakably that the inscription was not to be understood in a specifically Christian sense. The words were not meant to be an ecclesiastical "profession of faith"; what was affirmed here was rather God himself, "the ultimate question":

> It is a Delphic oracle though. It says: yes, the god will be on the spot, but in what form and to what purpose? I have put the inscription there to remind my patients and myself: *timor dei initium sapientiae* ["The fear of the Lord is the beginning of wisdom." Psalm 111:10].[8]

Thus it was a rather primitive religiosity under whose protection C. G. Jung placed himself and his family—consciously including his patients. For in this house, especially after giving up his position at the Burghölzli, he received the innumerable seekers of advice and help, visitors, and an international clientele.

Emma Jung was included in this work from the beginning. "She was known as an ideal hostess in a house where both parents' and children's friends were always coming and going. In her sense of reality she showed herself superior to her husband and hence was an indispensable help to him in many things. . . . Even though she was heavily taxed by the demands of her family and the large house, she learned mathematics,

Latin, and Greek, and devoted herself for decades to the study of Old French texts."[9] From these studies came the extensive work *Die Gralslegende in psychologischer Sicht* (*The Grail Legend from a Psychological Perspective*), which was completed by Marie-Louise von Franz after the author's death in 1955. This and a study of the animus and anima problem[10] were not Emma Jung's only contribution to Jung's analytical psychology. Her participation and collaboration in her husband's daily work also began in the early years of their marriage. At the close of his *Studies in Word Association* (1904, 1906), the author felt "indebted with special thanks to Mrs. Emma Jung for her active assistance with the repeated revision of this voluminous material."[11] Over the years she managed to grow ever deeper in practical experience in psychotherapy, so that she herself did analytical work, presented lectures and seminars, and was even active as a teaching analyst, that is, in the training of psychotherapists of the Jungian school. Thus when we look at the impressive photo of the psychoanalysts' congress of 1911 in Weimar, a group picture of all the founding figures of the psychoanalytic movement, we see Emma Jung sitting in the front row, not only her husband's wife, but here already his colleague as well.

We cannot fail to mention the fact that at times considerable difficulties arose for her in this role, precisely because the anima projection, as a vital problem facing every man, did not bypass C. G. Jung himself. Quite early an ever-growing crowd of "Jung ladies" began to form, who attached themselves to their master with great enthusiasm, partly in serious collaboration, but partly with the fanatical affection of people who believe they have found their guru. Two gifted Jungian women who were both students and loving admirers should be mentioned at this point: the young Russian Sabina Spielrein, who studied medicine in Zürich from 1905 and came under Jung's psychotherapeutic care from around 1906, at the age of twenty; and also Toni (Antonia) Wolff (1888–1953), whom Jung called in a letter to Freud in 1911 "a new discovery. . ., a remarkable intellect with excellent feeling for philosophy and religion." Close friendships and love relationships developed for both that were not without problems for Jung's marriage. Sabina Spielrein became Jung's student, and the relationship broke up after some years; Toni Wolff was for four decades Jung's closest coworker, next to his wife. Both women made independent contributions to psychoanalysis and Jungian analytical psychology.[12]

9

Sigmund Freud—"The First Man of Real Importance"

> Freud was the first man of real importance I had encountered; in my experience up to that time, no one else could compare with him. There was nothing the least trivial in his attitude. I found him extremely intelligent, shrewd, and altogether remarkable. And yet my first impressions of him remained somewhat tangled; I could not make him out.[1]

These lines from the elderly C. G. Jung's *Memories* express both the high esteem for the founder of modern research into the psyche that the young psychiatrist felt, still just at the beginning of his own great career, and a hint of the difficulties that attended the two men's relationship from the outset, becoming greater and greater until they finally led to their inevitable breakup. Decades later—Sigmund Freud died in exile in London on 23 September 1939—Jung extolled the master of Vienna and his work as "epoch-making." The intellectual history of the late nineteenth and early twentieth centuries, said Jung in his obituary in the Sunday supplement to the Basler *Nachrichten* of 1 October 1939,[2] could no longer be imagined without the name of the founder of psychoanalysis. The Freudian paradigm, whatever opinion one might have of its fundamentals or its details, had "touched nearly every sphere of contemporary intellectual life, with the exception of the exact sciences."

The gravity of this judgment can only be appreciated if one considers the time of its publication: National Socialism and Fascism—the system that had declared war on "Jewish psychoanalysis"—now ruled supreme in Europe. The Second World War had just begun, with the invasion and subjugation of Poland. And although Jung had departed from Freud's position decades earlier, he now referred to the latter's work as "probably the boldest attempt that has ever been made to master the riddles of the unconscious psyche upon the apparently firm ground of empiricism." And, referring to Freud's *Interpretation of Dreams*: "For us, then young psychiatrists, it was . . . a source of illumination, while for our older colleagues it was an object of mockery."[3]

This testimonial from the year 1939 is thoroughly confirmed by the positive assessment he had already made of psychoanalysis around the turn of the century, a generation before. Even in 1900, at twenty-five, he had seen the newly published *Interpretation of Dreams*. But at that time the young doctor was not in a position to recognize the pioneering efforts of his colleague from Vienna, nineteen years his senior:

> At the age of twenty-five I lacked the experience to appreciate Freud's theories. Such experience did not come until later. In 1903 I once more took up *The Interpretation of Dreams* and discovered how it all linked up with my own ideas.[4]

As Jung was becoming better acquainted with psychoanalytical research just after the turn of the century, it was still impossible to foresee how it was going to develop. After *Studies on Hysteria* (1895), published in collaboration with Josef Breuer, and the epochal *Interpretation of Dreams* (1899, 1900), other fundamental works by Freud appeared, such as *The Psychopathology of Everyday Life* (revised edition 1901), *Three Essays on the Theory of Sexuality*, and *Jokes and Their*

Relation to the Unconscious (both 1905). Among Freud's discoveries was the fact "that human affairs are more strongly directed by unconscious motives than . . . was earlier held to be possible; that repressed tendencies, rejected by the conscious mind and locked up in the unconscious, play an unsuspectedly large role in human life; that neuroses are not the result of small so-called functional changes in the brain tissue, but the outcome of complex psychic processes and powerful emotional conflicts, and that the knowledge of these facts can enable a doctor to understand psychic illnesses and in favorable cases even to cure them."[5]

Freud's scientific accomplishments had found the recognition they deserved, even if grudgingly, from both academic and public quarters; since 1885 he had been teaching as a *Privatdozent* in neuropathology at the University of Vienna. His appointment as a university lecturer was belated, to be sure, but at the request of Krafft-Ebing, among others, Emperor Franz-Joseph put his signature to the nomination papers on 5 March 1902. With this Freud achieved public legitimacy, although general acceptance would not come for some time. There was still no psychoanalytical organization, but the first steps had been taken: since 1902 a small circle of psychoanalysts had been meeting on Wednesdays in Freud's lodgings at Berggasse 19. Besides Freud there were Alfred Adler, Wilhelm Stekel, Max Kahane, and Rudolf Reitler, and within a year they were joined by Paul Federn. From 1910 on, this Wednesday club was designated the "Vienna Psychoanalytic Society." As it turned out, C. G. Jung was to become a vigorous supporter of this movement and of the whole subject of psychoanalysis, if only for the limited time of little more than a decade.

In a letter from 1908, Freud saw in Eugen Bleuler the "earliest and most important" of his adherents, whom he sought to interest in a leading role.[6] This high evaluation can be attributed to deliberate reflection, for Bleuler was a duly installed full professor and not merely a lecturer, a universally recognized practitioner and head of a respectable clinic. Furthermore, he and his Zürich coworkers, chief among them C. G. Jung, were non-Jews. This would serve to disarm the objections of those who considered Viennese psychoanalysis merely a more or less marginal Jewish sectarian doctrine within neurology and psychiatry. Thus, Freud must have said to himself, if psychoanalysis was to become a worldwide movement, it could only be with the support of the Zürich group. That Eugen Bleuler would soon dissociate himself, renouncing his membership within a few years (on 28 September 1911), was hardly expected at the time of this letter in 1908, least of all by Freud himself.

In the beginning, though, an extremely positive relationship, both professional and personal, developed between Vienna and Zürich. Bleuler began his correspondence with Freud in 1904. By all accounts, however, the Zürich professor left his Viennese colleague in no doubt that he could not consent to be bound to any dogmatic regulation dictated from Vienna.[7] Thus contact with those in Zürich—among whom were the Burghölzli coworkers Ludwig Binswanger, Franz Riklin, and Alphonse Maeder—devolved more and more onto Jung, who then became the de facto inheritor of the leadership role in the incipient psychoanalytic movement that had been intended for Bleuler. Freud learned with satisfaction from Bleuler that they had been working with his word-association method at Burghölzli for some two years, since 1902, and that Dr. Jung had not only applied it successfully, but largely affirmed the psychoanalytic approach. This was shown not only by his early review of *The Interpretation of Dreams* as an intern, but by his public references to Freud, for example in his dissertation.

In the Foreword to his study on "The Psychology of Dementia Praecox," written in July 1906, Jung commented on the origin of his work on schizophrenia, as Bleuler called it, at the same time revealing his attitude toward Freud:

> My observations are not spun from some brooding fancy, but thoughts that have ripened in almost daily contact with

> my respected supervisor, Professor Bleuler. For the considerable enlargement of my empirical material I owe special thanks to my friend Dr. Riklin in Rheinau. Even a superficial glance at the pages of my work will show how much I have to thank to the ingenious conceptions of Freud. As he has still not received due recognition and appreciation, but will be opposed by even the highest authorities, I hope I may be permitted to clarify somewhat my position with regard to Freud. . . . I can assure my readers that from the first I naturally made all the same objections to Freud that have been adduced in the literature. But I said to myself that Freud could only be refuted by one who had repeatedly applied the psychoanalytic method and actually inquired as Freud did, considering daily life, hysteria, and dreams from his point of view, patiently and at length. Whoever did not or could not do this should not pass judgment on Freud; otherwise he would be like the famous men of science who disdained to look through the telescope.[8]

Was Freud a modern-day Galileo? There is much to be said for this idea, at least as far as the stance of those in authority—once the church, now the scientific community—is concerned, but Wilhelm Weygandt, a professor of psychiatry and private consulting physician, expressed it perfectly on the occasion of a medical convention in Hamburg in 1910: "Freud's theories have nothing to do with science; they are more a matter for the police."[9] (Three years earlier Jung had said of this "scholar": "I know Weygandt personally, he is a hysteric par excellence, stuffed with complexes from top to bottom, so that he can't get a genuine word out of his throat. . . . I would never have thought German scholarship could have produced such meanness."[10]

In his text of 1906, however, Jung emphasized explicitly that doing justice to Freud by no means meant that one had to surrender oneself to a dogma. He himself was not even willing to grant the exclusive significance that Freud apparently saw in infantile sexual trauma. To be sure, "the undoubtedly powerful role of sexuality in the psyche" might suggest this, but Freudian therapy was at best just one of the possibilities,

> and perhaps does not always offer what it is theoretically supposed to. But all these are minor issues that vanish in the face of the psychological principles whose discovery we owe to Freud, and to which his critics have paid far too little attention.

In the long term, Jung remained true to this same statement of his position toward Freud and psychoanalysis in 1906. And, conversely, the strength of the young psychiatrist from Zürich was that he distinguished from the outset between the fundamental accomplishments of the Freudian theory and its critical shortcomings. But for the moment the bond of collegial solidarity with Freud outweighed the majority of the profession. And Jung was not lacking in this commitment. According to his *Memories*, he first entered the lists in defense of Freud in 1906, at a conference in Munich,[11] although in fact it was probably at the conference of Southwest German neurologists and psychiatrists in Baden-Baden in May, where the psychiatrist Gustav Aschaffenburg of Heidelberg attacked Freud's "Fragment of an Analysis of a Case of Hysteria." In the same year, in the *Münchener medizinische Wochenschrift*, Jung took up what was admittedly a rather cautiously defensive position: Freud was probably subject to many human errors, he said, but this by no means excluded the possibility that "beneath the tangled exterior lies hidden a kernel of truth of whose significance we can as yet form no adequate conception."[12] Furthermore, he claimed, written statements were incapable, even approximately, of reproducing the reality of psychoanalysis (Jung wrote "psychanalysis") sufficiently for the reader to understand it without any difficulty. It had been no different for him, Jung said, at his first reading of Freud; he had only been able to scribble question marks in the margins. And yet his experiments in word association were replicable, and their outcome agreed with Freud's results.

There was no shortage of reaction from the authorities. Two German professors made it known in correspondence that anyone who defended Freud in this manner and persisted in working along this line was risking his academic future. Jung's answer was clear:

> "If what Freud says is the truth, I am with him. I don't give a damn for a career if it has to be based on the premise of restricting research and concealing the truth." And I went on defending Freud and his ideas. But on the basis of my own findings I was still unable to feel that all neuroses were caused by sexual repression or sexual traumata. In certain cases this was so, but not in others. Nevertheless, Freud had opened up a new path of investigation, and the shocked outcries against him at the time seemed to me absurd.[13]

When *Studies in Word Association* reached print in 1905, Jung sent a copy of his new work to Freud, in order to show his colors to him as well. It turned out that Bleuler's references to his energetic assistant had not failed to have an affect on Freud, for on 11 April 1906 he informed his "very esteemed colleague" in Zürich that he had already procured a copy of the study "out of impatience." With this began the voluminous—and as Jung later said, "accursed"[14]—exchange of letters which continued until April 1914 (not counting one straggler in which Jung referred a patient to Freud in 1923). Almost six months elapsed until Jung's first letter. On 5 October he had occasion to thank Professor Freud for his "collection of monographs on studies of neurosis." His gratitude gave way immediately to practical discussion arising from the current controversy. Significantly, Jung made no secret in this first letter of his own position with regard to the Freudian sexual theory. Apart from his clinical observations, the schooling of Pierre Janet may have been at work here, which had similarly taken a stand rejecting psychoanalysis.

Freud's rejoinder took up this point by return mail. That

his sympathizers in Zürich reported such reservations cannot have gone overlooked in Vienna. But Freud was hopeful: "I have long suspected from your writings that your regard for my psychology does not fully extend to my views on questions of hysteria and sexuality, but I have not give up the expectation that in the course of the years you will come much closer to me than you now think possible."[15] Freud did not omit to remark incidentally that he himself would have judged his opponent Gustav Aschaffenburg "somewhat more harshly" than Jung had done, and that he could find in his statements nothing but silliness and an "enviable ignorance of the matters on which he is passing judgment."

Thus the differences between the two men were quite clearly marked—in all collegiality and good will, of course—even in the comments made in their first letters to each other. At that point there was—as yet—no cause to dig trenches between the two. For the younger man the dominant factor was his admiration for the pioneer of the investigation of the psyche, Jung's respect ("very esteemed Herr Professor") for "the first man of real importance" in this field; the older was stirred by the hope of a faithful following and even strict succession, such as one can only hope for from an adopted son and "crown prince." And Freud made use of just this title in a letter from the year 1909 that was also informative in other respects.[16] Perhaps the master was not quite sure of his hopes in his obviously rather independent "disciple," for as early as the eleventh of the 259 letters, we find the exhortation, dictated with Freudian clairvoyance, ". . .do not deviate too far from me, when in reality you are so close to me, otherwise we will yet see how they will play us off against one another."[17] The validity of his statement from 1 January 1907 is well known!

During the next seven years the correspondence between the two men became astonishingly massive. There was hardly a week—except for the last stage—in which one and often more letters were not sent back and forth between Vienna and Zürich. An extremely rich and varied conversation unfolded in these letters, providing a glimpse into the thought processes, the joys and cares of two doctors of thoroughly remarkable human and cultural stature. "There are in our century not many such first-rate records of human struggle, human error, human comedy, and human conflict," as Joachim Kaiser pointedly summed it up in his review of the excellently edited publication.[18] Going into more detail, Martin Grotjahn has said, "Freud seems to have been especially happy to have found in Switzerland a non-Jewish academic who was prepared to align himself with psychoanalysis as an ally and organizer. Both men candidly exchanged their views on their colleagues and the further steps by which the 'cause' should be advanced. They spoke of their experiences with patients and discussed questions and details of theory and practice, bringing to light a particular interest in schizophrenia, mythology, anthropology, and occultism. The early stages of many of Freud's later ideas can already be seen here, along with the genesis of psychoanalytical journals and the preparations for visits and international and local meetings."[19]

The younger man asked the older for advice, but increasingly revealed an ever greater self-confidence and professional maturity. The degree of intimacy between them grew. From October 1908 on, Jung was to Freud "my dear friend," while Jung used the salutation "Dear Professor," until finally the last letters stiffened into formality and ran out into silence. But none of Freud's correspondence with any of his other colleagues—be it Bleuler, Binswanger, Pfister, Abraham, Groddeck, Lou Andreas-Salomé, Reik, Reich, Weiss, Putnam, Ferenczi, Federn, or Rank—rivals that which he carried on with Jung in range, human depth, and forcefulness of expression.

Special mention may be made of a few letters scattered here and there in the collection from Emma Jung, who here also acted not only as the wife of her famous husband, but spoke for herself, standing on her own feet while at the same time taking sides with her spouse. With great maturity the young woman turned her attention to the problematic situation that had long been developing between the two men. Partly thanks to her feminine intuition, but also through the practical application of psychological understanding, she noted the complications that stood between "father" and "son" and searched for a humane solution. "Indeed, one can certainly not be the child of a great man with impunity, considering how much trouble it already takes to get away from even ordinary fathers. And then when this eminent father also has a patriarchal streak in him, as you said yourself!"—this last in reference to Freud's family circumstances. And, regarding Jung, "You can imagine how pleased and honored I am at the confidence which you place in Carl, but it would almost seem to me that sometimes you give him too much; do you not see in him more of a successor and fulfiller than is necessary? Doesn't one often give much because one wishes to hold much back?" A revealing question! Finally she made an urgent appeal: "Please think of Carl not with the feelings of a father: 'He will grow, but I must fade away,' but as one person to another, who like you must follow his own law."[20] So she wrote, at twenty-nine, to the father of psychoanalysis, who was fifty-five—spirited words from a mature woman!

After a few letters containing discussions of problems of work and dreams, a meeting in person was envisaged for early 1907. As the wish to visit America had appeared to Jung in a dream, Freud answered jokingly, why not Vienna first—"It is closer!" After some discussion back and forth, their first conversation in Freud's home was scheduled for Sunday, 3 March, at ten in the morning. Jung was accompanied by his wife and his colleague from Zürich Ludwig Binswanger. Sunday was chosen because by his own report Freud was in harness from eight to eight Monday through Saturday, practicing therapy on the average ten hours a day. Thus only Sunday was free, and also evenings after eight o'clock, which were also considered—for example Wednesday, the habitual meeting time for the colleagues from Vienna, whom Jung likewise met for the first time on this occasion. Naturally the main issue came up during the face-to-face conversation between Freud and

Jung: "We met at one o'clock in the afternoon and talked virtually without a pause for thirteen hours."[21] Jung acknowledged that Freud at first seemed to him, as he did to many of his contemporaries, "a rather strange phenomenon." He had to discover the Austrian's peculiar mentality, to examine how far the already suspected lines of division were valid and where he would be able to follow the founder of psychoanalysis. Regarding the opposition of Freud and Jung, it should also be made clear that the particular atmosphere of Vienna during the last decades of the old Austro-Hungarian empire, represented by a member of the Jewish intelligentsia, must have had a singular effect on Jung, who as a Swiss had been influenced by entirely different cultural traditions. To these dissimilarities of environment was added the difference in character and temperament which Jung later expressed by describing himself, according to his own typology, as an "introverted" type and Freud as a distinctly "extraverted" type. "But you must not think I am frantically out to contrast myself with you by holding the most divergent views possible," Jung had already said in his letter of 29 December 1906, in which he declared his upbringing, his environment, and his scientific premises to be "utterly different" from Freud's.[22]

How serious the differences between the two personalities were became evident on the objective and scientific level. There was as always Freud's sexual theory:

> What he said about his sexual theory impressed me. Nevertheless, his words could not remove my hesitations and doubts. I tried to advance these reservations of mine on several occasions, but each time he would attribute them to my lack of experience. Freud was right; in those days I had not enough experience to support my objections. I could see that his sexual theory was enormously important to him, both personally and philosophically. This impressed me, but I could not decide to what extent this strong emphasis on sexuality was connected with subjective prejudices of his, and to what extent it rested upon verifiable experiences.[23]

Then, too, Freud's view of the spirit seemed questionable to his visitor. The master tended to designate as "psychosexuality" whatever could not be explained as an outpouring of sexual libido. Although this hypothesis can in no way be dismissed as solely Freud's invention—one need only think of Richard Krafft-Ebing's *Psychopathia sexualis* (1886), or of Schopenhauer, Eduard von Hartmann, and even further back in religious and intellectual history!—Jung shrank from the thought that the whole of human culture could be thought of as the morbid product of repressed sexuality. Was not sexuality too a thoroughly numinous phenomenon, an unfathomably religious power that far surpassed human capacity? Some two years later[24] this first impression of Jung's appeared to be confirmed, as Freud enjoined him with great urgency: "My dear Jung, promise me never to abandon the sexual theory. That is the most essential thing of all. You see, we must make a dogma of it, an unshakable bulwark." And when Jung asked him in astonishment, a bulwark against what?, he answered, "Against the black tide of the mud . . . of occultism." In his *Memories*, Jung commented:

> First of all, it was the words "bulwark" and "dogma" that alarmed me; for a dogma, that is to say, an indisputable confession of faith, is set up only when the aim is to suppress doubts once and for all. But that no longer has anything to do with scientific judgment; only with a personal power drive.
>
> This was the thing that struck at the heart of our friendship. I knew that I would never be able to accept such an attitude.[25]

As far as "occultism" was concerned, Freud understood by this practically everything that philosophy and religion—and especially the parapsychology that was coming into fashion around the turn of the century—had to say about the human spirit. But this was by no means his final word on the subject; his skepticism did begin to give way. For Jung, in a peculiar way, it was precisely Freud's universally applied sexual theory that seemed "occult," an unproven hypothesis or a scientifically embellished dogma.

Yet Jung could have no doubt of Freud's greatness, his intelligence and sagacity. Thus his first impressions of him remained "unclear and partly not even understood." Only after they had gone some way together was he able to achieve the necessary clarity. In terms of Jung's life this meant that the parting of ways, the turning point, would only come when Jung had reached the critical stage of his own middle life, in which it became both possible and necessary for him to form a clearer idea of his own intellectual and above all existential point of view. As far as the meeting of the two men in general is concerned, clearly there was a combination of two factors here. On one hand there was the unenvious recognition of Freud's professional qualities and experience, and indeed his geniality and human greatness, while on the other hand considerable contrasts were evident, which could be traced to their difference in type, and also in large measure to the disparity in intellectual standpoint of the two researchers. These contrasts in any case could not have been entirely suppressed, as Jung of course recognized rightly from the outset. Born in 1856 and thus about nineteen years older, Freud was too settled in the intellectual prejudices of his century, as revealed in its one-sidedly materialistic natural science and the worldview built on it. Jung believed he had observed in Freud "the eruption of unconscious religious factors." Deeply impressed, he wrote later in his autobiography:

> Freud, who had always made much of his irreligiosity,[26] had now constructed a dogma; or rather, in the place of a jealous God whom he had lost, he had substituted another compelling image, that of sexuality. It was no less insistent, exacting, domineering, threatening, and orally ambivalent than the original one. Just as the psychically stronger agency is given "divine" or "daemonic" attributes, so the "sexual libido" took over the role of a *deus absconditus*, a hidden or concealed god.[27]

Strong as Jung's resistance was to an interpretation that was to his mind monotonously reduced to sexuality, nevertheless within a few years the personal relationship became quite intimate and friendly, including the two men's families (Freud's interest in Jung's family was much stronger than Jung's in that of Freud). Many things contributed to this, among them external pressure, which demanded solidarity of the small band of those who fought for the cause of psychoanalysis. Another reason was the time they spent together, although distance and professional duties severely restricted the frequency of their meetings. Freud made his first return visit to Zürich between 18 and 21 September 1908, when the Jung family still lived at the Burghölzli. As the lady of the house and the children were away and Eugen Bleuler had granted his senior doctor the necessary time off, the two men were able to concentrate completely on their topic. "I was not alone until late at night; we walked and debated until eight o'clock every day," Freud reported to Abraham in Berlin on 29 September. "As for Jung, he has so overcome his hesitation that he belongs to the cause without reservation, and even plans to go on working on the question of dementia praecox energetically along our lines. This suits me supremely."[28] Thus Freud wrapped up his stay in Zürich with relief and satisfaction.

From 25 to 30 March 1909, Carl Gustav and Emma Jung stayed with the Freuds in Vienna for a second time. At the time his relationship with the Burghölzli was due to end at the close of the month, although the family were forced to stay in their apartment at the clinic until the end of May because their own house in Küsnacht was not finished on time. This second stay in Vienna was marked by a spectacular occurrence, for, on the last evening the two men were together, as the conversation turned to matters of parapsychology and precognition, and Freud resolutely denied the existence of such things, Jung was possessed by a peculiar sensation, which he described thus:

It was as it my diaphragm were made of iron and were

> becoming red-hot—a glowing vault. And at that moment there was such a loud report in the bookcase, which stood right next to us, that we both started up in alarm, fearing the thing was going to topple over on us. I said to Freud: "There, that is an example of a so-called catalytic exteriorization phenomenon."
>
> "Oh come," he exclaimed. "that is sheer bosh."
>
> "It is not," I replied. "You are mistaken, Herr Professor. And to prove my point I now predict that in a moment there will be another such loud report!" Sure enough, no sooner had I said the words than the same detonation went off in the bookcase.
>
> To this day I do not know what gave me this certainty. But I knew beyond all doubt that the report would come again.[29]

Freud was astounded, particularly at this exact prediction of something that could not have been known. At any rate there was no room in his philosophy at that time for any such phenomena. That he had to admit in the end that they did occur, and indeed—to his further astonishment—even after Jung's departure, appears unmistakably in their subsequent correspondence. His colleague from Zürich seemed to him a bit uncanny, and his dissertation *On the Psychology and Pathology of So-Called Occult Phenomena* suddenly appeared to him in a new light. "I do not deny that your comments and your experiment made a powerful impression on me"—Freud actually spoke of an experiment, as if his visitor had intended to demonstrate some psychic ability, although this cannot have been the case. "After your departure I determined to make some observations, and here are the results. In my front room there are continual creaking noises, from where the two heavy Egyptian steles rest on the oak boards of the bookcase, so that's obvious. In the second room, where we heard the crash, such noises are very rare. At first I was inclined to ascribe some meaning to it if the noise we heard so frequently when you were here were never heard again after your departure. But since then it has happened over and over again, yet never in connection with my thoughts and never when I was considering you or your special problem," Freud added explicitly.[30] Of course the subject itself had become his special problem some time ago. Still, in this connection Freud had to recognize the "spell" of Jung's personal presence.

Jung, who had long been familiar with such "synchronistic" manifestations from his own experience, did not dwell any further on the phenomenon per se. But because at the time he had a patient in whose case apparitions of ghosts played a role, the event in Vienna prompted Jung to think further along psychoanalytic lines. He came to the conclusion that "if there is a psychanalysis [sic], then there must also be a 'psychosynthesis' which creates future events according to the same laws."[31] In particular, the Italian Roberto G. Assagioli (1888–1974), whom Jung met in the summer of 1909, had devoted his dissertation in Florence to psychosynthesis.[32] What Jung tried to make palatable to the master in Vienna was a final-prospective point of view, one oriented to the future development of the psyche, and which at the time had in fact already received due consideration—even in his own dissertation Jung had contrasted a final-prospective alternative to the causal-analytical approach to psychic data.

In Jung's view the real profit from the second meeting in Vienna was represented by something still different. Immediately after that ominous last evening he had begun to feel, "most happily, inwardly freed from the oppressive feeling of [Freud's] fatherly authority."[33] Freud, however, obviously did not share this opinion. He was convinced that something rather unfortunate had happened, when he replied on 16 April 1909: "It is remarkable that on the same evening that I formally adopted you as an eldest son, anointing you as my successor and crown prince—*in partibus infidelium*—that then and there you should have divested me of my paternal dignity, and that the divesting seems to have given you as much pleasure as investing your person gave me. Now I am afraid that I must fall back again into the role of father toward you in giving you my views on poltergeist phenomena. . . . I therefore don once more my horn-rimmed paternal spectacles and warn my dear son to keep a cool head and rather not understand something than make such great sacrifices for the sake of understanding."[34] And on the question of the purported psychosynthesis, Freud said, he shook his wise old head; thus there would be no discussion of a subject that Jung had no intention of losing sight of. Moreover Freud, as always, considered Jung's researches into the "spook complex" a "lovely delusion." And all this was amiably wrapped up "With cordial regards to yourself, your wife and children, Yours, Freud."

The need for an exchange of ideas and continued critical development of the psychoanalytic approach led its practitioners to establish a psychoanalytic association, beginning in Vienna with the "Wednesday society," and in Zürich drawn from the circle of coworkers at the Burghölzli under the rubric of the "Freudian Society." This existed from late September 1907 under the chairmanship of Ludwig Binswanger, a participant in Jung's association experiments and later the director for many years of the private Bellevue Clinic in Kreuzlingen on Lake Constance, who was also known as a cofounder of existential analysis. "Things are going very well." Jung reported to Vienna on 10 October 1907, "generally great interest, lively discussion. One has the enjoyable feeling of being involved in an endlessly fruitful work."[35] According to the same letter, he had also "converted" his first theologian. Above all, the common cause attracted further small groups. Karl Abraham, who had worked at the Burghölzli for some years, put together a psychoanalytic working group in Berlin, with Freud's lasting support. The American Abraham A. Brill, who had also been a student under Bleuler and Jung, brought the psychoanalytic doctrine to the United States, especially with the help of his translation of Freudian and Jungian writings into English. At the same time two other Americans, Charles Ricksher and Frederick W. Peterson, beat the drum of publicity there, seeing to it that Jung's association experiments became known in the States. In London a psychoanalytical society was formed by Freud's later biographer Ernest Jones; in Hungary Sandor Ferenczi, one of Freud's strictest students, collected a group of sympathetic doctors. Eventually it was also Ferenczi who stirred up the desire for the first great convention of psychoanalysts.[36] That the "First International Psychoanalytic Congress" was able to take place in Salzburg in April 1908 was unquestionably thanks to the strong organizational and intellectual commitment of C. G. Jung. The designation "First Congress for Freudian Psychology" was his idea; such at least was the heading over his draft of the written invitation, sent to Vienna for approval late in January.

With forty-two participants altogether, who gathered on 26 and 27 April 1908 in the Hotel Bristol on Makartplatz in Salzburg, the attendance was greater than had been anticipated, greater even than Freud wanted it. For because he was only too aware of the sometimes quite limited abilities of his colleagues in Vienna, who nonetheless energetically desired to express their opinions, from some of them he would rather have had refusals than acceptances to Jung's signed invitations. Since Freud had informed him of this, Jung once stated that Freud had no, or only a few, adherents of any importance in Vienna; rather he was surrounded there by a "degenerate gang of Bohemians" who did little credit to the common cause. Behind this disparaging remark Ernest Jones saw nothing but blatant anti-Semitism.[37] The letters, however, reveal how unjustified was this supposition, which was also made against the non-Jewish Jung in other circumstances. In fact, in the face of the upcoming Salzburg Congress, it was Freud who was afraid he might "all too obviously look ridiculous" in front of the Swiss, "for not all of them are anything to write home about. I am making do with very little here," he said prophylactically, confirming Jung's assessment in a letter from Vienna dated 17 February 1908. The hint that Jung might therefore consider limiting the time allotted for each speaker and politely reject "certain contributions" as unsuitable also came from Freud himself—in fairly clear language. A bit later, in contrast, he set Jung apart: "You are really the only one who even has anything original to offer."[38] And Freud once again:

"It is enough trouble for me to see that not too much incorrect and hasty comes out in the contributions of my Viennese companions."[39] So the worst of the Vienna circle were not included among those who were invited to present papers, namely Isidore Sadger, Wilhelm Stekel, and Alfred Adler. They were flanked by the foreigners Ernest Jones, Karl Abraham, and Jung himself. That Freud, with his contributions of case material, came first and received unlimited time to speak goes without saying. And after Eugen Bleuler, who was also present, had declined the flattering invitation to preside over the first congress of psychoanalysts, it fell to Jung to take over the office. This remained so for the subsequent congresses, and C. G. Jung officiated as president of the International Psychoanalytic Association until his resignation.

With this his representative role at the founder's side was clearly defined for all to see. Thus dissensions that could not be avoided, whether of a factual or a more temperamental and atmospheric nature, could always be smoothed over. Freud also performed no little service in resolving and reconciling the "quarrels" that began to arise here and there among his colleagues. His assessment of the Salzburg Congress, with which Abraham as well as others were in agreement, was extremely positive—on Jung's address he said: "It was very refreshing and left a pleasant aftertaste with me. I was glad to find you flourishing so well, and whatever resentment there might have been melted away as soon as I saw you again and understood you,"[40] expressing the father's delight in his "son and heir." One outcome of the Salzburg gathering was a resolution to begin producing a proper annual journal, in which exemplary works on psychoanalysis would be published. Freud and Bleuler were designated publishers, while the editorship of the new *Jahrbuch für psychoanalytische und psychopathologische Forschungen* went to C. G. Jung; thus once again two of Freud's colleagues from Zürich and none from Vienna figured as custodians both inward and outward. As Freud had to admit—even after the two great secessions under Adler and Jung (1914)—"The Zürich contingent were the picked troops of the little army fighting for the honor of analysis. They provided the only opportunity of acquiring the new art and working at it. Most of my adherents and coworkers today came to me by way of Zürich, even some who were geographically much closer to Vienna than to Zürich. . . . In the union that was formed between the Vienna and Zürich schools, the Swiss were by no means only on the receiving end. They had already produced respectable scientific work in their own right, the results of which benefited psychoanalysis."[41] Freud stated openly that these contributions from Bleuler's camp were connected above all with the name of C. G. Jung.

The first Freudians, Jung among them, could not complain of a lack of publicity. Certainly attacks from official academic circles were predominant, especially in the German-speaking world. So it was all the more surprising when an invitation came from the United States, where Freud's and Jung's output was being followed with intense interest and the necessary lack of prejudice. "In no other country was psychoanalysis adopted as early and as readily, and nowhere did it become as popular as in the U.S.A.," wrote Ulrike May.[42]

This invitation from America arrived in the same year in which Jung withdrew from his fatiguing work at the Burghölzli, moving into his home in Küsnacht and establishing his equally extensive private practice from there. Stanley Hall, himself a psychologist and president of Clark University in Worcester, Massachusetts, invited Freud, and a few weeks later Jung, to deliver a number of lectures in German on their field of research, on the occasion of the twentieth anniversary of its founding. The recipients were surprised at these invitations, considering the ingrained puritanism of the New England states, even though Jung was optimistically inclined to hope for great interest in psychoanalysis in the United States as early as 1907–1908. That there was nevertheless a certain willingness in medical circles to accept Freud's work, despite its sexual underpinnings, goes along with the general American readiness to become acquainted with new scientific, medical, and psychological achievements and make them more generally useful. As far as the new path of research and therapy of the psyche initiated by Freud was concerned, the conference's organizer had informed himself rather thoroughly about how its methods were evaluated and practiced. No less a figure than William James, author of the famous Gifford Lectures (Edinburgh, 1901–1902) on *The Varieties of Religious Experience*,[43] had spoken of the "marvelous investigations of Binet, Janet, Freud, Mason, Prince, and others into the subliminal consciousness"; he had followed Freud's early works with benevolent interest and kept his compatriots up to date with them through his reviews. Another, James Jackson Putnam, a well-known doctor in Boston and professor of neurology at Harvard, had begun to do psychoanalytical experiments. Brill's return to the States from Zürich and Ernest Jones's appointment to head the university psychiatric clinic in Toronto, both in 1908, provided for at least sporadic dissemination of the new ideas. Writing to Freud on 10 December 1908, Jones was not short of admonitions toward restraint: "The Americans are a peculiar people with customs all their own. They show curiosity, but seldom genuine interest (a distinction like that between the craving of the neurasthenic and the true desire of the normal lover). Their attitude toward progress is lamentable. They want to hear all about the 'latest' methods of treatment, with one eye firmly fixed on the almighty dollar, and they think only of the esteem, 'kudos' as they call it, which these will bring them. Many articles have recently been written in praise of Freudian psychotherapy, but they are absurdly superficial, and I fear they will judge it harshly as soon as they hear about its sexual foundation and grasp what it means. The best we can hope for are a few genuine converts who may be won for us and broaden their experience. Still we must do what we can in order to smooth the way for the future."[44]

Not just a cautious warning, then. Sobering experiences with American partisans were also exchanged in letters between Jung and Freud at this time. The correspondence shows how highly, on the whole, Jung rated the upcoming trip to America, and indeed not least for the positive reverse influence it might have on work in Europe. For when Freud had originally received the invitation, and had actually turned it down at first on account of the date and his finances, Jung had not neglected to point out all the potentially positive aspects to his friend in Vienna. As it turned out, the hosts shifted the arrangements to September, and Freud now promised to go. He was elated when a little later Jung was also asked to present some lectures, for the long ocean crossing and the stay in America itself would mean plenty of opportunity for the conversation between them that had been so painfully limited until then. On 20 August the small party of travelers, which had been joined by Sandor Ferenczi, embarked in Bremen, and the next day the steamer *George Washington* of the North German Lloyd line put off, beginning a journey of some seven weeks, all told.

Jung left no doubt about the importance of this event: "We were together every day, and analyzed each other's dreams," he reports in his *Memories*. Important dreams of all sorts appeared, but because of their collective and symbolic content the master of dream interpretation hardly seemed equal to them—the riddles were too much for Freud.

> It was a human failure, and I would never have wanted to discontinue our dream analyses on that account. On the contrary, they meant a great deal to me, and I found our relationship exceedingly valuable. I regarded Freud as an older, more mature and experienced personality, and felt like a son in that respect.[45]

Thus Jung himself fully affirmed the father-son relationship. But even this harmony did not remain undisturbed, and it was in their analytical dream work together during the voyage that serious personal and practical problems began to reveal themselves. Jung also had trouble understanding certain elements in the dream life of his analysand, and as usual he asked about certain details in Freud's private life, which in view of the openness and unreservedness they had always shared, both in person and in their letters, was nothing out of the ordinary. But suddenly now there was a remarkable block on the elder man's part, justified by the remark "But I cannot risk my authority!" Jung's reaction described the situation:

> At that moment he lost it altogether. That sentence burned itself into my memory; and in it the end of our relationship was already foreshadowed. Freud was placing personal authority above truth.[46]

Hardly less significant, in terms of its content, is a dream that Jung had at this time: He found himself in an unfamiliar two-story house. Upstairs in a kind of living room there were beautiful old pieces of rococo-style furniture, and one floor lower, furnishings from the fifteenth or sixteenth century. Much older still were the cellar and the rest of the basement, which seemed to date back to Roman times. Finally he lifted a stone slab to reveal narrow stone steps, leading still farther down into a cavelike depth where bones, broken pottery, and two very old and partly disintegrated human skulls were lying.

Naturally, according to psychoanalytical dream theory, Freud sought to find out what secret "wish" was being fulfilled here, what wish fulfillment might be reflected in the dream. Now it was Jung's turn to feel resistance. On the one hand he was convinced that the assumption of mere wish fulfillment did not fit in this case, but on the other hand his own divergent dream interpretation was still quite uncertain at the time. So he only pretended to respond to Freud's further analytical questions—certainly just as questionable a tactic! At any rate, such a thing was clearly bound to lead to error.

Obviously these differing approaches to the interpretation of dreams must be viewed within the existential and psychological contexts in which they were developed. And in Jung's case this means that one must always take into consideration his strong historical interest, which included archeology and ancient history. He himself referred to the intensely historical atmosphere that surrounded him during his school days at the end of the nineteenth century. Hence, understandably,

> when I thought about dreams and the contents of the unconscious, I never did so without making historical comparisons; in my student days I always used Krug's old dictionary of philosophy. I was especially familiar with the writers of the eighteenth and early nineteenth century. . . . By contrast, I had the impression that Freud's intellectual history began with Büchner, Moleschott, DuBois-Reymond, and Darwin.[47]

Disregarding for the moment the fact that this characterization of the master was at least an unwarranted inference—Freud's study, for instance, was filled with ancient relics of all kinds—Jung's dream must certainly be said to have had great significance for the further development of his thinking. According to his own interpretation, the various stories of the house, down to the cavelike hollow, symbolized dimensions of the human psyche. Thus the living room upstairs most likely corresponds to everyday consciousness, while beneath it lie levels reaching back into archaic spiritual pasts that are always present in every person all the way back to our animalistic roots, even though we are not always consciously aware of this. Therefore the meaning was not to be found in some kind of wish fulfillment (for example, that the dreamer unconsciously desired the deaths of two men), but in a fundamental insight:

> [The dream] was my first inkling of a collective a priori beneath the personal psyche. This I first took to be the traces of earlier modes of functioning. Later, with increasing experience and on the basis of more reliable knowledge, I recognized them as forms of instinct, that is, as archetypes.[48]

Of course the way to the archetypal dimension was still far from clear. But this dream presented Jung with an important stimulus to pursue further research in this area by recalling his old interests in archeology and immersing himself in the "symbolism and mythology of ancient peoples," for example with the help of Friedrich Creuzer's work of that title.[49] These interests, though, a field of investigation all its own, were at the time of his journey to the United States still far removed from the topics that were to be discussed there.

On the evening of 29 August, after a nine-day voyage, the three traveling companions arrived in New York.[50] Brill had come to welcome them, and two days later Jones arrived from Toronto. Before the journey on to Boston and Worcester began, the five men had time to tour New York. From Jung's letters to his wife we are rather well informed about his immediate impressions from this first trip to America. The gigantic size and bustle of this city of over a million inhabitants left the Swiss visitor breathless. A walk of several hours in Central Park did him good. Dinner at the Brills': "Imagine, a salad made of apples, cabbage, celery, nuts, etc., etc. But it was good anyway." Then from ten to twelve P.M., an automobile ride through Chinatown, "into the most dangerous part of New York," Jung thought. His letter went into vivid detail:

> It was filthy and exotic. The Chinese are all dressed in dark blue and wear their long black queues. We went to a Chinese temple that was in a horrible dump called a Josshouse. One could smell a murder in every corner. Then we went to a Chinese teahouse, where we had a really excellent tea, along with which they brought us rice and an unbelievable dish of chopped meat, which appeared to be completely covered with earthworms and onions. It looked frightful. The worms, though, turned out to be Chinese potato; I tried some of it and it wasn't bad. Otherwise the rowdies who were loitering about looked more dangerous than the Chinese. In Chinatown there are nine thousand Chinese men and only twenty-eight women. But because of this there are masses of white prostitutes, who have just now been cleared out by the police. After that we went to a real Apache music hall, where it was dismal. A singer got up, and people threw money on the floor in front of him for

payment. It was all strange and terribly unpleasant, but interesting.[51]

And so that his wife at home in Küsnacht would not worry about him enjoying the New York night life, he added: "Furthermore, like a true American woman, Mrs. Brill went everywhere with us. We finally got to bed at twelve o'clock. This morning—the thirty-first of August—the activity started up again."

This activity included a visit to an insane asylum, then to the Metropolitan Museum of Art for several hours, and in the evening to Coney Island, the "largest seaside holiday resort on the Atlantic coast." And all in fine weather and a pleasant breeze. There were pangs of homesickness, "and sometimes not small ones. I miss you, and I am always thinking how much you would like it here. It does not suit me terribly well, it is just extremely interesting."[52] So said the psychologist, who nonetheless was so busy viewing the paleontological collection with its huge fossils, "Lord God's anxiety dream of creation,"[53] that he put off preparing the details of his three lectures until he got to Worcester. But this real purpose of the journey was threatening to turn into an incidental episode, for in the same letter he mentioned his further plans: Niagara Falls, an excursion to Canada if possible; they would not be able to make it to Chicago—and by the way he would be on his way home again on 21 September.

Another voyage by steamer was in the offing, from the Hudson River around the point of Manhattan with its innumerable skyscrapers, and up the East River under the Brooklyn and Manhattan bridges. On 5 September they reached Fall River, Massachusetts, and on the same day took the train on to Boston and from there to Worcester, the goal of their journey. Jung took pleasure in the ever-changing scenery with its forests, meadows, and small lakes, partly dotted with tiny villages of wooden houses, whose construction and appearance reminded him of Holland. All in all it was "a refreshing relief after the life in New York."

Jung stressed in his letters the kindness with which the travelers had been welcomed. He and Freud lodged with Professor Stanley Hall, "a refined, distinguished old gentleman close on seventy." Once again, thanks to her husband's description, Emma Jung could imagine a colorful picture of his stay in Worcester.

> The house is furnished in an incredibly amusing fashion, everything roomy and comfortable. There is a splendid studio filled with thousands of books, and boxes of cigars everywhere. Two pitch-black Negroes in dinner jackets, the extreme of grotesque solemnity, perform as servants. Carpets everywhere, all the doors open, even the bathroom door and the front door; people going in and out all over the place; all the windows extend down to the floor. The house is surrounded by an English lawn, no garden fence. Half the city (about a hundred and eighty thousand inhabitants) stands in a regular forest of old trees which shade all the streets. Most of the houses are smaller than ours, charmingly surrounded by flowers and flowering shrubs, overgrown with Virginia creeper and wisteria; everything well tended, clean, cultivated, and exceedingly peaceful and congenial. A wholly different America![54]

Jung was unquestionable fascinated. But he too did not neglect to display his own charm, particularly in the company of the ladies. He had just had "a talk" with two very cultivated elderly ladies, he wrote to Küsnacht, adding that they had proved to be very well informed and even "free-thinking." Another five ladies crowded around the doctor from Switzerland to delight in the way he attempted to make jokes in English. In any event, all of his terror of his first lecture at the University was removed, "since the audience is harmless and merely eager to learn new things." This observation must certainly have applied to two personalities at least who made a lasting impression on Jung. These were, for one, Stanley Hall himself, who deserved much of the credit for the formation of the relatively small Clark University, and of course William James. "I spent two delightful evenings with William James alone and I was tremendously impressed by the clearness of his mind and the complete absence of intellectual prejudices. Stanley Hall was an equally clear-headed man, but decidedly of an academic brand," wrote Jung a generation later to an American who was engaged in writing a doctoral thesis on this Clark conference of 1909.[55]

After Freud's very positively received lectures, which were really five extemporaneous addresses, it was Jung's turn. His three lectures dealt with the association experiments, the investigations carried out at the Burghölzli through which he had eventually become known in the United States. A further lecture was devoted to "Psychic Conflicts in a Child."[56] One of the basic assumptions of the thesis maintained in this paper was that the interest in sexuality plays a not inconsiderable causal role in the developmental process of the child's thinking. Understandably, the presenter avoided going any further into the tension that existed between himself and Freud on this very point. This minor work, which later appeared in print and was included in the publication of the collected works, showed that even here Jung was referring to his own experience, as the father of a four-year-old child. Thus the assertion that these were the observations "of a father versed in psychoanalysis about his then four-year old daughter" was a veiled reference to himself and his little daughter Agathe, a suspicion confirmed by statements to this effect in his correspondence with Freud.[57]

The great recognition accorded to Freud and also Jung at Clark University culminated in the award of an honorary doctorate of law. Thus his communication to Emma Jung on 14 September 1909:

> Last night there was a tremendous amount of ceremony and fancy dress, with all sorts of red and black gowns and gold-tasseled square caps. In a grand and festive assemblage I was appointed Doctor of Laws *honoris causa* and Freud likewise. Now I may place an L.L.D. after my name. Impressive, what?[58]

Freud, for his part, considered his and Jung's appearance in the United States significant in another sense, as a recognition of the new science and the friendly reception of its representatives. In his own "Self-Portrayal" we find the lines: "The short stay in the new world was exceedingly good for my self-respect; in Europe I felt like an outlaw, but here I found myself accepted as an equal by the best. It was like the realization of an unbelievable daydream. . . . Thus psychoanalysis was no longer a flight of fancy; it had become a valuable piece of reality. Since our visit it has never lost ground in America."[59]

Before the travelers could begin their return trip they had a final sightseeing program to complete, which was a welcome change much less for Freud than for Jung, who thirsted for primitivity—although after the turbulent previous days he, too, had become "weary of America" and was, as he said in a letter to his wife, "looking forward enormously to getting back to the sea again." This time their host was J. J. Putnam, who owned a camp in the Keene Valley in the Adirondack Mountains where one could camp close to nature, in a peculiar, primitively elegant manner, away from the confusion of the city and society. Jung wrote to Küsnacht, the evening of 16 September:

> I am sitting in a large wooden cabin consisting of a single room, and before me is a mighty fireplace roughly built of bricks with huge wooden logs in front of it, and masses of tools, books, and the like on the walls. Around the cabin runs a covered porch, and when you step outside you see nothing at first but trees—beeches, firs, pines, and cedars, all a bit strange, with the rain softly rustling beneath them. Through the trees you see a mountainous landscape, all covered with trees. The cabin stands on a slope, and a little farther down there are about ten small wooden cottages—over there the women live, there the men, over there is the kitchen, there the dining cabin, and in between cows and horses are grazing. . . ."[60]

His description of a primitive landscape with wild animals

of all kinds goes on in this way, and one gains the impression that the American traveler from Küsnacht is already thinking of building a similar retreat in addition to his recently finished comfortable country home; at any rate it was a dream that was to come true a decade later.

Psychoanalysis around a campfire in a secluded corner of an American mountain—it is very easy to imagine Jung in this setting, but far less so Freud. The unregulated and improvised life thoroughly disagreed with him; he was irritated and developed an inflammation of the cecum and other such complaints. And so his dictum, reported by Jones, is also understandable: "America is a mistake, a gigantic mistake to be sure, but a mistake all the same."[61] Freud's biographer noted explicitly that it was very difficult for the master to get along at all with the easy and unforced manners of the New World. Jung meanwhile was enthralled with the wild forested mountain scenery, the "primitive virgin forest from the time of the glaciers, the bears, wolves, deer, moose, porcupines, and snakes of all kinds." And the contrasts could not have been greater: one day atop a rocky peak almost 5600 feet high, with a view open to the blue infinities of America, and the next day back in Albany, the bustling capital city of New York State. What remained with him, though, were his meetings with people and impressions of nature. Here, Jung said, "an ideal of what is possible in life" had been realized. He wrote further to his wife, two days before his departure:

> We have seen things here that inspire enthusiastic admiration, and things that make one ponder social evolution deeply. As far as technological culture is concerned, we lag miles behind America. But all that is frightfully costly and already carries the germ of the end in itself. . . . I shall never forget the experiences of this journey. Now we are tired of America.[62]

The next notes came from the North German Lloyd steamer *Kaiser Wilhelm der Grosse* of Bremen, on which the three travelers put to sea from New York Harbor on the morning of 21 September 1909. Once again Jung surrendered himself to the "cosmic grandeur and simplicity" of the sea, which compels man to silence

> when the ocean is alone with the starry sky[.] One looks out silently, surrendering all self-importance, and many old sayings and images scurry through the mind; a low voice says something about the age-oldness and infinitude of the "far-swelling, murmurous sea," of "the waves of the sea and of love," of Leukothea, the lovely goddess who appears in the foam of the seething waves to travel-weary Odysseus and gives him the pearly veil which saves him from Poseidon's storm. The sea is like music; it has all the dreams of the soul within itself and sounds them over. The beauty and grandeur of the sea consist in our being forced down into the fruitful bottom lands of our own psyches, where we confront and re-create ourselves. . . .[63]

And then came the day-long storm the next day, which Jung watched from an elevated spot beneath the bridge. Into his description of the outer drama of the elemental forces flowed the happenings of the soul, just as they were portrayed in the myth of storm-tossed Odysseus. Thus the real events on the sea and the mythical drama matched the experience from his own depths, pointing far beyond the personality to the transpersonal and the spiritual. Could anyone who was in the grip of this power be satisfied with a "psychoanalysis" limited to the ego and its instinctive fate, without opening up to the suprapersonal and collective unconscious? But with this the conflict with Freud was predestined, for he was such a person. What Jung had always wondered about—the philosophical and scientific premises on which Freud's entire psychoanalysis really rested—would have to come to light.

10

The Inevitable Break

Predictably, Freud and Jung's visit to America brought far-reaching consequences for the reception psychoanalysis received in the United States. Abraham A. Brill translated Jung's lectures, which had been given in German, and published them in American professional periodicals that had also reprinted Freud's texts. From then on the number of publications on psychoanalysis generally increased. Respected Americans, among them James J. Putnam, declared themselves in Freud's favor at medical conferences. Already in 1911 the American Psychoanalytic Association was formed in the United States, with Putnam as president and Ernest Jones as secretary. As was to be expected, Jung's contributions at this time made a strong case for psychoanalysis, and the two men's friendship still continued. The foreseeable shifts in emphasis, for example on the role assigned to sexuality, were scarcely noticed from the outside.

Since their journey, however, there was no question that Jung had recently been tending ever more strongly toward a mythopsychology that would enable him to get closer to the archetypal structural elements of the psyche. What he was striving to do, as his correspondence with Freud documents, was to put "the symbolic" on a "psychogenetic" footing. Hardly had he returned to his everyday work when Jung reported to Vienna on his intense activity and his heightened interest in mythology, as well as the archeology he had neglected for several years. He was studying Herodotus; all four volumes of Freidrich Creuzer's *Symbolism and Mythology of Ancient Peoples* were receiving a careful rereading, along with Jakob Burckhardt's four-volume *Cultural History of Greece* and Erwin Rohde's *Psyche*. The comparative mythological material revealed surprising prospects. In addition he read pertinent works by authors in English. And in the same letter of 8 November 1909 in which Jung reported all this, we find the oracular statement: "Sooner or later polemics are certainly going to arise within our camp."[1] The immediate reference was to Freud's Viennese disciple Wilhelm Stekel, whose style had long been difficult to tolerate. How little suspicion Freud and Jung had of the fundamental divergence in their assessments of mythical material is shown in Freud's answer: "I am glad that you share my conviction that we must thoroughly conquer mythology."[2] It remained to be seen, of course, in what sense this would have to happen. In any case, as early as late January 1910, Jung mentioned that he had given a whole series of lectures on the psychogenetic approach to symbolism, showing how essentially the fantasy life of the individual is connected with mythological material. This was about the time when the beginnings of Jung's later *Symbols of Transformation* first saw the light of day. The two correspondents were still unaware of the consequences that would result from this only a few years later—as much for the further development of psychoanalytical research as for the personal relationship between Freud and Jung. For Freud, Jung's mythological studies were still refreshing. Besides, there was hardly time for forebodings or suspicions, for both were thoroughly swamped with work. Jung's practice was for the moment relatively quiet, and therefore he turned his full attention to lecturing activity and the teaching of his students, with twelve weekly seminars of university training in psychoanalysis. One of these students to whom Jung devoted much time and individual attention was Johann Jakob Honegger (1885–1911), who had already been his assistant at the

Burghölzli and promised to become an important representative of psychoanalysis, until his suicide at the age of twenty-six.

Further adding to the extent of Jung's professional duties, the compiling and editing of the *Jahrbuch* that had been decided upon at Salzburg required some effort, and meanwhile the preparation and organization of a second Congress of Psychoanalysts had also become necessary. Moreover it should not be forgotten that the young father had his three children, Agathe, Gret, and Franz, to look after, and a fourth child was already on the way. Duties of quite another sort arose for the doctor in consequence of his permanent status in the military reserves, for he had to go on field maneuvers for some weeks every year, which time always had to be reconciled with the rest of his calendar. Jung knew from experience that conflicts could not always be avoided, for instance when in the midst of his conference preparations, on 8 March, he was called to Chicago for about a week by his patient Harold McCormick—a second trip to America. Of course he arranged for a substitute: the young Dr. Honegger took over his patients, and Emma Jung stepped in to do all that could be asked of the head secretary of a doctor with an international clientele. The experiment succeeded, plunging the master in Vienna into distinct agitation. He was anxious for Jung's prompt return and confided in the Swiss clergyman Oskar Pfister: "What will happen if my Zürichers forsake me?"[3] A word of ill omen!

But things did not—yet—go so far as this. In fact the psychoanalytical conference took place as planned on 30 and 31 March 1910 in the Grand Hotel in Nuremberg. Freud made some introductory remarks on the future prospects of psychotherapy; Abraham, Honegger, Ferenczi, Adler, Stekel, and Maeder gave reports. Jung reported on the Clark conference, as one who had just completed his second, albeit very short, stay in America, thus providing the virtue of immediacy. One notable result of the Nuremberg Congress was the establishment of the International Psychoanalytic Association, with

C. G. Jung as its president and its headquarters at the president's home, and thus not in Vienna but—for about four more years—in Zürich and Küsnacht. In addition the existing *Jahrbuch* was supplemented by the monthly newsletter *Zentralblatt für Psychoanalyse—Medizinische Monatsschrift für Seelenforschung*. What went on behind the scenes has been preserved in differing versions and sheds light on the predicament in which Freud found himself. His concern was that he would be forced by necessity into having to represent psychoanalysis to the world without the Zürich contingent. In order to be able to present a personality as well known as he was circumspect, and who was furthermore not of Jewish descent, the choice fell as one might expect on C. G. Jung, for an initial term of two years. A few days after the congress Freud wrote to Ferenczi, one of the very few—next to Jung—in whom he placed his undivided trust: "With the Nuremberg meeting our movement's infancy comes to a close; this is my impression. I hope that now there will come a rich and handsome youth."[4] All in all, it was a hope that was belied by the actual developments of the next few years. For the psychoanalytical movement these years were marked by the famous secessions, the withdrawals first of Alfred Adler and then Wilhelm Stekel. The correspondence between Freud and Jung, for the most part with great candidness, documents the persistent tensions that existed especially within the Vienna group, but also in the wider ranks of the young psychoanalytic movement, which despite furious assaults gained ground continually in the psychiatric profession as well as in public opinion. On European soil, alongside Vienna and Zürich, local groups sprang up in Berlin, Munich, London, and Budapest, and they were joined by psychoanalytic associations in the United States. Jung's qualifications to hold the office of president were universally acknowledged, but Ferenczi's proposal in Nuremberg, that his widely esteemed colleague from Zürich should be immediately entrusted with this leading role for an indefinite period, was bound to provoke the opposition of Adler and other Vienna members. On this account Freud saw himself compelled to make some compromises. The delegation of Adler and Stekel to edit the *Zentralblatt* represented one such concession, as did Freud's transferring the leadership of the Vienna Association to Adler—measures, as it turned out, that remained in effect for only a very limited time.

While Jung informed Vienna in the spring of 1910 that psychiatrists and authorities of the prestige of Emil Kraepelin were labeling the Zürich group—with Jung at their head—as "mystics and spiritualists," and that therefore only limited confidence could be placed in them, at the same time he reported the liveliness of his "mythological dreams." About these, he said, only a little was divulged even to friends, and he was consciously curbing his desire for publication. On the subject of his secret-enshrouded inner experiences, Jung's impression was: "It often seems to me as if I have been hauled alone into a strange land, and see wondrous things that no one has yet seen and which no one else even needs to see."

Reading the letters of the years from 1910 to 1912, one feels that Jung, who elsewhere was so communicative, when it came to discussing his mythopsychological investigations, made use of a decidedly theatrical technique of allusion, quotation, and intimation, along with a tactic of concealment. But this was clearly prompted by the subject matter itself and by the still wholly unfinished process of discovery and probing whose end he himself could not yet foresee. Repeatedly he lamented that he could not express himself adequately in written form. Nevertheless the process of development of his inquiries is visible: In May of 1910 Jung presented a lecture in Herisau "on symbolism. . . , mythological stuff which got the greatest applause." Freud, answering on 26 May, was already looking forward to reading "a fine piece soon" from Jung's pen. Then, in early June, "My mythology is oscillating in an inner motion of its own, and here and there meaningful pieces are 'proffered up.'"[5] The mystery cult of Mithras, the ancient Persian light-religion that once offered serious competition to Christianity, had stirred Jung's interest. On this he gathered important comparative religious data from such works as those of Albrecht Dieterich,[6] which had appeared a few years earlier.

Freud was by no means disinclined to such interests; on the contrary, his own study "Leonardo da Vinci and a Memory of His Childhood"[7] already pointed in this direction and was completed at the same time, in the summer of 1910. Jung was not only pleasantly surprised, but he remarked in it a transition to mythology, and this "out of inner necessity." Moreover this was the first writing of Freud's to which Jung felt himself "perfectly in tune" from the start.[8] Freud was gratified to note this affirmation. For his part the master in Vienna took satisfaction in observing that his spiritual "son and successor" worked exactly as he did himself: "You lie in wait to see where your inclination draws you, and leave the obvious straight way untrodden. I believe this is the right thing too; afterward one is astonished at how logical all these detours have been."[9] So it was only natural that "coincidence" should play into his hands with material showing similar motifs, for when Jung undertook a bicycling tour to Italy in October, he discovered in the Museo Civico in Verona a purportedly Mithraic sculpture, depicting a bull grasping a snake in its forefoot, like a Roman stele of Priapus, with the snake's bite aimed at the penis. Jung connected the phenomenon with the sacrificial notions that he thoroughly interpreted later in *Symbols of Transformation*.[10] His correspondence with Freud, particularly in the summer of 1910, also affords glimpses into the development of his thinking and theorizing with regard to the libido.

After his return from Italy it was back again "full steam" to the "mythology work," and along with his practice in Küsnacht the beginning of the upcoming semester created a further distraction for the Zürich lecturer. The bright tone of Jung's letters of the summer and fall of 1910 was not lost on his correspondent in Vienna. There were definite reasons for it: his family was getting on splendidly; his third daughter, Marianne, had just been born. This of course did not prevent the Jung family from also feeling a growing concern over "the blessing of too many children." "For"—as he once confided some months later to the fatherly Freud—"one seeks, with little confidence, every possible trick to stem the tide of this unstoppable blessing somewhat. One muddles through, so to speak, from one menstrual period to the next. . . ."[11] But on the whole the father from Küsnacht's love for his children won out. His good mood was further prompted by his growing clientele, which had long since assumed international dimensions. The house on Lake Street was filled "with the babble of German-French-English voices that my bloodsuckers raise."[12] Amid all this yet another quick consultation abroad was required, this time in London. Of course, this was only for patients who could also afford to pay their psychiatrist's fee. Thus in Jung's case the need to make money, of which Freud so often spoke, was hardly a problem.

Further variety, besides family, research, teaching, and practice, was provided by Swiss medical Captain Jung's annual two-week military exercises. As a passionate sailor with his own jolly-boat, built in 1907, he was also able to obtain the relaxation he needed, as for another fortnight during this autumn he cruised about Lake Constance under sail. Then, before the year's end, there came an incidental announcement that was bound to stir Freud's interest anew, concerning the growing mythology manuscript: "It seems as if I had hit the bull's-eye this time, or come very close, because the material is falling into place surprisingly well."[13] He did not reveal any more, but an explicit and eloquent warning for the further course of the two men's relationship went with it. Freud, Jung said, should be prepared for something strange, "the likes of which has never yet been heard from me." And, with a twinge of insecurity or worry, there followed his assertion that his conscience was clear. He had after all worked honestly and done nothing offhandedly—as if his "father" could have entertained any doubts on that score! When Jung saw a performance of Goethe's *Faust* in January 1911, he said regarding the mythology-steeped second part that his "respected great-grandfather" (Goethe) would have approved of what he was writing, because the great-grandson had "continued and extended his ancestor's thinking."[14] Although the self-mocking tone of this note should not be overlooked, it reverberated too with the satisfaction that with this work he could now stand up to Goethe. The analyst was certainly conscious of the fact that he needed this assurance, should criticism come from those in Vienna or from Freud himself, and the presentiment was not unfounded, for the book being prepared, its scope continually growing, was to bear the title *Wandlungen und Symbole der Libido*, "Transformations and Symbols of the Libido," translated as *Psychology of the Unconscious*. Part 1 appeared in the *Jahrbuch für psychoanalytische und psychopathologische Forschungen* in 1911, Part 2 in 1912. In the same year the separate book edition was published by the firm of Franz Deuticke of Leipzig and Vienna, which had also produced other psychoanalytical writings. At the age of seventy-five, offering the substantially revised, partly shortened and partly expanded work under the new title of *Symbols of Transformation*, Jung commented:

> This book was written in 1911, in my thirty-sixth year. The time is a critical one, for it marks the beginning of the second half of life, when a metanoia, a mental transformation, not infrequently occurs. I was acutely conscious, then, of the loss of friendly relations with Freud and of the lost comradeship of our work together. The practical and moral support which my wife gave me at that difficult period is something I shall always hold in grateful remembrance.[15]

But to return to the time when the first version of the work originated: Along with mythology, psychology of religion, and investigation of the manifestations of unconscious fantasies came a renewed interest in the occult. The motto was, "We shall also have to conquer occultism."[16] It dawned on Jung how informative the consideration of astrological aspects could be for the understanding of mythology as well as for psychotherapeutic practice. Thus he spent many an evening poring over horoscopic calculations, tracking down the true psychological content of astrological results. In the signs of the zodiac Jung recognized symbols of the libido, which indicated the typical qualities of the libido or character at a given time. There was one patient, for example, whose star chart tallied exactly with a definite character sketch, including a number of detailed predictions. But it turned out that one particular feature fit not the patient but her mother. The analyst's diagnosis, which could also serve as a clarification of the apparent contradictions, was that the patient was suffering from an extraordinary mother complex—undoubtedly an interesting problem for both psychologists and astrologers. For the most part, though, the Vienna master was willing to let his younger friend intoxicate himself "on magical fragrances for a while." After this, he thought, he would return in due time from the land of secrets with a rich booty for the knowledge of the human soul.

From previous experience Freud had long known of Jung's inclinations and talents with respect to parapsychology, and he had no doubt that he would "return home with a rich cargo." On the basis of what he had attained so far, he would not have to incur the "disgrace" (!) of having turned into a mystic. Freud even promised "to believe everything that can be made to seem the least bit reasonable. As you know, I do not do so gladly. But my hubris has been shattered."[17] But on the other hand he could not forbear to offer a serious admonition as well: "Only don't stay too long away from us in those lush tropical colonies; it is necessary to govern at home."[18] Under no circumstances—so he told Jones—could Freud participate in such "dangerous expeditions." Be that as it might, Jung's report on his lengthy work in the psychology of religion could not fail to have its effect on Freud, for he was working around the same time on related themes, which he published as *Totem and Taboo: Some Points of Agreement between the Mental Lives of Savages and Neurotics* (1913). The preface, written in Rome in 1913, mentions at least in passing pertinent works of the "Zürich school of psychoanalysis."[19] But during the book's composition, which was not entirely without problems,

At the Weimar Congress, September 1911. Emma Jung is seated at center, with Toni Wolff at the far right and Lou Andreas-Salomé at the far left. C. G. Jung is standing behind his wife, with Sigmund Freud to his right.

Freud once let the remark slip out to Jung, "why the devil did I have to let myself be incited to follow you into this field?"[20]

There are many convincing indications of the high degree of intimacy and personal closeness in the years-long friendship between Freud and Jung. One of these is surely the repeatedly expressed need they both felt, busy as they were, for face-to-face meetings and deep conversation. Of course this was also made necessary by the manifold troubles Jung was having in Zürich with Bleuler and the Burghölzli clan, and Freud with the "Adler gang" in Vienna. A brief encounter took place at the beginning of the Christmas holiday in Munich, and after this meeting Freud gave Ferenczi his opinion of Jung: "I am more than ever convinced that he is the man of the future."[21] But for how much longer?

More opportunity for an exchange of thoughts was afforded by the Third International Psychoanalytic Congress, which took place on 21 and 22 September 1911 in the Hotel Erbprinz in Weimar by way of Zürich. Jung picked up his visitor at the railroad station in Zürich early on the morning of 16 September. James Putnam had arrived from the United States. After seminars and receptions as well as intensive discussions in Jung's home, they departed from Zürich on the nineteenth. Together with Eugen Bleuler and eight or ten colleagues, the Zürich contingent represented a respectable delegation, making up about a fifth of the entire congress. The roster of participants numbered fifty-five persons.

About a dozen lectures and brief reports covered not only psychopathological topics, but for the first time also interdisciplinary ones, including for example philosophy (Putnam) and mythology and symbolism (Otto Rank and C. G. Jung).

Undoubtedly a novelty at the Weimar Congress was the participation of several women, as documented by the impressive group photo with the ladies included.[22] The fact that Emma Jung took her place in the first row not only as her husband's wife but also as his colleague was justified, for example, by her etymological contributions to *Wandlungen und Symbole der Libido*. Jung introduced as a "charming American lady" Dr. Beatrice M. Hinkle, one of the first woman psychiatrists; as a student of Freud and Jung she later translated his book into English as *The Psychology of the Unconscious.* Dr. Sabina Spielrein, Jung's erstwhile patient and sometime friend and student, is missing from the photo. In her place had come, as Jung customarily referred to her, "a new discovery of mine," Antonia (Toni) Wolff, his other close female friend and closest collaborator for some forty years. Finally, wrapped in a great long fur, Lou Andreas-Salomé appears in the picture, a youthful-appearing woman in her fifties who had once been courted unsuccessfully by both Nietzsche and his friend Reé, and who was the lover and traveling companion of the young Rilke. The Swedish physician and analyst Poul Bjerre, also a very close friend, had brought her with him to Weimar when he came from Stockholm. Anyone who might entertain the suspicion that Frau Lou was there merely to make an appearance, the avant-garde pioneers of psychoanalysis being just what she needed for the purpose, must stand corrected. A few months after the Weimar meeting, Abraham reported to Vienna how highly he regarded the professional abilities of this fascinating woman: "One attendee of the Weimar Congress, Frau Lou Andreas-Salomé, was recently in Berlin for some time. I have become closely acquainted with her and must say that I have never met with such an understanding of psychoanalysis down to the last and smallest detail."[23] Thus Lou brought the best qualifications with her when she found acceptance as a colleague "in the Freudian school."[24] And this was not all, for when it came—shortly after Weimar—to the first psychoanalytic secessions, Freud allowed her, as a rare exception, to be a regular visitor to the internal Wednesday gatherings at Berggasse 19 as well as to Alfred Adler's circle, and so she was able to evaluate independently the contributions made by both. Jung's efforts, especially his "disastrous recent work,"[25] found little favor with Frau Lou, and the two remained strangers.

From 1912 we turn back again to the fall of 1911: While Freud looked back in a radiant light on the days in Zürich and

Weimar, and Jung was snatched away on military service in the mountainous regions of the Swiss interior in October of that year, Freud received some unexpected mail from Küsnacht. In her husband's absence Emma Jung was writing to discuss her view of the state of affairs between the two men. It had occurred to her at any rate that the friendship that was valued so highly on both sides concealed an obviously deep-seated problem, which might well come into the open as a result of Jung's *Psychology of the Unconscious*. Thus the young wife advised the master in Vienna that the two men should "just talk this over quite thoroughly," much more thoroughly than had been the case—so far at least— of late.[26] We do not have the "nice kind letter," as Emma found it, with Freud's answer. But from Emma's second writing, which immediately followed, we know how anxiously Jung was awaiting Freud's opinion of his latest work. And sure enough, the plucky correspondent reached into the arsenal of psychoanalytical concepts to interpret the phenomenon. In her husband's case, she said, it was the remnant of an unresolved father or mother complex, for (so went her pointed argument): "actually Carl, when he thinks something is right, has never been able to care about any other opinion"—and thus not even Freud's. This is followed by a series of suggestions and bits of advice that attest impressively to the young woman's mature personality and her ability to stand up to the father of psychoanalysis. Finally this new letter ended with an emphatic recommendation: "Think of Carl not with the feelings of a father. . . , but as one person does of another, who like you must follow his own law." For the rest, she hoped the wise old master would not be angry with her.[27] How could he!

About a week after this pregnant epistle, the unsuspecting (of these events) Jung had Freud's reaction to Emma's letter in hand. According to it, the new volume was "one of the nicest works . . . of a well-known author," as Freud wrote to this very same author. It was, he said, certainly the best thing he had produced so far, though not the best that he would accomplish—an extremely cautious critique, to the extent that it was one at all. Freud's letter was dominated by the "many points of agreement" that he attested to. He even worried about how he, a successful master in the realm of the psychology of religion, could avoid appropriating relevant ideas from his more competent "successors" in these spiritual regions. One might have wondered where such scrupulous solicitude would end. After all, Part 2 of the work had not yet been finished in November 1911, and thus Freud had not seen it. It was this section that dealt with the controversial libido theory, the touchstone of all classical psychoanalysis. In his letters Jung revealed only that the purely sexually defined concept of libido, as it had been established in Freud's fundamental *Three Essays on the Theory of Sexuality* (1905), would have to be extended to include the "genetic factor," that is that the exclusively sexual motivation should be given up—the depths of heresy, and nothing less! The chosen crown prince must have forgotten what the elderly autobiographer recalled so vividly, the earnest commandment that Freud had impressed on him at their first meeting: "My dear Jung, promise me never to abandon the sexual theory. That is the most essential thing of all. You see, we must make a dogma of it, an unshakable bulwark."[28] Yet this very chosen successor was about to raze the bastions and relinquish the dogma.

Emma Jung appealed to Freud with two further letters in November 1911. Mirrored in these lines we see the anxious and uncertain side of C. G. Jung, who put the finishing touches on the portentous second part of his study only after grappling with hesitation and great inner resistances. Finally the young woman broached the problem she faced at the side of her (almost) universally respected husband, basking in the early glow of his fame as a doctor: "From time to time I am plagued by conflict as to how I can be noticed next to Carl; I find that I have no friends, but that everyone who comes to visit us really only wants to see Carl, aside from a few boring people who are totally uninteresting to me." And where in the previous letter Emma Jung had asked for discretion vis-à-vis her husband, adding expressly, "things are hard enough on me already," now she became somewhat more explicit, for she complained: "Naturally the women are all in love with him, and to the men I am off limits immediately, like the wife of one's father or friend. But I do have a strong need for people, and Carl also says I should stop concentrating as I have up to now on him and the children, but what am I supposed to do?"[29]

Naturally she was careful to avoid naming names in her complaint. But apart from the general crowd of women who accompanied Jung's life out of personal as well as professional interest, there were especially the two "affairs," first with Sabina Spielrein and then the very much longer one with Toni Wolff. But this was hardly a revelation to Freud; on the contrary, he had been quite well informed for some time, at least in the case of Spielrein, especially since Jung had taken him into his confidence. Here a brief flashback to the year 1908–1909 is necessary.

The young Russian Sabina Spielrein, some eleven years Jung's junior, had been studying medicine at the University of Zürich since 1905. Jung cured her of a severe neurosis and presented her case in his lecture at a conference in Amsterdam in 1907.[30] With her dissertation, "Concerning the Psychological Content of a Case of Schizophrenia (Dementia Praecox)" she earned the medical doctorate in 1911, showing herself in this as in a number of other works to be a gifted student of C. G. Jung, although late in 1911 she went to Vienna and attached herself to the Psychoanalytic Association there. Jung mentioned Spielrein's works several times in his own books. Eventually she made a name for herself as an analyst and later as a lecturer at the North Caucasus University in Rostov-on-Don, and while she was in Geneva, from 1921 to 1923, the famous child psychologist Jean Piaget underwent analysis with her. Hence there was no question about her high professional qualifications.

The transference that occurred during her own analysis with Jung (while he was at the Burghölzli) meanwhile led to an intense love affair. At the critical phase in this event he wrote to Freud on 7 March 1909—at first without mentioning any names:

> A patient whom I extricated years ago from the most severe neurosis has betrayed my confidence and my friendship in the most offensive way imaginable. She has caused a nasty scandal for me, simply because I chose to forgo the pleasure of begetting a child with her. I have always remained a perfect gentleman toward her, but before my somewhat too-sensitive conscience I still do not feel clean, and that is what hurts the most. . . . These painful and yet extremely salutary realizations have gnawed at me hellishly, but because of this they have, so I hope, ensured moral qualities in me that will be of the greatest benefit in my later life.[31]

His relationship with his wife, he said, had not been damaged at all; it had actually gained in depth and security. But he did have to admit that despite all his self-analysis it was only through the Spielrein affair that he first discovered his "polygamous components." Not unsympathetically, but with the requested sobriety, Freud answered: "Being slandered and singed by the love with which we operate are our occupational hazards, but we are not really going to give up the profession on their account."[32] And a few weeks later, on 7 June 1909: "Such experiences, although painful, are necessary and hard to avoid. Only with them does one really know life and the thing he has got hold of. I myself have never actually been taken in quite so badly," asserted the fifty-three-year-old, adding, "but I have been very close several times and had a narrow escape."[33] Moreover, in analysis one was of course "invariably" faced with the so-called countertransference; that is, the analyst was in a position not only to become the object of the patient's emotions, but in turn to develop feelings of personal sympathy and affection, if not love, toward the analysand.

It is true of course that this touches on only one side of the phenomenon, the side that Jung later referred to and set forth in more detail as the problem of a man's anima. This problem was posed in no less painful and significant a way for those concerned here. Sabina Spielrein, as we know today, kept a careful diary of her encounter with Jung.[34] Emma Jung, an extremely sensitive young wife and mother (some of her pregnancies fell during the time of the Spielrein affair), had a double burden to bear, especially with her knowledge of the tension that existed between Jung and Freud, which in loyalty to her husband she wished to help reduce. And just at this moment, when Sabina Spielrein had barely left the stage in Küsnacht, a new arrival came on the scene, the twenty-three-year-old Toni Wolff of Zürich (b. 1888), who became Jung's patient because of a severe depression after the sudden death of her father in 1909, and only two years later, of course, took part in the Weimar Congress of Psychoanalysts. But in the case of Toni Wolff it would certainly be a mistake to speak of a mere transference and countertransference in the analytical sense, or to proceed from the simple formula of "*cherchez la femme*." Such a superficial view is precluded especially by the larger biographical context, although Jung did make it extremely difficult for his biographers to shed any light on this intimate relationship. He destroyed his letters to Toni Wolff, which were returned to him after her death in 1953, together with those she had written to him.[35] On the other hand it is surely no coincidence that Emma Jung devoted a study to the anima- and animus-problem in men and women; certainly it was an opportunity for her to work out the difficulties in this regard which she faced in her own marriage. But between the composition of this text and Emma Jung's exchange of letters with Freud there was a gap of at least two decades.[36] Only after his break with Freud did Jung himself gain an insight into the nature of the so-called soul-images of animus and anima.[37]

As far as the relationship between Freud and Jung is concerned, this much at least is certain: It was not any affair with a woman—here that with Sabina Spielrein—that prompted their split, as has occasionally been suggested, for example by Bruno Bettelheim.[38] For Spielrein, who had been discussed from a professional and collegial point of view, was long out of the picture when the tensions arose which were to lead to the eventual break between Freud and Jung. And Freud would hardly have been considered a potential rival with regard to his much younger colleague. Far more weight must be given to the wider professional and theoretical differences between them. Thus, four weeks after the Weimar Congress, the suspicion surfaces in one of Jung's letters "that so-called 'early recollections of childhood' are not individual memories at all." Jung spoke of "phylogenetic reminiscences" and informed Freud of his conviction that it would be seen that "unbelievably many more things than we now suppose" could be traced to such nonpersonal or superpersonal recollections.[39] From here it was no longer a great step from Freud's personal unconscious to the "collective unconscious."

As yet the growing discrepancy between the two men's views remained unseen. And although, another four weeks later, Jung did see in Freud "a dangerous rival" in matters of the psychology of religion, this assessment was considerably mitigated by the context. Freud meanwhile remained anxious about what Jung really meant in practice by his occasional announcement of a widening of the sexually determined concept of the libido, and just this was to be the subject of the already mentioned Part 2. Tension was foreseen; an entire chapter would be devoted to the outcome of several years of deliberation. Jung attempted to forestall trouble by advising Freud, "You must allow my interpretation to work as a whole. Fragments are hardly intelligible."[40] For sometimes it is precisely the context of a statement that makes clear its scope and significance. From his return letter of 17 December 1911 it can be gathered that Freud even seems to have felt that Jung would be helping to illuminate "an obscure point" of psychoanalytic theory. But it was precisely the point on which Freud, in his quasidogmatic commitment, had no intention of retreating.

The rest of the news Jung sent from Zürich was positive. "The Psychoanalytic Association is thriving and growing," he said in mid-February 1912. He reported on successful lectures, one before six hundred Swiss teachers, another to 150 students. As an agitator for psychoanalysis he compared himself proudly with "Roland's Horn," probably referring to the Roland who figures as one of the paladins of Charlemagne in the *Karlssaga*. It would not have been hard for the analyst, thinking as he did in metaphors and analogies, to make the association that the nearly six-foot-one Carl from Küsnacht, whom his Jewish colleagues especially, including his friend Sabina, used to call the "blond Siegfried," was himself really a "Carlus Magnus."

In view of the strides that the psychoanalytic movement was making in Zürich, disagreement was unavoidable. Now it was set in motion by a publicity campaign that gave the Jungians, and Jung himself, the opportunity of placing their goals and methods in an accurate light, as opposed to popular vulgarizations and corruptions. In any case, the controversy showed that not only did people object to the Freudian sexual theory on the grounds of a Victorian pseudomorality, but a role was also played by a fear of wider circles that psychoanalysis was a materialistic and atheistic worldview comparable to the scarcely overcome monism of the likes of Ernest Haeckel.[41] And because the real opposition in such movements so often forms within their own ranks, Jung once remarked:

> Our real opponents will be those who commit the greatest atrocities with psychoanalysis, as they are already doing, according to their strengths, with all the means at their disposal. Woe to psychoanalysis in the hands of these fleecers and fools![42]

The further progress of the relationship between Freud and Jung was determined by various factors. At the center, becoming ever clearer to Freud, stood the discrepancy in the question of the nature of the libido, which Jung could no longer see as restricted to the sexual drive. For him libido was more and more a universal psychic or life energy, whose "transformations" or ability to be altered he was striving to show in the work in question. The beginnings of such a new conception of energy were of course already found in his writings on dementia praecox,[43] and in the above-mentioned publicity campaign he gave the impression that his own approach was equally universal:

> I have asserted consistently for years in my courses and writings that the concept of libido should be understood in an extremely general way, somewhat in the sense of the preservation of the species, referring, in psychoanalytical terminology, not to "local sexual excitation" but to all the urges and desires reaching beyond the area of self-preservation, and should be applied in this sense.[44]

But right here he came into conflict with Freud, who on 23 March 1912 voiced "strong antipathy" toward such innovations or extensions. At the same time he detected a fatal similarity to one of the theorems of Alfred Adler, who had finally withdrawn from the Vienna Psychoanalytic Society after the Weimar Congress and was in the process of developing his own psychology of the individual. Jung expressed sorrow, but in no way did he wish to emulate Adler's disloyalty, as he explicitly asserted.

In the same letter in which Freud expressed his displeasure—still as ever with the salutation "Dear friend"—we also find a note that he would be in Constance during Whitsuntide to visit the sickbed of their mutual colleague and friend Ludwig Binswanger, and thus would be rather close to Jung. But a meeting, which up to now they had both always tried hard to achieve, did not come about this time. Whereas Freud, in his letter of 13 June, was able to offer good reasons for this failure, Jung voiced the suspicion that he had to attribute Freud's forgoing a meeting "to your displeasure with my development of the theory." Of course, he said, he hoped they could come to an understanding later on the controversial points, but he also invoked his national mentality: "With the Swiss obstinacy which you know so well, it seems I must travel a longer stretch of road alone," reads his letter to Freud of 8 June.

Jung wrote these lines as he was engaged in the preparation of lectures that were about to bring the internal controversy in the profession out in the open. He had been invited for a second time to speak in the United States, this time on his own, at the Jesuit-run Fordham University in the Bronx. There were to be nine teaching sessions, which he took as an opportunity to present and defend in detail his most important divergences from Freud. Thus to the discord and partial distancing already mentioned was now added public criticism, even though in this presentation of "The Theory of Psychoanalysis" Jung still felt gratefully indebted to his "revered teacher Sigmund Freud." Jung's criticism, he said, had resulted not from academic reasoning,

> but from experiences that have forced themselves upon me through ten years of serious work in this field. I know that my experience in no way rivals the extraordinary experience and insight of Freud, but nevertheless it seems to me that certain of my formulations express the empirical facts more aptly than is the case with the Freudian model.

In this preface to the first German edition, written in the fall of 1912, Jung did not fail to add two further notes. One was the asseveration:

> I am far from seeing modest and sober criticism as a "defection" or a schism; on the contrary, through it I hope to further the continued flourishing and growth of the psychoanalytic movement, and also to open up an avenue to the treasures of knowledge of psychoanalysis for those who . . . have been unable before now to master the psychoanalytic method.[45]

In the other comment, Jung made the statement with regard to Alfred Adler's work *The Neurotic Constitution*, which had appeared in the meantime, that "Adler and I have at various points arrived at similar results"—an additional confirmation of Freud's suspicion, which under the circumstances Jung must have set down in writing with some satisfaction.

Jung could count his eight-week stay in America, beginning on 7 September, as a complete success. This time his lectures were translated into English, and thus his audience was not limited to the small circle of German-speaking participants and colleagues. Since the Clark conference in 1909 the young psychoanalytic movement had undergone a remarkable development, and this time the press was looking for further publicity. The *New York Times*, in its Sunday edition of 29 September, published a full-page interview with a photograph under the headline "America Facing Its Most Tragic Moment—Dr. Carl Jung."[46] Further lectures, for example at the New York Academy of Medicine, as well as visits to Chicago, Baltimore, and Washington, D.C., rounded out this tour of America. For letters, to Freud for instance, there was ostensibly no time during these two months, and above all there was "no desire," as Jung informed Freud with calculated boldness on 11 November. "I had an audience of about ninety psychiatrists and neurologists. . . . Naturally I also made room for my own views, which differ in places from previous conceptions."[47] He said he did not want to run away from Freud, but preferred direct confrontation, and he was, after all, only fighting for what he believed to be the truth. Their personal relationship he wished to maintain. For all that, he wanted objective judgment and no resentment.

> I think I deserve this much, if only from the standpoint of expediency, for the psychoanalytic movement is indebted to me for its promotion more than Rank, Stekel, Adler, and the rest of them put together. I can only assure you that there is no resistance on my part, unless it be that I refuse to be judged as a complex-laden idiot. . . .[48]

Is this not an expression of the fact that Jung had now thoroughly completed his detachment from his "father" and was willing to generously renounce his claim to the "succession" to Freud that had been offered him? The whole letter exudes self-confidence: he had lectured, performed demonstrations, and analyzed fifteen Negroes in several clinics; on the return trip he had presided over the founding of a local group in Amsterdam; and above all he had found that his own Jungian conception of the psychoanalytic libido theory had won a great many friends. In a word, triumph all the way down the line.

And Freud? It goes without saying that his dark suspicions had been more than realized. For hardly had Jung set out on his trip to America when Emma Jung sent the painfully awaited second part of *Wandlungen und Symbole der Libido* to Vienna. Hence there was no more room for further illusions. With suitable yet nonetheless restrained sobriety the first letter in response arrived from Vienna, now with the more distant salutation "Dear Doctor Jung"—"I greet you on your return from America no longer so affectionately as the last time in Nuremberg; you have successfully weaned me of that, but still with sufficient sympathy, interest, and gratification over your personal success." And in the way of countercriticism, Freud added, "the fact that you have reduced a good deal of resistance with your modifications should not be entered on the credit side of the ledger, for you know that the further you try to distance yourself from what is new in psychoanalysis, the surer you will be of applause, and the smaller will be the resistance."[49] Of Freud's objectivity and their continued relationship, however, Jung had no need for concern, he said. His commentary on the long-awaited Part 2 of the libido book proved, understandably, extremely brief: some details had pleased him, the whole had not; he had not been able to extract from it the desired clarification of Jung's innovations.

The general business of the International Association, of which Jung continued as president, made a conference of its chief spokesmen necessary. It took place on 24 November in a small group at the Park Hotel in Munich; along with Freud and Jung, Franz Riklin, Ernest Jones, Karl Abraham, Leonhard Seif, and J.H.W. van Ophuijsen attended. Among other things on the agenda was the advance planning of the next Congress, which was also to take place in Munich. It says something for the personal effect Freud and Jung had always had on one another that after what had happened the two remained by no means as distant as might have been expected. Rather they took advantage of a two-hour afternoon walk to put aside at least the more emotionally and atmospherically caused obstacles. There was even something of a reconciliation. But at the end of a dinner that was described as cheerful, when Freud was reproaching the Zürichers for having avoided mentioning his name in their publications of late, he fainted—just as he had in Bremen three years before—and fell to the floor. Jung recounted how he gave first aid: "I picked him up, carried him into the next room, and laid him on a sofa. As I was carrying him, he half came to, and I shall never forget the look he cast at me. In his weakness he looked at me as if I were his father."[50] As nearly five decades lay between the event and the recollection, shifts and errors are possible, of course—for example, Jung was confusing this presidents' conference with the Munich Congress of 1913—but his appraisal of it was undoubtedly right. For in fact a significant psychological turning point had been reached; for Jung, Freud's "fatherhood" seemed to be over, but not—not even yet—his friendship, for when Freud wrote on 28 November 1912 to James Putnam, who for his own part had voiced some criticism of Jung, he recorded his own immediate impressions of the gathering in Munich, writing: "My colleagues behaved charmingly toward me, Jung not least of all. A personal conversation between us cleared away a multitude of unnecessary sore spots."[51] Freud looked forward to further successful cooperation, untroubled by the theoretical differences that continued to exist. As for the libido question or even the problem of incest, however, he would be unable to accept any modification, for all his experiences argued against this conception. This was doubtless a powerful argument, but would it be able to carry any weight—with Jung—in the long run?

That such a short meeting and conversation should have disposed of every one of the points of disagreement seems

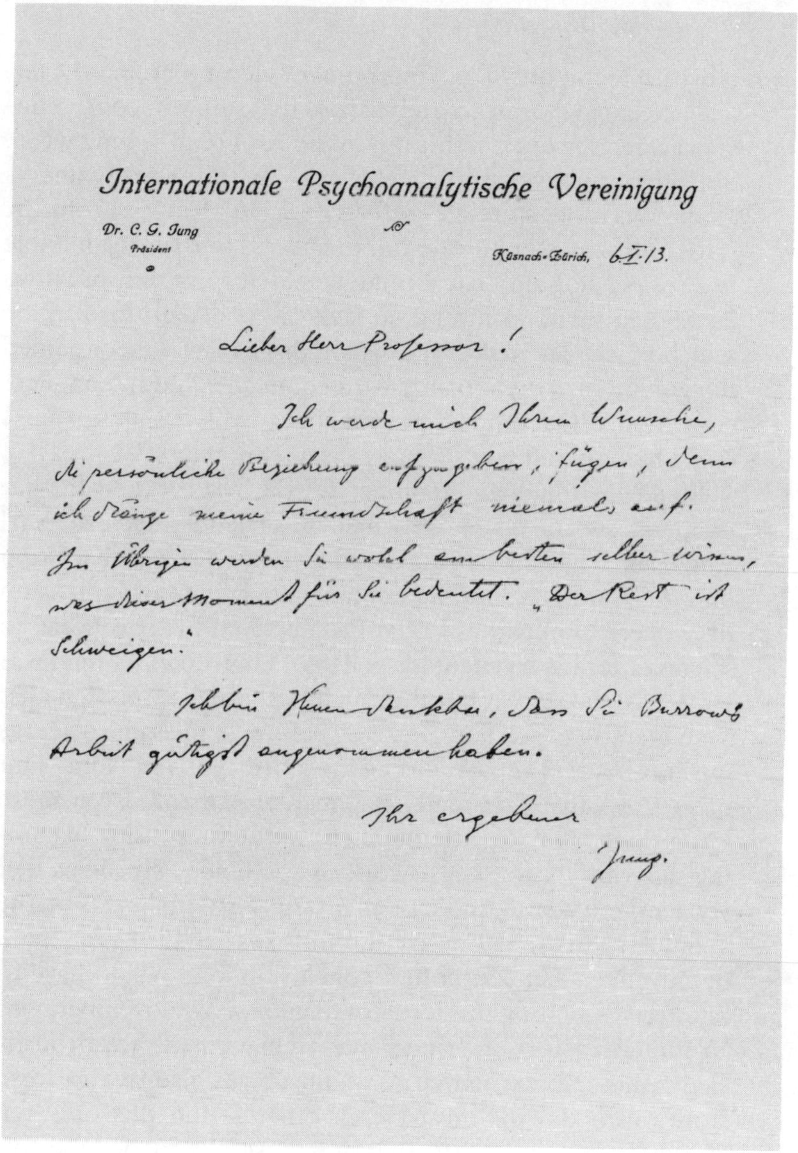

Internationale Psychoanalytische Vereinigung

Dr. C. G. Jung
Präsident

Küsnach-Zürich, 6.I.13.

Lieber Herr Professor!

Ich werde mich Ihrem Wunsche, die persönliche Beziehung aufzugeben, fügen, denn ich dränge meine Freundschaft niemals auf. Im Übrigen werden Sie wohl am besten selber wissen, was dieser Moment für Sie bedeutet. „Der Rest ist Schweigen."

Ich bin Ihnen dankbar, dass Sie Burrows Arbeit gütigst angenommen haben.

Ihr ergebener

Jung.

Jung's historic letter to Freud, dated 6 January 1913, marking the end of their collaboration and friendship of many years.

remarkable not only from our point of view today. Yet the letters exchanged immediately after the summit conference endeavored to confirm this impression of Freud's. Jung wrote on 26 November that he had "for the first time really understood" Freud despite all differences. He changed from the self-confident tone of one full of success to that of a humble *mea culpa*, hoping that Freud would forgive his previous errors and there would be no lack of good will. Instead, he said, he wished to make "the insight that has at last been gained the guiding principle of my own conduct." And in complete contrition: "It pains me that I did not gain this insight earlier. I could have spared you so many disappointments."[52]

Freud was touched. He hoped for the best for their further cooperation and even informed his friends, such as Karl Abraham, what an extremely kind letter Jung had written him.[53] Naturally it also had not failed to include an expression of concern about how Freud had survived his trip home to Vienna after his momentary collapse. How deeply Freud was moved is shown by his thoroughly unusual admission that such a fainting spell had occurred before, in the same place, as long as six years ago. And then his self-diagnosis: "Thus a bit of neurosis that one really ought to attend to." Even more astonishing is Freud's claim that he himself was "slowly coming to terms" with Jung's work on the libido. "It seems that you have solved the riddle of all mysticism, which rests on the symbolic utilization of complexes that have been deactivated"—all too bold a conclusion, one would have to say. Freud's signing this letter of thanks on 29 November with "Your untransformed friend" was ambiguous, although qualified by his conviction that "We must really also lay in a fresh store of good will toward each other"—and this only ten months before the end of their relationship as friends and colleagues! Thus the harmony of their reconciliation could not last long, as the next few letters already show. Jung continued to find his *Psychology of the Unconscious* undervalued by Freud. Then on 18 December came Jung's criticism that the techniques with which Freud treated patients and students alike constituted an interference, that he was begetting "slavish sons" for himself, who out of pure submissiveness did not dare to discover themselves and tug the prophet's beard. Publicly, of course, Jung would continue to support Freud, but with due recognition of his own views.

With this Freud felt it impossible to continue their private relationship. Indeed he would lose nothing by it, he said, for—despite their reconciliation and reciprocal confessions—the earlier disappointments he had suffered were always before him. At bottom, then, nothing had changed, wrote the "untransformed" Freud to the ever more changing Jung. The final break was now more a matter of time, a very short time. Jung's letter of 6 January 1913, on the letterhead of the International Psychoanalytic Association, is of a brevity that speaks for itself:

> Dear Professor Freud,
>
> I shall submit to your wish to discontinue our personal relationship, for I never force my friendship on anyone. For the rest, you yourself know best what this moment means to you. "The rest is silence."
>
> [Followed by one sentence concerning a business matter, then the closing:]
>
> Yours sincerely,
> Jung[54]

With this the days of the detailed and friendly epistles they had kept up were gone forever. Their formal association still existed, along with Jung's presidency and his editorship of the *Journal*, including the preparation of the Munich Congress. Besides this, Jung was in great demand in addition to his lecturing activity and his private practice. From March until early April he traveled a third time, for about five weeks, to lecture in the United States. The journey was planned so that he could go to Naples on the return trip and make an excursion to Pompeii. This trip to America was one of the many events of his life that remained unmentioned in the *Memories*, but his encounter with the world of Greek and Roman antiquity challenged his receptivity to a very high degree:

> I was able to visit Pompeii only after I had acquired, through my studies of 1910 to 1912, some insight into the psychology of classical antiquity. . . . Certainly Rome as well as [Paris or London] can be enjoyed esthetically; but if you are affected to the depths of your being at every step by the spirit that broods there, if a remnant of a wall here and a column there gaze upon you with a face instantly recognized, then it becomes another matter entirely. Even in Pompeii unforeseen vistas opened, unexpected things became conscious, and questions were posed which were beyond my powers to handle.[55]

This third lecture tour (counting the quick consultation in 1910, it was Jung's fourth trip to America) is as poorly documented as is a trip he made to England in August, during which he was to hold two lectures on "General Aspects of Psychoanalysis"[56] before the Psycho-Medical Society in London. This was the first time that Jung referred to his own newly originated psychological science, as distinct from that of Freud—which to a great extent he continued to endorse—by the new term "analytical psychology." Along with "complex psychology" this later became the standard designation for the Jungian orientation. Thus the child whose baptism he had sponsored long ago had at last been christened, although the name hardly stood in sufficiently clear contrast to that of psychoanalysis, considering that in Jung's work it was not only the analysis but the "psychosynthesis" that was to become at least as important. In the often-revised elementary text "On the Psychology of the Unconscious" (1917/1926/1943) Jung accorded particular attention to his synthetic or constructive method. Here we find the avowal:

> I had first to come to the fundamental realization that analysis, insofar as it is reduction and nothing more, must necessarily be followed by synthesis, and that certain kinds of psychic material mean next to nothing if simply broken

> down, but display a wealth of meaning if, instead of being broken down, that meaning is reinforced and extended by all the conscious means at our disposal—by the so-called method of amplification. The images or symbols of the collective unconscious yield their distinctive values only when subjected to a synthetic mode of treatment. Just as analysis breaks down the symbolical fantasy-material into its components, so the synthetic procedure integrates it into a universal and intelligible statement.[57]

Jung had encountered this synthetic method already in the early period of his psychoanalytic work, specifically in the psychiatrist Dumeng Bezzola of Graubünden[58] and in Roberto G. Assagioli, the Italian analyst whom Jung came to know and to think highly of in 1909.[59] When the Seventeenth International Congress of Medicine gathered in London from 6 to 12 August of 1913, Jung was once again on the list of speakers. He repeated the lecture "On Psychoanalysis," which he had given some ten months earlier in New York.[60] Here as before he sought to do justice to the Viennese founding father, but without disavowing his own perspective on the questions of libido and the interpretation of dreams. To outsiders, then, there was as yet no trace of a developing split within the movement.

Outwardly, this impression would still be corroborated by the subsequent Fourth Congress (the "Fourth Private Psychoanalytic Meeting"), although by the participants—who by this time reached the impressive figure of eighty-seven members and guests—the considerable tensions that had arisen in the meantime did not go wholly unnoticed. The affair took place in the Hotel Bayrischer Hof in Munich on 7 and 8 September 1913. As in the previous congresses of the psychoanalytic movement, this time too there was an extensive program of events to be completed within a relatively short time. In the two days no fewer than seventeen speakers were to take the podium, among them Ernest Jones, Hanns Sachs, Karl Abraham, Franz Riklin, Poul Bjerre, Sandor Ferenczi, and J. von Hattinberg. Hence the time allotted for discussion was limited to between twenty and twenty-five minutes each. Freud spoke on the problem of the choice of neurosis, whereas Jung considered the question of psychological types. This paper at Munich in 1913 represented his first preliminary contribution to the subject of typology, the theme that would be treated thoroughly in his work *Psychological Types* (1921),[61] starting from the idea of two opposite orientations of the libido or psychic energy, which Jung termed extraversion and introversion. Already at this point Jung made it clear that his approach should be seen in the context of other philosophical and psychological parallels, such as Binet and William James, Schiller's distinction between naive and sentimental types, or Nietzsche's demonstration of the opposition between Apollonian and Dionysian. Even Otto Gross[62] did not go unmentioned, a psychiatrist who had distinguished two forms of inferiority. Finally, Jung's lecture went on to make a typological comparison of the reductive-causalistic viewpoint of Freud with Alfred Adler's more final- and future-directed standpoint. "It will be a difficult task for the future," Jung said in closing, "to create a psychology that will do justice equally to both types."[63] Here too his endeavor was clear: it was not a rejection, but a widening, and in part also a transformation, of the results that had been gained so far from work in psychoanalysis, or depth psychology.

With this the speaker set a great task for himself and for the analytical psychology he represented, whose beginnings were now starting to become visible. Moreover, it brought to light a further aspect of Jung's unorthodox position. But the increasing need for a separation between the diverging orientations could no longer be kept quiet. At the Munich meeting this had already become evident through the fact that Freud and Jung, with their respective sympathizers, sat at separate tables. One participant who had already put in with the party of her choice some time ago, and who mentioned this in her report, was Lou Andreas-Salomé.[64] As Poul Bjerre had once brought her along as a guest to the Weimar Congress, so had she, having become a Freudian herself in the meantime, followed his lead. This time, on her way from Vienna, she had imported her young friend Rainer Maria Rilke and introduced him to Freud. The poet, the same age as Jung and by this time well known, among other things as the author of the *Book of Hours*, *New Poetry*, and *Malte Laurids Brigge*, had long been a famous personality and thus was able to provide the Congress with some glamor, even though he was only to become better acquainted with psychoanalysis through his companion. With some pride Frau Lou noted how well he and Freud understood each other, and that they were together until late at night. The gentlemen also exchanged greetings later. Freud had the poet, who was surrounded, informed via Lou that he had a daughter (Anna) who read Rilke's poems and could recite some of them by heart.[65] Under these circumstances any contact between Jung and Rilke was clearly out of the question. Nevertheless, with regard to Rilke, Jung had by his own admission always been conscious of "how much psychology is hidden in him,"[66] and that he as empiricist and Rilke as poet or visionary had ultimately drawn from the same source, the collective unconscious.[67]

After what had happened, the mood of the Munich Congress ranged from "disagreeable" (Jones) to "fatiguing and unedifying" (Freud). The atmosphere was mentioned several times in letters between the various participants. Freud's circle tried somehow to get rid of Jung and his followers. Since the reelection of the president was due and Jung had previously already announced his intention to resign, his removal from office was expected. But only twenty-two out of the total of fifty-two voting members in attendance abstained from voting for Jung, and thus he was effectively reelected as president of a society against whose theoretical basis he had voiced fundamental criticism. "The Jew endures," wrote Freud to his designated new successor, Karl Abraham, in Berlin. In his notes "On the History of the Psychoanalytic Movement" Freud felt himself compelled to point out vaguenesses and insincerities of the new secessionist movement, because it was opposing things that it had formerly defended on Freud's behalf. He continued: "At the Munich Congress I found myself obliged to illuminate this semi-darkness, and I did so with the explanation that I do not recognize the Swiss innovations as a legitimate continuation or further development of the psychoanalysis that started with me. . . . Abraham is correct in saying that Jung is in total retreat from psychoanalysis."[68] But Jung took the final step only when he heard through his colleague Alphonse Maeder that Freud had called his good faith ("bona fides") into question. Further hesitation was no longer possible, and on 27 October Jung wrote to the "Most esteemed Herr Professor":

> I would have expected you to have imparted something as weighty as this to me directly. Since this is the most serious accusation that can be made against a person, you make further collaboration with you impossible for me. Therefore I am resigning from the editorship of the *Jahrbuch* with which you entrusted me. I have also informed Bleuler and Deuticke [the publisher] of my decision.
>
> Most respectfully,
> Dr. C. G. Jung[69]

Volume 5, number 2 of the *Jahrbuch*, then, also carried Jung's notification that he had found it necessary to step down as editor. As Jung could not help seeing that his views stood "in such stark contrast to the ideas of the majority of members of our Association," on 20 April he also tendered to the board of directors his resignation as president. With this the "new era without Jung" had begun for the psychoanalysts. The majority of the local Zürich group joined ranks behind him and resolved to withdraw from the Association. "I cannot suppress a hurrah," Freud exulted in a letter to Abraham on 18 July. "And so we have gotten rid of them." And again a week later in the classic expression: "So we are finally rid of them, the brutish Saint Jung and his yes-men."[70]

The comments of other analysts from Freud's circle also bear witness to their happy relief at this separation. Already in April 1914, by telegraph from Berlin, Abraham and Eitingon had expressed their joy over the "tidings from Zürich" of Jung's resignation.[71] How the central figures concerned perceived the break, responded to it, and ultimately evaluated it for themselves is another matter. While Freud took a cool, reproachful, and aggressive stance in the *Journal*, declaring Jung's conduct an abandonment and a defection from analysis in his article on the history of the psychoanalytic movement,[72] Jung pointed out to his Zürich colleague Maeder the impossibility of further collaboration with Freud:

> I have by no means fallen into Freud's trap, for I consider it no advantage of Freud's if he disgusts me. . . . The outward impression will be very bad. But inner successes carry more weight than the howling of the crowd.[73]

In any case Jung's opponents could not deny the reaction he continued to excite in wider circles. Thus in late July 1914, on the occasion of the annual meeting of the British Medical Association in Aberdeen, Scotland, he spoke "On the Importance of the Unconscious in Psychopathology."[74] On this occasion there was no mention of psychoanalysis; the term was not used. But Jung did not hesitate to point out Freud's pioneering accomplishments in the field of dream interpretation. Thus he continued along the line which he had announced regarding Freud, namely of outward loyalty even though their personal relationship had ended. Jung held fast to this rule—*cum grano salis*—even in his autobiography, writing there:

> . . .my main concern has been to investigate, over and above [the] personal significance and biological function [which Freud attributed to sexuality], its spiritual aspect and its numinous meaning, and thus to explain what Freud was so fascinated by but was unable to grasp.[75]

How much the factor of human association was involved became clear in various letters, for example in 1949, ten years after Freud's death, in a letter to the son of his friend Théodore Flournoy, in which Jung said:

> [To Freud] belongs the honor of having discovered the first

archetype, the Oedipus complex. This is a motif that is as much mythological as it is psychological.[76]

Or to a doctor in 1957:

> In spite of the astonishing lack of appreciation I incurred on the part of Freud, I cannot fail to recognize his significance as a cultural critic and pioneer in the realm of psychology, even considering my own resentment. A correct assessment of Freud's efforts reaches into areas that concern not only the Jews but all European people, areas which I have tried to shed light on in my works. Without Freudian "psychoanalysis" I would have entirely lacked the key.[77]

But Freud, too, had not lightly forgotten the intensity of his many years of friendship with Jung. In those situations where he did not have to stand before the public primarily as the founder of psychoanalysis, some of this became visible, as for example in a letter to James Putnam in 1915: "He [Jung] was someone who was sympathetic to me, so long as he went along blindly and quietly as I did. Then came his religious and ethical crisis with its high morality, rebirth, and Bergson, together with lies, brutality, and anti-Semitic presumptions against me."[78] Or to Lou Andreas-Salomé in March 1914: "Naturally I also know that adversaries, popularizers, and distorters also serve an important purpose, in that they prepare otherwise unpalatable material for the digestive systems of the masses. But that should not be acknowledged aloud, and I support them only in the proper fulfillment of this mission, while I continue to curse the taint that the pure thing suffers through this procedure."[79] A singular note was surely sounded by a brief remark Freud made at the age of seventy-six to an American visitor, the physician E. A. Bennet, who visited him at his home in Vienna in 1932. Asked what effect the departures of Adler and Jung had had on him, Freud said that Adler's separation had not been a loss that he regretted, but that "Jung was a great loss."[80] All in all, it was the end of a "simple tragedy"—so says Alexander Mitscherlich on the relationship between Freud and Jung.[81] Only a simple tragedy?

11

Transformation Begins Within

Having arrived at the threshold that marks the transition from the first half to the significant second half of C. G. Jung's life, we pause, as observers and companions along the way, to take note of this change, which makes its more or less pronounced appearance in the course of every human life.

> . . .for there is no place
> That does not see you. You must change your life.
>
> —Rilke

Here was a man who drew from an extremely rich intellectual and spiritual heritage—or more precisely one from whom this heritage burst forth, striving for clarification and consciousness, and ultimately for the integration of the unconscious, demanding to become whole. It would not be enough simply to point to the psychic gifts of the Preiswerk family, for instance, reducing Jung to a psychological magician who manipulated atavistic psychic powers the way the alchemical magician did the elements. And yet the example, or rather analogy, of the alchemist is indeed applicable, for the goal of this ancient hermeneutic discipline was transubstantiation, the transmutation of substances through the creation of a new quality. In other words, it was meant to lift the inheritance of the soul out of the depths of the psyche, transforming it so that the treasures of the human spirit become clear and can be made accessible. And this had to happen at that moment in the historical development of consciousness when, as a consequence of rationalism and materialism, of extraversion and the conclusion that "God is dead," the spiritual dimension of the depths (but also the heights!) was lost to a large part of Western humanity. A religious vacuum had been created, because the traditional guardians of the religious life had themselves succumbed to this *Zeitgeist*, and there was no lack of signals to indicate that the consciousness of modern man was passing through a zero point. One thinks also of the various spiritist and spiritualist or theosophical movements that forced their way into the public eye around the turn of the nineteenth century, seeking to reactivate ancient psychic alternatives or borrowing from eastern religions. So it was no coincidence that Jung, while studying medicine around the turn of the century, read the spiritist and parapsychological literature and carried out his own experiments of this kind as a young man. It was also no coincidence that Jung was born in the same year, 1875, in which the Anglo-Indian Theosophical Society of the medium Helena Petrovna Blavatsky (1831–1891) and Henry Steel Olcott (1832–1907) was first formed in the United States.

But it is also important to make clear the enormous distinction between these ancient psychic faculties, as they appear in spiritism and mediumism, and the scientific mode of consciousness. In the end the modern technique, to be feasible and manageable, demands rationality in the highest degree, whereas the mediumistic and magical mind is firmly fixed in the prerational or irrational. The mere tacking on of magic and mystical elements to modern rationality clearly cannot solve the problem. The manufacture and operation of a complicated machine require quite a different mental and emotional disposition than does a religious practice, for instance, for here the mathematical mind is predominant; the whole world is looked upon as a machine. And yet to today's entirely outer-directed objective consciousness, the rehabilitation of the psychic and spiritual seems indispensable. The question is, how can an integration of the inner and outer worlds, the psychic and the material, be brought about, so that the disjointedness of modern man can be overcome?

One thing is clear: the process that leads to the integration of the person with the world (what the alchemists called the *mysterium coniunctionis*, the "secret of joining together") obviously must be set in motion *within the person himself*. The scientific demonstration of the existence of the unconscious that Freud and his school achieved at the threshold of the twentieth century had certainly been a pioneering accomplishment in this area, and this bridgehead to the territory of at least the personal unconscious, with its contents originating among other things in the process of repression, undoubtedly represented an epoch-making achievement. But for the time being, a wide field of psychic investigation was still hidden. It has been pointed out often enough how much Freud remained imprisoned by the intellectual presuppositions of his time, the nineteenth century. To get a look at the human psyche's tendency to unity, what was needed was a more profound method of inquiry, one that would give due recognition to the transpersonal. And someone was needed who would first experience the double face of the psyche within himself, who would learn firsthand the laws of integration, of individuation. What had seemed at first sight to be a dangerous split—Jung's experience of the No. 1 and No. 2 personalities—turned out more and more to be the indispensable prerequisite for any further realization of the human psyche as a whole. Only when the "two souls in his breast" had become a single symbolic and metaphorical experience could he set out on the way "to the mothers," to the archetypal powers.

We think, for example, of the suggestive dream Jung had during his trip to America with Freud, which the two pioneers of depth psychology attempted to elucidate each in his own characteristic and distinctive way—the multistory house with its contemporary furnishings in the upper story and the dead skeletons in the depths of the cellar. Whereas Freud, wholly in keeping with the psychology that was conditioned by his own view of the world, suspected individual death wishes on the dreamer's part, Jung's attention turned to the archaic, suprapersonal or collective roots that form just as much a part of the human psyche as the personal unconscious and its unrecognized drives, wishes, and repressions.

Jung, who had come to know the deep-lying psyche step by step through his own early inner experiences as well as his historical interests, and who as a psychiatrist had practiced testing the usefulness of the psychoanalytic method, could not stop at the borders asserted by Freudian views and methods. Even at the cost of a personal friendship with Freud that had lasted ten years, Jung had to go beyond the bounds of Freudian psychoanalysis, to extend its scope as well as its methods. The son was compelled to escape his "father," the "crown prince" to reject the inheritance—as Freud understood it—his Viennese master had intended for him. But clearly the separation, painful for both of them, did not accomplish this by itself. Whosoever would push forward into a new country must fulfil the necessary preconditions. One approaches the archetypal world not through mere reflection, and thus persisting in the rational mode of consciousness, but through transforming and deepening it. To reflection must be added a willingness to undergo a complete transformation of the human being, a change that begins *within*, in the confrontation with one's "own" suprapersonal unconscious. When this task arose for Jung at the middle period of his life, the outlines of the problems of consciousness and of an era merged with those of the individual.

12

The "Night Sea Journey" and the Confrontation with the Unconscious

The split with Sigmund Freud represented a profound, decisive break in C. G. Jung's life. Freud, of course, was deeply affected by it himself, but for him the basic positions of his work had long been firmly established. The founder of psychoanalysis was able to pursue the work he had begun without the spectacular modifications to which he had reacted so allergically in the cases of Adler and Jung. A serious disturbance of psychoanalytic activities began only with the onset of national socialism in Germany and Austria, hence from outside. And by this time Freud's life's work was finished.

Not so for Jung. At the ages of thirty-eight and thirty-nine he had to undergo a midlife crisis; his work on *Symbols of Transformation* was already an expression of this process. To be sure, in the public eye the doctor from Küsnacht was a renowned representative of his profession with a respectable international clientele. But Jung knew that merely continuing his work on the fringes of the psychoanalytic movement, or outside it altogether, was out of the question for him. He even went so far as to give up his position as a lecturer on the medical faculty of the University of Zürich, which he could have continued to hold independently of the Psychoanalytical Society. His resignation, dated 30 April 1914, was accepted by the cantonal board of education on 3 June, and with this Jung had, for the present, abandoned his academic career. Now he concentrated on his private practice, or more precisely on himself, harder than ever before, for a process had begun for Jung, some time before his outward break with Freud, which he himself called the "confrontation with the unconscious," and so he titled the corresponding, telling chapter of *Memories, Dreams, Reflections.* Now at last the fundamental meaning of Jung's Prologue to his autobiographical notes became clear: "My life is a story of the self-realization of the unconscious."[1] It is not the part which can be externally and biographically dated that constitutes the real life of a person, but its myth—the fateful, spiritual inner side of this life.

Because Jung repeatedly pointed out the necessity of relating this inner process of maturation and growth to one's concrete life, the larger historical context of his biography must not be neglected. In his correspondence and conversations with Freud, of course, social and political events had hardly played any role, and cultural ones for the most part only in the immediate context of their research, for example when mythological and artistic material was compared to mental processes or used as an interpretive tool. The pioneers of modern depth psychology were far too occupied with their analytic and therapeutic business, their patients and "cases," and with education, teaching, and warding off their opponents, to have sufficient time for the world's political incidents. But it was precisely during these months of tense confrontation and division that the catastrophe of the First World War began.

The external data are well known. On 28 June the successor to the Austrian throne, Archduke Franz Ferdinand, was murdered by Bosnian conspirators in Sarajevo. Within a few days this regional Balkan conflict had developed into a world war, which before long enveloped the entire continent. On 1 August a state of war was declared between the Kaiser's Germany and tsarist Russia; on 3 August France joined in, and the other nations followed. Suddenly neutral Switzerland found itself surrounded by warring powers, and Captain Carl Jung's compulsory military service had taken on a new dimension. Reading his *Memories*, one gets the impression that the outbreak of the war per se was very much of secondary importance to him. It was not entirely out of the picture, to be sure, but for Jung the real task even now was to work out the meaning of the unconscious.

> I had to try to understand what had happened and to what extent my own experience coincided with that of mankind in general. Therefore my first obligation was to probe the depths of my own psyche. I made a beginning by writing down the fantasies which had come to me. . . .[2]

Not coincidentally, the lecture he gave in Aberdeen in late July 1914—a few days before the outbreak of the war—was devoted to the importance of the unconscious in psychopathology.

How intensely the collective destiny of peoples must have concerned Jung from out of the unconscious is evident from an active imagination which occurred to him as early as October 1913, and then again a little later. He described this "vision" as follows:

> I saw a monstrous flood covering all the northern and low-lying lands between the North Sea and the Alps. When it came up to Switzerland I saw that the mountains grew higher and higher to protect our country. I realized that a frightful catastrophe was in progress. I saw the mighty yellow waves, the floating rubble of civilization, and the drowned bodies of uncounted thousands. Then the whole sea turned to blood.[3]

It is no wonder that he pondered in shock and confusion on the sight of this apocalyptic panorama, which had held him spellbound for an hour. Two weeks passed, and the vision was repeated under the same circumstances, but this time the transformation of the sea into blood took on a still more menacing form. The question was, what could all this mean?

Could it be a great revolution, of the same extent and fateful significance of the sixteenth-century German Peasants' War, which had once likewise been presaged in a great natural catastrophe? The thought of an imminent war did not occur to Jung, who considered the impending psychosis rather in relation to himself. But many other contemporaries of the world war, at least the more spiritually sensitive among them, could not but have recognized some inescapable doom. For even while the frenzied flush of victory lasted among the warring peoples—the Germans at least—for several months in 1914, one could read in the Sunday edition of the *Neue Zürcher Zeitung* for 14 August 1914, under the headline "War and the Word of God": "The monster has descended upon us. The time we live in is full of horrors; there is no one upon whose head its heavy fist has not fallen. . . . Everything around us has been changed. . . . The air around us is laden with tears suppressed, forgotten, and to come. The gravity of this hour cries aloud."[4] These are not the words of a preacher, nor indeed even of one sure of victory, but the opinion of a Jewish journalist, Margarete Susman, who was living in Zürich.

And as a sign that something extraordinary was about to happen, Jung was visited in the spring and summer of 1914 by a thrice-repeated dream: in the middle of summer there was a cold snap of gigantic proportions; the entire country became solid ice, and everything living froze to death.

> In the third dream frightful cold had again descended from out of the cosmos. This dream, however, had an unexpected end. There stood a leaf-bearing tree, but without fruit (my tree of life, I thought), whose leaves had been transformed by the effects of the frost into sweet grapes full of healing juices. I plucked the grapes and gave them to a large, waiting crowd.[5]

A surprising turn, then, the rescuer appearing in the face of the greatest danger! But the dreamer had to wonder to what extent he himself could act, if not as a numinous savior (grapes from a healing vine represent a numinous symbol), at least as a helper in time of need. For at this point in his life his outer and inner circumstances alike were more those of one deeply in need of help himself.

Following the break with Freud, Jung became aware of just how fundamentally alone he was. The much-touted "Zürich school" had effectively dwindled to an unpretentious little group; there remained his erstwhile colleagues from Burghölzli, Franz Riklin and Alphonse Maeder. The majority of his friends and acquaintances had turned away, and his status as a university lecturer had been given up. The large chapter on sacrifice in *Transformation* Jung now connected with himself. More strongly than ever he found himself faced with the question of what the language and imagery of myth had to say to him, or more precisely what myth he himself must live, according to what inner, superindividual life plan his personal life, with its highs and lows, was structured.

> I did not know that I was living a myth, and even if I had known it, I would not have known what sort of myth was ordering my life without my knowledge. So, in the most natural way, I took it upon myself to get to know "my" myth, and I regarded this as the task of tasks, for—so I told myself—how could I, when treating my patients, make due allowance for the personal factor, for my personal equation, which is yet so necessary for a knowledge of the other person, if I was unconscious of it? I simply had to know what unconscious or preconscious myth was forming me, from what rhizome I sprang.[6]

Remarkable as it seems at first that Jung should speak of a myth in looking back on this critical segment of his life, fundamentally it is a rather common human experience.[7] It happens whenever people learn to recognize a meaningful texture in seemingly coincidental outward facts, joys and sorrows, human encounters and fatefully interwoven patterns. And when Jung speaks of a confrontation with the unconscious, he means not only the contents of the personal unconscious in the Freudian sense, the sum of that which is forgotten and repressed, of instinctive factors and drives of all kinds. He means above all the collective unconscious, with its transpersonal factors extending beyond the personal. "Really," according to Marie-Louise von Franz, "it is a modern, scientific expression for an inner experience that has been known to mankind from time immemorial, the experience in which strange and unknown things from our own inner world happen to us, in which influences from within can suddenly alter us, in which we have dreams and ideas which we feel as if we are not doing ourselves, but which appear in us strangely and overwhelmingly. In earlier times these influences were attributed to a divine fluid (mana), or to a god, demon, or 'spirit,' a fitting expression of the feeling that this influence has an objective, quite foreign and autonomous existence, as well as the sense of its being something overpowering, which has the conscious ego at its mercy."[8]

At the time when this overpowering force first took possession of him, Jung could not yet suspect the scope of the events that awaited him in the days to come before and during the world war. For the clearly defined concepts of the collective unconscious and the archetype did not yet exist for him. The pertinent experiences of his childhood, such as the dream of the ritual phallus or the existence of the antique "No. 2" personality alongside the concrete everyday reality, had pointed in this direction, of course. The same is true for his dream of the multistory house with its ancient vault. But in order to be able to understand these sometimes fascinating images and integrate them into his conscious life, what was necessary was precisely this confrontation with the influences from the unconscious, in the form of a perilous time of uncertainty and spiritual and psychic disorientation. Jung saw his situation after the break with Freud thus:

> I felt totally suspended in mid-air, for I had not yet found my own footing. Above all, I felt it necessary to develop a new attitude toward my patients.[9]

Again it was dreams that occupied him, as enigmatic as they

were meaningful, for example one around Christmas in 1912, at a moment when Jung was not yet thinking of a final split from Freud and the Psychoanalytical Society, or still wished to avoid it. The action took place in the surroundings of an Italian renaissance palace. A white dove came to rest on a magnificent emerald table at which the dreamer was sitting. The dove spoke, with a human voice, about the possibility of her being transformed, along with twelve dead people who were also involved. Jung was unable to interpret the dream; in particular it was not clear whether the number twelve should be connected with the apostles, the signs of the zodiac, or some other manifestation of twelve. Should the emerald table be compared with the tradition-laden *tabula smaragdina* of Hermes Trismegistos, and thus with the ancient Egyptian mythical figure of Thot-Hermes, the representative of hermetic and alchemical wisdom?

There was still another dream, which took the dreamer to the region of Arles, where there was a row of sarcophagi. There the figures of knights were lying in full armor, as in ancient burial vaults, going back in chronological order to the twelfth century. The remarkable thing about it was that the dreamer observed, as he walked past the line of forms he had thought to be dead, how one figure after another came to life upon being looked at or touched. That Freudian dream theory proves a failure when faced with such motifs and forms is obvious. The recipient of this experience found it significant that "such contents are not dead, outmoded forms, but belong to our living being."[10] Only in the larger context of the gradually developing doctrine of the archetypes was some light shed on such dreams, although the details are bound to remain problematic when the rational and reductive method—or any other—is applied to them. And even this barely resolvable dream text was grounds enough for Jung to occupy himself for a long time with this matter, which led him gradually to his later doctrine of the archetypes. This took place under a considerable inner pressure, which

> at times . . . became so strong that I suspected there was some psychic disturbance in myself. Therefore I twice went over all the details of my entire life, with particular attention to childhood memories; for I thought there might be something in my past which I could not see and which might possibly be the cause of the disturbance. But this retrospection led to nothing but a fresh acknowledgment of my own ignorance.[11]

This statement is characteristic of Jung's predicament, in that while he was, to be sure, groping after the structures of the collective unconscious, on the other hand he was still seeking to apply the reductive and causal methodology relied upon by psychoanalysis, with whose help he thought he could uncover some kind of childhood traumas. The turning point in his destiny arrived only with the moment when Jung yielded to his inner impulse, the play instinct with which he had once manipulated building stones as a boy of ten or eleven. The image of how he had constructed his childish edifices in the surroundings of the parsonage in Klein-Hüningen was still vivid in his memory. He said to himself, "Here is a creative life that is not extinguished yet, but could be reactivated under the right circumstances." And then something clearly remarkable happened. Once he had wholeheartedly accepted the feeling of humiliation and the avowal of his complete helplessness, he began—a man in his late thirties with several elementary-school-age children of his own—to do the same thing all over again. Just as he had a generation ago, he collected little stones on the shore of Lake Zürich and began playfully building a whole village; a village with a church and finally also—after some hesitation—an altar. The sense of this as a numinosum, something sacred and belonging to the "wholly other," must have prompted him. But the decisive thing for Jung was that with his (we might say therapeutic) action, his thoughts began to clear and he began to find a certain contentment. He explained:

> I went on with my building game after the noon meal every day, whenever the weather permitted. As soon as I was

through eating, I began playing, and continued to do so until the patients arrived; and if I was finished with my work early enough in the evening, I went back to building. . . . Naturally, I thought about the significance of what I was doing, and asked myself, "Now, really, what are you about? You are building a small town, and doing it as if it were a rite!" I had no answer to my question, only the inner certainty that I was on the way to discovering my own myth. For the building game was only a beginning. It released a stream of fantasies which I later carefully wrote down.[12]

The need to master his inner vision, the inner urge which strove toward realization, through handcraft still had meaning for Jung even in his later years. As he recounted this stage of his autobiography in 1957, at the age of eighty-two, he drew particular attention to how important working with stones—whether as stonemason or as architect and bricklayer—had always been to him whenever specific problems had to be solved—inner stagnation in writing certain books, or even coping with the death of his wife, who died on 27 November 1955. Sometimes he would take up brush and colors and paint a picture. This creative activity had a revivifying effect on him, and he made a method of it in his therapeutic practice. But referring to the time of this crisis, Jung declared:

To the extent that I managed to translate the emotions into images—that is to say, to find the images which were concealed in the emotions—I was inwardly calmed and reassured. Had I left those images hidden in the emotions, I might have been torn to pieces by them. There is a chance that I might have succeeded in splitting them off; but in that case I would inexorably have fallen into a neurosis and so been ultimately destroyed by them anyhow. As a result of my experiment I learned how helpful it can be, from the therapeutic point of view, to find the particular images which lie behind emotions.[13]

Occasionally he would devote himself to yoga exercises in

order to find the peace necessary for working with the productions of the unconscious. But what was of crucial significance for him during those years of disorientation was being firmly anchored in his concrete life, his profession and his family, which not only made their own claims upon him, but for just this reason provided a handhold and a counterweight as well as any spiritual leader or guru could have done. Again and again it became clear that these things were the real base of his life, to which he must always return.

> The unconscious contents could have driven me out of my wits. But my family and the knowledge: I have a medical diploma from a Swiss university, I must help my patients, I have a wife and five children, I live at 228 Seestrasse in Küsnacht—these were actualities which made demands upon me and proved to me again and again that I really existed, that I was not a blank page whirling about in the winds of the spirit, like Nietzsche. Nietzsche had lost the ground under his feet because he possessed nothing more than the inner world of his thoughts—which incidentally possessed him more than he it. He was uprooted and hovered above the earth, and therefore he succumbed to exaggeration and irreality. For me, such irreality was the quintessence of horror, for I aimed, after all, at *this* world and *this* life.[14]

His affirmation of the concrete world also found expression in the fact that he once again took up his favorite sport, sailing, with the cooperation of friends. On one occasion he spent four days crisscrossing Lake Zürich, in the company of his boyhood friend Albert Oeri and three younger companions. On this occasion the voyage took on a special tone from Albert Oeri's reading from Homer's *Odyssey.* He deliberately selected the particularly fitting *nekyia*-episode, which describes Odysseus' voyage to the other-wordly shores of the realm of shadows and the abode of the departed. "The sails were taut," Homer's hero describes his ship to the listening Phaeacians,

> "as she sped all day across the sea till the sun sank and light thickened on every pathway. The vessel came to the bounds of eddying Ocean, where lie the land and the city of the Cimmerians, covered with mist and cloud. Never does the resplendent sun look on this people with his beams, neither when he climbs towards the stars of heaven nor when once more he comes earthwards from the sky; dismal night overhangs these wretches always. Arriving there, we beached the vessel, took out the sheep and then walked onwards beside the stream of Ocean until we came to the [rock and the confluence of the rivers of the dead] that Circe had told us of, [and there we sacrificed as she had prescribed]."[15]

Undoubtedly it was a pertinent text, for Jung too found himself in the midst of his own *nekyia*, in which he had to hold his ground against the superpersonal experience of the other side. Although there were no ghosts of the dead to be conjured up here, he would have to enter those precincts of spiritual and psychic reality which Sigmund Freud had once invoked when he prefaced his *Interpretation of Dreams* with the no less ominous lines:

> *Flectere si nequeo superos,*
> *acheronta movebo.*
>
> If I cannot turn the gods above,
> then shall I move the world below.

But who, in Jung's case, was moving whom? Was it not the inner conflicts, the disquieting dreams and overpowering fantasies and imaginations that were driving him to the edge of insanity? The doctor had become the patient, the psychiatrist a "borderline case" on the threshold between neurosis and psychosis.[16] Jung was clearly aware of the alarming precariousness of his predicament, and for this very reason he could not allow himself to lose his footing in reality. It would not have been the first time that a psychiatrist or psychoanalyst had been sacrificed to his own discipline. Jung had only to

The night sea journey: "I myself had to undergo the original experience, and, moreover, try to plant the results of my experience in the soil of reality."

think of his colleague and patient Otto Gross or the tragic suicide of his promising student Johann Jakob Honegger.

The motif of the ocean voyage, or that of the *nekyia*, cannot be grasped by means of academic psychopathological criteria alone. The "night sea journey," as Leo Frobenius called it early in this century,[17] is known in many mythologies, which is to say that it contains archetypal features common to all humankind. Thus as the sun is devoured day after day in the west to begin its night voyage in the womb of the cosmic mother before it can rise anew in the east, so too runs the course of the sun god, the primordial image of the (solar) hero who accepts being devoured as his destiny, and in this way experiences rebirth and resurrection. With this we encounter a primal motif of both humankind and the individual. Is it any coincidence that the much-discussed midlife crisis, the critical stage of middle life, comes at a time of change? The time when physical powers are on the increase is a climax and a conclusion only from a biological standpoint. Significantly, there is a "dead center" through which one has to pass in one's own individual way, in view of the new orientation to the completely altered contents and goals of the second half of life. Fundamentally every person is confronted with this problem, for practically speaking only a relatively few are destined to go fully conscious through the events of middle life, as even a glance at the spiritual and mystic history of humanity will show. But only one who has accepted this process of mystical death, who has undertaken the soul's journey to the other side and withstood the voyage on the night sea, into hell ("traveled down into the realm of the dead. . ."), can stand before his fellow men with this experience as one changed, even as "a new person," and bring them the knowledge of a new life. Only he is in a position to lead others on their own night voyages, whether as the psychopomp ("leader of the soul") of the ancient mysteries, or as guru, master, or spiritual leader in the various Eastern and Western systems of initiation. The history of Christian esoterism all the way to the present offers a wealth of examples of the ways and means of spiritual experience and guidance.[18]

Whereas the priest performs traditional rites of purification and sacrifice, and the scribe or the theologian interprets the texts of sacred tradition and unlocks them for the present day, the spiritual master draws from his own individual inner experience, whether by showing others the mystical path as a meditation teacher or advisor, or by helping as a therapist to release self-healing psychosomatic powers. In each case the process of individual maturation goes on after the experience of the zero-point of middle life. Merely countering the symptoms would be just as inadequate as merely adapting the individual to the respective norms and expectations of society. Self-realization—what Jung terms "individuation"—is the great theme of humanity; Nietzsche said, "You must become who you are!" The occasional reproach that Jung was a mystic, an esoteric (in the true sense of the word as one who is gifted with inner experience), can justifiably be applied to these experiences of his middle life, and Jung may be taken at his word when he says in his description of this time:

> I myself had to undergo the original experience, and, moreover, try to plant the results of my experience in the soil of reality; otherwise they would have remained subjective assumptions without validity. . . . Today I can say that I have never lost touch with my initial experiences. All my works, all my creative activity, has come from those initial fantasies and dreams.[19]

The process which had had its beginning for Jung in the year 1912 entered the crucial phase around Advent—on 12 December, to be exact—in 1913. He was ready to lay himself open to the flood of imaginations, fantasies, and dreams, to begin his own journey to the other side, as it had repeatedly been described for example in the Gnostic texts of antiquity. The impression made by the whole thing was, by his own report, quite frightening. To be sure, Jung meant to conceive what happened during these months as a scientific and medical experiment on himself, an experiment which the doctor seemed to owe to his patients if in future he wished to make it available to them as well. But his predicament took on unexpected dimensions.

> I was sitting at my desk once more, thinking over my fears. Then I let myself drop. Suddenly it was as though the ground literally gave way beneath my feet, and I plunged down into dark depths. I could not fend off a feeling of panic.[20]

Darkness and glittering light alternated, and among the forms that gradually emerged was a large black scarab, the ancient Egyptian symbol of death and rebirth. For Jung, the dismaying novelty in these experiences evidently lay in the fact that the distance between subject and object appeared to have been abolished. The experimenter no longer stood apart form the "object" of his investigation in the accustomed way; rather he himself had become the object of the experiment.

> It is of course ironical that I, a psychiatrist, should at almost every step of my experiment have run into the same psychic material which is the stuff of psychosis and is found in the insane. This is the fund of unconscious images which fatally confuse the mental patient. But it is also the matrix of a mythopoeic imagination which has vanished from our rational age.[21]

When the gigantic bloody vision from the fall of the same year appeared again, Jung was forced to give up trying to understand what he had seen. The images were too far removed from rational consciousness. Not until six days later (18 December 1913), when a dream appeared in which the dreamer found himself in a mountainous landscape, was it possible to guess the meaning: Over the mountain ridge the horn of Siegfried sounded. Suddenly his awesome figure appeared in the light of the rising sun and raced like the wind down toward the valley. Jung, who was accompanied by an unknown brown-skinned man, was convinced that they had to shoot Siegfried. After the deed was done he was "filled with disgust and remorse for having destroyed something so great and beautiful,"[22] and oppressed by an intolerable feeling of guilt.

Hardly had Jung awoken from this dream when he sensed an inner need to resolve it. He felt that if he did not succeed this time he would have to kill himself; the terse comment in his autopsychograph reads, "In the drawer of my night table lay a loaded revolver." And in fact it did become clear to him: Siegfried, a symbol of the German and idealistic ideal, is the quintessence of the self-conscious ego and the heroic ideal. He himself identified with Siegfried; indeed many of his Jewish colleagues had once looked upon him as just such a "gigantic blond Siegfried"! Siegfried was also the name of the son whom Sabina Spielrein longed for. And it was just this proud egoism to which he had to put an abrupt end, accompanied by the brown-skinned savage. In this strange figure Jung recognized an embodiment of his primitive shadow, which is to be seen as another component, the unconscious dark side, of the dreamer's being. The sensation that with this explanation he was on the right track, or at least heading in the right direction, afforded a certain feeling of confidence, although he had not yet by a long shot won the insights he was searching for. Before him lay a passage into the depths, an encounter with images that gave him the feeling of being "in the land of the dead":

> Near the steep slope of a rock I caught sight of two figures, an old man with a white beard and a beautiful young girl. I summoned up my courage and approached them as though they were real people, and listened attentively to what they told me. The old man explained that he was Elijah, and that gave me a shock. But the girl staggered me even more, for she called herself Salome! She was blind. What a strange couple: Salome and Elijah. But Elijah assured me that he and Salome had belonged together from all eternity, which completely astounded me. . . . They had a black serpent living with them which displayed an unmistakable fondness

> for me. I stuck close to Elijah because he seemed to be the most reasonable of the three, and to have a clear intelligence. Of Salome I was distinctly suspicious. Elijah and I had a long conversation which, however, I did not understand.[23]

Thus the dream of the killing of Siegfried had opened the doors to the other side, for the figures who meet Jung in his imagination and with whom—particularly Elijah—he agrees to converse clearly stand for factors in his unconscious. The religious tone is clear from the names given to the characters. The opposition between the reasonable old man and the beautiful but blind young woman stands out immediately. Those who are familiar with the history of mystery and myth will be reminded of similar couples, for example Klingsor and Kundry in the Grail legends, where the Merlinesque wise man is opposed by a sorceress. Jung himself thought of the sage Lao-tse and the dancer in Hölderlin's poem: "Who has thought of the deepest/Loves what is most living. He understands high virtue/Who has looked into the world. And the wise often bow/To beauty in the end." And because Jung had been absorbed, during his year of confrontation with the unconscious, in the gnosis of early Christianity, the Gnostic of the apostolic period, Simon Magus of Samaria, was also no stranger to him. To be sure, the New Testament Acts of the Apostles (chapter 8) is silent on Simon's possible following, but the church inquisitors of the second and third centuries reported that he had gone about with a woman by the name of Helen, thought to be a reincarnation of Helen of Troy, whom he had passed off as his "first intention" (that is, the first thought that had arisen in him). The gnosticism of the first centuries after Christ was of great importance for Jung's theme, because its polymorphous pantheon of spiritual beings included many such dual entities or syzygies,[24] a phenomenon known further from comparative religion. Finally, the presence of a snake points to a hero myth, not because it has to do with a battle with the snake or dragon, but because the snake, which sheds its skin, embodies a being that transforms itself, expressing the transformation of the hero.

But all these are of course only amplifications, embellishments of what is seen in the imagination by means of elements showing similar motifs. With their help Jung later achieved an interpretation which was to become important in Jungian psychotherapy, namely the concept of the soul-image. In a man it usually takes a feminine form (in dreams and fantasies, for example); this is the "anima," whereas in the same way a woman produces or imagines the oppositely sexed soul-image of the "animus." And this in itself serves to mark two typical, or archetypal, and primal forms of the unconscious. Hence Jung's explanation:

> Salome is an anima figure. She is blind because she does not see the meaning of things. Elijah is the figure of the wise old prophet and represents the factor of intelligence and knowledge; Salome, the erotic element. One might say that the two figures are personifications of Logos and Eros.[25]

Jung interrupts himself at this point in his interpretation to remark—correctly, of course—that a hasty intellectual definition of such soul-images is of little help. It is much more sensible, he says, to take the respective figures as what they represented, namely elucidations of unconscious background processes. As such they are by no means required to retain the same form or name. In Jung's later imaginations and dreams, for example, Elijah changed into another venerable figure, whom he named "Philemon." The name Philemon was not given by chance, for clearly this product of his unconscious was connected with the old Philemon, the husband of Baucis, whom Jung had met at the beginning of Act 5 of Goethe's *Faust*. To Jung this figure took on a new function, for the Jungian Philemon was not the companion of an equally old woman, but of the youthful Salome. The latest evidence that Jung had in mind a reference to Faust came from the stone-chiseled inscription which can be seen over the entrance to his tower in Bollingen:

Philemonis sacrum
Fausti poenitentia.

Shrine of Philemon,
Repentance of Faust.

As early as his first readings at the Gymnasium—not least of Ovid's *Metamorphoses*—he was familiar with these two hospitable old people who were to die a violent death in *Faust*. The lives of those who had once sheltered Zeus and Mercury beneath their poor roof had stood in the way of Faust's ambitious plans, and therefore they had become this murderer's victims. One day it became suddenly and alarmingly clear to Jung that he "had a legacy from Faust, as the advocate and avenger of Philemon and Baucis, who, at variance with Faust in his hubris, are the hosts of the gods in a time of wickedness and neglect of the gods. This became, one might say, a personal matter between me and my *proavus* Goethe." Jung suspected the existence of a Goethean world within himself, in which he had to play his corresponding part, in which he answered to Faust. "I would have given a world to know whether Goethe knew why he named the two old people 'Philemon' and 'Baucis.' Faust sinned against these ancestors (Philema and Baubo) from the beginning. Indeed, one really has to be almost dead before he understands this secret correctly," he wrote at sixty-six.[26] And again later in the *Memories*, Jung followed the thread of this thought further, remarking: "Later I consciously linked my work to what Faust had passed over: respect for the eternal rights of man, recognition of 'the ancient,' and the continuity of culture and intellectual history."[27]

One day this pagan and gnostic figure of Philemon emerged in an impressive dream. He had the horns of a bull and wings the characteristic color of a kingfisher, and in his hand was a bunch of four keys with which he was about to open a lock.

Hence Jung was deeply shaken when, a little later, he discovered a dead kingfisher on the shore of the lake in his garden; it had died relatively recently, two or three days before at the most, and had no visible injuries—a memorable coincidence. Anyone with psychotherapeutic experience knows that in everyday life similar or analogous "coincidences" can be associated with inner images or dream motifs. But what of the dream? Jung once again took up his paintbrushes to preserve the image of Philemon. Anyone who has seen Jung's tower in Bollingen at first hand has encountered Philemon's portrait there, for it hangs on the wall of the cell-like sleeping chamber in which Jung used to spend the nights when he would retreat for days or weeks at a time into the quiet solitude of his tower. The fact that he continued to paint this figure from his imagination into the twenties shows how deep an impression this "wise old man" must have made on him a decade earlier. Psychologically speaking, Philemon represented for him a superior insight, or at any rate one that was not achieved by virtue of his own intellectual efforts but managed to unfold its own unique life. As C. G. Jung's example shows, this is so true that in some cases one can speak with such "fantasy figures," who may have ready answers and advice that can be of extraordinary significance for the person concerned—the significance of an inspiration which stems, in the esoteric sense, from the "spiritual world" and therefore is equivalent to spiritual guidance. It was the certainty that he was not alone with his problem, that he had a psychagogue, a spiritual guide or guru with whose support he could withstand the inner darkness, that afforded Jung some confidence during this time of his journey to the other side. "This task was undertaken by the figure of Philemon, whom in this respect I had willy-nilly to recognize as my psychagogue. And the fact was that he conveyed to me many an illuminating idea."[28]

To this spiritual aspect of the unconscious psyche was later added another idea, which was more an embodiment of the chthonic, the spiritual in nature. The Egyptians had known this principle as the *ka*, a kind of double which accompanies the person. The *ka* was "an expression of the creative and preserving power of life; in earliest times it referred specifically to the masculine power of procreation. . . , but early on it was applied to spiritual and psychic power. . . . The *ka* was born together with the person."[29] In Jung's fantasy the *ka* came up out of the earth as if from a deep pit, and suddenly the image of the ritual phallus he had seen in his childhood dream comes to mind. He painted this chthonic figure from his imagination as one of the hermae (Greek *hérma*, "prop, support") which stood before houses in ancient Greece as (phallic) stone pillars intended to protect them from the evil of the world outside. But just as with the mythical drama, what is essential does not lie in any particular concrete, external form, and thus it does not really depend upon the assigning of this or that specific name or shape. All that matters is that the one who experiences these active imaginations should learn to recognize, resolve, and integrate them as spiritual and psychic signatures. Thus one would be wholly mistaken to cling to these images and personifications as if they were beings existing in themselves. For they are "only" markers and indicators; as such they need to be transformed to the point that with their help—much as in dealing with a dream—the meaning of the dream is perceived. Hence the reality lies *behind* Jung's terse concluding comment on Philemon and Ka: "In time I was able to integrate both figures."

Because this is in every case a very individual process, it is impossible to recommend any universal method. But certainly the representation of the experience, whether in clay or color or by recording it in written form, is one invaluable aid in mastering the productions of the unconscious. As a scientifically trained doctor, Jung was bound to wonder what he was really doing with this activity, whether this could still be called science, an experiment that nonetheless largely eluded complete scientific controls, or whether his fantasy images belonged in the category of art. While he was struggling with this question, a woman's feminine voice intruded itself, one which he recognized as the voice of one of his patients, "a gifted psychopath who had a strong transference to me." Naturally, as became gradually clear to him, it was not simply a particular patient who was speaking; for one thing she could not have known what was going on within her doctor's psyche or what her voice was inaudibly saying to him. Yet this aspect of their relationship was no coincidence, for Jung realized that it was that archetypal figure in the man's unconscious which he later termed the anima. Furthermore, in the course of his studies he came to the conclusion that the man's soul-image, the anima, was unconsciously projected onto certain feminine figures, which could then hold a correspondingly strong fascination for him. Put more generally:

> Wherever there exists an absolutely magical relationship, as it were, between the two sexes, it is a matter of projection of the soul-image [in this case the anima]. Now since these relationships are so common, the psyche must frequently be unconscious; that is, many people must be unconscious of how they are related to their inner psychic processes. . . . If the soul-image is projected, an unconditional affective tie to the object of the projection appears. If it is not projected, a relatively unadapted condition arises which Freud described in part as "narcissism." The projection of the soul-image is a release from concern with the inner processes, so long as the behavior of the object corresponds to the soul-image.[30]

It is significant for Jung's biography to note that this unnamed "gifted" patient had had "a strong transference" to him. This brings to mind in the first place the erotic relationship which is conditioned by, while at the same time making possible, the process of analysis. The autobiography is silent on this point. Above all, it says nothing about whether Jung's unconscious may have answered with a countertransference of its own,[31] which, as Freud declared in the case of Sabina Spielrein, is by no means an uncommon problem of the psychotherapist—quite apart from the question of the value or uselessness of the transference and countertransference phenomenon. That Jung makes no further reference to the person's identity beyond the fact that she was a gifted patient is understandable on the grounds of his professional duty to maintain confidentiality. Or could this refusal also have been because any further information would have shed definitive light on his relationship with a specific woman? He did after all destroy his correspondence with Toni Wolff, for example. The fact that this particular "gifted" woman, who was very close to him for over forty years, received not a single word of mention in the *Memories*, reveals an eloquent silence. But it was at precisely this point in his extremely active confrontation with the unconscious that his relationship with the young Toni must have played an important role—clearly not only in the erotic sense of the reciprocal "transference" between man and woman or doctor and patient, but also with respect to his *nekyia* in the inner world of the unconscious. In his emphatically polemically oriented study on Jung, Paul J. Stern asks whether Toni Wolff could perhaps have provided her friend with an Ariadne's thread for his escape from the labyrinth of psychic confusion and obscurity.[32] In the absence of evidence, a satisfactory answer to this question remains impossible.

Already in the Alexandrian era, alchemy was familiar with the *soror mystica* ("mystical sister"), the spiritual companion of the adept. She stood by him and, through her presence, as a symbol of totality, brought about the desired work. On the artistic plane there is the well-known *femme inspiratrice*, the woman whose inspiration makes possible the realization of works of art (even though this state of affairs, lying as it does partly in the unconscious, is not always clear to those involved); to say nothing of the negative aspect of femininity as seen in the *femme fatale*. In psychological terms, there are clearly various "structural forms of the feminine psyche" (a formulation of Toni Wolff's!),[33] be they those of mother or hetaira, medium or amazon. Noteworthy in this connection is the typology which Toni Wolff attributed to the structural form of the hetaira, as a companion who accompanies the man's scientific or artistic creation: "The hetaira or companion is instinctively related to the personal psychology of the man. . . . The man's individual interests, tendencies, and, if need be, problems lie within the purview of her consciousness, and through her they are stimulated and advanced. She gives him a sense of personal value apart from collective values, for her own development requires that an individual relationship be drawn out and realized in all its nuance and depth. . . . The function of the hetaira would be to awaken in the man the individual psychic life which goes beyond his masculine responsibility, to make him a whole personality. This development generally becomes a task only for the second half of life, after his social existence has been established."[34]

And it was in exactly this situation that Jung found himself at the time in question. The age gap of some thirteen years was not that of an old man and a young woman, considering the imaginary figures of Philemon and Salome. Anyone who knew both Jung and Toni Wolff well, and had had ample opportunity to observe them carefully together in private as well as in the professional sphere, would have to agree with the judgment of Barbara Hannah, who recalled that even by his schoolmates at the Gymnasium Jung was called "Father Abraham." In her experience and that of others who knew the two well and often saw them together, he was "the prototype of the wise old man," whereas Toni Wolff enjoyed "the quality of eternal youth." "At much the same time of the fantasy he made the extraordinary discovery that of all his friends and acquaintances only one young girl [Toni] was able to follow his extraordinary experiences and to accompany him intrepidly on his Nekyia to the underworld. . . . It was anything but easy at first for him to find a *modus vivendi* by which she could give him her extraordinary gift—it would not be an exaggeration to call it her genius—for companionship in the 'confrontation with the unconscious.'"[35]

The interpersonal problem is obvious, for on the one hand there was Emma Jung, a mother of five children and moreover a scarcely less insightful companion and collaborator beside her husband. On the other hand, Toni Wolff was described as a woman who clearly could not be dismissed by anyone—not even Emma Jung—as a mere *femme fatale* or willful home-wrecker. And in fact Toni, in her mid-twenties, did have her placed in the maturing process in which Jung found himself; above all she had her place in the "experiment" whose results included the insight into the anima archetype without which analytical psychology's picture of the human being is unthinkable. The Jungian analyst Barbara Hannah said flatly that Emma and Toni, the mother figure and the hetaira figure, were the two fundamentally inseparable sides of a single problem. In her judgment, "Toni Wolff was perhaps—of all the 'anima types' I have ever known—the most suited to carry the projection of this figure. She was not beautiful in the strictly classical sense, but she could look far more than beautiful, more like a goddess than a mortal woman. She had an extraordinary genius for accompanying men—and sometimes women too, in a different way—whose destiny it was to enter the unconscious. Indeed, she learned of this gift through her relation to Jung, but she afterward showed the same gift when she became an analyst; in fact it was her most valuable quality as an analyst. Curiously enough, she did not ever enter the unconscious on her own account."[36] Late in his life Jung came to speak of the problem of the hetaira.[37]

It would hardly be possible to achieve a proper evaluation of this fateful constellation from outside. Many people, though, might have found the problems of this three-way relationship unacceptable, making it all the more astonishing that a modus vivendi was in fact found and practiced which lasted for decades. With the reservations that must necessarily be held toward the testimony of even a close observer, the floor goes once again to Barbara Hannah, who wrote: "What saved the situation was that there was no 'lack of love' in any of the three. Jung was able to give both his wife and Toni a most satisfactory amount, and *both* women *really* loved him. Therefore, although for a long while they were at times most painfully jealous of each other, love always won out in the end and prevented any destructive action on either side. Emma Jung even said years later: 'You see, he never took anything from me to give to Toni, but the more he gave her, the more he seemed able to give me.'" The eyewitness added tersely, "Of course, this amazing insight was not reached early or without suffering, but that it was reached at all is the amazing thing. . . ."[38] There is no question that Emma Jung had an important say. For a person who is concerned—as Jung was at this period in his life—to become acquainted with his own inner world, it is very important, however, not to make this descent into the unconscious without guidance or relationship. Jung himself pointed in his autobiography to the great help his family and his work offered him; of Toni Wolff's accompanying function of *soror mystica* he occasionally spoke to his most intimate friends. As Barbara Hannah conjectured, "I think he was doubtful that he could have survived this most difficult of all journeys had he been entirely alone in it."[39] And she pointed out in this connection how indispensable a reliable interpersonal relationship is whenever one enters this inner path through one's own "active imagination."

Because dreams and fantasies such as have been described sometimes prove to be very fleeting, it is necessary to fix them in writing, even if in notes which are not much more than an insufficient suggestion of the inner vision. Jung had entered a part of his written record first in the so-called Black Book, which Aniela Jaffé described as series of "six black-bound, smallish leather notebooks." These descriptions took their final form in the Red Book, written in a calligraphic script and illustrated with numerous full-sized drawings in color, also depictions of what he had seen.[40] Jung noted in the *Memories*:

> In the Red Book I tried an esthetic elaboration of my fantasies, but never finished it. I became aware that I had not yet found the right language, that I still had to translate it into something else. Therefore I gave up this estheticizing ten-

> dency in good time, in favor of a rigorous process of *understanding.* I saw that so much fantasy needed firm ground underfoot, and that I must first return wholly to reality. For me, reality meant scientific comprehension. I had to draw concrete conclusions from the insights the unconscious had given me—and that task was to become a life work.[41]

But in practice this meant that he had to present his dealings with the unconscious, his dialogues with his anima (Salome) and the wise old Philemon, in such a way as to make his experience generally assimilable and usable. The means of dealing with the emotions, affects, fantasy-obsessing thoughts, melodies, or dream-images and of discerning their secrets found its expression in Jung's method of active imagination.[42] But the process itself represented for him a drama of self-rescue from the grip of the unconscious. It was for this very reason that he could not keep to himself the course or the results of these events which had extended over some five years. These "building blocks of psychosis" had revealed themselves to be equally a "matrix of mythopoeic imagination," which, like the unconscious itself, had a compensating function to fulfill in a rationalistic and nonspiritual age. To the extension of consciousness was thus added an ethical obligation, the doctor's duty to make what he had won by experience bear therapeutic fruit. The old admonition "Physician, heal thyself" is nowhere more warranted than here. Jung recalled Goethe's dictum: "Dare to storm those gates which everyone gladly sneaks past," referring to the common deep-rooted human aversion to looking behind the pleasant facade of self-deception and coming to know oneself.

Gradually a change began to be apparent. It turned out that the measures Jung had found by instinct and intuition had been the right ones for his spiritual and psychic predicament. They had helped him not only to come to an understanding of these "initial imaginations and dreams," but also to maintain his contact with everyday reality and his obligations to society.

And still the world war raged on. Jung was not allowed to bring his experimental night voyage of the soul to a close in the relatively sheltered atmosphere of his home in Küsnacht, for as part of his recurring compulsory duties as a captain in the medical corps, he served from 1916 to 1918 as commander of a training camp for British troops at Châteaux-d'Oex, a few kilometers south of Fribourg in the lower Alps region of French-speaking Switzerland. The various writings from the year 1916 were themselves of great significance for the progress of Jung's inner development. He perceived an inner need to put the flood of images and thoughts into literary and artistic form, and what emerged was the *Septem Sermones ad Mortuos*, the "seven sermons to the dead." Who "the dead" were was not explained in more detail; Jung went only so far as to say that he had in mind the "voices of the unanswered, the unreleased and unredeemed." But ambiguity arises even from the real fact of the great war: in the same year, 1916, more than half a million men bled to death before Verdun alone. On the other hand the fateful confrontation with the world of the departed came up also in Odysseus' *nekyia*. It goes without saying that Jung had no truck with any spiritism, even though he had occasion to speak of the presence of ghosts in the context of the *Sermones*. Ultimately they were personifications of his own inner being. Thus the *Septem Sermones ad Mortuos* represent the written record of psychic processes which needed to be elucidated from the point of view of consciousness. To be sure, the circumstances under which these writings came about were remarkable enough.

At first there was a great restlessness, but who or what was causing it Jung did not know. The whole atmosphere in his house was, as it were, oppressed, "filled with ghostly entities." And then a regular haunting began, in which the entire family was included. One night his eldest daughter saw a white figure passing through the room. Independently of her, his second daughter reported that twice during the night her blankets had been pulled away. The next morning his nine-year-old son asked his mother for crayons in order to draw his dream of the previous night, and he called the result "The Picture of the Fisherman," itself an extremely puzzling imagery. This happened on a Saturday morning. Jung's account continues:

> Around five o'clock in the afternoon on Sunday the front doorbell began ringing frantically. It was a bright summer day; the two maids were in the kitchen, from which the open square outside the front door could be seen. Everyone immediately looked to see who was there, but there was no one in sight. I was sitting near the doorbell, and not only heard it but saw it moving. We all simply stared at one another. The atmosphere was thick, believe me! Then I knew that something had to happen. The whole house was filled as if there were a crowd present, crammed full of spirits. They were packed deep right up to the door, and the air was so thick it was scarcely possible to breathe. As for myself, I was all a-quiver with the question: "For God's sake, what in the world is this?" Then they cried out in chorus, "We have come back from Jerusalem where we found not what we sought."[43]

A mysterious occurrence indeed, disregarding for the moment that such manifestations (poltergeists and so on) are not at all rare in the vicinity of young people in puberty, and that Jung could have been no stranger to such things on the basis of his own earlier experiences in his parents' house. But what could be done to diminish this tension coming from the unconscious, within whose field the whole family seemed to be living? Once again Jung reached for his pen. Instinctively seizing on the sentence the "spirits" had uttered, he began the first of the seven *Sermones* with the declaration, "The dead came back from Jerusalem, where they found not what they sought. They prayed me let them in and besought my word, and thus I began my teaching."[44] The *Sermones* were subtitled

"The seven instructions to the dead. Written by Basilides in Alexandria, the city where the East touches the West."

Basilides (Basileides) was one of the famous gnostics and thus heretical figures of the second century C.E. Already Hegel had referred to him, in his lectures on the history of philosophy, as one of "the most excellent gnostics."[45] He lived in Alexandria during the reigns of the Roman emperors Hadrian and Antoninus Pius (117-161). The midpoint of the culture of the ancient world, the city on the Nile delta was indeed a place where the East touched the West, as well as a significant center of Gnosticism and early Christian heresy.[46] Naturally the text Jung was drawing up was not really to be seen as a treatise on the interpretation of Gnosis. For he was, for one thing, more the recorder than the author of this text, which might have been inspired by "Philemon." For another, the effect of writing it down was striking, for hardly had Jung picked up his pen when the haunting was released. The tension evaporated, the air cleared, the "spirits" had vanished. Within three evenings the putative gnostic text was complete. It spoke from the very outset of the "pleroma," the "fullness" of a divine, spiritual world, which contrasts with that of created things. Then came the significant point:

> We are, however, the pleroma itself, for we are a part of the eternal and infinite. But we have no share thereof, as we are from the pleroma infinitely removed; not spiritually or temporally, but essentially, since we are distinguished from the pleroma in our essence as creature, which is confined within time and space.[47]

Characteristic of the pleroma are a number of pairs of opposites such as good and evil, time and space, light and dark, living and dead—all qualities inherent in human beings. There is only one drive, namely the aspiration toward our individual nature or self-existence.

In the second sermon the dead ask for instruction about God. The Basilides of these discourses answers, attesting not only to the fullness of life that is in God and its opposite in the

Devil, but also to the "God above God," the unknown and unconscious which stands above God and Devil as "the effective itself," embodying force, duration, and change. Its name is Abraxas. Then the dead demand further information about this primal being, which is neither the *summum bonum* nor limitless evil; Abraxas is life, "the mother of good and evil." Hence Abraxas begets truth and falsehood. The third sermon continues:

> It is the hermaphrodite of the earliest beginning.
> . . .
> It is abundance that seeketh union with emptiness.
> It is holy begetting.
> It is love and love's murder.
> It is the saint and his betrayer.
> It is the brightest light of day and the darkest night of madness.
> To look upon it is blindness.
> to know it is sickness.
> To worship it is death.
> To fear it is wisdom.
> To resist it not is redemption.[48]

It is mostly beside the point that the historical Basilides, according to the records of Irenaeus of Lyon and Hippolytus of Rome, made many statements concerning an Arbraxas or Abrasax. Rather one gets the impression, in reading the individual *sermones*, that these utterances in their hieratic language allowed some of what would enfold in the course of the years as the contents of Jung's archetypal psychology to show through; later, however, it would be cloaked not in the mythological enigmas borrowed from Alexandrian gnosticism but in the expository prose of analytical psychology, where it would receive its allotted place in the context of anamnesis, analysis, and synthesis. This psychology can dispense with the mythologizing and even the estheticizing treatment of unconscious contents, to the extent that it succeeds in leaving behind the images, voices, and figures and in maturing by recognizing them.

In the years after 1912, precisely this happened to Jung himself, and often in such a dismaying fashion that he must have been concerned for his own psychic equilibrium and the preservation of his inner sense of direction. But at the end of this journey into the depths it became clear to him that the insights he had won were not intended only for him. The experience he had gained proved to be a healing one for others as well:

> From then on, my life belonged to the generality. The knowledge I was concerned with, or was seeking, still could not be found in the science of those days. I myself had to undergo the original experience, and, moreover, try to plant the results of my experience in the soil of reality; otherwise they would have remained subjective assumptions without validity. It was then that I dedicated myself to service of the psyche. I loved it and hated it, but it was my greatest wealth. My delivering myself over to it, as it were, was the only way by which I could endure my existence and live it as fully as possible.[49]

These words were written from the perspective of hindsight. But the pictorial representation of psychic wholeness goes back to the last years of the war. At that time, in 1916, an inner urge prompted Jung to begin sketching and painting clearly structured pictures. What emerged were the circular figures known to Indian esoterism as mandalas (Sanskrit *maṇḍala*, "circle"). Basically the mandala is a primal symbol of the energy of the human form, which appears in all cultures and religions as the "holy circle" and can also be found in profusion in nature, in the shapes of flowers or radiolarians. This circumstance itself explains the mandala's deep-rootedness in the unconscious. At first Jung, in command of the camp at Châteaux d'Oex, drew such a circle every day. It was a kind of test; from the spontaneously formed circular structure the experimenter would read his psychic state of affairs at the time.

> Only gradually did I discover what the mandala really is: "Formation, Transformation, Eternal Mind's eternal recreation." And that is the self, the wholeness of the personality, which if all goes well is harmonious, but which cannot tolerate self-deceptions.
>
> My mandalas were cryptograms concerning the state of the self which were presented to me anew each day. In them I saw the self—that is, my whole being—actively at work.[50]

These lines already contain an important element in the interpretation and significance of all that the years between 1912 and 1918 had brought, while at the same time leading toward the answer to the question which Jung had had to ask himself during these years, namely: What is the real goal of this process, the goal of the *nekyia*, the journey into the inner depths? What results does it produce?

In the beginning the dominant role had been played by the dynamics of the unconscious itself, the superior power of its images and other manifestations, up to and including the parapsychic phenomena. The mandalas were already signs that an important point had been reached, the center of which announced unity and psychic completeness (but not completion!). In this context came the growing insight that the real source of the inner images and voices was not the everyday ego, influenced as it was by desires and interests of all kinds, but an authority superordinate to this ego, which could provide wisdom and leadership, be it through the figure of the wise old Philemon or in the energy lines and ordered structures of the individual mandalas. Thus Jung was able to say that the goal of psychic development is clearly the process of self-realization or individuation, in the course of which the great polarities or pairs of opposites in life are merged into a unity: the conscious and (at least partially) the unconscious, the light and the dark, and the masculine and the feminine, in the form of the soul-image which constitutes the inner femininity of the man (anima) and the inner masculinity of the woman (animus).

Several more years had still to pass before the inner experience could be confirmed and secured through definite evidence, for example the encounter with the spiritual world of the East as provided by such personalities as Richard Wilhelm and Heinrich Zimmer, as well as many more years of investigations into alchemy. Thus the expenditure of time which C. G. Jung's work demanded was considerable. He himself spoke of the forty-five years that had been necessary before his unique experience could be scientifically formulated and converted into therapy and practice. This is what must be borne in mind when we are confronted, unprepared, with certain statements of analytical psychology which cannot be unlocked by rational effort alone, but require patient acceptance.

On the question of what his period of confrontation with the unconscious had produced, and what value it could claim within the larger context of his biography and his work, Jung concluded:

> the early imaginations and dreams were like a fiery stream of basalt; out of them crystallized the stone which I could then work on.[51]

> The years when I was pursuing my inner images were the most important in my life—in them everything essential was decided. It all began then; the later details are only supplements and clarifications of the material that burst forth from the unconscious, and at first swamped me. It was the *prima materia* for a lifetime's work.[52]

13

The Work

In the early years of his activity as a psychiatrist and analytical psychologist, Jung repeatedly found himself pressed to define his position and to distinguish it from those of Freud's "psychoanalysis" and Adler's "psychology of the individual." Distinctions of this kind had already been made before his formal separation from the Psychoanalytic Association; as we have seen, the consequential *Transformations and Symbols of the Libido*, the roughly contemporary lectures on "The Theory of Psychoanalysis" presented at Fordham University in New York in 1912 and 1913, and others were among them. He gave a brief definition of his standpoint in the preface to his *Collected Papers on Analytical Psychology* (1916–1917), a collection of his pertinent works that had managed to appear in London during the First World War. This very place and date of publication were themselves remarkable, being (from the point of view of Germany and Austria) in foreign, enemy territory.

On the other hand, after his intense confrontation with the unconscious, Jung achieved a certain distance, so that it was now possible for him to sketch the first outlines of his emerging analytical psychology, although a well-rounded treatment would still be out of the question for some time to come. It was no coincidence that the years from 1913 to 1921 saw a conspicuous dearth of publications, during which Jung published only a few studies, all of them short. Still, there was a definite continuity between Jung's early work and the later work that appeared after the critical phase of his middle life. Jung regarded the individual essays of his *Collected Papers* as, at best, stations along the way to more general views, though they had nevertheless been achieved on the basis of empirical experience and thorough reflection.

As always, the author of these papers credited the discovery of the new analytical methods of general psychology to Sigmund Freud, whose original interpretations, however, "would have to undergo many important modifications," as he said in the preface.[1] The terminology of the time spoke of the "Vienna school," with its exclusively sexualist perspective, as opposed to the "Zürich school," represented chiefly by Jung, which held a "symbolistic interpretation." The distinction between Jung and Freud began with the concept of the symbol. Whereas the Vienna school viewed the symbol in psychology semiotically, that is, as merely a sign of certain primitive psychosexual processes, and then proceeded to explain it analytically or causally, the Zürich group took a more critical stance. Of course they did recognize the scientific possibility of the Freudian position, as the elderly C. G. Jung still acknowledged in his *Memories*, noting:

> It is a widespread error to imagine that I do not see the value of sexuality. On the contrary, it plays a large part in my psychology as an essential—though not the sole—expression of psychic wholeness.[2]

Thus Jung added to the analytic method, as has already been mentioned, a combinative, constructive, and prospective point of view, one which was aimed at the goal of human maturation. This was also an approach long championed, for example, by Jung's Zürich colleague Alphonse Maeder.

Already at an early date, for instance at the Munich Congress in 1913, Jung acknowledged the views of Alfred Adler, which also departed from Freud's. In the briefest terms, Jung felt that whereas Freud had helped to validate the pleasure principle, thereby (as also in other ways) setting out on the path to a more materialist and mechanistic world view, Adler, approaching to a certain extent the philosophy (or at least terminology) of Nietzsche, stressed the primacy of the so-called power principle. On this point Jung found himself in the intellectual vicinity of a William James, who granted a relative validity to both interpretations, but only—as Jung put it—"within the confines of their corresponding types"; thus excluding any universal validity of one or the other. With this Jung emphasized once again how important it is, in applying either method, to be aware also of the typological state of affairs, a factor that was to undergo necessary development in Jung's typological studies. By the same token, it is not a matter of indifference what psychological types the analyst and analysand belong to. Quite practical consequences arise from this, such as the fact that Jung would in certain cases refer one patient or another to other doctors. This practice was based both on typological considerations and on the fact that the psychoanalytical procedure as such, in the wider sense of the term, is applicable only in a limited number of cases. Hence as early as his correspondence with R. Löy, a leading sanatorium physician in Montreaux-Territet, we find the comment:

> There are cases where psychoanalysis works worse than anything else. But who said that psychoanalysis was to be applied always and everywhere? Only a fanatic could maintain such a thing. Patients must be selected for psychoanalysis. . . . Any preconceived scheme in these matters makes one shudder.[3]

Biographically speaking, these lines of 4 February 1913 were written before the famous parting of the ways. They could claim equal validity for the later analytical psychology which remained to be worked out, but at the same time they indicate a transition that one might call the road "from Freud to Jung." In her study of the same name Liliane Frey-Rohn described this transitional character, insofar as it applied to the emerging work, as follows: "It is fascinating and at the same time heart-wrenching to follow the inner split with which Jung struggled in his efforts to do justice to Freud's findings on the one hand, while remaining true to his own inner demons on the other. Not only did the first part of *Symbols of Transformation* reveal clear signs of this inner disunity, but the second part especially, which appeared somewhat later, made obvious his increasing distance from Freud. As positively as Jung had accepted his friend's early writings, he maintained an attitude of corresponding reservation toward the sexual theory that had been published in the meantime[4] and the works based on it."[5]

Jung's unremitting insistence that he wished to be known not as a theorist (or even dogmatist), but as an empiricist who had first had to test his insights thoroughly, was not without its consequences. For decades there was a certain fluidity in his psychological statements. This lasted a relatively long time, up until—to retain Jung's metaphor—the "fiery stream of basalt" of his imaginations, but his attempt at a theoretical formulation had also come to something of a standstill. (Of course, it could never have stopped completely, if he was to do justice to the ever-changing nature of the human soul. Some of Jung's critics failed to make allowance for this requirement, demanding clearly defined concepts, even though Heraclitus' *pánta rheî* requires intellectual flexibility of the psychologist more than anyone.)

As a typical example of the potential and the necessity for continuing development within Jung's work, we may adduce the early and then repeatedly revised text "On the Psychology of the Unconscious," which appeared under various titles between 1912 and 1942.[6] The repeated changes in its title corresponded to his ongoing interest in the archetypal dream material that he discussed, as well as the necessity for changes in content, for eventually the dynamic manifestations of the psyche demanded adequate treatment. Time after time the confrontation with the unconscious, as Jung himself had had to master it, provided evidence for the correctness of his statements. In the foreword to the second edition he made clear the necessity of such a confrontation, writing in 1918, the last year of the World War:

> But still too few look inward, to their own selves, and still too few ask themselves whether the ends of human society might not best be served if each man tried to abolish the old order in himself, and to practice in his own person and in his own inward state those precepts and victories which he preaches at every street-corner, instead of always expecting these things of his fellow men.

How closely Jung connected the forms of the external catastrophe with the inner revolution that was becoming so necessary, and how he spoke here from his own often painful experience, becomes evident in this same passage:

> Every individual needs revolution, inner division, overthrow of the existing order, and renewal, but not by forcing these things upon his neighbors under the hypocritical cloak of Christian love or the sense of social responsibility. . . . Individual self-reflection, return of the individual to the ground of human nature, to his own deepest being with its individual and social destiny—here is the beginning of a cure for that blindness which reigns at the present hour.[7]

The therapeutic concern was unmistakable. But Jung also left no doubt about the provisional character of his work. In any case his book could under no circumstances give a comprehensive idea of the total scope of analytical psychology, as he noted in the fourth edition of 1936. And by the time the fifth edition became necessary, in 1942, Europe had been invaded for a second time by world war. In the meantime fully three decades had passed since the first version, and hence the concluding lines of his new foreword were meant rather literally:

> New ideas, if they are not just a flash in the pan, generally require at least a generation to take root. Psychological innovations probably take much longer, since in this field

> more than in any other practically everybody sets himself up as an authority.[8]

Thus Jung realized that his orientation to research and therapy would only slowly be accepted by his contemporaries. Even in his old age had had cause to complain of being continually misunderstood and misinterpreted, but it is hardly surprising when one considers that he was comparing the results of his own investigations with historical material that was rather far removed from the general consciousness. Even upon reading the text on "Transformation," many of his readers had grumbled at how the author pulled out practically every stop of humanistic, religious, and comparative intellectual tradition, and recited all of his sources in great detail. Indeed, the psychotherapist from Küsnacht had become familiar with some very specialized areas of knowledge. The strange *Septem Sermones ad Mortuos* already signaled Jung's interest in early Christian gnosticism, which was deepened in the years between 1918 and 1926. He saw that the exponents of this brand of mythological knowledge also

> had been confronted with the primal world of the unconscious and had dealt with its contents, with images that were obviously contaminated with the world of instinct. Just how they understood these images remains difficult to say, in view of the paucity of the accounts—which, moreover, mostly stem from their opponents, the Church Fathers. It seems to me highly unlikely that they had a psychological conception of them.[9]

As is attested to by the bibliographies in his books, during these years Jung assembled the standard works of Gnostic scholarship up to the beginning of the century. The great find of Gnostic texts that were original—and thus not mediated by the opponents of Gnosticism—that was made a generation later (1945) at Nag Hammadi in upper Egypt, was therefore not yet available to him. Thus he could not have known of the "Codex Jung," later named for him, which formed part of the Gnostic corpus. The redaction, translation, and classification of this extremely important codex was to take up several more decades, as we know,[10] and hence these texts remained unavailable for Jung's examination. But regardless of these facts, Jung was compelled to the conclusion that the distance in time, and above all in consciousness, between this ancient gnosis and the modern problems of the soul was far too great for him to achieve effective results in that direction. Thus this first attempt at bridge-building was unsuccessful. Only when he became better acquainted with medieval alchemy did he discover the possibility of drawing parallels between modern productions of the unconscious and alchemical terminology and symbolism. It was only closer familiarity with alchemy that enabled him to speak of a spiritual and psychic continuity between past and present. "Grounded in the natural philosophy of the Middle Ages, alchemy formed the bridge on the one hand into the past, to Gnosticism, and on the other into the future, to the modern psychology of the unconscious,"[11] although certain central themes, for example the important gnostic motif of sexuality, already bore a resemblance to Freudian psychoanalysis.

Also to be considered in this connection is the great theme of the *coniunctio* ("joining together") of the masculine and the feminine, at the level of the spiritual world as described by the Gnostics. The same is true of the "sacred marriage," the *hierós gámos* that was supposed to take place between God and man, between the divine *pneuma* and the ground of the human soul.[12] But what happens in the ground of the human soul is the central theme not only of the Gnostics, and mystics of all eras, but also of any psychologist who attaches as much importance as Jung did to understanding the peculiarities and the fulfillment of the psyche, and hence of the total personality. And precisely around the time of his work with the Gnostic texts, around 1921–1922, this interpretation of the process of individuation was entering more and more into Jung's consciousness. Individuation, as the process of self-realization that determines the humanness of the human being, was gradually shifting toward the center of analytical psychology. The concept itself had emerged as early as 1916, though defined differently.[13] Several years were to pass before Jung was able to express more precisely what he had in mind.

> Individuation means becoming a single, homogeneous being, and, insofar as "individuality" embraces our innermost, last, and incomparable uniqueness, it also implies becoming one's own self. We could therefore translate individuation as "coming to selfhood" or "self-realization."[14]

This process of development, then, is not one that goes on aimlessly, but one through which the human being's true nature and innate gifts are to take shape. Of course it is not some duty imposed on the psyche from without; rather the goal lies hidden within the person himself, as a self-regulating principle superordinate to the everyday ego. It plays a considerable role in the confrontation between the ego and the unconscious, an insight Jung had gained in the tension-filled years of his midlife crisis. At the same time, around 1916, he began to discern the workings of a function that served to mediate between consciousness and the unconscious, the so-called transcendent function.[15] It is this which forms the bridge between conscious and unconscious, between rational and irrational.

> It is a natural process, a manifestation of the energy that springs from the tension of opposites, and it consists in a sequence of fantasy-occurrences which appear spontaneously in dreams and visions.[16]

On the whole, then, the transcendent function is a symbolizing one. In the process of self-realization it operates to help unify the conflict within the human psyche. We shall return to this central theme of the unification of the opposites (*mysterium coniunctionis*), as it both represents the theme of Jung's middle life and marks the culmination of his later work.

The first significant book that can be seen as the fruit of his own confrontation with the unconscious after his middle life was *Psychological Types* in 1921, although in his preface from

1920 its author could point to nearly twenty years of interest in this problem of practical psychology, which means that the study of the typical structures and functions of the psyche had occupied Jung since the beginning of his psychiatric career. Because every person (regardless of the typological approach applied) can be classified as a particular psychological type, typology represents an important aid in the understanding of any person. It is no coincidence that *Psychological Types* stands as one of Jung's best-known works, and the subject itself deserves to be discussed in more detail.

For more than two thousand years attempts have been made to come to grips with the physical, mental, and emotional phenotype of humankind by reducing it to a common denominator of typical characteristics. The early Greek thinkers and physicians all made their contributions to this effort, embedded within the view of man and the world that prevailed at this time. The most famous of these is the division into the "four temperaments," associated with the four elements of Empedocles, Hippocrates' doctrine of bodily humors, or Aristotle's blood-conditions. Beside these ancient temperament types, modern psychology had developed a wide array of typologies. In 1921, virtually coinciding with Jung's, Hermann Rorschach[17] and Ernst Kretschmer[18] published their own characteristic typological schemes. That the appearance of Jung's typology was not entirely sudden is shown by the already mentioned paper "A Contribution to the Study of Psychological Types" at the Munich Congress in 1913, reprinted in volume 6 of the *Collected Works*. Here we can observe the genesis of this aspect of his work. On the basis of many years of experience as a doctor, Jung was eventually able to conclude:

> What I have to say in this book has been tested line by line, so to speak, a hundred times in the practical treatment of sick people, and was originally inspired by such treatment. . . . Hence the layman cannot be blamed if certain statements strike him as odd, or if he should even suspect

> that my typology comes out of some idyllically undisturbed study.[19]

Jung's typological scheme was characterized by the point of view from which he looked upon psychological types, seeking to determine the relationship of the personality in question to its environment and those around it. He asked, then, whether the person was more inclined toward or away from the environment, whether directed outward or inward, whether he could be seen as an "extravert" or an "introvert." At first sight this approach seems almost simplistic, though it cannot be denied that posing the question in this way already points to certain basic underlying assumptions. Detailed experience shows that the Jungian typology not only makes possible a rich differentiation of types, but can also accommodate the uniqueness of the individual which is beyond the scope of typology. No special proof was needed to show that despite many points of typological comparison, the uniqueness of any person could not be sufficiently "grasped" by means of any of the available systems.

Jung had observed two psychic "mechanisms," which were distinguished by a difference in goal-orientation. Psychic energy directed outward produced extraversion, a "shift of interest toward the object. A shift of interest away from the object to the subject and his own psychological processes" Jung referred to as introversion. Thinking, feeling, and wishing were subordinate in their turn to one of these two basic attitudes. Jung had noted a parallel in Goethe's conception of diastole (expansion) and systole (contraction), and accordingly extraversion could be classified as "a diastolic going out to and taking hold of the object," whereas introversion represented "a systolic concentration and detachment of energy from the grasped object." In his early article "On the Psychology of the Unconscious" (1916, etc.), the author defined the two basic attitudes of the introvert and the extravert as follows:

> The first attitude is normally characterized by a hesitant,

> reflective, retiring nature that keeps itself to itself, shrinks from objects, is always slightly on the defensive, and prefers to hide behind mistrustful scrutiny. The second is normally characterized by an outgoing, candid, and accommodating nature that adapts easily to a given situation, quickly forms attachments, and, setting aside any possible misgivings, will often venture forth with careless confidence into unknown situations.[20]

Consequently in the first case it is the subject, and in the second the object that should claim decisive importance. The voluminous book *Psychological Types* proceeds to unfold these twin themes, beginning with historical interpretations of the problem of types from antiquity, the Middle Ages, and the various formulations developed in modern times, with particular consideration of writers such as Carl Spitteler and Goethe.

It goes without saying that the designations *introvert* and *extravert* were intended to be completely value-free, Jung himself being assignable to the introverted attitude type. This was documented especially by the whole of his psychotherapeutic and literary work. In his *Memories* he understood his individual works as stations in his own life and expressions of his own inner development:

> All my writings may be considered tasks imposed from within; their source was a fateful compulsion. What I wrote were things that assailed me from within myself. I permitted the spirit that moved me to speak out.[21]

Certainly many an author could make such an avowal. To this assertion Jung added the suggestion that he had never counted on any strong positive response to his writings. His books represented as it were a compensation for the world of his contemporaries, and so he was bound to say much which no one really wanted to hear. One who works in this introverted way cannot allow himself to be overly concerned with public taste or the reactions of readers, although to be sure it is quite another matter how keenly such a person senses rejection and lack of interest or understanding.

To return to Jung's typological studies, a clear distinction must be made between "type" and "attitude." According to Jung, only when extraversion or introversion assumes the nature of a habitual trait and thus represents a constant can we speak of a "type" in the full sense. The "attitude," in contrast, is the variable. It can change over the course of a person's life, for example in the form of a fundamental change of opinion or inner "conversion." The emphasis can shift from the extraverted side to the introverted, and vice versa. Type is clearly an expression of the respective underlying psychic structure.

But now Jung discovered still further distinguishing criteria, noting especially that people who shared the same basic psychic structure could nevertheless be stamped in very different ways. The possible distinctions arose from the consideration of four "basic functions," including two rational functions, *thinking* and *feeling*, and two irrational ones, *sensation* and *intuition*. At first sight this scheme seems to allow, at least to begin with, only eight different possible variations, and therefore a thorough familiarity and practical experience is necessary in order to become acquainted with further modes of variation. In the view of the Jungian approach, the typological factor also comes into play, for

> from the extraverted, rational standpoint these [irrational] types are probably the most useless of all people. But seen in a wider perspective, such people are living testimony to the fact that the rich, eventful world with its overflowing and intoxicating life lies not only outside, but also within. Certainly these types are one-sided manifestations of nature, but they are instructive for one who does not allow himself to be blinded by the intellectual modalities of the day. People of this attitude are promoters of culture and educators after their own fashion. Their lives teach more than what they say. . . .[22]

To the typological studies, which take up more than six hundred pages in the collected works, Jung added a detailed appendix containing definitions of psychological concepts, seeking to accommodate the widespread need for as clear a formulation of these concepts as possible. How strictly circumscribed such an intention must be becomes clear even from the preface to these definitions. That which can be grasped by means of size and number, with the scientific methods of measurement and calculation, can never reveal more than a piece, a single dimension of reality, and not the whole extent of it. Therefore Jung explicitly called attention to the fact

> that no experimental methodology ever has or ever will succeed in capturing the essence of the human soul, or even so much as tracing out an approximately faithful picture of its complex manifestations.[23]

For this reason it was necessary to consult, as Jung did, the insights of philosophers, theologians, scientific theorists, and poets in developing a doctrine of psychological types. Once again he quoted extensively from the records of cultural history, for example the theological oppositions between Tertullian and Origines, Augustinus and Pelagius, the opponents and defenders of the Catholic doctrine of transsubstantiation, and the so-called problem of universals between realists and nominalists in the Middle Ages. Jung saw the influence of a typological factor in the conflict between Luther and Zwingli over Holy Communion, and he thought also of Schiller's distinction between sentimental and naive poetry or the opposition of Apollonian and Dionysian principles in Nietzsche. The contents of this "book which is just as fat as it is hard to understand"—as Jung once jokingly said of his typological studies[24]—served above all as a "critical apparatus" in his practical work. He employed it only on a case-by-case basis, "mostly only when I have to clarify for certain patients disequilibria in their behavior, remarkable relationships to other people, and such things."[25]

As literary products of his decades-long concern with the psyche and its unceasing process of transformation, we may mention two texts from the year 1928. One of them, "The Relations between the Ego and the Unconscious,"[26] developed from an article that had been published in 1916 in French and then also in English. Thus we have yet another indication that even though Jung had discussed a number of topics even in the early days of his work as a psychiatrist and psychotherapist, these provisional drafts could only be rounded out after several years of maturation of his own personality and further professional experience.

The other text, "On Psychic Energy,"[27] constituted a defense and an extension of what had been said in *Symbols of Transformation*, while at the same time allowing Jung an opportunity to comment upon his particular approach to energy and its application. Both of these texts are among the basic writings of analytical psychology. In them we learn, for example, the extent to which psychic energy (libido) parallels physical energy. Psychic energy can be accumulated or blocked and transformed. It can be projected onto forms in the external world, or it can be introjected and thus absorbed internally. Jung discussed the nature of the unconscious, which comprises much more than simply those contents that have been repressed from consciousness or sunk into forgetfulness. The total scope of the unconscious, and thus the human psyche, also includes psychic factors that have never been the object of individual experience, and consequently could not have been repressed or forgotten. With this we contact the world of the "archetypes," in which Jung clearly distinguished between the still-nebulous hypothetical archetypes and the archetypal images. The archetype, as Jung employed the concept, is derived from such things as myths, folk tales, and religious traditions. As soon as dreams or even hallucinations appear with archetypal motifs, the vague and indefinable content of the archetype starts to become discernible and describable in the archetypal image. Jung subsumed the archetypes under the concept of the "collective unconscious," that dimension of the unconscious which transcends the individual psyche and thus cannot be attributed to forgotten or repressed contents.

Indisputably, the unconscious with its energetic properties forms part of the totality of the psyche. Together with the conscious mind, it constitutes the human soul. The unconscious develops autonomously—that is, independently of the conscious life—and for this reason Jung spoke of its compensatory or complementary character with respect to the conscious state at a given time. This character becomes clear especially in dreams, and thus as a rule of thumb:

> The more unbalanced the conscious attitude is, and the further removed from the optimum of life's potentialities, the greater the possibility that vivid dreams of a strongly contrasting, suitably compensatory aspect will appear, as an expression of the psychological self-regulation of the individual. Just as the body reacts in appropriate ways to injuries, infections, or abnormal habits, so too the psychic functions react to unnatural or dangerous disturbances with suitable defensive measures.[28]

At this point the obvious thing might be to continue with an enumeration of further writings and published books, thus providing an overview of C. G. Jung's literary output. But such a procedure would fail to do justice to the reality of life as he lived it. By his own account, Jung's work grew step by step out of his life, a life that included the intimacy of his family and friends on workdays and holidays, as well as the no less intimate sphere of the consultation room from which the psychotherapist showed his patients and students the way within. When the season and the weather permitted, he often moved his analysis and discussion sessions to his spacious garden on the shore of Lake Zürich, and this was not the only indication of the great importance Jung placed on remaining in living, creative contact with nature and the concrete world. His self-forgetting play with his children was also an expression of it, as were his various works of handicraft, such as building, carving, woodcutting, and cooking. In this way his analysands received various hints as to how to regain their own relationship to the fullness of life. Also part of this life was meeting with people, the exchange of views in person and in a correspondence whose richness is so impressively attested to by the three-volume edition of his letters. And just as on days off Jung launched his sailboat, or climbed aboard his bicycle or later his own automobile to tour his Swiss homeland, so his numerous travels abroad and overseas cannot be left out of his biography. All these elements represent important aspects of an astonishingly multifaceted life, one which shows that introversion, turning within, does not necessarily mean isolation or reclusiveness. Only from a life lived with the intensity of all one's senses can a work like that of C. G. Jung's emerge, a work that points the way toward wholeness and self-realization.

14

Traveling and Tower-Building

Without stirring abroad
One can know the whole world;
Without looking out of the window
One can see the way of heaven.
The further one goes
The less one knows.
Therefore the sage knows without having to stir,
Identifies without having to see,
Accomplishes without having to act.[1]

These lines from the forty-seventh section of Lao-tse's *Tao Te Ching* (as rendered into English by D. C. Lau) might come to mind if one wished to characterize the mental attitude of an introverted person—someone who seems to see no need for roaming about in the world, who is horrified at the thought of protracted travel. But Jung, the confirmed introvert, was living proof that this assumption is wrong, or at least represents an undue oversimplification. In any case, this revision becomes necessary when we see how, inwardly directed and concerned with problems of the psyche as he was, yet he did not hesitate to undertake extended journeys, precisely so that he could return once again, "amplified" and enriched by encounters and impressions of the outer world, to concentrate on the great theme of his life and work. For here Aniela Jaffé's statement is relevant: "Like every true introvert, Jung thoroughly enjoyed the positive aspects of extraversion—travel and success—from the very beginning."[2] When he traveled to America with Freud, for instance, to present a series of lectures at Clark University on the association experiment he had developed, he wrote to his wife from there in 1909: "We are the men of the hour here. It is very good to be able to spread oneself in this way one in a while. I can feel that my libido is gulping it in with vast enjoyment. . . ."[3]

One who regularly crosses over into the realm of the psyche, whose task is to mediate between consciousness and the unconscious in order to achieve a "psychosynthesis" which will embrace the whole of reality, cannot heedlessly overlook the reality of other peoples and cultures. On the contrary, it is only by juxtaposing the mentality of European, Western people, ruled by everyday consciousness, with that of the Far East or Africa, more strongly anchored in the archaic and unconscious, that the *unus mundus* becomes visible, the reality of oneness which dissolves the oppositions and one-sidednesses of a view that considers only the foreground. Hence Jung's almost unrelenting effort to attain an Archimedean point, "an outside point to stand on." This applies even to the interpersonal I-Thou relationship. It is all the more regrettable not only that the analytical psychologist's special interests were not understood by contemporary dialogue-thinkers of the likes of Martin Buber, but also that Jung himself was in no position to do justice to this concern for the perspective and the dimensions of the Thou, and thus to arrive at a fruitful synthesis. Jung was surely aware that such an external standpoint is especially indispensable in psychology, considering the subjective bias which is greater here than in any other scientific discipline.

> How, for example, can we become conscious of national peculiarities if we have never had the opportunity to regard our own nation from outside? Regarding it from outside means regarding it from the standpoint of another nation. To do so, we must acquire sufficient knowledge of the for-

> eign collective psyche, and in the course of this process of assimilation we encounter all those incompatibilities which constitute the national bias and the national peculiarity. Everything that irritates us about others can lead us to an understanding of ourselves.[4]

But this is not merely a late insight on Jung's part. He was an eager traveler his whole life. Even as a young man he made excursions of all kinds, trips to the mountains and extended bicycling tours, the travels by boat that have already been mentioned, sailing tours and travels in his own car, and in his later years automobile trips with friends, in which—as Aniela Jaffé once noted—the reconnoitering of good restaurants played an important part. Jung, himself an avid cook, was well known as a patron of the culinary arts and a connoisseur of noble spirits.

After the manuscript of *Psychological Types* was completed in 1920, and after having long been preoccupied with himself and restricted by military service during the war years, Jung felt an urge to get out into the open. The Anglo-Saxon world had held a particular attraction for him throughout his life, and within only a few months after the end of the First World War, in the summer of 1919, he spent several weeks there. We do not know what the real reason for this trip was, but we do have one letter, written in London on 1 July 1919 and addressed to his nine-year-old daughter Marianne. Naturally, as a communicative father, he knew what would interest his little daughter and the other children too. At the same time the reader gets the impression that the traveler himself had become fascinated all over again with the great city on the Thames, for the citizen of Küsnacht found it really something to be able to report, in 1919, that some five thousand automobiles drove past his quarters in London.

> Every morning at half past ten the cuirassiers ride by in their golden armor with red helmet plumes and black cloaks. They go to the royal palace and guard the king and the princes and princesses.

Astonishing sights were everywhere:

> . . . the king has his golden throne and his golden scepter in another castle, in a high tower, with thick fences and iron gates. In the daytime the crown is up in the tower and you can see it, but at night it and the scepter sink down into a deep cellar that is shut up with plates of armor, so no one can steal them. There are jewels in the crown as big as dove's eggs. . . .[5]

Truly, little Marianne's country had nothing like this to show for itself. And the fact that the great river flowed downstream for six hours and then for six hours turned around and flowed upstream—this bordered on the miraculous! What else might Father have had to tell, when even his letters were filled with such amazing things?

Within a year Jung accepted an invitation from English friends and colleagues to his first seminar in England, which took place in the summer of 1920 at Sennen Cove in Cornwall. The assembly was a small one. Esther Harding remembered about twelve participants, among them the later Jungian Eleanor Bertine, a doctor at Bellevue Hospital in New York. Dr. Helton Godwin Baynes of London, Jung's assistant intermittently in Zürich for many years, probably made the arrangements. Barbara Hannah described him as an unusually amiable person, whom Emma Jung and Toni Wolff also especially liked; the circle of friends, including Jung, always called him Peter. "In many ways he was the best assistant Jung ever had."[6] Jung loved gatherings and seminars in small groups, because these afforded the best possibilities for personal exchange. For the same reason he saw to it that the Psychological Club in Zürich, an informal society of former patients and students which had existed since 1916, did not grow unnecessarily large. Despite keeping it small in number, however, Jung was unable to restrain all the unavoidable jealousies that arose in the club, which was composed mainly of women and had been formed at the suggestion of Toni Wolff.

Hence when his friend Hermann Sigg, a Swiss businessman, invited him to go along on a business trip to North Africa, Jung eagerly agreed: at last there was the prospect of being able to meet non-European, noncivilized people at first hand on the spot, and study the primitivity of their psyche! In early March 1920, and thus before the seminar in England, the two departed for Tunisia via Algiers. "After cold, heavy weather at sea" they reached Tunis and the city of Sousse with its whitewashed walls and towers, its harbor, and "beyond the harbor wall the deep blue sea, and in the port lies the sailing ship with two lateen sails which I once painted," Jung reported to his wife from the Grand Hotel in Sousse. The date was 15 March 1920. Jung lamented bitterly that he could not write coherently because the impressions were too numerous and strange, for "this Africa is incredible!" This was his first step onto the threshold of the dark continent. And yet its flashes of light let him paint quite a colorful picture:

> Bright houses and streets, dark green clumps of trees, tall palms' crowns rising among them. White burnooses, red fezzes, and among these the yellow uniforms of the Tirailleurs d'Afrique, the red of the Spahis, then the Botanical Gardens, an enchanted tropical forest, an Indian vision, holy *acvatta* trees with gigantic aerial roots like monsters, fantastic dwellings of the gods, enormous in extent, heavy, dark green foliage rustling in the sea wind.

After a thirty-hour rail journey they reached Tunis, a city where the ancient world blended in a unique way with the Moorish Middle Ages, the Moorish Granada with the fairy tale of Baghdad. And the effect?

> You no longer think of yourself; you are dissolved in this potpourri which cannot be evaluated, still less described: a Roman column stands here as part of a wall; an old Jewish woman of unspeakable ugliness goes by in white baggy breeches; a crier with a load of burnooses pushes through the crowd, shouting in gutturals that might have come straight from the canton of Zürich; a patch of deep blue sky, a snow-white mosque dome; a shoemaker busily stitching

> away at shoes in a small vaulted niche, with a hot, dazzling patch of sunlight on the mat before him; blind musicians with a drum and tiny three-stringed lute; a beggar who consists of nothing but rags; smoke from oil cakes, and swarms of flies; up above, on a white minaret in the blissful ether, a muezzin sings the midday chant; below, a cool, shady, colonnaded yard with horseshoe portal framed in glazed tiles; on the wall a mangy cat lies in the sun; a coming and going of red, white, yellow, blue, brown mantles, white turbans, red fezzes, uniforms, faces ranging from white and light yellow to deep black; a shuffling of yellow and red slippers, a noiseless scurrying of naked black feet, and so on and so on.

The psychologist became a writer of travelogues, a painter. He knew that his hurried jottings could be nothing but "miserable stammering," to say nothing of what Africa was "really" saying to him. But there was no doubt of one thing—"It speaks!" Jung could not avoid the magic of the continent; he had to stand up to it if he did not wish to fall under its spell. For "going black under the skin"—that is, becoming virtually swamped by the strangeness of an exotic mentality and deeper unconsciousness—represents a danger of which the "white man" is not always sufficiently aware. Jung was at least strongly moved by this magical aura:

> In the morning the great god rises and fills both horizons with his joy and power, and all living things obey him. At night the moon is so silvery and glows with such divine clarity that no one can doubt the existence of Astarte.[7]

While Hermann Sigg went about his business in Sousse as planned, Jung traveled further into the country on his own, southward toward the Sahara. Finally he had come to where he had so often longed to be:

> . . .in a non-European country where no European language was spoken and no Christian conceptions prevailed, where a different race lived and a different historical tradition and philosophy had set its stamp upon the face of the

> crowd. I had often wished to be able for once to see the European from outside, his image reflected back at him by an altogether foreign milieu.[8]

The language barrier presented a not inconsiderable obstacle. Only in the large hotels in the cities was French spoken, and Jung had no command of Arabic, not in spite of the fact that his father, as a certified Arabicist, had mastered the language of the prophet Muhammad, but because of it. He once told Barbara Hannah that Arabic was the one language he was totally unable to learn. He attributed this seemingly remarkable circumstance to the fact that his father had had such a good command of that language,[9] hinting at a not yet fully resolved father complex. So Jung made do by sitting in one of the Arabic cafés along the main street and carefully observing the people, their speech, their sign language and gestures. Being accustomed to riding from his days in the military, the psychologist mounted a mule to ride to the oasis of Nefta. A whole new world opened up, even though it lay only some twenty-four kilometers distant from Tozeur, another stop on the journey. And because this could not be done entirely without an escort, he hired a guide. It was advisable to go armed. Lacking a pith helmet, Jung wrapped a white hand towel around his head as a short of turban, and off they went with an "*as-salaam aleikum*." Again he sent a detailed report to Küsnacht. Scenes out of a world like that of the *Thousand and One Nights* came to life, and then the surprising confession: "There is nothing more magnificent than the desert."

What moved him most strongly about his journey into the Sahara was the timelessness, the change in the perception of time, and the feeling-oriented directness of the North African people. The *Memories* comment on this point: "The deeper we penetrated into the Sahara, the more time slowed down for me; it even threatened to move backward."[10] The sense of an "age-old existence" began to grow, a particularly consciousness-altering factor. And although this North African trip of only a few weeks did not yield the scientifically reportable results that the traveler might have hoped for, Jung did not underestimate the importance of this first experience in itself. It had affected him much more strongly than he had thought at first. Accompanied by an infectious enteritis which Europeans have to take in stride in these latitudes, dreams began to appear that indicated how the dark side of his own psyche had been activated by these impressions of Africa. Thus just as Jacob in the Old Testament had once had to grapple with the angel of Yahweh at the border stream of Jabbok, so now Jung had to hold a life-and-death combat with a young Arab prince in a dream. The opponent was forced to give in, but dangerous as he had been to the dreamer, Jung could not deny feeling admiration for him. Clearly the process of maturation is always a matter of recognizing and accepting the dark side of one's own self and its inherent potential for resistance. Hence Jung made clear in his *Memories* the extent to which his journey to Africa corresponded to his own search for that part of his personality which had become invisible under the influence and the pressure of his Europeanness, but which was waiting—up to a point—to be made conscious. Or in other words:

> Obviously, my encounter with Arab culture had struck me with overwhelming force. The emotional nature of these unreflective people who are so much closer to life than we are exerts a strong suggestive influence upon those historical layers in ourselves which we have just overcome and left behind, or which we think we have overcome. It is like the paradise of childhood from which we imagine we have emerged, but which at the slightest provocation imposes fresh defeats on us.[11]

In this connection Jung mentioned the naive faith in progress of the "white man," who he said is all the more ready to abandon himself to even more childish dreams of the future, the further our consciousness pulls away from the past which has not yet been sufficiently "mastered."

After his return home by way of Algiers and Marseilles,

Jung's resolve was firmly fixed to continue his exploration on the ground he had trodden, far from civilization, at the next opportunity, be it among the Indians of New Mexico, in East Africa, or, at another point in his life, in India. There is much to suggest that Jung's travels represented a kind of continuation, a variation on another level of the confrontation with the unconscious that had begun with his *nekyia*. But some years would pass before his next excursion, for the medical profession was his first duty. Not every psychotherapeutic case could stand an interruption of several months, and every day eight or ten patients arrived at Dr. Jung's for analytical discussions lasting as a rule an hour each. It is appropriate in Jung's case to speak of conversations, because—unlike Freud—he managed without the classical analyst's couch. For whereas the Freudian analyst simply wrote down the analysand's so-called free associations, or spontaneous ideas, as a seemingly indifferent secretary who remained in the background, the Jungian "analysis" could unfold fully only through a reciprocal dialogue. Of course here too the patient brought along dream images and ideas, but this took place in a fully personal face-to-face relationship, so that the analysand stepped out of his initially passive role to become a collaborator in a mutual effort. The individual sessions were like way-stations along a road—the analyst offered his guidance and leadership, but to *travel* the road, to *live* what was experienced in the confrontation with his own unconscious in everyday life, remained the task of the analysand. In this there could be no representation by proxy. For the same reason the Jungian analyst considered it very important that there should be a sufficiently large ration of this "life" and confrontation with the concrete world of everyday reality between sessions.

The variety of paths which life and the soul may take lay claim on the doctor of the psyche in many respects, for he can be for others only what he is for himself. Thus the need for a counterpoise to the stresses of his daily work, and even more the necessity of his own mental and spiritual growth, becomes an indispensable requirement for any psychotherapist. That a teacher must possess more than his students in the way of knowledge and training is indisputable; above all one ought to expect superior experience and maturity of a person from whom one seeks personal leadership and inner guidance. Early in the twenties, Jung was on the lookout for a place to concentrate on his own self-realization. What he was seeking was therefore not simply some sort of vacation home in the usual sense. It dawned on him that such a refuge should be built with his own hands. In contrast with the house in Küsnacht that his cousin Ernest Fiechter had designed, the new abode should have none of the character of a bourgeois villa, matching the role and the prestige of a much-in-demand physician. This time too it was certain that he had to build on the water, the symbol of psychic depth and vitality. The enchanting island in Lake Zürich, where he had so often landed his boat and where aquatic creatures of all sorts, wild ducks, peewits, and crested grebes had found a home among the reeds, seemed to offer an idea location. But then a parcel of land came up for sale in Bollingen, likewise situated on the upper lake. Jung seized the chance and acquired it in 1922. Originally he had in mind a kind of hut such as are known among primitive communities, "a dwelling-place which corresponds to the person's primitive consciousness. It should impart the feeling of being born—not only in the physical, but also the psychic sense." The building site turned out to be ideal, open to the lake, but screened off from the town on the landward side by trees and shrubbery. There was no need for an architect, since the owner and later inhabitant would follow his own plans, in both the design and the building. Two local workmen were sufficient to act as helpers and mason's assistants. How to cut stone Dr. Jung learned in the Bollingen quarries. Anyone who saw the grown man in his late forties working with hammer and trowel in his gray work clothes would have taken him for one of the anonymous country laborers; certainly no one would have thought that this work with stone and building had anything to do with psychology. And yet for the Bollingen house especially, a tower with a round foundation, the saying is true: the building becomes human.

> From the beginning I felt the Tower as in some way a place of maturation—a maternal womb or a maternal figure in which I could become what I was, what I am and will be.[12]

The reference to the maternal principle and to the fundamentality of the circle as an expression of wholeness did not come by chance. Two months before the building began, Jung's mother, Emilie Jung-Preiswerk, died, who in the last few years had maintained her own household in Küsnacht, primarily to be close to her grandchildren, whose religious instruction she saw to as an erstwhile parson's wife. Jung had always emphasized that no one could relieve him of the trouble of the building, and this was also the reason for his thorough description of it in the *Memories*. Here he reported the various phases and units of the multipartite structure, which had taken its present form in intervals of four years each, beginning in the year of his mother's death and concluding, after Emma Jung's death in 1955, with a tower which was connected in some secret way with the dead.

The Tower gave its builder a feeling of having been born again in stone, as if the architecture were a realization of his own individuation process. For this very reason the secluded building, connected to neither the water supply nor the community electric lines, bore no trace of civilized amenities. For the one who put up here from time to time was not Dr. C. G. Jung, the No. 1, but the timeless No. 2 of his personality, rooted in his psychic past:

> At Bollingen I am in the midst of my true life, I am most deeply myself. Here I am, as it were, the "age-old son of the mother." That is how alchemy puts it, very wisely, for the "old man," the "ancient," whom I had already experienced as a child, is personality No. 2, who has always been and always will be. He exists outside time and is the son of the maternal unconscious. In my fantasies he took the form of Philemon, and he comes to life again at Bollingen.[13]

At the very entrance to the Tower one encounters him in an inscription, and as a colorful fresco in Jung's monasterylike sleeping chamber. The simple life of Bollingen was no fashionable flight from civilization, but rather a kind of homecoming.

> At times I feel as if I am spread out over the landscape and inside things, and I am myself living in every tree, in the plashing of the waves, in the clouds and the animals that come and go, in the procession of the seasons. There is nothing in the Tower that has not grown into its own form over the decades, nothing with which I am not linked. Here everything has its history, and mine; here is space for the spaceless kingdom of the world and the psyche's hinterland.[14]

The house's simple furnishings, the open hearth in a smoke-smudged kitchen, held the presence not only of life in the present, but the depths of the soul's past. In a letter to a colleague in Zürich Jung once explained how important the historical form of this frugal space was to him, smelling of smoke and oatmeal mush, and sometimes of wine and smoked bacon. Finally the ancestral souls, the *lares* and *penates*, tutelary spirits of Roman antiquity, had once lived in the pots and pans of the kitchen. "The lares and penates are important psychological quantities which whenever possible should not be frightened by too much modernity."[15] Indeed, who wants his wood-chopping and fire-making, his water-pumping and cooking, to be disturbed by people who might intrude the obnoxious, hectic breathlessness of the intellectual and technological world into this realm of retreat and self-discovery! Probably one would actually have to have lived for many years among people of primitive societies, in remote parts of Africa for instance, to comprehend how the inhabitant of the Bollingen Tower acted. It was not to be equated with some eccentric wish to be a child of nature, any more than with what we might call "alternative lifestyles." What was involved here was making contact with the primeval, a return to the elementary. The African expert Laurens van der Post, who in later years often met the psychologist from Küsnacht and remarked in him a deep sympathy with the psyche of primitive people, found an expression of this in his dealings with things and elements, for example in his attitude toward fire: "He never took it as something obvious. It always remained a wonder to him and was sacred to him. He had a way all his own of piling the wood and kindling the flame; indeed there was even something in it of the way in which fire was made with such trouble by primitives, who prepared it with endless patience, as if it were a matter of life of death and must never, once it was kindled, be allowed to die. Jung did this instinctively, as if he were carrying out a religious ritual, and then when the Hindu flame flickered up, in its light his face would take on an expression of godliness like that of an ancient priest."[16]

Thus Jung's journeys among the peoples of older (that is, more naturalistic) cultures were closely connected to the building of his Tower, as well as his stays for days or weeks at a time in Bollingen while his family remained behind in Küsnacht. Because his preoccupation with stones and his ritual and creative activity with wood and fire had held a firm place in his life even in childhood, it need not be particularly stressed that in the Tower at Bollingen he was not imitating the primitive life of someone else, but living his own, impelled by an urgent inner need. The various works of his stonemasonry, which can still be seen in and around the Tower, bear emphatic witness to this fact, for it was always a matter of expressing in image and form something created out of inner experience. Hence, although the psychiatrist's skill in sculpture remains astonishing, it should not be judged primarily on the basis of artistic and aesthetic standards.

Therefore, as Jung set out on two further journeys abroad in order to meet people who lived in harmony with nature and the elements, he already brought with him the necessary sensibility. Barely four years after the brief North African trip he was ready, and late in 1924 Jung sojourned once again in North America. In Chicago he met up with Fowler

McCormick, with whose parents he had been close friends for a number of years. The couple had made a name for themselves as promoters of Jungian psychology; suffice it to say that Fowler's mother, Edith McCormick, had undergone an analysis with Jung. As the daughter of John D. Rockefeller, Sr., she had used her considerable means to make a strong contribution toward the foundation and endowment of the Psychological Club in 1916. His father, Harold, one of Jung's first American patients, had also been active as a supporting charter member. Early in January 1925, Jung and the young McCormick left Chicago for New Mexico. Also in the party were George Porter, and, from Santa Fe on, Jaime de Angulo, both men interested in Jungian psychology. Traveling at first by car and later by mule, the real goal of the trip was the settlements of the Pueblo Indians, though Jung made sure to miss neither the powerful natural impression of the Grand Canyon nor a visit to the Indians living in small huts in the Cañon de los Frijoles in New Mexico. After riding and hiking for several days they reached the Taos plateau, a gently rolling landscape of valleys at an altitude of over seven thousand feet above sea level, with the conical peaks of long-extinct volcanoes towering in the distance to a height of twelve thousand feet. Here lived the Taos Pueblos. They were called the "city-building" Indians, for their large villages were built of square houses of air-dried adobe brick layered atop one another in stories like building blocks. Of this plateau Jung reported:

> Behind us a clear stream purled past the houses, and on its opposite bank stood a second pueblo of reddish adobe houses, built one atop the other toward the center of the settlement, thus strangely anticipating the perspective of an American metropolis with its skyscrapers in the center. Perhaps half an hour's journey upriver rose a mighty isolated mountain, *the* mountain, which has no name. The story goes that on days when the mountain is wrapped in clouds the men vanish in that direction to perform mysterious rites.[17]

An air of secrecy surrounded this mountain and its dark-skinned people, huddled—it being winter—in their woolen blankets. Jung struck up a conversation with one of them, Ochwiay Biano or "Mountain Lake," whose legal name was Antonio Mirabal, a chief of the Taos Pueblos. Jung estimated him to be forty or fifty years old, and found the encounter with him especially fortunate, for it was his first opportunity to speak with a non-European who was still closely in tune with his own religious tradition. An approach opened up to the "age-old knowledge that has almost been forgotten," the vantage point at last outside his own culture and civilization. Ochwiay Biano gained confidence. He openly criticized the Americans, and with them the white man in general, who struck him as mad because he thought not with his heart but with his head, and therefore was estranged from that dimension of reality which eludes the calculating grasp of human rationalization. Jung was taken aback:

> For the first time in my life, so it seemed to me, someone had drawn for me a picture of the real white man. It was as though until now I had seen nothing but sentimental, prettified color prints. This Indian had struck our vulnerable spot, unveiled a truth to which we are blind. I felt rising within me like a shapeless mist something unknown and yet deeply familiar. And out of this mist, image upon image detached itself. . . .[18]

For Ochwiay Biano had noted how the loss of the soul was reflected even in physiognomy, in the expression and facial features. Now Jung could see the cultural and religious history of two thousand years in a new light: the invasion of the Roman legions into Celtic Gaul, the sharply chiseled features of Julius Caesar, Scipio Africanus, and Pompey; he saw Augustinus the monk and how he had imparted the Christian creed to the Britons "on the points of Roman spears." Here came holy wars, the missions of Charlemagne, when plundering, murdering bands, the mantle of the crusader thrown over the martial trappings of the knight, drew their bloody tracks across history for centuries; "to the greater glory of God" they conquered the New World, and with it the habitations of the Indians—Columbus, Cortez, the armies of the Conquistadors; always with the sword and the cross in one hand, and wherever in the world the modern division of labor presented itself, there discovery, colonization, missionizing, exploitation, slavery and degradation of all kinds could go hand in hand. . . . In 1925 the problems of the Third World were still far distant from the general consciousness, and to the Reformed parson's son all this was eye-opening.

There was yet another aspect to which the psychologist's eyes were opened, a problem which on the whole remains hidden from most people. To the extent to which the Christian sacraments have ceased to be mysteries, antiquity's spiritual understanding of the world of mystery has been lost, and with it the ability to perceive that "vital secret" which naturalistic peoples still have, but whose loss robs them of their identity and inner security. Jung saw now how emotionally Ochwiay Biano reacted when the conversation touched upon this secret realm. The sun was a central mystery for the Indians and their race: "The sun is God. Anyone can see that." Jung commented:

> Although no one can help feeling the tremendous impress of the sun, it was a novel and deeply affecting experience for me to see these mature, dignified men in the grip of an overmastering emotion when they spoke of it.[19]

This was also the cause of their strained relationship with the American authorities, who sought to curtail the Pueblos' ritual life. Jung's interlocutor found this least comprehensible of all, since indeed—of this he was thoroughly convinced—it was precisely they, the Indians, who through their worship performed an indispensable service for the Americans and the whole world as well. The question of how this was so Mountain Lake answered in a manner that revealed something of the incontrovertible secret:

> "After all," he said, "we are a people who live on the roof of the world; we are the sons of Father Sun, and with our religion we daily help our father to go across the sky. We do this not only for ourselves, but for the whole world. If we were to cease practicing our religion, in ten years the sun would no longer rise. Then it would be night forever."[20]

Here, then, the life of the individual, like that of a whole culture or nature religion, is bound up in the cosmos and therefore meaningful, as expressed in the consciousness: "All life comes from the mountain" and "We are the sons of Father Sun." Certainly Jung could not be suspected of wishing to turn back the wheel of the history of consciousness or to recommend a general psychic regression. But in his autobiography he called for understanding for this attitude of the soul, which should neither be extinguished forcibly nor even taken lightly:

> If for a moment we put away all European rationalism and transport ourselves into the clear mountain air of that solitary plateau, which drops off on one side into the broad continental prairies and on the other into the Pacific Ocean; if we also set aside our intimate knowledge of the world and exchange it for a horizon that seems immeasurable, and an ignorance of what lies beyond it, we will begin to achieve an inner comprehension of the Pueblo Indian's point of view. . . . That man feels capable of formulating valid replies to the overpowering influence of God, and that he can render back something which is essential even to God, induces pride, for it raises the human individual to the dignity of a metaphysical factor. "God and us". . .[21]

How strong and lasting an effect his encounter with Ochwiay Biano must have had on Jung is shown by a detailed letter he wrote to the Chilean ambassador, Miguel Serrano, in September 1960, the last year of his life, at age eight-five. Here he came to speak of the spiritual poverty of contemporary mankind, saying among other things:

> We are sorely in need of a truth or a self-understanding similar to that of Ancient Egypt, which I have found still living with the Taos Pueblos.[22]

For several more years Jung kept in touch with Ochwiay Biano, alias Antonio Mirabal, alias Mountain Lake. They exchanged letters, and Jung inquired whether the young men still worshiped "Father Sun," whether they sometimes created mandalalike sand paintings such as were common among the Navajo. Above all he averred his continuing interest in everything to do with the Pueblos' religious life. "Times are very hard indeed and unfortunately I can't travel as far as I used to do," he wrote on 21 October 132 to Antonio Mirabal in Taos, New Mexico. "All you tell me about religion is good news to me. There are no interesting religious things over here, only remnants of old things."[23] Indeed, religious originality and vitality were of great consequence to Jung; hence his introversion, the depth of his own soul, and his retreat into his tower, but hence also his extraversion in the form of the journeys that brought him into contact with the "world unconscious."

The discoveries he made in these travels were put to use in C. G. Jung's everyday psychotherapeutic practice, where it was always important for modern people, cut off from their spiritual and religious roots, to gain a new "ground" to stand on. His experiences abroad also made their way into his literary output, as expressed for example in a paper on "Mind and Earth," presented to the Gesellschaft für freie Philosophie under the auspices of Count Hermann Keyserling in 1927, and in one on "Archaic Man" in Zürich in 1930.[24] Also to be mentioned in this context is "The Spiritual Problem of Modern Man," given in Prague in 1928. For the often-referred-to modern man, living entirely within his present consciousness, past levels of consciousness and psychic possibilities have faded away, and therefore he is psychically isolated and impoverished,

> because every step toward higher and wider consciousness further distances him from the original, purely animal mys-

> tical participation with the herd, the state of immersion in a universal unconscious. Every step forward means a tearing away from this all-encompassing maternal womb of initial unconsciousness, in which the bulk of humanity, for the most part, persist.[25]

There was also another perspective that had motivated Jung's travels, especially his trip to the land of the Pueblos, and on account of which he made a side trip to New Orleans. Acquaintance with his growing number of North American patients had confronted him with the phenomenon that even when no blood relationship was apparent between them, white Americans exhibited a strong psychic influence from Indians and blacks. In his paper of 1927, for example, he mentioned the amazingly Negroid laugh and the sauntering, hip-swaying gait one can often observe in North Americans.

> Thus the American presents us with an odd picture: a European with the manner of a Negro and the soul of an Indian. In this he shares the fate of all usurpers of foreign soil. Certain Australian primitives claim that one can never possess a foreign land, because in foreign ground there live foreign ancestral spirits, and so those who are born there are incarnations of foreign spirits. There is a great psychological truth in this; foreign soil assimilates the conqueror. . . . It is the way of virgin land everywhere that at least the unconscious of the conqueror sinks down to the level of the autochthonous inhabitants. Thus in the American there is a distance between conscious and unconscious that is not found in the European, a tension between advanced conscious culture and unconscious primitivity. . . .[26]

For C. G. Jung, now exactly fifty, 1925 was a year of extensive traveling. He began it, as we have seen, in America; he closed it in Africa. But the intervening months too saw him only intermittently at home and with his patients. For his many, mostly anglophone patients and students abroad, Jung held a seminar in Zürich from 23 March to 6 July, consisting of sixteen lectures in which he allowed autobiographical material to enter for the first time in such a forum.[27] Thereafter he traveled to England for a few weeks, to give another seminar of twelve lectures at Swanage in Dorset, this time with special attention to his practice of dream analysis.[28] From Swanage he visited the Wembley Exhibition in London, where he gained a lasting impression of life in the colonies under the British flag, and he resolved to undertake a journey to tropical Africa as soon as possible. And so it came about. Jung was quite clear that such a journey, in contrast to the short North Africa trip organized by Hermann Sigg, would be of the nature of an expedition into a completely unknown land. Thorough preparation was therefore indispensable, particularly as neither he nor his two traveling companions had any experience in the tropics. The party this time consisted of his young American friend George Beckwith, an excellent hunter, and "Peter," his English colleague Helton Godwin Baynes. Fowler McCormick, who would also have liked to join them, was unable to go. Jung made use of the weeks between the return to Küsnacht and the Bollingen tower and his departure for Africa to prepare, in particular by learning Swahili, in order to be able to speak with at least some of the natives. Apart from the outfitting and provisioning, the necessary entrance papers for Kenya and Uganda had to be obtained from the mandate administration in Britain.

On his life's important decisions Jung customarily consulted the *I Ching*, having known and used this ancient Chinese book of oracular wisdom since the early twenties. Richard Wilhlem's often-used translation from 1923 showed him the way, particularly as he had known the famed sinologist from Frankfurt personally since they had met under the auspices of Count Keyserling's "School of Wisdom." Because the consultation of the *I Ching*—traditionally done with yarrow stalks or coins—is only meaningful in an environment that provides the requisite quiet and composure, the retreat at Bollingen was obviously the most suitable place for it. In place of the Chinese yarrow stalks, Jung had carefully cut a corresponding number (fifty minus one) of small reeds, and sitting under a hundred-year-old pear tree he had in years past acquainted himself with the art of taking the oracle. This involves the production of a hexagram, a sign made up of six horizontal lines, some solid, some broken. In all, sixty-four variations are possible. These are further "changed" and converted into their opposites, according to the polarity principle of the masculine/positive/light/creative Yang and the feminine/negative/dark/receptive Yin. In consulting the oracle one or two specific hexagrams are formed, for which there are corresponding prophetic texts in the *I Ching* or "Book of Changes." Of course the interpretation and individual application of these dicta, couched in mythical imagery, pose a problem in themselves. For Jung it was above all a matter of illuminating the parallelism that existed between the "coincidental" result of the hexagram he obtained, on one side, and the psychic or physical and factual situation on the other.[29] Thus it involved a phenomenon that Jung later customarily termed "synchronicity," referring to the simultaneity of two meaningfully but not causally connected events or situations. It comes into play, for example, when dreams, premonitions, or visions point "coincidentally" to definite external occurrences in the future.

When Jung consulted the *I Ching* shortly before beginning his journey, hexagram number 53 fell to him. It is called "*Chien*—Development" and stands for "gradual progress." Psychologically speaking, this meant that the unconscious was basically in agreement with his plans. But the third line seemed troublesome, for the *I Ching*'s commentary read: "The wild goose gradually draws near the plateau. The man goes forth and does not return. . . ," posing a problem of interpretation, for in what literal or somehow metaphorical sense was this nonreturn of the man meant? Hence Jung prepared himself for dangers. He felt called upon to take the utmost precautions, indeed considering, if worst came to worse, the possibility of his own death. He did not let this stop him, however, and the Woerman steamer put to sea from England on 15 October. The next ports of call were Lisbon, Malaga,

Marseille, and Genoa, and on 7 November they reached Port Said in Egypt. They traversed the Suez Canal and the Red Sea in temperatures of up to 32° C. in early November. Numerous young Englishmen were aboard, on their way to take up service in various African colonies of the United Kingdom.

> It was evident from the atmosphere aboard ship that these passengers were not traveling for pleasure, but were entering upon their destiny. To be sure, there was a good deal of gay exuberance, but the serious undertone was also evident. As a matter of fact, I heard of the fate of several of my fellow voyagers even before my own return trip. Several met death in the tropics in the course of the next two months. They died of tropical malaria, amoebic dysentery, and pneumonia. Among those who died was the young man who sat opposite me at table. . . .[30]

Thus the oracle's warning of the nearness of the threat of death was borne out by events. A few years later the young George Beckwith became the victim of a traffic accident.

On 12 November they reached Mombasa on the east coast of Africa. Here Jung went ashore with his two companions. "The whole city consist of huts roofed with grass, nothing but Negroes and Indians," he wrote in a letter to his youthful assistant in Bollingen, the sixteen-year-old Hans Kuhn.[31] Such was the "skyline" of Mombasa in 1925. What remained in the traveler's memory was the humid, hot climate of this city on the Indian Ocean, overshadowed by an old Portuguese fort. After a two-day layover the journey continued by narrow-gauge railroad on into the interior for twenty-four hours. "The soil there is quite red," he wrote to Hans Kuhn, "and red dust swirled around the train until our white clothes became completely red. We saw wild Masai Negroes with long spears and shields. They were completely naked and had only hung an ox-skin over themselves." Skirting a region of virgin forest, they went on into the east African plains, where herds of antelope and zebra rushed past and ostriches followed the train. In the distance Nairobi emerged, the capital of Kenya.

Here they were to replenish their supplies, among other things with two firearms, a shotgun for hunting and a nine-mm. rifle with a few hundred rounds of ammunition. The rail journey continued to the end of the line, where three natives and a cook were engaged. Two tropic-worthy trucks picked up their tents, provisions, and other equipment, and they continued inland toward Mount Elgon. Francis Daniel Hislop, a British government official of the Nandi district in Kenya, who long afterward recorded his recollections[32] of his meeting with the Jung expedition (officially known as the Bugishu Psychological Expedition), gave the members of the safari, who seemed to him peculiar and hence were viewed with skepticism, what information he could. Characteristically, Hislop recalled C. G. Jung's roaring laughter. The three-man company was unexpectedly supplemented by a fourth person, a woman. This was the young Englishwoman Ruth Bailey, who had served as a nurse in the war and whom the English governor provided as a guide.

Before them stood five days' trek on foot through pathless country. Forty-eight bearers had to be hired to carry all the freight from the trucks on their shoulders, but they reached the Elgon region:

> We drew up to the mountain some twelve kilometers away, until we came to the great, impassable primeval forests. There we set up camp. Almost every night we heard lions; often leopards and hyenas crept around the camp. We stayed there three weeks and climbed the mountain and looked at the wild Negroes there. . . . The camp was 6900 feet high. I went up to 9600 feet. Up there the bamboo forests are full of black buffalo and rhinoceros.

Here in his letter to Hans Kuhn as well as in the *Memories*, Jung described in detail the adventures and perils of life on safari. He enjoyed it. At last he had arrived in the interior of the continent as he had longed to. He felt enchanted at being for the first time among people some of whom had never come in contact with a white man before. So strong was this confrontation that he felt, at least once, that truly he had been here ages ago, no longer within the reach of individual memory.

> It was as if I were this moment returning to the land of my youth, and as if I knew that dark-skinned man who had been waiting for me for five thousand years. The feeling-tone of this curious experience accompanied me throughout my whole journey through savage Africa.[33]

As soon as he saw the great game preserve of the Athi Plains outside Nairobi, Jung became conscious of the uniqueness of this experience of nature, and the "cosmic meaning of consciousness" became clear to him. Just as the Pueblo chief had spoken of the Indian peoples' indispensable task of helping their solar Father in heaven by their actions, so the insight arose in Jung that only through human beings was the seemingly unceasing creation completed in all its enormity. In this way man actually becomes a second creator. It is human consciousness that creates meaning and grants man a firm place in the great process of cosmic evolution.

A particularly interesting experience for the psychologist was conversing with the black people, still undisturbed by any civilization, who squatted around the whites' camp day after day and watched them curiously. The campsite lay at some distance from a waterfall, whose basin served as a bath.

> Nearby—that is, about fifteen minutes' walk away—was a native kraal which consisted of a few huts and a *boma*—a yard surrounded by a hedge of wait-a-bit thorn. This kraal provided us with our water bearers, a woman and her two half-grown daughters, who were naked except for a belt of cowries. They were chocolate-brown and strikingly pretty, with fine slim figures and an aristocratic leisureliness about their movements. It was a pleasure for me each morning to hear the soft *cling-clang* of their iron ankle rings as they came up from the brook, and soon afterward to see their swaying gait as they emerged from the tall yellow elephant grass, balancing the amphorae of water on their heads.

> They were adorned with ankle rings, brass bracelets and necklaces, earrings of copper or wood in the shape of small spools. Their lower lips were pierced with either a bone or iron nail. They had very good manners, and always greeted us with shy, charming smiles.[34]

Jung consciously avoided speaking with native women, in order to avoid disastrous misunderstandings. This made all the more intensive his conversations with the chief, the medicine man, and a young prince of a Elgonyi tribe who made Jung acquainted with his sister's family, and so introduced him to the social life of the Elgonyi. While it fell to the women to care for the huts, the children, and the animals, it was exclusively men who contested the daily palaver. Jung's knowledge of Swahili and theirs was just enough for them to strike up a conversation, above all on the subject of their religious rituals and the inhabitants' dream life. But on this topic his normally talkative companions became quite reticent. Jung found out one of the reasons for this when an old *laibon*, a medicine man, explained to him with tears in his eyes, "In old days the *laibons* had dreams, and knew whether there is war or sickness or whether rain comes and where the herds should be driven."[35] His grandfather had still had dreams of this sort, but since the whites had come to the country these dreams had stopped. They were no longer needed anyway, for the Englishmen always knew what to do. The twilight of the gods had already begun.

Jung did manage to learn something of sun and moon worship among the Elgonyi. The sun was sacred, but only at the moment when it began to rise above the horizon with its glowing light. At this numinous instant the men would hurry out of their huts, spit into their hands, and hold their palms up to the sun with great emotion. Why they did this they could not say. For them it was enough to perform the rite of worship. The act of worship evidently no longer required any theological explanation. And just as the rising dawn represented the divine presence, so too did the first, equally golden, shimmering crescent of the new moon. Jung translated the wordless prayer thus: "I offer to God my living soul." On the other hand, the visitor to Africa found it informative that the power of darkness and the demonic abyss also held a firm place in Elgonyi religious life, and that the fear of demons had nonetheless left the inhabitants of Mount Elgon capable of an optimistic outlook on life.

But Jung had not gone to Africa only as a collector or recorder of facts about the psychology of religion. His notes and oral reports repeatedly show his ability to open himself up to the numinous and the extraordinary experience of nature, from the overwhelming event of sunrise in these latitudes to the manifold adventures that every day in Africa holds in store for the European. Jung spoke of the "profoundly moving experience" of being at the sources of the Nile and discovering anew the wisdom of the ancient Egyptian concepts, referring to the knowledge of the mystery god Osiris, with the solar falcon or sky-god Horus and his dangerous adversary Seth. In the great dualism of day and dark, of glittering sunlight and deep black night, Jung recognized the primal yearning of the soul to free itself from the darkness and enter the light, an "inexpressible longing for light." He could perceive it in the glance of the primitive, indeed even in the eyes of animals.

> That sadness also reflects the mood of Africa, the experience of its solitudes. It is a maternal mystery, this primordial darkness. That is why the sun's birth in the morning strikes the natives as so overwhelmingly meaningful. The *moment* in which light comes *is* God. That moment brings redemption, release. To say that the *sun* is God is to blur and forget the archetypal experience of that moment.[36]

For this meant already to rationalize or theologize the numinosum, to turn it into an expressible, conceptually graspable object.

In late December 1925 the time had come to strike their tents on the slopes of Mount Elgon and begin their return home. This occasioned sorrow, though it was eased by the promise that they must not fail to make another journey to the Elgonyi. In the *Memories* Jung still remarked that at the time he could not imagine that he would never return to this undreamt-of splendor.

> My companions and I had the good fortune to taste the world of Africa, with its incredible beauty and its equally incredible suffering, before the end came. Our camp life proved to be one of the loveliest interludes in my life. I enjoyed the "divine peace" of a still primeval country. . . . My liberated psychic forces poured blissfully back to the primeval expanses.[37]

The South African-born travel writer and noted African expert Laurens van der Post, who had traveled large portions of the continent on foot, remarked in his memoirs of C. G. Jung: "I thought that if there was anything at all which I knew and could understand, it was Africa and its people. But when we talked about Africa, I had to realize that Jung knew the archaic pattern of African life even better than I did, and revered it if possible even more deeply. There were a few moments when I felt a little disconcerted that a Swiss—and so of course he still was—seemed to understand the deepest nature of my native continent better than I."[38]

Now, rather than retrace their steps southeast via Nairobi to the port of Mombasa, the trek set out westward toward Lake Victoria. Gradually the landscape and its people changed. They reached the province of Bugishu, where a stirring view opened out over the valley of the upper Nile. Partly by truck and partly by means of a wood-fired stern-wheeled steamer, the journey continued onto Lake Kioga toward Lake Albert. Further adventures lay in store. Jung reported one "unforgettable experience" when they stopped in a village en route from Lake Albert to Rejaf in the Sudan: A young chief appeared with his warlike and not altogether confidence-inspiring retinue, and a kind of war dance began. Jung was so thrilled by this that he sprang up and joined in with the dancers, who brandished their spears, swords, and clubs with an ever-increasing rhythm. The situation became threatening, not only because no one could foresee what spontaneous actions the ecstatically raving natives might be capable of, but because Jung suddenly became aware of the inner danger of an identification, the danger of "going native" or "going black," which can cause the European to lose himself in the archaic psyche. Sobered, Jung tried to calm the warriors. When handing out tobacco failed to do the trick, he began, half in earnest and half jokingly, to crack his rhinoceros whip menacingly, cursing loudly in Swiss German. Laurens van der Post, who could imagine himself in this situation only too well, remarked on this account of Jung's: "His eyes flashed as he told me of the tension of that moment. This was also the turning point in his relationship to Africa. . . ."[39]

Jung was forced to realize that he had reached the limit of his ability to assimilate such new and strange impressions, and that there was also an inner necessity that compelled him to continue his return without delay. He also received a corresponding signal from the unconscious, for whereas until now he had dreamed only of people and motifs from his homeland, now a dream appeared in which a black man played a part. It concerned an American Negro; it was Jung's barber in Chattanooga, Tennessee. And indeed he was about to make Jung's hair kinky, like a black man's, with a huge red-hot curling iron.

> I could already feel the painful heat, and awoke with a sense of terror. I took this dream as a warning from the unconscious; it was saying that the primitive was a danger to me. At that time I was obviously all too close to "going black."[40]

Little by little it occurred to him not only that his months-long expedition might have served as an encounter with the psyche of the African people, but that this excursion also represented an important stage on the path of his own self-examination and self-discovery. What would happen to C. G. Jung the psychologist when confronted with the wildness of Africa? It was a question he might rather have avoided, despite his intention to investigate the reaction to the European to primitive conditions.

> It became clear to me that this study had been not so much an objective scientific project as an intensely personal one, and that any attempt to go deeper into it touched every possible sore spot in my own psychology. I had to admit to myself that it was scarcely the Wembley Exhibition which had begotten my decision to travel, but rather the fact that the atmosphere had become too highly charged for me in Europe.
>
> Amid such thoughts I glided on the peaceful waters of the Nile toward the north—toward Europe, toward the future.[41]

As Jung felt he had found the origin of the Egyptian Horus-concept on the flanks of Mount Elgon, it was very important to him to come to Egypt down the Nile from this geographical starting point, and not upriver from the Mediterranean as was usual. He was less interested in the Asiatic influence on the great kingdoms of the upper and lower Nile than in the Hamitic contribution to Egyptian culture. And the Horus myth was the story of the newly risen light that the Elgonyi worshiped in their peculiar way as a divine phenomenon.

> Thus the journey from the heart of Africa to Egypt became, for me, a kind of drama of the birth of light. That drama was intimately connected with me, with my own psychology. I realized this, but felt incapable of formulating it in words.[42]

What were all the other little curios, hunting trophies, weapons, or exotic jewelry, compared with such experiences! No wonder that even months after his return, Jung declared—to the American analyst Frances G. Wickes from Sils-Maria in August—that he was still far from having "entirely worked through" all this. Africa itself, he said, affected one. "The realizations which Jung made in Africa still took him some years to digest and work out," commented Barbara Hannah, to whom—she met Jung in 1929—he repeatedly recounted these events. Among these, finally, there was also his encounter with Islamic Egypt. Jung who had discovered for himself the importance of the mandala for psychic wholeness some seven years earlier, witnessed a mosque in Cairo. Barbara Hannah followed Jung's description:

> . . .it was a perfect square with very beautiful broad pillared corridors on each side. The House of Ablution, where the ritual washings take place, was in the center. A spring of water welled forth there and formed the bath of rejuvenation, of spiritual rebirth. Jung described the dusty, crowded streets outside, and said that this vast hall seemed like entering the Court of Heaven, as if it were heaven itself. He had the impression of perfected concentration and of being accepted in the immense void of heaven, and this religion, where God is really a call, at last became comprehensible to him. . . . He spoke of hearing the call—"Allah!"—echoing through this vast hall, and of feeling that the call itself penetrated to heaven. Such impressions and those of the far more ancient culture were so enthralling to Jung. . . .[43]

Thus over and over it was immediate experiences that had to be assimilated and integrated over the course of many years before the psychologist, in his empirical work, felt justified in making the results of his research public. Several more years passed before he could speak comprehensively about the nature and significance of the mandala as a primary religious symbol. But the same was true in an even more drastic sense for the theory of the collective unconscious which seemed to be represented by "black Africa." To this extent Jung's African journey represented an essential episode in his life and work, and an important biographical element which was to be joined by many others.

15

The Encounter with Alchemy

One of the most remarkable elements of C. G. Jung's activity is undoubtedly the numerous works that he devoted to alchemy and its significance for psychology. This line of research continued for decades, extending from his middle life to the end of his productive period, and fascinated him as virtually no other area of work and knowledge. Entering Jung's study and library at his home in Küsnacht today, one finds along one wall, protected from the direct light, an impressive collection of rare and valuable alchemical texts. As an "eminently historically minded researcher," in the words of Aniela Jaffé, it was not simply a hobby that made him assemble all these manuscripts and even produce extensive hand-copied excerpts from these alchemical editions, in order to surround himself with curiosities for their own sake. Rather, he was guided by his need to document, by means of "historical prefigurations," what he had experienced for himself and explored psychologically, to place the productions of the unconscious of modern people in a larger historical context. Looking back upon this critical stage in his own life, he asked himself what examples of these inner experiences there might be in history, and where. In the *Memories* he put it this way:

> If I had not succeeded in finding such evidence, I would never have been able to substantiate my ideas. Therefore,

> my encounter with alchemy was decisive for me, as it provided me with the historical basis which I had hitherto lacked.[1]

In approaching Jung's work, therefore, we cannot avoid regarding alchemy as more than just the "prescientific" expression of the scientific techniques of chemistry. It does not mean the art of turning lead into gold, which became decadent and disrespectable in past centuries, and in which error—not to mention (self-)deception—and truth were so oddly combined. Those who sought in earnest the *lapis philosophorum* or "philosophers' stone," striving to express it in chemical form, referred to a practice that presented in the imagery of material "transmutation" what was primarily a path to spiritual and physical knowledge, a way of self-transformation. One of the few in our century who have sought to connect the meditative and the operative aspects of alchemical practice, the writer and pharmacist Alexander von Bernus, explains:

> The background of alchemy is initiation, an indoctrination into the mysteries that dates back millennia. Originating in the Egyptian-Chaldean Hellenistic universal consciousness in the pre-Christian era, and later flowing into the West via the Arabic cultural orbit, it became tinged with the substance of Christianity. . . . To be sure, the idea of transmutation stands at the center of alchemical initiation; not, however, that of the transformation of metals but rather the mystical process of inner transmutation, of which the outward chemical and physical transformation of metals is but the external manifestation, realized and made visible in the material world.[2]

Mircea Eliade, who in his studies of comparative religion investigated the attitude of people in primitive communities toward the material world, also stressed the mystery character of this "discipline," referring to the initiation rituals practiced among smelters, smiths, and alchemists. Accordingly, he says, given certain assumptions, alchemy can hardly be viewed as an early form of modern chemistry. From a historical point of view, however, a different development presents itself.

> Alchemy came into being as a sacred science, whereas chemistry was consolidated only after it had cast off its sacred elements. Hence there is necessarily a break in the continuity between the spheres of sacred and profane experience. . . . There is an immense distance between one who is religiously moved to take part in the sacred mystery of a liturgy and the aesthete who enjoys its gorgeous beauty and the music that goes with it.
>
> Of course the techniques of the alchemists had more than merely a symbolic character. They were real procedures in the laboratory, but their aims were different from those of chemistry. The chemist's work consisted in the precise observation of physical and chemical processes and systematic experimentation to investigate the structure of matter, whereas the alchemist concerned himself with the "suffering," the "death," and the "marriage" of matter, insofar as these were necessary for the transformation of matter (the philosophers' stone) and of human life (the elixir of life).[3]

That the nonchemical and thus nonoperative factor could sometimes predominate in alchemy can be gathered from the fact that it was the mystical element of religious experience that became its real content—that is, although the alchemical terminology and symbolism were used in individual cases, they referred not to the work in the alchemist's lab, but to the person who was to be transmuted, transformed into a new type. Jakob Böhme could be considered a proponent of this mystical alchemy, as could the Rosicrucians as seen in Andreae.[4] And from there the step to depth psychology is not so large. But Jung was not the first to consider the psychological aspects of alchemy in detail. The psychoanalyst Herbert Silberer, who is mentioned repeatedly in Jung's correspondence with Freud, had made a beginning as early as 1914 in a study[5] in which—starting with the "secret figures of the Rosicrucians from the sixteenth and seventeenth centuries"

(Altona 1785ff.)—he tied alchemy, hermeticism, Rosicrucianism, and freemasonry into his interpretation of depth psychology. It was already clear to Jung when he entered this field that one could no longer be content with such relatively young texts as Silberer had used, but would have to go back to the original alchemical sources, back if need be to the beginnings of Western alchemy. These lay in Alexandrian times, when the Greek spirit merged with the technical magic of the Near East.[6]

Only with this do we come to the pivotal point in intellectual history. Because Jung's interests were directed only to the process of inner transformation, to individuation and hence self-development, it is understandable that the decisive impetus for his absorption in the alchemical tradition came from the unconscious. Behind it lay several years of the study of ancient Gnosticism. Interesting as the Gnostic imagery was for him, Jung could not find in it the sought-after "historical prefiguration" of his own results, for the gulf in consciousness between the gnostic symbolism and the inner experiences of modern people turned out to be too great and unbridgeable. In the realm of intellectual history and the history of consciousness, what was lacking was something like a bridge-piling in the stream of the human psyche. Hence it is also clear that in the mid-twenties Jung was on the lookout for the possibility of building such a bridge.

In 1925 and after, he had a number of dreams which all revolved around a similar motif: Beside his own house there stood another one, or an annex, which struck the dreamer as strange and which he did not seem to recognize, although it seemed that it must always have been there. And one day, when the dream led him into this house, he discovered there

> a wonderful library, dating largely from the sixteenth and seventeenth centuries. Large, fat folio volumes, bound in pigskin, stood along the walls. Among them were a number of books embellished with copper engravings of a strange

> character, and illustrations containing curious symbols such as I had never seen before.[7]

With this dream Jung was staring the answer directly in the face, for it later turned out that the emblems and signs in these folios came, or were to come, from alchemical contexts. That Jung would possess a similar collection of alchemical texts of his own ten or fifteen years after this dream is certainly of some biographical interest, but what was more essential for him was the insight that this unknown wing of his house, with its peculiar library, embodied a part of his own personality, one which would soon be explored still more closely. Finally, around 1926, another dream appeared, set during the war in South Tyrol and the North Italian countryside, which Jung interpreted as a portent of his encounter with alchemy. A figure in the dream, a peasant, uttered the noteworthy remark, "Now we are caught in the seventeenth century!"[8] For Jung, who had become accustomed from childhood to similar indications of how he was rooted in past epochs, this was actually no particular news. He construed it rather as a matter-of-fact task of his life, to which he would have to devote himself in order to get out again from this "seventeenth century," years later, matured and transformed.

Many years were to pass, then, before the writing and publication of *Psychology and Alchemy* (1944), one of Jung's major works. They were years of absorption in alchemical texts and their decipherment and psychological interpretation, the process of which suggested a close parallel with the shared experience of analyst and client in their work together. Jung commissioned resourceful antiquarians to provide him with the most important of the now rare original texts—a rather expensive undertaking. And the young classical scholar Marie-Louise von Franz, who had already come to Bollingen as a student, paid for her analysis with Jung by helping him with the translation of the Latin and Greek authors. Also necessary was a thorough familiarity with the extremely abundant pictures that the early authors and printers had added to their

▲ C. G. Jung in his library, 1946.

◀ (*Above*) The alchemist as geometer: "Make a circle of man and woman, from it draw a square, and from the square a triangle. Make a circle and you will have the philosophers' stone."

◀ The *coniunctio* in the alchemical vessel. It was Jung who rediscovered the correspondence between the union of opposites in the alchemical procedure and the processes of integration leading to individuation.

works in order to illustrate at least a suggestion of that which could not be expressed conceptually. Jung pointed out that the astonishing parallelism between certain unconscious productions of modern people and the results of alchemistic researchers already begins wherever there are formal and substantive correspondences, for example between dream images and alchemistic copperplates.

The longer Jung worked in his new field, the clearer it became to him that alchemy had represented something of an esoteric undercurrent within official Christianity.[9] Put differently, alchemy was related to ecclesiastical Christianity as a dream to consciousness. And just as the dream, through its images, compensates for the conflicts of the everyday conscious life, so alchemy strove to expose something of the tension that was present—acknowledged or not—within Christianity. Such problems there clearly were—for example, we notice that there is no feminine figure in the traditional image of God in the Trinity, and that the factor of evil is generally treated as if it lay outside God's will, seeing the devil as the dark opposite number of a God of light. In this connection Jung argues:

> Evil needs to be taken into account just as much as good, for good and evil are ultimately nothing but the idealized extensions and abstractions of action, and both are part of the chiaroscuro phenomenon of life. In the end, after all, there is no good that cannot produce evil, and no evil from which some good cannot come.[10]

So the encounter with the shadow, along with the integration of this dark side of the human psyche that belongs to the total personality, is part of the process leading to psychic wholeness. Something analogous occurred in the first stage of the alchemistic process, known as *nigredo* or "blackening." Here, generally speaking, it was the dynamic aspect of development that played the dominant role, whereas the dogma of the confessional was formulated once and for all, statically as an article of faith. The alchemist was primarily an experimenter, a seeker. He himself stood in the midst of a process from which (in contrast to modern science!) he could not separate himself. Ultimately the goal of the multistage process, accompanied by manifold phenomena of color and shape, was the "chemical marriage," an expression of the successful unification of the opposites, be they light and dark or masculine and feminine, without which the "philosophers' stone" could not grow. What religions had known for ages as the "sacred marriage," and what the mystic hoped for "within" as "mystical union" through the bestowal of the grace of God, the chemical marriage was to these seekers. And in alchemy this marriage took place within *and* without—externally in the form of material transformation, inwardly in the process of turning to gold within oneself. Not without reason did the alchemists have as their motto *Aurum nostrum non aurum vulgi*—"Our gold is not ordinary gold."

What they meant by marriage was also—in the strict sense of the word—extraordinary. The motif of the sacred marriage can be traced back to the Egyptian rites for the dead, where marriage and death are intimately connected. "For love is strong as death," says the wedding song of Solomon (8:6). At the death of the symbolic figure of the Kabbalah, the great Rabbi Simon bar Yochai, his marriage in the other world was celebrated, according to the *Zohar*. As we shall see, Jung himself gained experience in the immediate vicinity of death that touched upon the *mysterium coniunctionis*, that dimension of individual and transpersonal reality which the alchemist designated—in Goethe's sense— as the "open and secret" goal of the *opus alchymicum*, the work of preparing the philosophers' stone (*lapis philosophorum*). In terms of Jungian psychology, it involves nothing less than the accomplishment of individuation or self-becoming, which ultimately embraces the whole process of life, including death itself. Thus this process cannot be completed during one's incarnation on earth. No one can say, "I have gotten through it!"

From this point of view the *mysterium coniunctionis*, even from the psychological standpoint, as Jung understood it, presents a problem whose difficulties he expressed in all of his books on the subject. One troublesome point consisted in the fact that though the birth of more enlightened rationalism did indeed bring with it an illumination and strengthening of ego-consciousness, at the same time, once the world had been stripped of its gods, matter too was now rendered lifeless. The world in its entirety, it seemed, could now be viewed in a purely materialistic way, and indeed the measuring, weighing, calculating mind did bring about, in the form of modern technology, a manipulation of matter that had never before been possible. Matter and spirit, or psyche—insofar as the latter was recognized at all—were separated from one another as unconnected entities. It is doubtless interesting that Jung's alchemy dream went back to the seventeenth century, to a time, historically speaking, when this tendency to dissociate spirit and matter was prevalent, resulting on the one hand in the physical sciences, and on the other—with repeated delays—in a "psychology without a soul." Jung's task clearly was to pick up the threads of spiritual development and grasp of reality where they had once been broken off. But instead of simply satisfying the historical, reliquarian interests of a backward-directed consciousness, what concerned him was something quite different. For one thing, by comparing the alchemical symbolic world with the dream symbolism of people living today (for example in *Psychology and Alchemy*), he gained insights into the individuation process and also into such important matters as the phenomenon of the transference, so significant for every therapist.[11] The alchemists' techniques for transformation shed crucial light on those of freeing oneself from neurosis and one-sided conscious orientation, so that the conscious and unconscious psyche finds wholeness in the Self. Furthermore, this work with the problems of alchemy and psychology encouraged a dialogue with modern physics, because the atomic world of microphysics showed signs of being essentially related to the psychic world. Indeed, there was no lack of indications that physical and psychic energy—ultimately—represent two aspects of one and the same reality, and this brings within sight the realization of a single unified view of reality that the late medieval alchemists and philosophers called the *unus mundus*, the one, or unified, world.[12]

In concrete terms this meant that Jung, as a psychologist, was broadening his own outlook, by opening himself up afresh—as he had once done as a result of his studies in the physical sciences—to questions of natural science. This he did while at the same time interesting physicists, in turn, in the application of the physical approach to the psychological. Thus it is understandable that two noted physicists were exchanging views with the psychologist as early as the mid-thirties, when he was beginning to put forward the first demonstrable results of his alchemy research. These were Wolfgang Pauli, Professor of Theoretical Physics at the Swiss Institute of Technology and winner of the Nobel Prize for physics in 1945, and Professor Pascual Jordan, director (after 1930) of the Physical Institute of the University of Rostock. On his first studies in this area, Jordan wrote to Jung: "I am very impressed to see a belated appreciation even for alchemy beginning to develop here again; I have long felt, you know, that the wholly superficial assessment of alchemy that has persisted up to this time stood in need of liquidation, but until now I had looked in vain for a more incisive explanation of what really lay behind this phenomenon that is so important in the history of our culture."[13]

Before Jung could make the dialogue on the foundations of natural science bear fruit in this way, he found himself on the receiving end. Along with the dreams, already mentioned, that pointed toward alchemy came an acquaintance with an ancient Taoist text that treated Chinese yoga as well as Chinese alchemy. This was *The Secret of the Golden Flower*, as translated into German by Richard Wilhelm. In the Preface to the second edition of the work which he himself annotated, Jung wrote:

> My late friend Richard Wilhelm sent me the text of *The Secret of the Golden Flower* in 1928, at a moment that was full of problems for my own work. Since 1913 I had been engaged in investigating the processes of the collective unconscious, and I had obtained results which struck me as difficult in more than one respect. Not only were they far removed from anything known to "academic" psychology, but they also went beyond the bounds of medical, purely personalistic psychology. It was an extensive phenomenology to which hitherto known categories and methods could no longer be applied. My results, which rested on the efforts of fifteen years, seemed to be hanging in midair, for there was nothing anywhere to compare them with.[14]

It was the ancient Chinese alchemists' text that put Jung on the right track, so that he was at last able to uncover in alchemy, and Western alchemy in particular, the comparative material he needed for his own psychological investigations. Thus the text itself was only a sort of catalyst, an impulse, not really a pattern by means of which one could get a feeling for Far Eastern spirituality. In the same place Jung objected to the misconception that his psychological commentary described his therapeutic methods. Rather, the situation here was much as it was with the *I Ching*, also translated into German by Wilhelm, which represented a challenge to the analytical psychologist and the physicist alike, being grounded in the principle of synchronicity, of parallelism in time. This refers to a noncausal "ordering" of both psychic and physical facts, in which a definite archetype must be postulated as the ordering factor. As for this subject, several years passed before Jung, in collaboration with Wolfgang Pauli, explained "Synchronicity: An Acausal Connecting Principle."[15] He made first intimations of this at the time of his preoccupation with alchemy, for example in his English seminar in the fall of 1929 and his obituary for Richard Wilhelm in 1930.

Through his pursuit of alchemy (before and around 1940),

all the elements that had previously lain disconnectedly side by side fell into place for Jung:

> . . .the fantasy-images, the empirical material I had gathered in my practice, and the conclusions I had drawn from it. I now began to understand what these psychic contents meant when seen in historical perspective. My understanding of their typical character, which had already begun with my investigation of myths, was deepened. The primordial images and the nature of the archetype took a central place in my researches, and it became clear to me that without history there can be no psychology, and certainly no psychology of the unconscious. A psychology of consciousness can, to be sure, content itself with material drawn from personal life, but as soon as we wish to explain a neurosis we require an anamnesis which reaches deeper than the knowledge of consciousness. And when in the course of treatment unusual decisions are called for, dreams occur that need more than personal memories for their interpretation.[16]

With this the circle was closed. What might be misunderstood, if considered only superficially, as a ludicrous escapade in a marginal field actually turned out to be a helpful insight for the everyday practice of the psychotherapist who was familiar with the symbolism of alchemy.

In fact, his research into alchemy could not help but take on a central, or one might say centralizing, role in C. G. Jung's life. In his work with it he saw his inner relationship to Goethe.

> Goethe's secret was that he was in the grip of the process of archetypal transformation which has gone on through the centuries. He regarded his *Faust* as an *opus magnus* or *divinum*.[17]

In a letter dated 1955, when he was eighty, Jung characterized *Faust* as nothing less than an "*opus alchymicum* in the best sense." The mystery of the *coniunctio*, he said, was like a leitmotif pervading the whole of Goethe's work. At the same time Jung hinted that even *Faust*, which had been with him his whole life, had not become intelligible to him until the mid-thirties, when he read J. V. Andreae's *The Chemical Marriage of Christian Rosenkreutz*,[18] the famous basic text of Rosicrucianism which narrated the path of alchemical initiation and maturation of the fictional Christian Rosenkreutz over the span of "seven days."[19]

At the same time Jung's understanding of religious reality, which he discussed in lectures in the mid-thirties and also in book form after 1940 (*Psychology and Religion*) and subsequently in *Paracelsica* (1942), was appreciably deepened. More and more his attention was drawn to the figure of Christ as the *anthropos* or true human being, the quintessence of the Self, for Western people at any rate. Alchemy dealt with this Christ-self in the form of the philosophers' stone that was to be prepared, and thus it is possible to speak of a parallel between Christ and the stone. In *Psychology and Alchemy* this important aspect is clearly elaborated and thoroughly documented,[20] from the third-century Gnostic and alchemist Zosimos of Panoplis, whose *Visions* Jung annotated in detail,[21] down to Jakob Böhme in the seventeenth century, who of course was not a practicing alchemist, but who did make use of alchemical symbolism. From this Jung arrived at the conclusion:

> From this material it appears quite clearly what alchemy was seeking, in the last analysis. It wished to produce a *corpus subtile*, the transfigured body of the resurrection—a body that is simultaneously spirit. In this it matches Chinese alchemy, as it has become known to us through the text of *The Secret of the Golden Flower.* This is the "diamond body," that is immortality, attained through the transformation of the body. Because of its transparency, its brilliance, and its hardness, the diamond is a fitting symbol.[22]

And always, the one who performs the operation is included in the process. Hence if we seek to understand the significance of alchemy for C. G. Jung's psychology, the picture we arrive at, in a nutshell, is this: In his "work" (*opus alchymicum*), the alchemist is confronted with a task, as one who no longer can or will remain what he is. He has to undergo a total, inner transformation. This is why Gerhard Dorn (Dorneus), the sixteenth-century Paracelsist often quoted by Jung, programmatically demanded:

> *Transmutemini in vivos lapides philosophicos.*
> Transform yourselves into living philosophic stones!

This means: Find within yourselves the "philosophers' stone"; prepare it by recasting your own nature, and be not content with the conventional chemical practices of the alchemist's kitchen! The procedures, beginning with the *prima materia*, the still-untransformed yet mysterious initial substance, allow the technician, who must always be also a meditator, a contemplative worker, to pass through a definite series of developmental stages. The first stage involves the *nigredo* or "blackening," a dangerous stage that can confound the technician through the production of fumes and poisons. In the path of psychological individuation this corresponds to the confrontation with the "shadow." The second stage is called *albedo*, "whitening," and can be compared with the integration of the soul-image, the anima or animus. Turning to the phenomenon of the transference between patient and therapist, which can cause such difficulties in analysis, the motif of the "mystical marriage" comes into play. In this regard, the early practitioner had at his side a *soror mystica*, a spiritual sister or helper. Lastly, the alchemistic opus proceeds to the third stage of *rubedo* or *citrinitas*, "reddening" or "yellowing," that is, turning to gold. The longed-for philosophers' stone appears to have come close enough to realize; in it—in psychological terms, in the self—the opposites of spirit and matter, light and darkness, masculine and feminine, are united. With this the alchemist's path of initiation, so far as this is possible, has reached its end. The mystical work along its sorrowful road, beset with so many errors and obstacles, is finished—to the extent that it can ever be so.

This work kept C. G. Jung busy for more than a decade, haunting him to the last phase of his late work. The question of why he had undertaken a task that demanded so much trouble and patience he answered in his memoirs:

> The experiences of the alchemists were, in a sense, my experiences, and their world was my world.[23]
>
> Thus I had at last reached the ground which underlay my own experiences of the years 1913 to 1917; for the process through which I had passed at that time corresponded to the process of alchemical transformation discussed in [*Psychology and Alchemy*].[24]

In the Epilogue to that fundamental work, Jung stated clearly that what the alchemist did was project (unconsciously) the stages occurring in his own individuation into the process of chemical transformation he had set in motion—that is, that which he experimented with was his own transformation and growth. And the term "individuation" should in no way be taken to mean a totally known and enlightened, or enlightenable, state.

> It denotes merely the realm of the process of personality-forming centralization in the unconscious, which is still very obscure and in need of further investigation. It has to do with vital processes which from time immemorial, because of their numinous character, have been the most significant initiators of symbol-formation. And these processes are mysterious, in that they present the human intellect with riddles for whose solution it will continue to struggle for a long time to come, and perhaps in vain. For it is entirely doubtful whether, in the last analysis, the intellect is or is not the appropriate instrument for this. Not for nothing did alchemy style itself an "art," sensing correctly that it had to do with processes of development that could really be comprehended only through experience, and intellectually only labeled.[25]

Jung's lifelong insistence on learning through his own experience, regardless of the grand words of the great authorities (though these should be respected all the same), serves here as a path of spiritual instruction for everyone:

> *Rumpite libros, ne corda vestra rumpantur.*
> Tear up your books, that your hearts may not be torn!

The alchemist must persist in his study of books, but he must also be sure that the experience of his spirit is not masked by the letters on the page. The letter kills, the spirit bring to life!

As C. G. Jung's interest in alchemy covered more than three decades, it is a thread of his life that we shall take up several more times during the thirties, in considering not only the biographically and historically crucial phase of the era of National Socialism, but also the contributions it made to his work during this time, whether in regard to the psychology of religion, his several months long journey to India, or his encounters in the circle of Eranos.

16

Eranos—A "Navel of the World"

"Eranos is really an extended, relatively narrow garden that falls away in terraces down to the shore of Lago Maggiore from the road that skirts the lake hard by the cliffs on its way from Ascona to Brissago. The areas was originally a vineyard—hence the terraces—and in a spiritual sense it remains so today, for there the wine of wisdom is pressed from the knowledge of thinkers and scholars as they meet and blend with one another."[1] Here Alfons Rosenberg, the expert in symbolism, meditation teacher and author, referred to the place where for more than half a century the internationally known Eranos conferences took place. The Dutchwoman Olga Fröbe-Kapteyn, coming from the Anglo-Indian theosophical tradition, began them in the Villa Gabriella on 14 August 1933, with a lecture series that was repeated at the same time every year thereafter. In the beginning she was advised by the religious scholar Rudolf Otto of Marburg, who had become known for his landmark standard work, *Das Heilige* (1917), and it was he who suggested the name for the annual meeting. Eranos, in ancient Greece, was the name of a gathering for a more or less impromptu common meal, to which each participant was supposed to bring along some edible or artistic contribution. In the Foreword to the first *Eranos Yearbook* (1933), in which the texts of the individual lectures were printed in their respective original languages (German,

English, and French), the founder described her original intention thus:

"The Eranos conferences have set themselves the goal of mediating between East and West. The task of this mediation, and the need to create a place for the promotion of such an understanding of the spiritual realm, have become ever clearer. . . . The question of a fruitful confrontation of East and West is above all a psychological one. The clear-cut questions posed by Western people in matters of religion and psychology can undoubtedly find added, meaningful fructification in the wisdom of the Orient. It is not the emulation of Eastern methods and teachings that is important, nor the neglecting or replacing of Western knowledge about these things, but the fact that Eastern wisdom, symbolism, and methods can help us to rediscover the spiritual values that are most distinctively our own."[2]

"Rediscovery," and even more, "rebirth," were words whose manifold permutations had already been propagated and tested for some decades in other places around Ascona, in particular on Monte Verità, the "Mountain of Truth," overlooking the fishing village and thus immediately nearby. Here at the beginning of the century idealists and world- and self-changers of all sorts settled for varying periods to practice their alternative styles of life, welfare, and art. The Russian anarchist Mikhail Aleksandrovich Bakunin had been residing in neighboring Locarno at the end of the nineteenth century, and Monte Verità, with its spa and open-air park, saw artists and writers of the most varied colors, Dadaists and expressionists, painters, sculptors, and dancers, for example Rudolf von Laban and his dance school, utopians and socialists such as Erich Mühsam, and occasionally men like Martin Buber or Hermann Hesse as well. The industrious Countess Franziska von Reventlow put up here, and the ill-fated psychoanalyst Otto Gross, the colleague and sometime patient of C. G. Jung, as did Theosophists and Freemasons, be it Franz Hartmann or the notorious Theodor Reuss with his Ordo Templi Orientis, the "Order of the Temple of the East."[3] And off

Porto Ronco in Lago Maggiore there were the charming islands of Brissago, also known as the "Islands of the Blessed."[4]

But the Casa Eranos and the conferences held there each August had little in common with Monte Verità, if only because C. G. Jung had put his stamp on the lecture cycles for years to come. This manifested itself on one hand in the international character of the gatherings, and on the other in the fact that representatives of various disciplines would each contribute a share of their specialized knowledge to a common theme. In the beginning the humanistic sciences were predominant; after World War II the natural scientist won a greater hearing, for example the biologist Adolf Portmann from Basel, the physicists Erwin Schrödinger and Max Knoll, the ethnologist Jean Servier, the physician Manfred Porkert, or the paleo-anthropologist Kurt Gerhardt. When Eranos opened its portals for the first time, the topic under discussion was "Yoga and Meditation in East and West"; thus the speakers included the Indologist Heinrich Zimmer of Heidelberg ("On the Significance of Indian Tantra Yoga") and the Sinologist Erwin Rousselle, Director of the China Institute of the University of Frankfurt. Whereas the Western tradition was represented by two (formerly) Catholic theologians, the convert Friedrich Heiler ("Contemplation in Christian Mysticism") and the excommunicate Ernesto Buonaiuti[5] of the University of Rome ("Meditation and Contemplation in the Roman Catholic Church"), Jung's student and friend Gustav Richard Heyer spoke on "The Meaning and Significance of Oriental Wisdom for Western Spiritual Leadership." Jung himself delivered "A Study in the Process of Individuation." Whereas it fell to the religious historians and theologians in the main to discuss the historical facts and developments, the two psychologists directed their audience's attention above all to the experiential potentialities of modern people, in an attempt at building a bridge to the inner world of the unconscious. Jungian psychology, Heyer explained,[6] was barely at the point of assembling the building blocks for such an effort, particularly for those contemporaries who, though they had lost touch with the tradition of the church, still felt themselves inwardly impelled toward a path to individual self-awareness.

Jung shed light on one of the possible forms which this process can take by the example of a fifty-five-year-old American woman and the story of her particular illness; that is, he presented a case history and described her dreams, and by way of illustration he showed a series of pictures that his client had made as productions of her unconscious, not works of art, but rather a graphic record of her experience. His lecture discussed the stages of individuation as a process of self-development, and in marked contrast to the rest of the participants in Eranos he spoke extempore. Of course Jung had already been involved with this central theme of analytical psychology for many years, but he had made it his duty to present a work to the wider public only when he, as an author, had formed a sufficiently clear idea of his subject. Consequently, the Eranos conference was for Jung the beginning of a preliminary, still relatively intimate platform for the development of his emerging work. In the first volume of proceedings, therefore, Jung's contribution turned out to be comparatively short, as it was drawn from the sketchy notes taken by Toni Wolff. Not until seventeen years later, in 1950, was a thoroughly revised and expanded version included in the volume *Gestaltungen des Unbewussten*.[7]

An element of the *provocateur* must also have been at work in Jung's debut performance, for in the beginning Olga Fröbe's connection had been with a theosophical group in America; originally she had wished to offer them a place to hold meetings and lectures. In any case Alfons Rosenberg, who was closely acquainted with the lady, reported a serious clash between Mrs. Fröbe and C. G. Jung. The latter had unmistakably voiced his displeasure with the large-sized paintings on display in the lecture hall, "roughly geometric shapes, without exception blue, black, and gold in color. These stiff pictures had a stark, mysterious, and solemn effect, but they radiated an atmosphere of dismaying coldness—they had been painted with the intellect and not with the heart; effective, but unsympathetic. Jung criticized them harshly and ruthlessly—one in particular, which Olga Fröbe had covered with a black latticework formed from the Om, the hallowed word and sign of India. The Golden Temple rose in the background, but it was separated from the observer by this black, Om-shaped grille. Jung had the hardest words for this composition, saying that its creator had put the devil between herself and the shrine, the symbol of godliness—that she had an affair with the devil. So shaken by this analysis was Olga Fröbe that she not only was able to escape the influence of the theosophical but actually changed its direction. . . ."[8] Rosenberg intimated that this was the real moment of Eranos' birth, and consequently that it was Jung who had stood godfather to it.

Now it is obvious how great a distance there is bound to be between paintings that have been made on the basis of a more or less abstract theory or "theosophical" system, and those that owe their origin to the vitality and spontaneity of the psyche. And still another note can be detected in Toni Wolff's lecture notes: to follow the previous contributions of his Eranos colleagues, Jung, it seems, opened with a line from Lao-tse's *Tao Te Ching*: "Exterminate learning and there will no longer be worries" (chap. 20), but then he explained:

> After the pleasant fragrance of the Orient comes the European: disagreeable, a pirate, a conquistador, dripping with the "religion of love," an opium trafficker, disoriented and miserable in spite of his superabundance of knowledge and his intellectual arrogance. This is the picture of Western man. . . .[9]

From this unvarnished avowal of the spiritual emptiness and destitution of the "Christian" European, however, Jung by no means proceeded to an exhortation to borrow from the Orient, as seemed to be recommended by the theme of the conference and as at least some of its participants undoubtedly would have expected. Rather than allowing himself to be forced into the mold of propagandist for the precedents of the East, he argued:

> The essential thing can only grow out of ourselves. Hence if the white man is true to his instinct, he reacts with instinctive defensiveness against everything that one might tell him or advise him. And what he has already swallowed, he must excrete again as a *corpus alienum*, for his blood rejects that which has grown on foreign soil.[10]

A few years later, Jung was to experience this in his own body, on his journey to India.

When Olga Fröbe invited the psychologist from Küsnacht to the second Eranos conference in 1934, she could already boast of a considerable staff of co-workers. The circle of speakers had substantially increased, and so the topic that had begun could be continued under the rubric of "East-West Symbolism and Spiritual Guidance."[11] The new collaborators included an Indian representative from the Ramakrishna Mission in Madras, who considered Hindu religious symbolism in connection with methods of spiritual practice. The place of art in the psychological view of life was discussed in a paper by Moritz Carl von Cammerloher of Vienna. The Zürich art historian Rudolf Bernoulli dealt with number symbolism in the system of the Tarot, and a young woman, Sigrid Strauss-Kloebe, a student of Jung and Heyer, was also one of the group on this occasion ("On the Psychological Significance of the Astrological Symbol"). Because the philosophical conflict in Germany was growing ever sharper in 1934, it is noteworthy that two men at least between whom there was a profound ideological gulf spoke alongside each other in the Eranos collegium: the Tübingen theologian Jakob Wilhelm Hauer, who on the masthead of his own *Kommende Gemeinde* had welcomed the rise of National Socialism as "a new faith,"[12] and the Jewish philosopher Martin Buber. His double lecture on "Symbolic and Sacramental Existence in Judaism" characterized the nature of Chasidism, in clear distinction to the mystical Kabbalah and all varieties of gnosticism. Jung's relationship was that he had invited Hauer, as an Indologist, to collaborate in the Psychological Club and his seminars,[13] and thus a fierce controversy was to arise between Jung and Buber after the end of World War II, as will be discussed in more detail later.

In view of this richly varied palette, Jung looked upon his own participation as superfluous; he wished to allow the Sinologists and Indologists to take precedence. Moreover it was his opinion that to "laymen of an Asiatic bent," psychology would seem "a difficult and unpalatable field." In his experience the only ones who hankered after psychology were those for whom every other avenue had failed, and this also applied, by the way, to the practical use of the *I Ching*. "Too much Eastern wisdom, however, takes the place of immediate experience, and thus the way to psychology is cut off."[14] Ultimately, he wanted to remain in the background, "taking part as a sympathizer." But things did not turn out this way. In the end, rather, Olga Fröbe succeeded in moving Jung to active collaboration. Reading, in this context, the Foreword to the second *Eranos Yearbook* (1934), it becomes clear that Mrs. Fröbe too now allowed herself to be guided by his thinking: the concern with Oriental symbolism was, to be sure, a significant enrichment, but it was crucial that it should be firmly rooted "in our own indigenous Western symbolism." "The Western road to health must be built upon Western ground, work with Western symbols, and be formed from Western material."[15] From this dictum it is not hard to discern Jung's intentions. This time—in August 1934—he gave not an off-the-cuff presentation, but a prepared written lecture on "Archetypes of the Collective Unconscious," that dimension of spiritual knowledge that goes beyond the individual psyche and its experience and allows people to take part in the religious and spiritual experience of all humanity. As far as this concept was concerned, here Jung reached back into the religious philosophy and theology of ancient times, where the designation "archetype" had been used already in the *Corpus Hermeticum*, in Augustine, Dionysus the Areopagite, and others. In short order Jung came to today's problems, placing under his lens the alarming loss of imagery and symbol among modern people, particularly those who come from the tradition of Protestantism. Rather than simply establishing the facts and lamenting the loss in the usual way, Jung showed the extent to which this impoverishment nonetheless could and in fact did have meaning, that is insofar as proper use was made of this spiritual poverty. It would be wrong for religiously estranged people, figuratively speaking, to attempt somehow to cover up this inadequacy in "robes of Oriental splendor" in the manner of the Theosophists. One could not allow the house of his own fathers to go to ruin, and then attempt to break into "Oriental palaces,"[16] to borrow rashly from the religions of the East. Once again, Jung bluntly criticized the orientalizing tendency he had perceived in certain Eranos participants in earlier years. In a series of examples he showed how the loss of the power of traditional symbols would point people to the collective unconscious and its archetypal figures, and then to the process of individuation which the individual can go through, a process that is solitary and therefore unappreciated and unimagined. Jung closed this sketch with an unmistakable warning, one which he made available to a wider readership only two decades later in "The Roots of Consciousness":

> To me it seems risky, on the whole, to bring too many of these dark things to light; but sometimes a wanderer in the darkness of night is grateful for the faltering yellow glow of a lone lantern, or the pale streaks of the first light of dawn.[17]

Thus from the first days of the conference Jung was among the supporting group of those who, in concert with Olga Fröbe, determined the spiritual direction of Eranos. And because the annual gatherings represented a lasting component of his work process and his calendar, between 1933 and 1951 he was never allowed to be absent as a speaker. Only during the time of his serious illness in the war years 1943–1944 was he forced to forgo his participation. In all he gave fourteen lectures at Eranos, among them groundbreaking contribu-

▲ The Casa Eranos in Ascona and its hostess, Olga Fröbe-Kapteyn. Jung occupied the upper room during the Eranos conferences.

◀ Jung in conversation on his favorite wall by the lake.

▲ Jung in the audience at Eranos (about 1942).

tions from his alchemy research, on the psychology of the Trinity, and the symbolism of transformation in the Mass as well as the psychology of the spirit. His last lecture, in 1951, was devoted to the phenomenon of synchronicity, the range of problems in which the depth psychologist's work shared such close theoretical foundations with that of the physicist. In no way, as he repeatedly stressed, did he wish to give the impression that he wanted to thrust himself into the foreground. In a letter to the lady of the house on 27 September 1943, he said:

> Under no circumstances do I wish it to seem as if the independent and spontaneous collaboration of others has been as it were shunted by me onto a psychological track, and thus pressed into my service. It is extraordinarily important, for Eranos in particular, that each individual speaker has the feeling that he is providing an independent contribution, not one that serves some other goal.[18]

Part of the special charm of the gatherings in this secluded garden landscape on the lake beneath the Ticino sun was that of meetings between people, including those at the occasions of their eating and drinking together. On the great round, tree-shadowed table in front of the Villa Gabriella, the hostess had the midday meal set out, at which the speakers, and every day a few other guests from among the audience, were assembled. Here Jung's extraordinary gift for establishing contact and firing conversation with his own unique spirit and humor could unfold fully. It even happened once that a passer-by outside stopped at Mrs. Fröbe's to inquire about the gentleman who had just given out with such a powerful and infectious laugh—an infallible sign of the presence of C. G. Jung! One time, Aniela Jaffé reports, the routine of the conference was interrupted by an unusual event, namely a nighttime party, which was celebrated partly inside the Casa Eranos and partly on the terrace outside. On this occasion Jung impressed himself on the memories not only of those who were direct witnesses, but also of the neighbors living in more distant yards: "Even today a kind of legend survives of a 'night sea journey,' which is not really accurate; one can hardly imagine a night sea journey as ear-splittingly loud as our nekyia was. It was tremendously boisterous and drunken. Baron von der Heydt (the owner of the hotel on Monte Verità) had donated the wine. Although there was no music for the dancing, the sound of it echoed far across the lake. The whole neighborhood near and far sent messages to Mrs. Fröbe complaining about the unaccustomed disturbance of the peace, but it did no good. Jung was pretty tipsy, and the words his friend and student comrade Albert Oeri had written in his memoirs of him came to my mind: 'Jung's drunks were rare, but they were loud!' But it was not only Jung who was tipsy; everybody else was too. Jung was very pleased at this, and he roused those who were too sober to render due homage to Dionysos. Plunging in now here, now there, he sparkled with wit, banter, and drunken high spirits. This, though, was the only party that was ever held at the Eranos conferences. Apparently Dionysos was satisfied once and for all with this sacrifice in wine and drunkenness."[19]

The banquets at Eranos evidently could not be considered overly opulent, particularly by the standards of C. G. Jung, who was accustomed to good eating and noble spirits. Thus Mircea Eliade, who met Jung repeatedly in Ascona and in Moscia, confided to his diary what he had heard from Henry Corbin's wife: "Jung is a gourmet, and really knows his way around the kitchen. Since he knows that the dining at Mrs. Fröbe-Kapteyn's is not too good, he buys himself little snacks in secret and eats them alone in his room at night. But eventually word of this got out, and one of his admiring young ladies from Ascona, also in secret, sent him a roast chicken." From the same journal, the entry from 23 August 1950, obviously about a dinner together in an Ascona restaurant: "I eat with Jung, on his left, and we converse from twelve-thirty until three o'clock. He is a captivating old gentleman, utterly without conceit, who is as happy to talk as he is to listen. What could I write down here first of this long conversation? Perhaps his bitter reproaches of 'official science'? In university circles he is not taken seriously. 'Scholars have no curiosity,' he says with Anatole France. Professors are satisfied with recapitulating what they learned in their youth and what does not cause any trouble; above all, their spiritual world is in balance. . . . For all that, I sense that at the bottom of his heart Jung is a little troubled by this indifference. That is why he is so interested in a scholar, in any line of research, who takes him seriously, or quotes or comments on him."[20]

Besides the lectures in the Eranos hall, one particular custom was soon adopted in which Jung's students especially took part. These were the sessions on the "little wall," the informal gatherings during intermissions and after lectures—actually, whenever Jung was present. Aniela Jaffé described these wall sessions from her own experience: Jung used to sit on the small terrace wall, "and right away listeners and students, but above all his female students, would cluster around him like a bunch of grapes. Jung gave a psychological commentary on every lecture, and even the shortest and simplest question received a detailed answer. These sessions were the most impressive and vital instruction in psychology we had ever been able to get. Jung's intellectual generosity was wonderful. The little wall sessions took on a special character whenever Erich Neumann was there from Tel Aviv: then there was—as there was not when we asked the questions—a dialogue, with speeches and contradictions. We listened."[21]

Occasionally what was heard in these inter- and after-sessions was written down and circulated in private, primarily among participants and friends; the notes taken by Margret Ostrowski-Sachs, a neighbor of Hermann Hesse's in Montagnola, should be mentioned in this connection. It goes without saying that the statements attributed to Jung in this form are fully understandable only in the context of his work as a whole. They cannot, however, be granted the authenticity of an exact stenographic record. Rather, these texts have the character of notations recorded in a diary immediately after the event, and hence they are somewhat more reliable than the memoirs, written for the most part from a greater distance in time. From this point of view it deserves to be mentioned why Jung placed such a high value on conversation in intimate groups, and that indeed he could never resist it. According to Margret Ostrowski, he once said:

"What troubles me is that I seldom get to have a conversation with an adequate partner—Father White is in England, Neumann lives in Israel; women of my circle do understand me, but with women their home, their husband, and their children always come first. If all these things are in order, then a woman also has some time for the spirit, and then it is interesting. But talking with a man, one listens to the reverberation from the cosmic spaces of the spirit."[22]

What Jung had to say did not always go unchallenged. Once, for example, when he was propounding his much-discussed theory of the quaternity, and the need for the Trinity to be augmented, be it through the principle of the feminine (Sophia/Mary) or that of darkness (Satan), opposition did arise. Alfons Rosenberg, himself a fairly regular visitor to Eranos and a welcome guest at Olga Fröbe's, launched a small counterevent in the form of a lecture at a friend's home, which was attended by many of the Eranos audience. He remarked: "It was an exciting evening of fiercely partisan arguments, which might have brought to mind the climax of the guild congress in Mailand in 1366, where it was debated whether the cathedral should be designed according to the law of the square or of the triangle. In any case, I resisted the notion that, as I and many others understood Jung to mean, the Trinity needed to be "completed" by the addition of a fourth principle, be it Mary, Satan, or even Man. I was, traditionally, of the opposite opinion, namely that trinity could, and must, constitute the counterprinciple to quaternity. Naturally, Jung heard about this lecture I gave in response to his own. The next day, I noticed that he kept a thoughtful eye on me, giving me critical looks. But he did not discuss the problem with me—not even later, when I met and talked with him frequently."[23]

Unquestionably, though, approval of Jung's personality and his work were by far predominant. This was still perceptible in the Eranos collegium decades after his death, even though after his departure, as a consequence of the arrival of new speakers and guests, new thematic emphases arose. Finally, part of the enduring legacy of the *Eranos* yearbooks, which documented the important stages in the development of Jung's work as we have noted, are two separate volumes that were personally dedicated to him. One of these was the testimonial volume for his seventieth birthday, *The Idea of the Archetypes* (1945), with contributions from Hugo Rahner, John Layard, Louis Massignon, Andreas Speiser, Karl Kerényi, and others, a remarkably substantial hardbound book to be published in wartime or immediately thereafter. The still more extensive anniversary volume for his seventy-fifth birthday was entitled *From the World of the Archetypes* (1950). A new group of contributors was assembled to mark out wider perspectives from their own fields of specialization; thus among others there were Henry Corbin, the expert on Islamic mysticism and Shiite esoterism teaching in Teheran; the philosopher Hans Leisegang with a paper on the God-man as archetype; two Dutchmen, the religious scholar Gerardus van der Leeuw and the gnostic researcher Gilles Quispel; as well as Erich Neumann from Tel Aviv, the ethnologist Paul Radin from Berkeley, the New Testament scholar Karl Ludwig Schmidt of the University of Basel, and also from Basel the biologist Adolf Portmann, who shed light on the problem of the archetypes from his own perspective. In her Foreword, Olga Fröbe-Kapteyn emphasized that the increasing realization of the inner world and man's relationship to it was owed above all to C. G. Jung and his work. "The nature and the influence of these dynamically charged archetypes were first recognized and interpreted for us through his work. In the course of his fifteen years of cooperation with the Eranos conferences he has created an authoritative body of work and earned our deepest thanks."[24]

All this notwithstanding, Jung and those who worked with him did their part to see that it did not develop into a personal cult. Alluding to the hermetic *Aurea Catena*, which according to ancient tradition bound the students of the mythical Trismegistos, the thrice-great Hermes, to one another, but above all linked together heaven and earth, Erich Neumann noted: "Eranos—lakeside scene, garden and house. Inconspicuous and out of the way, and yet a navel of the world, a small link in the Golden Chain."

How Jung's collaboration in the Eranos assembly was judged in retrospect can be gathered from a statement by Adolf Portmann, coming from the year of Jung's death, on the celebration of Olga Fröbe's eightieth birthday in Ascona in 19 October 1961: "the encounter with Carl Gustav Jung, the great researcher of the psyche, was decisive for the first period of Eranos, and even in later years, when it was no longer possible for Jung to take an active part, his silent presence and his inner participation contributed materially to the spirit of this gathering. To all those who shared the good fortune of being able to witness this volcanic spirit in action, these encounters with a great man remain unforgettable and alive."[25]

The events of Eranos, chronologically speaking, represented only a series of episodes—though important ones—in Jung's life. Hence in continuing the biography of C. G. Jung, we must make clear what other events directed his life and work during the time in question, in and around 1933. Along with his study of alchemy, we should mention the studies in the psychology of religion that continued for many years, as well as the further episode of his journey to India. The time of National Socialism of course demands particular attention, as do the war and its aftermath. Although a biography cannot be a mere chronology, affording separate treatment to each individual unit of life and work, because naturally they are all tightly interwoven, nevertheless when brought together thematically there is no other way to present them than in sequence. At this juncture the obvious next step is to report on Jung's trip to India.

17

The Remarkable Journey to India

C. G. Jung's assistant and later successor at the Swiss Institute of Technology in Zürich, C. A. Meier,[1] gave an account of a private seminar in 1930 in which Jung discussed the case of a patient who in the course of her analysis described the inner pictures she had seen in "active imagination"—a practice that Jung felt was indicated in certain cases for activating the unconscious.[2] But he was unable to unravel the images this patient had produced until he became familiar with the work of the well-known English Indologist Sir John Woodroffe (pseudonym Arthur Avalon). This work, first published in Madras in 1918 under the title *The Serpent Power*, contained a discussion of Kundalini-Shakti or "serpent power," from two texts translated from the Sanskrit with commentary by Avalon.[3] *Kuṇḍalinī* refers to the spiritual and psychic energy—the libido, as it were, in its original elementary form—that is liberated in the process of (tantric) yoga. It rises up through the seven spiritual energy centers, or *cakras*, from the lowest, the *mūladhara-cakra*, located in the area of the sexual organs, to the *sahasrara-cakra* beneath the top of the skull. In connection with a definite system of spiritual practices, the idea is to awaken the Kundalini serpent slumbering, so to speak, at the root of one's being, and lead it upward to an experience of unification and enlightenment.[4] In the Sahasrara center the Kundalini, or Shakti, thought of as feminine, is united with Shiva; a *hieros gamos* or sacred marriage takes place. Before this awakening, the Kundalini persists in the unconscious state. A comparison with the alchemists' experience of transformation suggests itself.

When J. W. Hauer, with Heinrich Zimmer present, held a seminar on Kundalini yoga at the Zürich Psychological Club for several days in October 1932, Jung had supplied detailed commentary and was even available for discussion.[5] The papers and personal meetings at the first Eranos conferences had undoubtedly contributed to strengthening Jung's interest in Indian philosophy and religion, particularly as he admits expressly in his *Memories* to his conviction about the value of Eastern spirituality. It is all the more surprising, then, that Jung did not consider traveling to India of his own accord. To be sure there was talk once of a trip to China, which Erwin Rousselle suggested to him. It was to take up about half a year, but it did not come off, probably owing to lack of time and his intensive involvement with his alchemical studies. Jung also had to defer his attempt to learn Chinese, which he had taken up particularly on account of the *I Ching*. The fact that in December 1937—in the company of Fowler McCormick—he did at last embark on a journey to India that was to last a scant three months was due rather to external circumstances.

In the summer of 1937 Jung had two guests from India. These were V. Subramanya Iyer, the guru of the Maharaja of Mysore, and the English writer on yoga and India specialist Paul Brunton, a pupil of the famous Ramana Maharshi (1879–1950), the saint of Tiruvannamalai, of whom, besides Brunton, Heinrich Zimmer, Arthur Osborne, Hans-Hasso von Veltheim-Ostrau, and Lucy Cornelsson have also given extensive accounts. V. S. Iyer had taken part as the Indian representative at the International Philosophy Congress at the Sorbonne in Paris in 1937. From a letter of Jung's to Iyer on 16 September[6] we learn that at this time he already had in hand an invitation from the (British) Indian government to take part in the festivities that were to take place in January 1938 to mark the twenty-fifth year of existence of the University of Calcutta. Thus the motivation for this trip to India was quite different than it had been in the twenties, when he had wanted to visit the Pueblos or the East African Elgonyi in order to gain insight into the psyche of people still undisturbed by civilization. This time his travel would have to be, so to speak, "self-supporting." He fancied himself "like a homunculus in the retort," Jung said.

> India gave me my first direct experience of an alien, highly differentiated culture. Altogether different elements had ruled my Central African journey; culture had not predominated. As for North Africa, I had never had the opportunity there to talk with a person capable of putting his culture into words. In India, however, I had the chance to speak with representatives of the Indian mentality, and to compare it with the European.[7]

This assertion, however, cannot obscure the fact that Jung maintained a definite distance toward India and specifically Indian spirituality, be it of Hindu or Buddhist origin—a distance that on one hand was justified, and on the other gives rises to critical questions. Undoubtedly well founded was the need for the Western doctor, during his travels to Calcutta, Benares, Allahabad, and Agra, as well as a number of Indian temple sites, to remain in touch with the "fundamental strata of European thought," and not to lose himself in the hypnotic quality of Eastern religiosity. For just this reason he brought with him one of his books on alchemy, the first volume of the *Theatrum Chemicum* from 1602, and "studied the book from beginning to end." This was the volume that contained the most important writings of Gerardus Dorneus, so often referred to by Jung. Thus we see the noteworthy fact that not even for a few months would Jung detach himself from the traditions which dealt with the secret of transformation and self-development as it existed in the Western alchemy that grew out of Christian esoterism. Clearly, he was not prepared to exchange the one spiritual approach for another, even one as wide-ranging and venerable as Indian tradition.

The travelers came ashore at Bombay, the city of over a million inhabitants on the west coast. The broad expanse of a sea of houses and low green hills silhouetted against the horizon intimated to the newcomers a huge continent, an unknown land filled with mysteries, secrets, and contradictions of all kinds. The doctor from Europe spoke only English and so could make himself understood to only a small portion of the inhabitants of India. The fact that the population was split into a multitude of languages, religions, and social classes (castes), with mutually conflicting interests and needs, makes any assertion about "India" seem a totally inadequate, indeed arbitrary statement of opinion. Jung was fully aware of this fact, yet he attempted to bring together his impressions under a valid common denominator. He spoke of the "dreamlike world of India," into which he had plunged for several weeks and from which he drew his selective observations.

Renting a car, Jung had himself driven out of the city and into the countryside:

> There I felt a great deal better—yellow grass, dusty fields, native huts, great, dark-green, weird banyan trees, sickly palmyra palms sucked dry of their life-juice (it is run into bottles near the top to make palm wine, which I never tasted), emaciated cattle, thin-legged men, the colourful saris of women, all in leisurely haste or in hasty leisure, with no need of being explained or of explaining themselves, because obviously they are what they are. They were unconcerned and unimpressed; I was the only one who did not belong to India.[8]

This consciousness of not belonging, of having to remain at a distance, stayed with him. It was relieved only when he was able to speak with people like himself, Europeans or intellectual, that is Europeanized, Indians. But this India with its jumble of haphazardly piled-up human habitations and its masses of people vegetating there as if in a dream, seemed filled with

Shiva dancing in the circle of fire: "India gave my first direct experience of an alien, highly differentiated culture."

the monotony of endlessly repeated life. There seemed to be nothing here that had not already been a hundred thousand times before. Was this not the ideally favorable soil for the "transmigration of souls," and not of egoistic individual entities in the sense of Western consciousness, but a transmigration of nameless souls? Time was relative, space was relative. Jung went for a stroll through the hustle and bustle of Bombay's bazaar.

> I had felt the impact of the dreamlike world of India. . . . Perhaps I myself had been thrown into a dreamlike state by moving among fairytale figures of the Thousand and One Nights. My own world of European consciousness had become peculiarly thin, like a network of telegraph wires high above the ground, stretching in straight lines all over the surface of an earth looking treacherously like a geographic globe.[9]

For a moment the thought even flashed through the psychologist's mind that this India, with its sentimental, monstrous images of gods, might be the real world, while the white man lived in a "madhouse of abstractions"—a depressing thought! Just as in Africa he had had to escape the danger of "going black," so here he was threatened by the endless dream sequences of India's dreamlike world.

And yet even in India in the thirties there were factors that were willing to lead the way in social and political life, on the one hand, and on the road to spiritual awakening and growing consciousness on the other: Mohandas Karamchand Gandhi, the Mahatma or Great Soul, had stood up for years in word, writing, and exemplary deed for the equality of the casteless and for the unity and independence of India. In the West, too, Mahatma Gandhi had long since become a moral force. Jung left him unmentioned, as he did Sri Aurobindo Ghose, the creator of Integral Yoga, who strove to bring about a spiritual synthesis of East and West, and who with his ashram in Pondicherry in Southeast India stood out at the time from the profusion of Indian gurus and yoga masters. The very silence of Jung's *Memories* on these two men strikes one as remarkable, for one would have thought it was precisely efforts of this kind that must have challenged the psychologist. At all events he was concerned with the question of the ominous population explosion; twenty years after his Indian journey Jung characterized the problem of overpopulation as more serious and more urgent for the future of humankind than that of the atomic bomb.[10]

The Indian subcontinent exerted a powerful suction, from the point of view alone of the great distances that had to be covered within the space of a few weeks. It was well over a thousand kilometers from Bombay to Calcutta, and from there another thousand and a half kilometers to Ceylon, where the homeward journey was to begin. At various places lectures were expected of Jung; the Islamic University of Allahabad as well as two universities of a more Hindu or English character, those of Benares and Calcutta, distinguished the European guest with honorary doctorates. More important to the honoree than the academic ceremony were meetings and conversations. His observations related, for example, to the manner in which Europeans spoke English here. It gave the impression, he thought, of being somehow superimposed, affected and insincere. The Swiss, known for his own unreservedness and sometimes stubborn frankness, noted: "It makes you tired listening to these unnatural sounds, and you long for somebody to say something unkind or brutally offensive."[11] Above all, even in his voice the still-dominant Englishman displayed his position and the respect it demanded. The appearance of the Indian women made a somewhat more positive impression on Jung, the dignity and elegance with which they wore the traditional clothing that suited them, whereas he heaped bitter scorn on the fashion of the Western woman, largely designed by men—one need think only of the ladies' fashions of the mid-thirties! "Even fat women have a chance in India; with us they can only starve themselves to death." Trousered women parading about in their finery the traveler found "mercilessly ugly."

Quite otherwise were his impressions of the Indian temple buildings, the Hindu temples, stuffed with Hindu mythology and also with noise and dirt, of the destroying Shiva, the terrifying Kali, and fat, elephant-headed Ganesha, who is supposed to bring luck. The religion of Islam, more highly developed and in some respects superior, stood in marked contrast.

> Its mosques are pure and beautiful, and of course wholly Asiatic. There is not much mind about it, but a great deal of feeling. The cult is one wailing outcry for the All-Merciful. It is a desire, an ardent longing and even greed for God; I would not call it love. But there is love, the most poetic, most exquisite love of beauty in these old Moguls.[12]

With this the reporter came to speak of the Taj Mahal, which has always been prized as a miracle of architectural beauty, "a heavenly dream in stone." The visitor was filled with unbounded admiration. In this gigantic burial monument, which Shah Jehan had erected to his wife in the seventeenth century, Jung saw a tool for self-realization. This, he felt, was the one place in the world where the all too invisible and jealously guarded beauty of the Islamic Eros had become manifest through an almost divine miracle. Jung was enthralled:

> It is the delicate secret of the rose gardens of Shiraz and of the silent patios of Arabian palaces, torn out of the heart of a great lover by a cruel and incurable loss. The mosques of the Moguls and their tombs may be pure and austere, their *divans*, or audience halls, may be of impeccable beauty, but the Taj Mahal is a revelation. It is thoroughly un-Indian. It is more like a plant that could thrive and flower in the rich Indian earth as it could nowhere else. It is Eros in its purest form; there is nothing mysterious, nothing symbolic about it. It is the sublime expression of human love for a human being.[13]

Without question, Jung was deeply moved.

As he was in quite a different way, more as a curiosity, by the equally gigantic dimensions of the Sūrya-temple at Konarak in the eastern state of Orissa, not far from the sea in the Bay of Bengal. The thirteenth-century structure was patterned after the chariot of the sun. What created a sensation—for the Western observer—were the representations, some small, some larger than life, of erotic lovemaking, an expression of fruitfulness and above all of the union of the human being with God. Jung spoke of the "exquisitely obscene sculptures," which were explained to him by the pandit who accompanied him. What was the real meaning of these Kamasutras hewn in stone in every barely conceivable position of amorous union, which were also to be found in other parts of India? Jung talked with his guide for a long time about these remarkable figures, which he said were meant to evoke spiritualization in the visitor to the temple:

> I objected—pointing to a group of young peasants who were standing open-mouthed before the monument, admiring these splendors—that such young men were scarcely undergoing spiritualization at the moment, but were much more likely having their heads filled with sexual fantasies. Whereupon he replied, "But that is just the point. How can they ever become spiritualized if they do not first fulfill their karma? These admittedly obscene images are here for the very purpose of recalling to the people their dharma [law]; otherwise these unconscious fellows might forget it."[14]

Quite a remarkable interpretation, indeed. "At last I have heard something real about India for a change!" remarked Heinrich Zimmer, when Jung told him of the event after his return.

Finally, among the unforgettable impressions were those of the stupas of Sanchi, which bore the imprint of Buddhist spirituality. "They gripped me with an unexpected power," Jung admitted, after he had climbed up to the temple precinct one brisk morning. The extraordinary clarity of the air set off every detail of the hemispherical structure, with its circular paths which one followed clockwise, in the direction of the sun. The stupas lay on a rocky hill, with a pleasant path over large stone slabs leading to the top through a green meadow. "The stupas are tombs or containers of relics, hemispherical in shape, like two gigantic rice bowls placed one on top of the other (concavity upon concavity), according to the prescripts of the Buddha himself in the *Mahā-Parinibbāna-Sutta*."[15] Hence to walk meditatively around the circular structure, the representation of totality, was to take part oneself in the process of becoming whole, of becoming oneself. Here Jung grasped the basis for an understanding of the Buddha, who embodied the reality of the Self for Eastern people as did Christ for those in the West—to the extent that such a sweeping, stereotyped comparison is possible. But whereas Buddha stood before people as the world conqueror, showing the Eightfold Path to a spiritual transformation that was meant to lead to overcoming the world within oneself, in Christ the dominant factor was the vicarious sacrifice. Suffering was judged to be a positive thing by one, a negative by the other.

> . . .Christ is an examplar who dwells in every Christian as his integral personality. But historical trends led to the *imitatio Christi*, whereby the individual does not pursue his own destined road to wholeness, but attempts to imitate the way taken by Christ. Similarly in the East, historical trends led to a devout imitation of the Buddha. That Buddha should have become a model to be imitated was in itself a weakening of his idea, just as the *imitatio Christi* was a forerunner of the fateful stasis in the evolution of the Christian idea.[16]

Certainly a notion that called for further elucidation!

The abundance and the vehemence of the manifold impressions stretching over so many weeks left traces with Jung that extended to somatic symptoms. Thus he was able to consider it almost a bit of good fortune that he was taken seriously ill for a short time, when for the space of about ten days he was forced to check into a hospital with dysentery. Could this have been the physical expression of overindulgence in the many indigestible things that India has to offer the European? Thus the stay in the clinic actually afforded a few days of reflection.

Hardly was the patient sufficiently restored to his usual robust constitution to continue the journey and bring it to a close, when he was caught unawares by a great dream, great particularly in view of its subject and the existential force of what it had to say. The dreamer saw himself, completely removed from India, transported to an island, which seemed to lie near the coast of southern England. First there appeared before him a castle with a flight of broad stone stairs leading up to a columned hall dimly illuminated by the glow of candles. This, he knew, was the castle of the Grail, where the Grail was celebrated. Next Jung found himself at the shoreline in an unpopulated and desolate area. And as neither footbridge nor boat was anywhere to be seen, it became clear to him that he would have to swim across the strait alone and fetch the Grail. Then he awoke. Understandably, he was greatly taken aback. Here in the midst of India was a dream that recalled a part of the central core of Christian and Occidental esoterism, without a trace of any connection to Eastern spirituality, whether Hindu, Buddhist, or Islamic. All the more startled was Jung as he could not help thinking of the correspondences between the poetic Grail myth and the tenets of alchemy, for there too there were the *unum vas* ("one vessel"), the *una medicina*, and the *unus lapis*. All at once the past had come to life, for alchemy, of course, had long been no mere museum piece or research object for Jung, but something that concerned himself and his own self-development:

> Imperiously, the dream wiped away all the intense impressions of India and swept me back to the too-long-neglected concerns of the Occident, which had formerly been expressed in the quest for the Holy Grail as well as in the search for the philosophers' stone. I was taken out of the world of India, and reminded that India was not my task,

> but only a part of the way—admittedly a significant one—which should carry me closer to my goal. It was as though the dream were asking me, "What are you doing in India? Rather seek for yourself and your fellows the healing vessel, the *salvator mundi*, which you urgently need. For your state is perilous; you are all in imminent danger of destroying all that centuries have built up."[17]

This, then, expressed Jung's evaluation of his trip to India, directly from the unconscious as well as its interpretation.

Once again Jung put to sea by passenger liner, another thousand kilometers and more southward to Ceylon; from the port city of Colombo to the ancient capital of Kandy in the interior, where the extraordinary relic of the holy tooth of Buddha was venerated. Again there were unforgettable ceremonies, this time devoted exclusively to the "Enlightened One," the dominant force in the life of most Ceylonese. What Jung had consciously avoided, however, even while still on the Indian mainland, was a meeting with one of the many Indian gurus or spiritual masters who had traveled the path of enlightenment or self-realization and now taught this path to their innumerable pupils. Thus Heinrich Zimmer's first question on Jung's return was whether he had ever sought out Ramana Maharshi of Tiruvannamalai, a wish that never came to pass for the prematurely deceased Indologist. Jung had to admit that the possibility of such a meeting had indeed presented itself in Madras. "Probably I ought to have visited Sri Ramana after all," Jung said after Zimmer's death, in his Foreword to the latter's book on the great Hindu (*Der Weg zum Selbst*).[18] But at the same time he added the defense that even the spiritual Maharishi was not so unique; Jung had actually seen him everywhere in India, the "true Son of Man of the land of India." He even conceded that figures such as the earlier Ramakrishna or the saint of Tiruvannamalai, who was then becoming known, could be compared with the prophets of ancient Israel, whose role in relation to their people was a compensatory one, inasmuch as they too had wished to show their "unfaithful" people the way to the true sources of spiritual life. But at bottom, Jung said to himself, the truth of these initiates of the East is not a truth for all the world. He himself must be satisfied with his own truth.

> I would have felt it as a theft had I attempted to learn from the holy men and to accept their truth for myself. [Their wisdom belongs to them, and what belongs to me is only that which comes from within myself.] Neither in Europe can I make any borrowings from the East, but must shape my life out of myself—out of what my inner being tells me, or what nature brings to me.[19]

An unmistakable hint for, or rather against, those who wished to make Jung into a trailblazer of Eastern spirituality in the West!

All in all, India did not pass him over without a trace. Jung also said unmistakably, "What India Can Teach Us." His prescription from the year 1939 was: One should wrap oneself in the mantle of one's moral superiority and stand before the Black Pagoda of Konarak, covered with its erotic obscenities, and then one should analyze with care and utmost honesty one's own reactions, feelings, and thoughts.

> It will take you quite a while, but in the end, if you have done good work, you will have learned something about yourself, and about the white man in general, which you have probably never heard from any one else. I think, if you can afford it, a trip to India is on the whole most edifying and, from a psychological point of view, most advisable, although it may give you considerable headaches.[20]

Indeed, quite a remarkable piece of advice, after a remarkable journey to India! Thus it will be necessary for us to return, in a later chapter, to Jung's assessment of Western thought and Eastern spirituality.

18

Again and Again, the Religious Question

The basis of analytical psychology's significance for the psychology of religion, including its practical therapeutic application, lies in C. G. Jung's discovery of how archetypal images, events, and experiences, individually and in groups, are the essential determinants of the religious life in history and in the present.

The birth of the divine child, the life of the God-man who acts as a savior, his death and return to life, his historical connection and mystical factuality as an individual—behind all these there clearly lies an ordering, sense-making, numinous factor which Jung termed the (invisible) "archetype." It becomes perceptible in a specific archetypal image, for example in the Christ of history and belief, in the path of his followers, and so on. Wherever people are gripped by the image and the content of an archetype that they believe in, symbolizing and demonstrating their belief in ritual or sacramental performances, there the archetype is virulent; it is alive and active, providing sense, offering comfort, inspiring hope and confidence. Anyone with an inner interest in what is done has a share in the religious experience. Psychologically speaking, a process of self-becoming unfolds. Clearly a need for this kind of experience is innate in the human soul, even if from time to time it is expressed in forms that differ from those of any particular denomination.

To the extent to which Jung gained insight into the nature of archetypal reality, it was also possible for him, from his psychological point of view, to make corresponding assertions concerning the nature of psychology and religion. And this was so long before the composition of the text of his book *Psychology and Religion*, that is before 1937 or 1940. For instance, with regard to the religious claims of the human soul Jung said in a paper from the year 1929:

> The psychologist of today has at last had to realize that it has long since been a matter not of dogmas and creeds, but rather of a religious attitude, a psychic function whose importance can hardly be imagined. And for the religious function especially, historical continuity is indispensable.[1]

Hence as a doctor Jung took the religious problems mentioned by patients seriously, as the real problems in their situations. Practical experience likewise led him to the conclusion that the general decline of the religious life in modern people must have considerably increased the number of neurotic complaints. The loss of living piety, quite apart from external membership in a religious organization, consequently led to a disorientation in world view and a loss of spiritual equilibrium. Before a conference of Alsatian ministers in Strassburg in May 1932, he announced:

> Of all my patients past middle life, that is, past thirty-five, there is not one whose ultimate problem is not one of religious attitude. Indeed, in the end every one suffered from having lost that which living religions of every age have given to their believers, and none is really cured who has not regained his religious attitude, which naturally has nothing to do with creeds or belonging to a church.[2]

Thus Jung always used the terms religion and psychotherapy in a comprehensive sense. "God is a primal experience of the human being."[3] Through the desire for knowledge and through "preaching" that mistakes "the words for the Word," as Karl Barth put it, this primal experience is lost, and replaced by the sense that "God is dead." In a paper from 1935 on the fundamentals of psychotherapy, Jung commented:

> Not only Christianity with its salvation symbolism, but all religions, down to the forms of magical religion of primitives, are psychotherapies, which treat and heal the sufferings of the soul, and those of the body that come from the soul.[4]

As we have seen, it was not these observations alone that formed the basis of the physician's insights, but above all his own experiences, which can be traced back to Jung's childhood, not so much because of his having grown up in a Calvinist parsonage, but rather despite the fact that he was a parson's son—precisely because he could not help but see in his own parents how ineffectual the traditional "devoutness" had become. Thus Jung's first religious experiences for the most past lay outside the realm of the church, in that of the elementary and immediate: "The farther away I was from church, the better I felt,"[5] noted this parson's son! Though Jung was not, nor wished to be, either a mystic in the traditional sense of the word nor a religious reformer, he did undoubtedly have a tendency toward the *homo religiosus*. If in Jung's case the connection between psychology and religion was regarded in a clearly positive light, this had nothing to do with current theology, particularly since the majority of theologists, especially the Protestants, failed in principle to understand the psychologists they spoke with as a consequence of their own religious isolation. To this lack of understanding, at any rate, we owe a number of detailed letters Jung wrote, especially late in his life, on this central theme of his life. With Goethe's *Faust*, which along with the Gospel of John he had learned to value early on, Jung realized that in the end it was not the critically explainable "parchment" of the "holy sources" that offered refreshment to the spiritual seeker, but that the ineffable divine word was to be found in the underlying springs of one's own soul. Here, of course, the doctor from Küsnacht was in agreement with all supporters of mystical experience! Hence no one who wishes to inquire into Jung's relationship to religion can limit his study to those of his books whose titles have to do with religion; besides, the profit from this would be relatively meager. Including *Psychological Types*, there is hardly a work from the second half of Jung's life in which the religious function does not play an important part.

Like so many of the years before it, 1937 was tightly crammed with work. Much time was taken up with the preparations for the Eranos conference in August. This time Jung was to lecture on the visions of the early alchemist Zosimos, one of the preliminary exercises for his treatment of the subject which later appeared in print. Then of course the invitation to India was on the agenda for the end of the year. Between these came a commitment to present the three honorary Terry Lectures at Yale University in New Haven, which were devoted to the great subject of religion. For the first time Emma Jung accompanied her husband—the children had become self-sufficient in the meantime—to the States. There the Jungian school was rapidly growing, and so Jung could not refuse his friends in the U.S.A. an additional seminar on the same topic. It was to be Jung's last visit to America. Through Barbara Hannah we know that Jung took this internal seminar as an opportunity to discuss the theme of religion as reflected in the times. "All-out peace" still prevailed; no one suspected that the Second World War would break out a short two years later. In her memoirs, Barbara Hannah wrote of one of the last evening events in New York:

"As I have often heard him remark on other occasions, he spoke that night of what difficult days we live in, for the archetypal images of the collective unconscious are no longer content to flow into the prevailing religion. They have come loose from their moorings, so to speak, and are troubling modern man with the restless state of the energy which has been contained in the Christian religion for the last two thousand years. Some of this energy has gone into science, it is true, but that is too narrow and rational to satisfy anything like all of the floating archetypal images. This is the reason for our many isms today, and it confronts the modern free individual with the task of coming to terms with them in his own life. . . .

"Then Jung said to his audience—and this is what struck so many of them as last words—that we could only follow Christ's example and live our lives as fully as possible, even if it is based on a mistake. . . . No one has ever found the whole truth; but if we will only live with the same integrity and devotion as Christ, he hoped we would all, like Christ, win through to a resurrected body."[6]

Surely an unusual word, and legacy, to come from a psychologist, who as a scientist took great care as a rule to keep investigation on a strictly empirical footing and to abstain in principle from any philosophical or theological and metaphysical assertions! But it must be understood that these words belonged to those candid and even confessional utterances which Jung made in the closed company of friends or in private letters. On the other hand, critics, especially those in church and denominational circles, occasionally felt called upon to object that Jung's statements on religious matters were all too noncommittal, even ambiguous. Hence his affirmation "I am an empiricist, and as such I adhere to the phenomenological standpoint" stands at the very opening of his Terry Lectures on "Psychology and Religion." Because their author saw in religion one of the earliest and most universal expressions of the human soul, these talks took it for granted that any kind of psychology that dealt with the psychological structure of the human personality would take religion seriously, and not only as a sociological or historical fact, but as an "important personal concern for a great many people."[7]

Jung's own understanding largely coincided with that of Rudolf Otto,[8] according to which religion is a careful and conscientious consideration of what Otto called the "numinous," an experience that bestows on the human being a feeling of dependence on and coming face to face with a "wholly other," something superhuman that is precisely the divine. This *mysterium tremendum* is perceived on the one hand as the epitome of awe-inspiring fear, but on the other also as the *fascinans*, the attracting, rapturous, blissful thing through which the human being is lifted above the everyday ego. Against this background Jung formulated his own paraphrase, one that did not so much give clear definitions as encourage individual verification and practical experience:

> Religion seems to me to be a distinctive attitude of the human spirit, which one could formulate, in keeping with the original use of the concept of *religio*, as an attentive consideration and observation of certain dynamic factors that are interpreted as "powers": spirits, demons, gods, laws, ideas, ideals—whatever man has called such factors in his world as he has found powerful, dangerous, or helpful enough to be accorded careful consideration, or great, beautiful, and meaningful enough to be prayed to devoutly and loved.[9]

The present, Jung wrote in this context, was "a time of the death of God and the disappearance of God."[10] Not only in Protestantism, but quite generally since the beginning of the Reformation, the age that was closely linked to the unfolding of scientific thought and a consciousness oriented to the individual ego, traditional spirituality, with its wealth of images and signs, of symbols and mysteries, had been lost. The enlightenment of individual consciousness and the awakening of the autonomous human ego since the Renaissance had thus carried a high price. Three Protestants—Jean Paul ("Speech of the Dead Christ from the Cosmic Spheres That There Is No God"), Hegel, and above all Nietzsche—had dreamed, reasoned, and proclaimed the death of God as an imminent event. Modern man looked proudly back upon the cloud of superstition, of medieval and primitive gullibility, entirely forgetting that it was this spiritual past of his with its primitive images that supported his proud rational consciousness. But without its anchor in the deep layers of the psyche, Jung argued, the human spirit hangs in midair. Hence the great nervousness, the insecurity and growing disorientation regarding the basic questions of human existence today and tomorrow. The true story of the spirit, then, was not really preserved in learned books, nor guaranteed by the measurement-data of science, but in and through the "living spiritual organism of every individual."

Jung had already referred emphatically, some years before the Terry Lectures, to the underlying facts which are empirically demonstrated to the psychologist in the dream productions of the unconscious, for example when he spoke "On the Archetypes of the Collective Unconscious" at the second Eranos conference in August 1934. Here he made plain what tremendous things the human intellect had accomplished, and how Western man, European and American alike, had allowed his "spiritual house" to fall into ruin. Already here we find the hopeful-sounding comment that the death of God, the estrangement from spiritual and religious tradition, by no means necessarily represented a total loss. This was precisely the hour for depth psychology, the time for the psychology of the archetypes, according to which the emptying of the soul, felt by many contemporaries to be a sad loss of spiritual substance, turned out unexpectedly to be an unlooked for gain. The time of a world of the gods, or God, projected into an "upper" sphere was probably past; it could not—here we see an agreement with Rudolf Bultmann!—be somehow "repristinized"[11] or restored. But the human unconscious—not the individual, but rather the collective unconscious, filled with archetypally active powers—harbors an extremely multifarious spiritual life. Precisely this impoverishment in symbolism and inherited religious feeling was needed in order to make the fertile soil of primal religious experience bear fruit in new ways—a discovery, as Jung had to admit for his own time, that was for the time being still not entirely believable. But it gains in credibility to the extent that today original experience is being gained and the mental and spiritual world—Jung called it simply the world of the psyche—is being opened up anew in ever more individual ways. And now came a significant observation:

> Since the stars fell from heaven and our highest symbols faded, a secret life has held sway in the unconscious. That is why nowadays we have psychology, and why we speak of the unconscious. All this would be, and in fact is, entirely superfluous in a time and a culture that has symbols. For these are spirit from above, and when they are present the spirit, too, is above. For such people, therefore, it would be a foolish, senseless undertaking to experience or investigate an unconscious that contains nothing but the still, undisturbed powers of nature. But our unconscious holds turbulent water, that is spirit become part of nature, on account of which it has been stirred up. Heaven, to us, has become physical space, and the divine empyreum a fond remembrance of how it used to be. But "our hearts still burn," and a secret unease gnaws at the roots of our being.[12]

Because this is so, Jung arrived at the insight that the concern with the unconscious represents an inevitably vital question. The path which he adopted in analytical psychology and recommended as a therapeutic method was twofold: it consisted on the one hand in bringing the unconscious contents to consciousness, and on the other in striving toward a psychosynthesis. What was necessary was to take up the task of integration, to lift into consciousness the unconscious contents which had become recognizable through the epochal "fall of the stars." This was something qualitatively more than the mere "pious" acceptance of dogmatic maxims.

Seen in this light, depth psychology takes the place as the "correlate to the secularization of thought," as Ulrich Mann put it, that had once been held by practicing religion,[13] not because, as is sometimes assumed, psychology seeks to offer a substitute for religion, but because and insofar as a gigantic process of impoverishment and secularization was gaining ground, while at the same time the spiritually troubled psyche was beginning to make itself felt as we have discussed, making available extraordinary experiences.

> Of course I do not refer to the *beati possidentes* [those who are happily still in possession] of the faith, but to the many for whom the light has gone out, the mystery has vanished, and God has died. For most there is no going back, and indeed one does not really know for certain whether the way back is always the better one. Today, probably the only way to an understanding of religious matters is the psychological approach, and this is why I endeavor to melt down historically solidified ways of thinking again and recast them in the light of immediate experience.[14]

Jung's object, in fact, was nothing less than to build a spiritual bridge between traditional dogma and immediate experience. In both, the same factor—the archetype—was, or is, at work. Put differently:

> That psychological fact which possesses the greatest power in a person acts as a god, because it is always the overpowering psychic factor that is called "God." . . . The place of the godhead seems to have been taken by the totality of humanity.[15]

Statements like this are significant because they are to be neither accepted blindly nor conveniently thrown to the winds. They are worth thinking about and, in the true sense, "question-able." Beyond this, Jung left it to his readers to determine for themselves what consequences arose from his results, which experience shows is a difficult task. When *Psychology and Religion* appeared in book form, critical reaction, psychological and theological alike, ranged from reserved to perplexed. Even positively disposed readers, such as the Calvinist theologian Hans Schär, had to admit that the book was difficult if not impossible to understand on its own: "It is an important and informative publication for one who is versed in Jung's other writings. But those who do not meet this condition are bound to be rather perplexed in the face of Jung's assertions. The reviews of this book that were written at the time confirm this. . . . Many readers, after reading this work, seem to have been more irritated and uncertain than if they had really understood Jung's views."[16] Certainly not an ideal beginning for the reception of C. G. Jung's plans for the psychology of religion.

It cannot be denied, of course, that Jung demanded a great deal of his theological colleagues; for example, he took for granted in the average theologian much that patently did not exist in general, namely a comprehensive familiarity with religious and intellectual history, and above all an individual religious consciousness that went beyond the denominationally restricted "experience of faith." Hence Hans Schär points out the extent of the knowledge with which the theologian must be prepared in reading Jung. "In this regard his knowledge is unique, and among both theologians and other people there are very few who possess such an awareness of the religious life in all its forms as one finds in Jung. With him one never has the impression that his explanations of religion are brilliant flashbulbs by an author who busies himself with everything possible and thus religion along with it, but where an interesting presentation has had to substitute for thoroughness and soundness of the thoughts advanced. Even those who cannot declare themselves in agreement with all of Jung's opinions will have to recognize his credentials for the treatment of religion. . . ."[17] It only remains to be noted that this only tells something about a subset of the material which Jung drew upon.

In the meantime the evidence to which Jung gradually directed his readers' attention did at first seem irritating: part of it was the figure of totality, which was not yet fully expressed by the Trinity. Totality—so psychological research confirms—is only achieved where the Three are joined by the fourth principle, whether it be that of the feminine, or that of darkness or evil. The number four symbolizes the parts, qualities, and aspects of the One. In terms of God, the quaternity reveals "a more or less direct representation of God as manifested in his creation."[18] These audacious notions were first cautiously suggested in *Psychology and Religion* and in the Eranos lecture "A Psychological Approach to the Dogma of the Trinity," as well as other works (as also in the essay "Brother Klaus," 1933). Here and in later works, for example "Answer to Job," Jung's concern was to show that it was a matter not of idle speculation, but of how the archetype overpowers people, reaching deep into their religious experience and changing them from the ground up. And in fact the history of the church alone provides examples enough for this, be it Paul of Damascus or the fifteenth-century Swiss hermit Niklaus von der Flüe, in the presence of his vision of the terrible image of God, or the Silesian Protestant Jakob Böhme (1575–1624), who bore witness to the fire of divine wrath but was also the messenger of the divine maiden Sophia.

His communications did not flow from his pen unimpeded; rather what he said or wrote often called for long years of testing, meditation, and reflection. Then, of course, sometimes a certain moment, a particular situation, was needed to be able to give form to what had been ripening. Thus Aniela Jaffé recounted one shining August day in 1940: the war had been under way for a year, and this time a particularly small crowd had gathered for the eight days of Eranos in Ascona-Moscia. Actually only one lecture was scheduled, by the Basel mathematician Andreas Speiser on the Platonic doctrine of the unknown god and the Christian Trinity. It was not desired to cancel the event altogether, and hence there was only this token short form among a small cadre. But of course matters did not stop with this one lecture. Aniela Jaffé recalled: "In the afternoon C. G. Jung, who was among the guests, withdrew to the shady garden on the shore of the lake. Taking a Bible from the library, he sat reading and making notes. The next day he surprised the crowd of anxious listeners with a reply to his Basel colleague's arguments, which he supplemented *ex tempore* on the subject of 'The Psychology of the Trinity.'[19] In his characteristically cautious and occasionally hesitant way, he formulated thoughts that he had carried about with him for years but to which he had not yet given final shape. Jung's improvisations, recorded in shorthand, later turned out to be practically ready for publication; only voluminous extensions were later added. . . . Jung's improvisation on the psychology of the Trinity brought the conference in Moscia to a close. There followed another earnest and heated conversation on the terrace of Casa Eranos, with its distant view over the lake and mountains. Jung was relaxed and—a rarity, especially in those years of the catastrophe—pleased with what he had done." It was the satisfaction of one who had found his *kairos*, the indispensably inspired time for his creative work and his say. And partly in explanation, partly in apology, Jung added the comment: "I can only formulate my thoughts as they escape from me, like a geyser. Those who come after me will have to put them in order!"[20]

What burst forth from him with elemental power, like an eruption, did indeed require a special interpretation. Jung himself never tired of contributing to this, for his own part, and since the forties this had been variously reflected in his letters. Above all in the correspondence with Christian theologians which he carried on with great patience, Jung sought to clarify the theme of his life's work, that of the primal experience of wholeness, whether by clarifying matters of cognitive theory or by establishing existential and confessional points, for example to H. Irminger in Zürich, to whom he devoted a lengthy epistle in late 1944, saying:

> I practice science, not apologetics and not philosophy, and I have neither the competence nor the desire to found a religion. My interest is a scientific one. . . . I proceed from a positive Christianity that is as much Catholic as Protestant, and my concern is to point out in a scientifically responsible way those empirically tangible facts which would at least make plausible the legitimacy of Christian and especially Catholic dogma.

Then an observation for his critics: "One ought to read and consider authors who take as positive a stance toward Christianity as I do somewhat more carefully, before wishing to convert them to what has already been a matter of the greatest concern to them."[21] In the same letter, not without some bitterness, he asks, at the age of sixty-nine, "Why do people not read my books conscientiously? Why do they skip over the facts?"

And Jung's attitude toward and interpretation of religious reality demanded to be understood on yet a deeper level, not only that of the investigative ascertainment or scientific presentation of his reconnaissance in depth psychology and intellectual history. Such intimate expressions of C. G. Jung the person, the *homo religiosus*, were naturally found in letters addressed to people of a similar turn of mind. Erich Neumann, his Jewish colleague in Tel Aviv, was one of these few; hence with him he could be brief, without running the risk of being misinterpreted by his self-reliant pupil and friend:

> I am not pushing any philosophy of religion, rather I am seized, almost struck down, and am defending myself as best I can. . . . [My living emotion] is local, barbaric, infantile, and abysmally unscientific. . . .[22]

This passage from a letter of 5 January 1952 is a far-reaching one, and yet it belongs at the center of the same theme that dominates Jung's later work, which remains to be discussed separately. First, however, we must examine the events that fundamentally altered the face of Europe, and also did not pass C. G. Jung by without a trace—the outbreak of National Socialism in Germany, and the Second World War and its devastating consequences.

19

National Socialism: "Yes, I Slipped Up"

When the International Psychoanalytic Association gathered for its twelfth congress in Wiesbaden in 1932, its president, Max Eitingon, had pointed out that "in Germany, under the influence of the ever-deepening financial and social crisis, interest in psychological problems has been overshadowed by economic and sociological ones," adding: "which is understandable, but which hopefully will pass quickly."[1] The political development that would be taken by the Weimar Republic, backed by fewer and fewer Germans, was at the time the last thing that could have been foreseen. In the July elections of 1932 the National Socialists had captured a 37 percent share of the vote, which meant 230 seats in the Reichstag. And although the November elections of that year produced a decline in their number of votes, the Nazis still made up a third of the delegates. The full implications for the psychotherapeutic movement in Germany (and later in Austria) of Hitler's seizure of power on 30 January 1933, and the pronouncement of the dictator's "empowerment" through a law to that effect in the German parliament on 24 March, were not widely recognized. This is the more astonishing as the majority of analysts, whether they followed Freud or Adler, were Jewish, and what Hitler had in mind for the Jews he had bruited about in speeches and in writing for a full decade. That no "Jewish science" or any other discipline would be allowed to survive must have been well known. But analysts too—Jewish and non-Jewish alike—shared the hope of others of their contemporaries, for example with the words Freud wrote in passing in July 1933: "Maybe it will not turn out too badly."[2]

In any case, the marks of the "national upheaval" are known to all. A few particulars will serve to refresh the memory. The beacon of the Reichstag fire on 27 February 1933 was followed in March by the setting up of the first concentration camps for the isolation of "undesirable members of the community." On 1 April, with the installation of national governors in the states, began the so-called "coordination" according to the brown-shirt ideology and its principle of authoritarian leadership. No longer were Jews allowed to hold public posts. On 10 April, in front of the opera in Berlin and in many other German cities, the funeral pyres of the book-burnings blazed up. With the words "against the soul-destroying overestimation of the sexual life and for the nobility of the human soul," "the writings of a certain Sigmund Freud" were consigned to the flames. Freud's commentary and his poor consolation were: "At least I am burning in the best of company."

By reason of his typological nature—introversion—and of his wide-ranging scientific interests and his exacting medical duties as a psychotherapist, Jung's personality was anything but inclined to political activity. Once he even referred to himself self-mockingly (in 1934!) as a "Swiss Philistine residing at 228 Seestrasse, Küsnacht, Zürich." Of course this self-accusation should be taken with a grain of salt, for one thing because it was addressed to James Kirsch, a close Jewish friend and student, and for another because Jung had always regarded himself as a European, following with a wary eye the events of the day, whose psychological background he analyzed no less attentively, and left no room for doubt as to his Swiss-tinged, fundamentally democratic stance. Marie-Louise von Franz commented on this fact on the strength of her many years of close collaboration with her teacher:

"His passionate commitment was to the *droits de l'homme*, the fundamental rights of man and the greatest possible freedom of the individual, which are guaranteed on one hand by the federal state, and on the other even more by the maturity, wisdom, and conscientiousness of the individual members of a community. The individual, in this sense, is even more important than the system. Naturally he repudiated any sort of dictatorship or tyranny; he did not believe in forcible 'improvements' in a system as long as the individual had not changed himself."[3]

As characteristic of Jung's way of understanding the phenomena and tendencies of his time from the perspective of depth psychology, we may take for example his remarks on "The Development of Personality," which he had first presented in Vienna in November 1932—only a few weeks before Hitler seized power—under the title "The Voice from Within." From Jung's title one would hardly have suspected that the discussion was aimed at a symptomatology of current events. Whereas Freud had once sought to trace people's faith in authority to a primitive herd-mentality,[4] and Wilhelm Reich was the first to derive National Socialism from a specific attitude of the sexually repressed petite bourgeoisie,[5] Jung took a different tack in his Vienna lecture. He looked at the opposition between the individual maturing toward its personality, which follows an inner voice of its own destiny, and the mass or social group, guided by convention. Whereas every individual attains a particular degree of consciousness, the mass persists by nature in a dull, thoroughly unconscious we-instinct. At the same time it tends to back the "personality" or "strong man," yet it is blind to whether he is a true leader toward the self-fulfillment of the individual and the community, or a dangerous misleader. For

> that is the great and redeeming thing about every genuine personality, that it voluntarily decides to sacrifice itself to its destiny, consciously translating into its own individual

> reality that which, if lived unconsciously by the group, would only lead to ruin.[6]

Historically speaking, the person and life of Jesus represented for Jung a paradigmatic example of such genuine leadership, for Jesus embodied the "prototype of the uniquely meaningful life" in contrast to the power-mad delusions of a Caesar, the religion of love in contradistinction to the Roman power-devilry. Jung placed the events in central Europe in November 1932 into this same context. While the general consciousness was taken up solely with problems of everyday politics, such as domestic peace and high unemployment, Jung was already speaking of "gigantic catastrophes that threaten us," catastrophes that were not primarily of a physical or biological nature, but rather to be traced back to psychic facts and processes. As early as 1932, fourteen years after the end of the First World War and seven years before the outbreak of the Second, Jung made a diagnosis:

> We are menaced to a terrifying degree by wars and revolutions that are nothing other than psychic epidemics. At any time several million people can be stricken with madness, and then we have another world war or a devastating revolution. Rather than wild animals, falling rocks, and flooding waters, man is now exposed to the elemental powers of his own soul. The psyche holds a great power, one that surpasses by many times all the forces of the earth.[7]

The words of a clairvoyant?

These warnings of Jung's, bordering on the prophetic, were by no means anything new. Even before he was able to give clearer contours to his psychology of the archetypes, at the end of World War I in 1918 he had already referred to the latent peril that could come from the psyche of the "Germanic barbarian." Christianity, he said, had split this barbarian, as it were, into a light upper half and a repression-filled lower, darker one. Only the light side had been domesticated and civilized, and against it traces of the heathen Germanic prehistory rumbled in the collective unconscious of central Europeans. And this was no laughing matter, for:

> The more the absolute authority of the Christian worldview is lost, the more perceptibly the "blond beast" will turn over in its subterranean prison and threaten us with the outbreak of devastating consequences. This takes place as a psychological revolution in the individual just as it can also appear as a social phenomenon.[8]

Even Jung's early experiences in America are reflected here, for there he had seen how the earth exercises an influence on the human psyche that must not be underestimated. Hence every piece of ground holds its own secret, and this in itself was sufficient, he said, to account for the difference of the Jewish people, for example, who had in the course of their very much longer history assimilated far more culture, and so been "domesticized" to a greater degree, but at the same time had lost some of their contact with the earth. It goes without saying that no value judgment was intended by this observation, least of all one that could have anything to do with the National Socialist racial doctrine; it was not the faceless collective but the individual, on the road to self-development in and for the community, that was Jung's chief concern. Hence his statements on the time and the situation of people troubled by the problems of the day were meant to be understood as exhortations to foresight and wake-up calls to increased consciousness. The fact that they were barely heard, much less understood or followed, is another matter. In any case they were by no means the accidental productions of an unsuspecting "Philistine." On the basis of these examples it is not hard to detect a definite continuity and a repeated insistence in Jung.

As a further indication of this, hardly had enraptured crowds in Germany begun pledging their allegiance to the Führer when in February 1933 Jung spoke in Cologne and Essen on "The Meaning of Psychology for Modern Man," scrutinizing the "overwhelming magnetism" which no one seemed able to avoid, for one person was being swept along by the next among the greater part of the German people, right up to the realm of the church. Jung argued that the tendency to individualism that had gained ground since the time of the Reformation was being answered by a "compensatory reaction toward the collective man," which dominated and held sway over the masses. And then in clear text, for those few who allowed themselves to be sensitized to the signs of the times:

> The collective man threatens to suffocate the individual, on whose responsibility all the work of man ultimately rests. The mass as such is always anonymous and unaccountable, and so-called Führers are the inevitable symptoms of a mass movement. The true leaders of humanity are always those who look after themselves, relieving the heavy burden of the masses of their own weight at least, by consciously keeping aloof from the masses' blind subjection to the laws of nature.[9]

Hence if one wishes to understand Jung's attitude toward the events in Germany of 1933 and after, one must bear in mind the factors that played a decisive role in it.

At that time Jung, according to many, was the only student of Sigmund Freud who had turned his back on psychoanalysis—"a bright but somewhat ungrateful offspring," as Thomas Mann saw fit to label him on the occasion of Freud's eightieth birthday in 1936.[10] It is not entirely incomprehensible why possible anti-Semitic motives were imputed to him, partly in the open and partly veiled, when one considers that this same supposed apostate along with his colleagues in Zürich had once had to serve as an alibi for psychoanalysis' not being bound to the Judaism of its first spokesman. With the rift between Freud and Jung, which was demonstrably due to other causes, Freud's original hopes were shattered. Yet the share of Jewish colleagues and friends of C. G. Jung remained remarkably large, as ever, in terms of both quantity and quality. Jung's most independent and most productive student was

Erich Neumann, a Jew who emigrated to Israel and met an early death, and who furthermore had delivered a study on the unconscious Jewish roots of psychoanalysis.[11] Aniela Jaffé, who took down Jung's *Memories* and who together with Gerhard Adler undertook the German and English edition of his letters, was likewise of Jewish extraction, and the same was true of a number of other colleagues. Independently of this there were, as always, considerable tensions between psychoanalysts and adherents of Jung's analytical psychology, whether occasioned by practical matters or by personal animosities. The young discipline, divided into schools, was a long way from being universally recognized, and the National Socialist program posed a serious danger to its continued existence in Europe, particularly since Germany and Austria contributed the largest numerical share of psychotherapists working in depth psychology. For this reason alone any professional agency was presented with a twofold task: for one thing it was a matter of developing an activity that would mediate between the divergent schools and orientations, and for another it was necessary to work hard for international cooperation, precisely because nationalistic tendencies demanded this kind of countermovement.

At this crucial moment this task fell specifically to Jung. Indeed he could not avoid it, because in March 1933 Ernst Kretschmer, at the time Professor of Psychiatry and Neurology at the University of Marburg and well known for his theory of physical constitution in *Physique and Character*, stepped down from the office of president of the General Medical Society for Psychotherapy, an association of which Jung had been vice-president since 1930. Asked by a number of his medical colleagues, for obvious reasons, to take over the presidency and the editorship of the *Zentralblatt für Psychotherapie und ihre Grenzgebiete*, which went with this post, Jung volunteered, "until further notice, that is until such time as the tangle of emerging problems should be definitively settled," to take over the chair. He named as his deputy his colleague and friend Gustav Richard Heyer.[12] Active in the

National Socialist camp was Dr. M. H. Göring, a psychiatrist from Wuppertal-Elberfeld and cousin of the Prussian prime minister and later Reichsmarshal. Jung took on the assignment at a time when the Society was in what amounted to an interim status, for the "revolutionary changes in Germany" demanded an uncompromising "coordination" in all areas of social and cultural life, and with it the introduction of the "Führer principle" based on the ideology of National Socialism. The so-called Aryan paragraph excluded Jewish, or rather non-Aryan, public officials and doctors in principle. Jung, as a Swiss, took advantage of his opportunity to lessen the effect of this compulsory standardization on the psychotherapeutic society by initiating the formation of an International Society and drafting its official constitution. In concrete terms this meant that it would be formed of national groups, for example German, Swiss, Dutch, and Danish, but only the German section, with M. H. Göring as its "Führer," could be subject to the requirements of coordination. For individuals who did not choose to be affiliated with any national section it was still possible to join the new International Society. In this way access to the common organization was still open to Jewish colleagues in particular, the Aryan paragraph and the coordination principle notwithstanding. In addition, in order to prevent any one nation's becoming predominant in the "supranational" society—in practical terms this could only apply to the "coordinated" German group—the statutes as devised by Jung stipulated that no national group would be able to hold more than 40 percent of the present votes. Moreover, Jung endeavored to strengthen the international basis of the new society and also to advertise the cause among his Swiss countrymen, whose political shortsightedness he bemoaned. To his Zürich colleague Alphonse Maeder in January 1934 Jung appeared to be thoroughly optimistic, believing that in this way he could be of help to the now-isolated German science.

That is precisely why I find it necessary for neutrals on the

> outside to provide it with the possibility of international connections through the foundation of a general organization. Germany is at present more cut off intellectually from other countries than during the war, and as a consequence is more in need of contact with the rest of the intellectual world than ever.[13]

In any event, the statutes of the International General Medical Society for Psychotherapy were ratified at its seventh congress in Bad Nauheim in May 1934. With this Jung also became *de jure* the president of this "supranational" association. Against the misunderstandings that are occasionally voiced even now, it must be emphasized that he had nothing to do with the coordinated German national group under Professor Göring. In a circular letter signed by Jung and dated 1 December 1934, the medical psychotherapists were informed that a "determination had been made that affiliation with a national group is purely optional, that is, it is possible to hold individual membership within the framework of the Supranational General Medical Society for Psychotherapy. The Supranational Society is politically and doctrinally neutral."[14]

This emphasis on "supranationality" speaks for itself, especially when one considers what it meant in practice against the background of National Socialist politics and pressure. That Jung consistently pursued this line through the unrest of the thirties—resigning the post of president only in 1939—can be verified in various ways. Thus for example he did not hesitate, in his book *The Reality of the Soul* (1934), to include a work by his Jewish colleague Hugo Rosenthal (*Typological Opposition in the History of the Jewish Religion*). A year later, in a comment published in the *Schweizerische Ärztezeitung*, he advocated "understanding among the various psychotherapeutic schools," setting forth as synoptic works, alongside those of W. M. Kranefeldt and the National Socialist party member G. R. Heyer, a study by his Jewish colleague Gerhard Adler in particular. In the same place Jung stressed his regard for the "European," transnational status of psychotherapy. It was high time, he said, for the individual psychotherapist to become aware also of his social responsibility.[15] And when, another year later, Jung greeted those who appeared for the ninth Congress for Psychotherapy in Copenhagen in October 1937, he accentuated how important it was to open up the widest possible horizons for this science.

> In view of this necessity, any overnarrow restriction to artificial boundaries of whatever kind, be they of national, political, linguistic, doctrinal, or philosophical nature, would be a catastrophe for our science. . . . The nations of Europe form a European family, which like every family has its own distinctive spirit. Far apart as our political aims may lie, they rest in the last analysis on a common European soul, of whose aspects and facets a practical psychology cannot afford to remain unaware.[16]

In any event, the internationality which Jung so vigorously advocated could not be reconciled with the dogma of the supposed Aryan superiority. The "supranational" society made possible precisely what the coordinated German national group strictly prohibited!

Although a practicable way seemed to have been discovered for the continued existence of medical psychotherapy, one that was also justified according to the rules of the international movement, it led to trouble. There were two developments in particular that made Jung the target of vehement assaults and reproaches shortly after his assuming the presidency, triggered by two items published in the *Zentralblatt*. One was more formal in nature and went back to the fact that Professor Göring, as leader of the German national section, had published in the December 1933 issue of the *Zentralblatt* a kind of manifesto urging the subordination of German psychotherapists to National Socialist principles. Jung had admittedly agreed to publish such an article—not, however, for printing in the *Zentralblatt*, but rather in a German supplement, for of course only the members of the "coordinated"

German group could be called upon to make such a "pledge of allegiance." As for the area of his own jurisdiction, anyway, Jung saw no reason to exclude Jewish colleagues from continued collaboration in the future. Thus, for example, even in late December 1933 he enlisted the Viennese physician Rudolf Allers to take on the editing of the review section. However, the publisher did find it advisable to turn over the general editorship of the new periodical "unconditionally" to a "coordinated" member of the profession. During several weeks in which the further course of events remained somewhat unclear to the parties concerned, including Jung,[17] the editor responsible, Dr. Walter Cimbal of Hamburg, neglected to keep Jung, as publisher, informed of what he was doing in good time, which is to say he acted on his own initiative. To his colleague in Copenhagen, the founder of the Danish national section Oluf Brüel, Jung defended the editor regarding "this irregularity," but at the same time (2 March 1934) he expressed his displeasure to Cimbal:

> As you will remember, I informed you of my express wish that the German volume should be signed by Professor Göring. As a foreigner, German domestic policy does not suit me. And with regard to the foreign subscriber to the *Zentralblatt*, it is a regrettable tactical error for platforms dealing purely with domestic politics, which one can if one must understand as necessities for Germans, to be shoved down the throat of the foreign reader who is critical as it is. . . . I would like to urge you most strongly to keep the *Zentralblatt*, which is intended for external circulation, in every respect nonpolitical.[18]

And once again Jung closed by stressing that he, as president of the supranational society, had to maintain a scientific attitude, "apart from any politics."

But the damage was already done. Jung spoke of the "smear campaign" that the *Zentralblatt* article had stirred up in Zürich. But the readers, especially those outside Germany, could not have been aware of the background of this oversight (or perhaps intentional exposure of Jung?). For another thing, Jung had also left himself open when it came to matters of content in the *Zentralblatt*. Thus he promised in his prefatory remarks in volume 3 (1933):

> . . .the differences between Germanic and Jewish psychology, which actually exist and which have long been known to sensible people . . . should no longer be glossed over. . . . I would like to state expressly that this is not meant to suggest any depreciation of Semitic psychology, any more than a depreciation of that of the Chinese is intended when speaking of the characteristic psychology of the people of the Far East.[19]

Harmless as this statement might be in itself, and especially when considered in the larger context of Jung's work and indeed of Freud's psychoanalysis, at *this* point in time and in view of the constellation of objective and personal factors, these words could fuel disastrous misunderstandings. So it came about that the Swiss psychoanalyst Gustav Bally made a scathing attack on Jung in the *Neue Zürcher Zeitung* of 27 February 1934. In his article entitled "Germanic Therapy" he said: "The well-known publisher of this coordinated periodical is Dr. C. G. Jung. . . . thus a Swiss edits the official organ of a society which, in the words of one of its leading members, Dr. M. H. Göring, 'expects of all its actively contributing members that they have thoroughly studied Adolf Hitler's fundamental book *Mein Kampf* in all scientific earnest and recognize it as a basis.'"[20] That this statement rests on a double misconception emerges only when one is aware of the circumstances we have described.

With this an avalanche was set in motion. Jung responded, also in the *Neue Zürcher Zeitung*, on 13 and 14 March, with an addendum on the fifteenth. He asked his opponent, who had been joined by others, to consider whether in this difficult predicament for psychotherapy he ought to have retreated "to the security on my own side of the border as a cautious neutral," or—as it actually turned out—stuck his neck out and exposed himself to the danger of misunderstanding.

> Was I supposed to sacrifice the interests of science, collegiality, and the friendship which binds me to several German doctors in the vital context of intellectual culture in the German language to my own egoistic well-being and my differing political convictions? I have seen too much of the agony of the German middle class, felt too much of the often unbounded misery of the life of a doctor in Germany at the present time, and I know too much of spiritual anguish to be able to withdraw from my clear duty as a man behind the shabby cloak of political pretense. So there was nothing left for me but to stand up for my friends with the weight of my reputation and my independent position.[21]

If the doctors in communist Russia had sought his help, he said, he would have defended them in the same way without hesitation, "for the sake of the human soul." Furthermore, we do not consider as a traitor to his country one who as a doctor, in time of war, proffers help to a wounded enemy, for:

> As doctors we are first of all human beings, who perform their service for their fellow men, if need be, despite all the impediments of a given political situation.[22]

At the same time Jung admitted to having been quite careless, so careless that as a psychologist he took care of the Jewish question by pointing out the "difference between Jewish and 'Aryan-Germanic-Christian-European' psychology." Naturally this referred not to psychology or psychotherapy as a scientific discipline, but to the fact that the practitioner of psychoanalysis or psychotherapy brings to the interaction between analyst and analysand, in his own person, a "subjective predisposition" that conditions any interpersonal relationship, particularly the psychotherapeutic process with its transference and countertransference. From this point of view, he said, one could not disregard the "psychic differences" that exist among all nations and races, even among Zürichers, Baslers, and Berners. Once again, that no kind of value judgment could be expressed by this was obvious in any case. Jung stressed this many times *expressis verbis*. Above all, he said, no psychology, including Jewish psychology, could claim to be universal, and the desire to establish and investigate this fact should not be subjected to accusations of anti-Semitism. Just such charges, however, have been raised against Jung time and again.

It would be interesting to know what Freud might have thought of the position Jung took during the days of the Third Reich, but apparently there is no evidence on this. As for Jung's thesis of the dissimilarities among psychologies, though, long before him Freud himself had stressed the emphatically Jewish character of his own ideas and of psychoanalysis, for example in a letter to Karl Abraham on 3 May 1908. Here he said: "Be tolerant, and do not forget that you actually have it easier than Jung in following my ideas, for in the first place you are totally independent, and then you come much closer to my intellectual constitution through being racially related, whereas he as a Christian and a pastor's son finds his way to me only against great resistances. This makes his association all the more valuable. I would almost have said that his appearance rescued psychoanalysis from the danger of becoming a Jewish-national matter."[23] According to Aniela Jaffé, Freud's words showed the "awareness and the attitude of a great Jewish man who understood the psychic circumstances and saw beyond the human limitations of the moment. For him, recognizing the Jewish character of psychoanalysis in no way represented a depreciation."[24] Thus we see how manifestly important it is to know by whom and when a thing is said or done.

Of course Jung lamented this "extremely unfortunate and confusing encounter" of the researches he had been carrying on for many years with the "Nazi storm," but as far as the question of the evaluation or devaluation of various psychologies was concerned, it must be said that Jung did after all allow himself to be carried away into statements which, if taken at face value, could and indeed were bound to be interpreted as serious discrimination. This was true, for example, of formulations found in his essay on "The State of Psychotherapy Today," also reprinted in the *Zentralblatt für Psychotherapie*.[25] Here Jung contrasted the Jews, members of a race whose culture was some three thousand years old, with the very much younger Aryan people, who as a result of this youthful immaturity were capable, he said, of creating new forms of culture that were as yet still slumbering in their unconscious. In this case Jung was speaking of the positive aspect of the same situation he had characterized negatively about a decade and a half before, as the dangerous potential of the "blond beast." If one consults the texts that emerged later (but likewise still in the thirties), such as the essay "Wotan" (1936), it becomes reasonable to think that Jung could not have helped being aware of the archetypal menace of what had come to pass in Germany since the rise of National Socialism. But at the time of his essay Jung managed to represent the unconscious of the "Jewish race as a whole" as less creative. His words then were:

> Apart from certain creative individuals, the average Jew is, I dare say, much too conscious and differentiated to labor with the tensions of an unborn future too. The Aryan unconscious has a greater potential than the Jewish; this is the advantage and the disadvantage of a youthfulness that is not yet fully estranged from barbarism.[26]

For this very reason, he said, it was a grave mistake of medical psychology up to that time that it had indiscriminately applied Jewish categories—which were not even binding upon all Jews—to the Christian Germanic and Slavic peoples. Anyone who was aware of Hitler's *Mein Kampf* and Alfred Rosenberg's *The Myth of the Twentieth Century*, as well as all kinds of neo-Germanic and "German faith" writings such as Wilhelm Hauer's *The German Vision of God*[27]—and not a few of Jung's adherents found themselves in Hauer's *Kommende Gemeinde*!—was bound to assume in Jung an effective empathizer of his cause, for in the same connection he spoke of the "precious secret of the Germanic people"; he pronounced an oracle on the "creatively ominous ground of their soul"; he apostrophized "the powerful phenomenon of National Socialism, on which the whole world gazes with astonished eyes. . . ." Of course the context shows that the author was referring to a view that extended beyond the personal unconscious, arising out of that which has been forgotten and repressed, to the supra-individual and collective unconscious, with its highly active archetypes. But time and circumstance, indeed even his choice of words, were bound to leave open the door to misunderstanding, especially because C. G. Jung, about to complete his sixtieth year, had long since achieved worldwide recognition as the "famed Swiss psychologist."

In 1932 the city of Zürich awarded him its prize for literature. In 1935 the Swiss Institute of Technology, where he had been teaching for two years, named him an honorary professor. In September 1936 Jung spoke on the occasion of the three hundredth anniversary of Harvard University in Cambridge, Massachusetts, where he received the degree of Doctor of Science *honoris causa*. Further honorary doctorates followed, including those from the universities of Calcutta, Benares, Allahabad, and Oxford in the year 1938. Tributes from Swiss academies came comparatively late. The University of Basel named him Professor of Medical Psychology on 15 October 1944, during the war. On 26 July 1945 he became an honorary doctor at Geneva University, and finally as an octogenarian the Swiss Institute of Technology conferred on him the honorary doctorate in science. In addition there were commitments now and again to international speaking engagements, such as the Tavistock Lectures "On the Foundations of Analytical Psychology" in London in 1935, or the honorable Terry Lectures at Yale University, which appeared in book form under the title *Psychology and Religion*, and Jung's substantial contribution to the genesis and formation of the likewise international and interdisciplinary Eranos conferences in Ascona on Lago Maggiore from 1933 on has already been thoroughly discussed. Renown, then, wherever one looks!

Certainly there was no question about the helpfulness of Jung's activity. He was neither a Nazi partisan nor anti-Semitic. This is shown even by his activities as president of the international society of medical psychotherapists. Beyond this, he aided many individual Jews by word and deed; thus Aniela Jaffé emphasized, as one of those affected: "However, the fact that Jung came out in public with this [his distinction between Jewish and non-Jewish psychology] at a time when being Jewish was a threat to one's life, and that he placed the psychological and racial distinctions on the scientific program of the International Society, has to be regarded as a serious mistake. Even if the most abysmal consequences of the hatred of Jews only became known later, any reference to the differentness of Jews was at that time fuel for further fanaticism. In this case the doctor's silence, which we rely on and so often impose upon him, would have been the order of the day." Such was Aniela Jaffé's judgment on her own doctor and teacher.[28]

It was not only in the professional press, as we have described, that Jung spoke out quite unnecessarily on the subject of National Socialism. When he held a seminar in Berlin between 26 June and 1 July, 1933, the Jungian Adolf Weizsäcker, a practicing psychologist, conducted an interview with him on Radio Berlin.[29] Weizsäcker succeeded in eliciting from (as he said) "the most progressive researcher in psychology today" all manner of statements that, from the very way in which the announcer presented them and in which the questions were phrased, were calculated to produce misconception. Thus Jung's "constructive psychology" was contrasted with the "demoralizing psychoanalysis," and Jung advised that at this moment in history the older generation should be wise enough to leave leadership to youth and resign themselves "to this natural course of events." Further, there was much talk of the hour of the "leader" and the "times of leadership," for "only in times of aimless quiescence" was "the aimless conversation of parliamentary deliberation" called for, and generally speaking "democracy or no democracy." It was, in a word, a thoroughly shameful business. Although the interviewee did point out the danger to those who are swept along by uprisings of this sort, because it is a characteristic of mass movements that they overpower the individual through mass suggestion and make him unconscious—as had been happening for more than twelve years—under the circumstances this warning was hardly likely to be understood as such or taken seriously.

When Jung began his Zarathustra seminars in Zürich in the spring of 1934, in the more intimate circle of his students, he was able to say much in clear words and with appropriate critical distance. Here he described the prevailing situation in National Socialist Germany as that prefigured in Nietzsche's *Thus Spake Zarathustra*: man lives in order to live or to die, no one knows what for; basically the Nazi party offered no real plan; its leaders did not know what they were risking; from the rational standpoint the Nazis' entire undertaking was pure madness—one could call it completely pathological, a divine or demonic madness; Nietzsche, in this light, had become a great prophet of what was now happening in Germany.[30]

What he had said in the inner circle of his students and friends in the form of a very exhaustive exegesis of Nietzsche's *Zarathustra*, Jung published, with similar emphasis, in the spring of 1936,[31] at a time when National Socialist Germany, with enormous propaganda, was sending out invitations to the Olympic Games in Berlin. In view of Hitler's brown and black storm troops (SA, SS, and so on), whose marching and drum-beating had long been impressed on the consciousness of their contemporaries, Jung characterized National Socialism, in his essay "Wotan," as the outbreak of an archetype. Wotan himself was "a god of storm and agitation, an unleasher of passion and lust for battle, as well as a sorcerer and master of illusion who is woven into all secrets of an occult nature."[32] This was a rude awakening for those who had believed up to now that they lived in a civilized country far removed from the Middle Ages. And this ancient Wotan, he said, with his abysmally deep but never exhausted character, revealed more of the essential nature of National Socialism than attempts at rational explanation did. Consequently Jung saw in the Wotan archetype an autonomous factor that produced collective influences, by seducing people who went along with the masses, and

> where it is not the individual but the mass that is moving, there people's self-regulation ceases and the archetypes begin to be effective, as also happens in the life of the individual when he finds himself faced with situations that can no longer be mastered with the categories he knows. But what a so-called Führer does vis-à-vis the restless mass, we can observe . . . with all the clarity one could ask for.[33]

And finally the oracular note again, according to which National Socialism might perhaps be far from the last word:

> . . .rather, things may be expected to come out of the background, in the coming years or decades, of which right now we can likely form only a poor conception. . . .[34]

These sentences were written three and a half years before the outbreak of World War II, only a few years before the installation of the brown-shirt extermination camps. But since what Jung understood by the term "archetype" was not a factor that could be confined within national boundaries, in the end it was also necessary to think of the destructive potential that a somehow or other misguided humanity had meanwhile amassed around itself, to its own self-destruction.

Aside from the "Wotan" essay, published in the *Schweizer Monatshefte*n, Jung had repeatedly made no secret of his attitude toward dictators, and especially the events in the Third Reich, to the international press as well. In October 1938 the well-known American journalist H. R. Knickerbocker called at Jung's home in Küsnacht, in order to conduct a detailed interview with him for the January 1939 edition of *Hearst's International-Cosmopolitan*. This happened in the same year that brought the annexation of Austria to Hitler's Germany in March. Furthermore, after the so-called Sudeten crisis and

Hitler's threat of war, the two interlocutors were still under the immediate impact of the ominous Munich accord of 29 September 1938. In the presence of Benito Mussolini, Hitler had had himself given the approval of France under Premier Edouard Daladier and Great Britain under Neville Chamberlain for his entry into the Sudetenland. At this moment when Hitler came to be validated by nations outside Germany as well, Jung depicted the brown dictator as a kind of medicine man or shaman. Quite a meaningless figure in himself, he nonetheless reflected the unconscious of the Germans. He gave voice (too) loudly to that which the German people unconsciously expected of him. The man from Braunau, Jung said, was not a political but actually a magical celebrity. This set in motion processes of unconscious projection between the collective unconscious of the people, which had been possessed by the impetuous god Wotan, and this person, irrelevant in himself, who had been highly stylized into a kind of German messiah.

On the question of Hitler's attitude toward women and marriage, Jung prophesied: "He cannot marry. . . . Hitler's real passion, of course, is Germany."[35] Then, with a shot of Jungian irony, he said that this was the only reason Hitler talked so loudly, even in private conversation, because he always spoke with seventy-eight million voices. Such a nation, together with its leader, was at bottom a monster; everyone should fear the terrible being, for "Big nations mean big catastrophes." The telephone rang, and Jung answered. Knickerbocker heard a patient crying that a hurricane was threatening to sweep him out of his bedroom. "Lie down on the floor and you will be safe," the doctor reassured him. And Knickerbocker commented, "It is the same advice the sage physician now gives to Europe and America, as the high wind of dictatorship rages at the foundations of Democracy."[36] Barely a year after this interview, the Second World War had begun.

We know what an impression Jung made on the American journalist from a comment by his English colleague Laurens van de Post: "He [Knickerbocker] had just returned from

Zürich, where he had interviewed Jung for his newspaper. He could talk of nothing else. Over and over he said that Jung was the only person who really knew what was going on in Europe, that none of the statesmen or politicians had any idea at all of what the growing volcanic rumbling on the European scene heralded. Only Jung knew it."[37] And Knickerbocker had been familiar with the phenomenon for at least fifteen years—he had been studying psychiatry in Munich when Hitler's Beerhall Putsch took place there in 1923.

After everything that may be assembled in the way of facts, impressions, and interpretations of Jung's attitude during the national Socialist period, the question of a conclusive assessment presents itself. How difficult, if not impossible, it is to give a valid answer is shown by the conflict of opinion among Jung's critics, which blazed anew after the catastrophe of the world war and the Holocaust of the Jews. Some tended to exonerate the "Swiss Philistine" entirely, as if a jointly responsible contemporary society condoned taking up a standpoint beyond good and evil. There is no denying that Jung indeed comes off relatively well when one compares his early diagnosis of National Socialism and its leader with the questionable verdicts or positions that appealed to a majority of his contemporaries in politics and culture, among them Christian theologians (even those from the confessional church), philosophers such as Martin Heidegger, who was "optimistic" in 1933, or such prominent Jews as Martin Buber, among many others.[38]

On the other hand Jung was cursed hatefully as a "pimp of power" (J. H. Herwig). Excess on one side or the other need not be discussed here. Nevertheless, if one applies Jung's psychological picture of man to the founder of analytical psychology himself, the factor of the personal "shadow" cannot be overlooked. According to Jung, the shadow personifies the dark side, generally unrecognized by the subject and so denied and projected onto others. It is one's own weakness of character, one's own inferiority and deficiency, that one sees in others. Hence Aniela Jaffé spoke in Jung's case—and probably with good reason—of a manifestation of his shadow. This archetype belongs, like the ego and the persona, whose role relationships are directed toward the outer world, to the totality of the human self, and for the sake of psychic wholeness it must never be denied. And where there is much light, there is also much shadow! Or, in Aniela Jaffé's words: "Jung gave too much to the world and to mankind for his shadow ever to jeopardize his spiritual significance and his greatness as a man."[39] As a coworker for many years— analysis with Jung in 1937, secretary of the C. G. Jung Institute in 1947, and Jung's personal secretary from 1955—Mrs. Jaffé attested to how clearly one became aware of this shadow in dealing with him in person, but also to the fact that one could accept this dark side.

On this point Jung's biographer refers to a letter she had received from the well-known Kabbalah scholar Gershom Scholem in Jerusalem, in which he gave an account of a conversation about C. G. Jung with Leo Baeck.[40] The Berlin rabbi, at the age of sixty-nine, had followed his congregation to the concentration camp at Theresienstadt and had been one of the few to survive. He knew Jung personally from the meetings at Count Keyserling's in his "School of Wisdom" in Darmstadt. Hence he had not thought him capable of any National Socialist or even anti-Semitic sentiment, and had been all the more dismayed by the publications of 1933 and 1934. Returning to Zürich shortly after the liberation, he quite intentionally did not seek Jung out, and declined an invitation to his home in Küsnacht. "Whereupon," Scholem wrote, "Jung went to see him [Baeck] at his hotel, and they had a confrontation, two hours long and at times thoroughly lively, in which Baeck threw up to him everything he had heard about him. Jung defended himself, with appeal to the special circumstances in Germany, but he also confessed to him: 'Yes, I slipped up,' when it came to his position on the Nazis and his expectation that perhaps this might have been the start of something great. This phrase, 'I slipped up,' which Baeck repeated to me several times, is vivid in my memory. Baeck said that in this conversation they had cleared up everything that stood between them and were reconciled with each other once again."[41]

The importance of a communication of this kind may be assessed by anyone who knows the great sensitivity of Jewish people and comprehends the sense of injury in the deepest part of their fate, especially when it is a statement that has come from the likes of a Leo Baeck and been vouched for by a Gershom Scholem. Taken by itself, the phrase "I slipped up" admittedly had seemed rather like an irritating minimization, and many took offense at it. But here again the essential thing is the context. In the same connection it is worth noting also that at the time of his conversation with Baeck, Scholem was faced with the question of whether, in view of Jung's dominant position there, he too should accept an invitation to participate in the international Eranos conferences. Thus Scholem's decision was a further indication that Jung's admission must have been far more than merely a casual, empty flourish. Hence Scholem closed his letter to Aniela Jaffé with the words: "On the basis of this explanation by Baeck, I also then accepted the invitation to Eranos, when it came a second time. . . ."[42]

The events of the Third Reich, in which Jung was so tensely entangled, should not make us forget that this involved only a portion of his life and activity. The decade of the thirties primarily represented for Jung a further important stage in his creative work. As much as the No. 1 of his personality was engaged with the issues of the day, the No. 2 devoted himself concentratedly and almost undisturbed to his own work—to research, to teaching, as lecturer and speaker both at home and abroad, as writer and author of numerous articles and essays as well as book reviews, and not least as psychotherapist in demand on all sides from his home in Küsnacht.

Between 1930 and 1934 he conducted his English seminars in the Psychological Club of Zürich. They bore the title "Interpretation of Visions" and consisted of lectures and question-and-answer sessions that were recorded and made available to students in typewritten form, totaling eleven volumes.[43] These were followed by the seminars on the "Psychological Analysis of Nietzsche's Zarathustra," which continued until 1939. This must have been the most exhaustive interpretation of this famous work to date, making up another eleven volumes of typewritten reports. In the framework of his series of *Psychological Essays* he brought out numerous essays and revised articles in the volume of collected papers *Seelenprobleme der Gegenwart* (1931) and *Wirklichkeit der Seele* (1934).[44] These were more of an introductory character, as was also true of the five lectures he held in 1935 before some two hundred English doctors at the "Institute of Medical Psychology" in London, the so-called Tavistock Lectures ("On the Foundations of Analytical Psychology"), named for the Tavistock Square Clinic founded in 1920. As E. A. Bennet remarked in his foreword to the first English edition: "His lectures attracted a representative group of psychiatrists and psychotherapists from all schools, as well as many doctors from neurological clinics and even a few general practitioners. . . . His finding that bodies and souls react as a unit made Jung the first clinician to recognize the importance of the physiological concomitants of emotion that are familiar to everyone today as psychosomatic phenomena."[45]

Also in the year 1935 came Jung's sixtieth birthday. An outward sign of how the Jungian school was taking shape was represented by the numerous contributions to the comprehensive testimonial volume compiled for the occasion by Toni Wolff, on behalf of the Psychological Club in Zürich, under the title *The Cultural Significance of Complex Psychology*.[46] The wording of this title alone reveals that Jung's work had gone beyond the more narrow bounds of medical psychotherapy and become a factor in interdisciplinary discussion. Among other places, this came to light in the context of the already mentioned annual Eranos conferences in Ascona, as well as a series of further international meetings and congresses. The Terry Lectures of 1938 should be mentioned again here, with the important study "Psychology and Religion." This opened the eleventh volume of the *Collected Works*, in which Jung's writings on Western and Eastern religion were brought together, including other texts from the thirties, some of which originated in collaboration with the Sinologist Richard Wilhelm or the Indologist Heinrich Zimmer. Jung's invitation to academic gatherings at Indian universities also came at this time.

But as university ceremony was basically distasteful to him, he was always happy to be invited to events in smaller groups, where he could speak without preconceived notions and generally "cut loose," unconstrained by protocol or strict conventions. Thus for example early in 1937 the Köngener League asked the Swiss psychologist to its annual conference at Königsfeld in the Black Forest. Jung's co-speaker was the theologian, then of Münster and later Bishop of Oldenburg, Wilhelm Stählin. Reading the accounts, which reflect the impression both men made on their audience from the realms of theology, pedagogy, and social work, it is obvious that many found the Swiss guest's "refreshing honesty" and his "wonderfully earthy matter-of-factness"—as organizer Rudi Daur put it—more appealing than the "much more strictly circumscribed accountability of expression" (in Alfons Paquet's words) of the German theology professor. Paquet reported: "From the first moment Jung had a significant, very independent, very open-minded, and at the same time somewhat Mephistophelian effect on this society. He finds great fun in unmasking things. He unmasks the fervor and the sourness of temper with which many pious people destroy themselves and others."[47]

The Swabian theologian Rudi Daur fared similarly: "Here stood before us one who, when asked what mission he was on when he spoke, took care of people, showed them paths, quite modestly but quite definitely rejected the question. . . . Several felt, here is a person with whom you could really trust all the questions, needs, all the confusions and mistakes of your soul." Daur also reported what Jung had answered when asked—a typical pious churchman's question!—who his client really was. The speaker, who was not easily rattled, appeared exceedingly surprised, but replied:

> I am Herr Jung and nobody else, and there is Miss so-and-so. It would not be nice at all if I could not treat such sick people. Besides, I have a certain zest for work. I am enterprising; I have a pioneering spirit. If any kind of screwball at all comes to the door, the explorer in me is awakened, my curiosity, my spirit of adventure, my sympathy. It touches my heart, which is too soft—and people my size usually have something of this; they try to conceal it, but like fools they don't succeed—and I enjoy seeing what can be done with such a crazy fellow. I have made a game out of healing even difficult cases. This is simply a kind of curiosity and sense of adventure.[48]

Moreover there was also the whole usual necessity of making a living, the mundane reason of earning money, and so no trace of a pastoral mission as far as that went. How did he, Jung, of all people, come to wish to care for the souls of others? Jung evidently had tremendous fun giving the creeps to the "aroused" among his audience from Baden and Swabia. In any case he made no bones about it when he continued:

> I can tell you this: When you have to exhaust yourself terribly for a person and you don't get paid for it, in time you lose your taste for it. So I confront the patient as a completely ordinary person, with all his pros and cons.

The reporter could only add: "How cool this man stays at the mention of great, high-sounding words! How relentlessly he asks: what is really behind these high and mighty speeches? What does someone who talks this way have to hide? What is he trying to gain with such peremptory verbiage?" And finally, "Then a profoundly wise man with practically universal knowledge at his command stands with the deepest humility before the secrets of life. What he has read and learned in colleges and from books is not enough for him. . . ."[49]

Finally, still in the thirties, came the death of Sigmund Freud, who died on 23 September 1939, at the age of eighty-three, in exile in London after having been driven out of Austria by the Nazis. Just as Jung had already praised the Viennese master, earlier in the decade (1932), as a cultural-historical phenomenon and a man who left behind a "glorious life's work,"[50] so now he dedicated a long obituary to the deceased in the Basler *Nachrichten*. Here praise and criticism were joined, tied together with the avowal:

> In the course of a personal friendship of many years which bound me to him, I had the privilege of looking deeply into the soul of this singular human being: he was a man "possessed," one in whom a light has simply opened up with an overpowering impression, taken possession of his soul and not let it go.[51]

Undoubtedly, this sentence about Freud can be applied word for word to Jung himself. As he penned these lines, the horrors of World War Two had already begun.

20

Night over Europe: The Second World War

"Hitler is reaching his climax and with him the German psychosis." This sentence is found in a letter of 2 September 1939 to Jung's English medical colleague Hugh Crichton-Miller in London. After stepping down from the chair of the International Society for Psychotherapy in July of that year, Jung in his turn tried to find a suitable specialist from a democratically ruled country to succeed him, while his student C. A. Meier served as managing secretary from Zürich in the interim. But it was too late, for the previous day German troops marched into Poland. World War II had begun. It would have taken a certain clairvoyance to know, or suspect, as Jung did, that with this the "German psychosis" would reach its high, or rather low, point. This referred above all to the symptoms of mass hysteria that Jung had already diagnosed as a psychotic manifestation some years earlier. The German people's expectations—and not only in the first weeks of the war—were kept at a high pitch, constantly spurred on anew by the victory fanfares of the sometimes weekly, sometimes daily "special announcements from the Führer's headquarters." In any case very few Germans, owing to the propagandistic information policy and lack of critical appraisal, were able to see Hitler's military campaigns for what they were.

For the neutral Swiss the events of 1939 took on quite a different aspect. Whereas for a few weeks at first the attention of the German and foreign public was directed to the *Blitzkrieg* of the Poland campaign, for Jung there was "no doubt and no question": Germany had to a great extent lost its national honor. In contrast to World War I, the majority of Swiss this time were in sympathy with the Allies, and Jung made it no secret that he shared this view. The letters from this period show it, from the beginning. In time the little country was hemmed in by three warring powers, particularly Nationalist Socialist "Greater Germany" and Benito Mussolini's Fascist Italy. "We feel the sword of Damocles over our heads," Jung wrote to an American woman in the fifth week of the war. He rejected a notion by his friend Esther Harding, a psychotherapist practicing in the United States, that he might travel in the United States during the war. Such a thing, he felt, would mean virtual exile. His son Franz was in the army, as were three sons-in-law. At the age of sixty-four Jung himself was too old to be on active medical duty in the service as in World War I, but he stood ready to assist in various relief organizations. The apolitical Jung even let himself be talked into standing as a candidate in the elections for the Swiss national assembly, but then he did not receive enough votes. A short exchange of letters with national councilman Gottfried Duttweiler, the well-known economist, shows that Jung had practical suggestions to offer for the present situation, in order to distribute the burden of the war onto the shoulders of as many of the nation's people as possible.

The feeling that motivated him he called already in the first weeks "apocalyptic." And in May 1940, when German troops rolled over France: "We are all terribly sorry for England and France. If they should lose the war, we also shall not escape the reign of the Antichrist"[1]—doubtless a surprising thing to say at this moment! The sense of sitting atop a powderkeg was something Jung shared especially with those of his fellow citizens who lived within range of the (assumed) front line of Swiss defense, of which the area around Zürich formed a part.

For this reason Jung fled for a short time with his large family, which by this time included twelve grandchildren, to the mountains near Saanen. An attack had been expected, and a hint to this effect had come from Bern.[2] But it was not just this individual fear alone that made him, as early as June 1940, write the sentence: "Night has descended over Europe." From the time of their work together on *Memories, Dreams, Reflections*, Aniela Jaffé recounted one particular recollection of Jung's. Immediately after the peace treaty in 1918 he had already had a prophetic dream in which, covered with burns, he had become a witness to the consumption of Germany in a rain of fire. And with this had been connected the "key year of 1940." Hence 1940 came up over and over in Jung's letters as "the fateful year," for example when he wrote to England on 12 August 1940 to his friend "Peter," the London physician Helton Godwin Baynes. France and Belgium had capitulated; English cities had been exposed to the hail of the Luftwaffe's bombs, before the German ones were reduced to soot and ashes. The climax of the war had not yet been reached; its expansion into the Balkan Peninsula and above all Hitler's sudden assault on the Soviet Union in June 1941 were still to come, and yet Jung even now spoke of a "catastrophe" of which he had suspected nothing despite his visionary prophetic gift. The year 1940 reminded him of the powerful earthquake of 26 B.C.E., when the temple of Karnak collapsed, a prelude to later destructions. In the same place he made the significant remark: "1940 is the year when we approach the meridian of the first star in Aquarius. It is the premonitory earthquake of the New Age."[3] We see how Jung considered earthly occurrences in a cosmic context, with an eye toward the approach of the Age of Aquarius,[4] which was supposed to come after the Age of Pisces in the global calendar.[5] This fact, differently interpreted by the various esoteric groups, was frequently connected with an "age of enlightenment" and great steps forward in spiritual progress. But it is not seldom forgotten that spiritual maturity carries the price of great suffering and severe trials. And Jung was certainly clearly aware of this aspect, even if there was still no clear notion of what the thoroughly sorrowful historical experience and entanglements of the coming years would bring to mankind. Jung lamented that at his age and in his position he felt as helpless as if he were living in a prison, and more than anything else he had to hear that his extensive interview with H. R. Knickerbocker, published in New York in January 1939, had gone unread by British Prime Minister Chamberlain, for there Jung had argued, from his own psychological understanding, that Hitler's aggressive tendencies would have to be turned against the Soviet Union. What the western and central Europeans could not do—putting a stop to the brown dictator and usurper—would be possible from the East. How correct Jung's hypothesis was would soon be verified in a well-known and staggering way, amid great bloody sacrifices on both sides.

Jung's everyday life was not altered substantially during the war years. Understandably, the number of his foreign patients was seriously curtailed, but he remained abundantly occupied nevertheless, as numerous younger colleagues were called into the military. His lectures at the Swiss Institute of Technology continued for a few more years. After dealing with Eastern and Far Eastern themes, from 16 June 1939 until March 1940 he concerned himself with the *Exercitia Spiritualia* of Ignatius of Loyola,[6] comparing them (as one might expect) with alchemistic and—from time to time—Far Eastern parallels. His Eranos lectures of 1940 and 1941 were devoted to "A Psychological Approach to the Dogma of the Trinity" and "Transformation Symbolism in the Mass."[7] And since only a few members of the Psychological Club were able to travel to the conferences at Ascona in Ticino during the war, Jung repeated his performance in the Club in Zürich, which had been holding its regular Saturday evening meetings at fortnightly intervals during the semester since 1916. Jung of course acted as "honorary president," but resigned himself to "the ruling matriarchy in the club," as he jokingly said. Besides Toni Wolff and Emma Jung, Jolande Jacobi, Barbara

Hannah, Marie-Louise von Franz, Liliane Frey-Rohn, and others had a say.

Even if Switzerland managed to preserve its neutrality as always, still all manner of wartime restrictions made themselves felt, such as the rationing of food and luxuries. The limited gasoline allowance cut back to a minimum the automobile outings of which Jung was so fond. When the Swiss monthly *Du* asked him in the spring of 1941 about the significance of the simple life, the answer came out as one might have expected from the occupant, landlord, and porter of the Bollingen tower:

> The return to the simple life can be regarded as an unexpected stroke of luck, even if such a "return" requires no little sacrifice and is not even voluntary. . . . All time-saving measures, which include easier communications and other conveniences, paradoxically do not save any time, but merely serve to fill up what time there is so that one really has no more time at all. This inevitably gives rise to breathless haste, superficiality, and nervous exhaustion, with all the attendant symptoms such as craving for stimulation, impatience, irritability, and vacillation. Such a condition leads to many things, but never to increased refinement of mind or heart.[8]

For this reason Bollingen remained his inalienable refuge, even in midwinter. Physical exercise was richly provided there; thus in December 1942 three trees needed felling. The young Bollingen resident Hans Kuhn was handy at the time, but Jung would not allow anyone to relieve him of the work of cutting the trees up and chopping them into pieces. Here, far from the world of the city, he received desired provisions now and again, for example from the American actress Alice Lewisohn-Crowley, who was living in Zürich, and his client, or coworker, Aniela Jaffé. Moreover, he had also laid in an additional large potato patch for himself in the garden of his place in Küsnacht, in order to supplement the food supply of his large extended family.

His most important field of activity during the war was undoubtedly alchemy. The pursuit of the ancient texts and their psychological significance that had been going on for more than ten years was now at last yielding its first written results. An additional external impetus was provided by an invitation to present a paper in 1941 in honor of Paracelsus, his great colleague and physician from the sixteenth century, on the occasion of the four hundredth anniversary of his death. Under the title "Paracelsus the Physician,"[9] Jung read it to the Swiss Society for the History of Medicine and the Natural Sciences in Basel on 7 September. On 5 October he spoke at the Swiss Paracelsus festival in nearby Einsiedeln, the birthplace of that great doctor, on "Paracelsus as a Spiritual Phenomenon."[10] Jung had accepted both invitations even though he expressly did not style himself an authority on Paracelsus. A reading of his pertinent works, after all, shows that he had been stimulated in particular by Paracelsists, and thus by such authors as Gerhard Dorn (Dornaeus), and in part by texts which, although they had been published under the name of Paracelsus, at best stemmed from his school. In the knowledge that he could say nothing conclusive about this difficult issue, and conscious of his many inadequacies, Jung wrote in the foreword to the first edition, partially enlarged, of these two papers:

> My intention could go no further than to open up a way that would lead to the roots and the psychic background of his so-called philosophy. Along with everything else that Paracelsus is, he is perhaps most profoundly an alchemistic "philosopher," whose religious worldview stood in a contrast to the Christian thought and belief of his time that was unknown to himself and almost inextricable for us. But in this philosophy lay a promising start for philosophical, psychological, and religious problems which in our epoch are beginning to take on clearer shape.[11]

All in all, this was grounds enough for Jung to lecture, in the place where Paracelsus was born and had once been active, on one who seemed to be "always underrated or overrated."

Concerning the preparations for his Eranos lecture in 1942 on "The Spirit Mercurius,"[12] Jung was visited by a number of dreams of this central figure in the process of alchemical transformation, dreams which had a lasting effect on him. He felt his anima was moved and "seized by the spirit of life (Mercury!)," as he remarked in a letter of 20 July 1942.[13] The material to be mastered and harnessed in literary form was powerful. The results of his study included first the introductory primer *Psychology and Alchemy* (1944), which—to conclude from the foreword to the first edition—must already have been completed in manuscript in January 1943. His students, or coworkers, Marie-Louise von Franz, Riwka Schärf, Liliane Frey, and Jolande Jacobi looked after translations and citations, and Olga Fröbe-Kapteyn had on Jung's instructions collected photocopies of alchemistic copperplate engravings and thereby enhanced the book's clarity. At the same time Jung was also already at work on his alchemical *magnum opus*, the *Mysterium Coniunctionis*, at the center of which stood the guiding theme of the *coniunctio*, the unification of the opposites. This referred to the problem of the masculine and feminine halves of the self, of psychic integration and maturity. And here it does not seem to have been the author who took on this task, but the task and its great theme that seized hold of the author. It was an inner compulsion which he could not help but obey. "I am just wrestling with this problem of the coniunctio," he wrote to Aniela Jaffé on 3 November 1943, "which I have to work out now as an introduction to the *Aurora Consurgens*. It is unbelievably difficult."[14] What he referred to here, with something more than understatement, as an "introduction" comprises two volumes and over eight hundred printed pages in the edition of his works. A third volume, overseen by Marie-Louise von Franz, was assigned to the alchemistic text attributed to Thomas Aquinas. "In the overall output of C. G. Jung the *Mysterium Coniunctionis* is the most important work of his later years," noted the editor in her preface.[15]

After Jung found himself obliged to suspend his regular lecturing activity at the Swiss Technical Institute in Zürich, on account of his workload and the heart troubles that were appearing now and then, he was named professor in ordinary of medical psychology and psychotherapy by the government councillor of the canton of Basel City, effective 15 October 1943—a tribute that came rather late, as the honoree himself declared. But the unforeseen arose, and so matters stopped at the receipt of this title, and the scheduled teaching activity in Basel never came about.

One day in February 1944, at barely sixty-nine years of age, Jung was out for an extended hike, one of the regular walks he had been in the habit of taking since his return from India. Suddenly, a few kilometers away from home, he slipped on a patch of snow, falling and suffering a broken fibula. Luckily he was able with some effort to drag himself to the nearest house and call a taxi to take him to the doctor. The treatment of the injury at the Hirslanden private hospital near Zürich required above all that the patient remain motionless. "At first Jung read his alchemistic books quite happily," reported Barbara Hannah, "but soon his active body rebelled against inactivity, and about ten days after entering the hospital he had a very bad thrombosis of the heart and two others which went to his lungs. It was totally unexpected. Emma Jung was in town and was contacted with great difficulty. She stayed in the hospital with him—she was able to obtain a room in another wing but quite close—until he could go home. Jung was at death's door and remained so for several weeks."[16]

This of course relates only the external, outwardly visible incident. In his memoirs Jung, who had been deeply moved, described vividly what he went through inwardly. As a result of the coronary infarct he had experiences in a state of deep unconsciousness, deliriums, and unexpectedly grandiose visions, together with the knowledge that he was about to depart from this life.

> The images were so tremendous that I myself concluded that I was close to death. My nurse afterward told me, "It was as if you were surrounded by a bright glow." That was a phenomenon she had sometimes observed in the dying, she added. I had reached the outermost limit, and do not know whether I was in a dream or an ecstasy. At any rate, extremely strange things began to happen to me.[17]

Jung saw himself hovering high up in space, while far below him, perhaps 1500 kilometers down, lay the globe of the earth, bathed in a glorious blue light, with the oceans and continents clearly visible. "It was the most marvelous and magical thing I had ever experienced." A temple appeared, like those he had once seen in Kandy in Ceylon. He went up the sacred steps. At the same time, in a painful process, everything earthly, everything that had been, fell away from him. All that remained was the unchanging identity of the "I am."

> This experience gave me a feeling of extreme poverty, but at the same time of great fullness. There was no longer anything I wanted or desired. I existed in an objective form; I was what I had been and lived. . . . There was no longer any regret that something had dropped away or been taken away. On the contrary: I had everything that I was, and that was everything.[18]

Now he was filled with the certainty that at last he was coming to where he really belonged, after perceiving his life up to that point as a "historical fragment," a slender clipping out of a larger context of whose total scope one normally knows nothing in one's earthly incarnation.

Another image emerged. It seemed to come out of ancient Europe; a priest-physician appeared from Cos, the birthplace of the great Hippocrates. In the primal form of the physician Jung recognized the doctor who was treating him, Dr. Theodor Haemmerlei-Schindler, who had a message to deliver. Jung, he said, must not leave the earth yet, since a protest had been raised against it on the planet, and so he would have to return. Hardly was he conscious of this message when the vision ceased.

> I was profoundly disappointed, for now it all seemed to have been for nothing. The painful process of defoliation had been in vain, and I was not to be allowed to enter the temple, to join the people in whose company I belonged.
>
> . . .Disappointed, I thought, "Now I must return to the 'box system' again." For it seemed to me as if behind the horizon of the cosmos a three-dimensional world had been artificially built up, in which each person sat by himself in a little box. And now I should have to convince myself all over again that this was important! Life and the whole world struck me as a prison, and it bothered me beyond measure that I should again be finding all that quite in order.[19]

And in fact the improvement that everyone hoped for did set in, while Jung's doctor himself became gravely ill and died shortly after. This was a remarkable synchronism, whose meaning Jung believed he had perceived in his paranormal state. From her detailed knowledge of the Zürich scene, Barbara Hannah reported further occurrences of this kind which Jung later referred to as synchronistic events or phenomena of synchronicity. Thus, at the time when Jung was wresting with death, one of his students suffered from a life-threatening attack of influenza. She was near death when suddenly she saw her teacher, who said to her, "I have decided to go back to the earth; get back into your own body as quickly as you can!" "Another pupil, who also had a very bad attack of that year's virulent flu, was suddenly horrified to find that her watch and the clock beside her bed had stopped at exactly the same moment. She was terrified that this might mean that Jung had died at that moment."[20] But the real inner experience of those weeks of illness in the spring of 1944 was represented by a series of visions of whose overwhelming beauty and sublimity Jung also tried to give an idea in his *Memories*. As these imaginations belong to the peak experiences of mystical knowledge, they defy adequate description, and symbols from religious tradition must serve as metaphors.

Jung saw himself as if held in the lap of the cosmos, in a state of the highest bliss, while he felt physically—in early April 1944—still very weak and miserable. But what he perceived spiritually, what he partook of, was what the religious documents of all ages call the experience of the "sacred marriage" (*hieros gamos*),[21] the highest union (*unio mystica*), which is seen sometimes in the meeting of God and man, sometimes in the image of God himself, where death—in Dietrich Bonhoeffer's words "the highest celebration on the way to eternal freedom"—and this marriage are intimately interconnected. It is this proximity that marks the outermost boundaries of the possibilities of human experience. Described also in the Old and New Testaments in the images of a religious eroticism, it becomes a most intense experience that appears repeatedly to those who are gravely ill.

Jung found himself in the *pardes rimmonim*, the garden of pomegranates, the place of the sacred marriage according to the Jewish Kabbalah, whose major work, the *Zohar* or *Book of Splendor*, goes back in turn to the Wedding Song of Solomon, while at the same time celebrating the death of the legendary Rabbi Simon bar Yochai in the form of his marriage in the other world.[22] And because, in the ten-branched tree of Sefiroth (the Tree of Life, which forms the pictorial image of the perception of God in Jewish mysticism), masculine and feminine are represented by Tifereth (Beauty) and Malkhuth (Kingdom), the real location of the mystical marriage is already in God himself, or rather the emanations or "reflections" of God. It is impossible to describe all this as an individual experience, and so Jung had to confess to the recorder of his *Memories*:

> I cannot tell you how wonderful it was. I could only think continually, "Now this is the garden of pomegranates! Now this is the marriage of Malkhuth with Tifereth!" I do not know exactly what part I played in it. At bottom it was I

myself: I was the marriage. And my beatitude was that of a blissful wedding.

Gradually the garden of pomegranates faded away and changed. There followed the Marriage of the Lamb, in a Jerusalem festively bedecked. I cannot describe what it was like in detail. These were ineffable states of joy. Angels were present, and light. I myself was the "Marriage of the Lamb."[23]

Here, then, we have the Old Testament wedding song, combined thematically with the New Testament Revelation of Saint John and brought into the present in the individual experience of a twentieth-century man! Certainly the marriage motif did not come to Jung entirely from out of the blue, for of course he had long been engrossed in alchemy and its relationship to the process of maturation or integration of the human psyche. The first chapter of his great late work *Mysterium Coniunctionis* was already written. And what could chiefly be looked upon at first in this book as the product of historical and psychological interpretation had—in part retroactively and in part prospectively—been legitimated by lived experience. In this very book spoke one who not only knew but had experienced these things. Hence when he spoke of these matters after his recovery with his coworker Marie-Louise von Franz, he intimated to her: "Everything I have written is right. I do not need to change a word of it, but only now do I realize the full reality of it." And to Barbara Hannah he said that his illness had been a virtual necessity in order for him to become aware of the full reality of the *mysterium coniunctionis*.[24]

Another aspect of his serious illness was touched on now and again in letters and conversations. It was Jung's opinion that it is the fate of the pioneer to be too early himself; what he longs for, in contrast, comes too late.[25] And if the recognition due him does come, then he is somehow threatened. Thus he wrote to the psychologist Alwine von Keller at the time of the Eranos conference in 1944 that he could not come:

> In fact there is great danger in being praised prematurely. That is why fate always strives for posthumous recognition. After all, it nearly bumped me off too, just on account of my being named a professor in Basel.[26]

This attempt at explanation, though, touched as it were only the more exoteric aspect, on which discussion was possible. What was thoroughly indisputable and could only occasionally be proved, on the other hand, was the esoteric perspective on the experience of death. As one who had been through it in the way he himself described, he was able to write to a terminally ill American colleague, Kristine Mann, on 1 February 1945 that he had gotten, as she herself had, a glimpse behind the veil. The only difficult thing was to get away from one's body, to become as it were totally naked, emptied of all wordly will, even down to one's own ego.

> When you can give up the crazy will to live and when you seemingly fall into a bottomless mist, then the truly *real* life begins with everything which you were meant to be and never reached. It is something ineffably grand. . . .

And returning once more to the climax of this experience that had presented itself to his inner vision:

> Not I was united with somebody or something—*it* was united, *it* was the hieros gamos, the mystic Agnus. It was a silent invisible festival permeated by an incomparable, indescribable feeling of eternal bliss, such as I never could have imagined as being within reach of human experience. Death is the hardest thing from the outside and as long as we are outside of it. But once inside you taste of such completeness and peace and fulfillment that you don't want to return.[27]

Thus in the last year of the war Jung's attention was much too strongly focused on himself, and the slow progress of his convalescence, to be able once again to devote his still greatly reduced capacity for work fully to the problems of the day. But once having overcome his illness, he began to consider world events with renewed interest, for example in the propaganda methods of the Germans and the Allies. In early 1945 he shared his thoughts on this with his American friend Allen Welsh Dulles. During the war Dulles (later head of the CIA) was chief of the U.S. Intelligence Service in Europe, headquartered in Bern, in which capacity he had called on Jung several times in Küsnacht. In the meantime the Americans and British had landed in northern France. The Eastern Front drew ever closer to the borders of the Reich, and from the south Allied troops took large areas of Italy. The failure of the assassination attempt on Hitler on 20 July 1944 could not conceal the fact that the final phase of World War II had begun. It ended in Europe with the surrender of the German Wehrmacht on 8 May 1945, with the devastation of large parts of the Continent apocalyptically eclipsed in East Asia by the two atomic bombs dropped on Himoshima on 6 August and Nagasaki on the ninth.

Jung was deeply disturbed by the deployment of these weapons of mass destruction. He felt that civilized humanity had reached its crossroads. As early as December 1945, when most Europeans had problems of existence of another kind to contend with, Jung's gaze was already turning to the question of the existence of planet Earth. Also striking is the moment when he acquainted a Zürich theologian with his concerns and hopes. Again he saw the events of the time within the much more sweeping framework of the Platonic cosmic year.

> Almost two thousand years ago the world entered the last month of the Platonic year, the age of Pisces [the Fish], and chiliastic forebodings developed. One thousand years ago it came more clearly, and around the year 2000 C.E. humanity already has in its hands the very instrument with which it can bring about and even ensure its own end, unless a third world war comes in which that group of people who could use the atomic bomb is utterly smashed to pieces; this would mean—and this is the only chance—the coming . . . of the great Return, by which I can only imagine absolutely nothing other than a real religious, worldwide movement

> which alone could head off the diabolic impulse toward destruction.

Jung referred to the Christian church, insofar as it (still) represented a spiritual quantity, seeing its great task as that of staving off the immediate threat of disaster. With skeptical realism he added, "Of course I know that it does no good for one single person to rack his brains over this. But one has to say something about it nonetheless. . . ."[28]

21

After the War

Jung closed out his seventh decade a man marked by serious illness. His full recovery took several months, and for a while very strict limits were imposed on his once-considerable physical capacities. For the time being he had to content himself with two hours of daily work at his desk. But this work he could not do without, for he was full of ideas and scientific and literary plans. It was as if the inner experiences of the previous weeks and months had opened up to him entirely new dimensions of spiritual reality. And there is no doubt about this. But what he had received when near death needed to be intellectually penetrated, scientifically organized, and above all existentially integrated. In turn, it pointed beyond Jung in both biographical and historical terms, as can be imagined by anyone who follows the "doctor of the soul" to the point where he crosses from the realm of scientific understanding and empiricism into that of the numinous, where the psychologist and therapist becomes a "psychagogue," a pioneer in the territory of spiritual growth.

Comparing the experiences which Jung described, on the one hand, as a "night journey" of the soul and, on the other, in the image of an ascent high above planet Earth, one could say that in the course of his fateful confrontation with the unconscious he combined the dimension of psychic *depth* with that of spiritual *height*. Anyone who devotes himself to this is at the point of crossing from the space of psychological presuppositions to that of the transpersonal and even pneumatic. It is no coincidence that religion comes ever more to the fore during the second half of his life. Jung recognized early on that the soul produces images whose content is religious, thereby activating meaning-giving factors, and thus that the psyche is to this extent *naturaliter christiana*, "Christian" by nature. It is superfluous to stress yet again that this does not entail any canonical or dogmatic assertions. And yet it is striking how, in his seventh decade (or more exactly in the last seven years before his seventieth year), this religious aspect was magnified in Jung's life and work, intensifying into a new therapeutic quality. And if one had asked the septuagenarian whether he was, after all, still a doctor in the traditional sense, he would have given a clearly affirmative answer, while of course he *extended* the picture of the traditional psychotherapist. A wholly new emphasis had been added to his previous practice, when he wrote on 20 August 1945:

> . . .the main interest of my work is not concerned with the treatment of neuroses but rather with the approach to the numinous. But the fact is that the approach to the numinous is the real therapy and inasmuch as you attain to the numinous experiences you are released from the curse of pathology.[1]

And this is so, one might add, even when a physical cure remains lacking, and must remain so, insofar as the meaning of an ailment consists precisely in the fact that it is affirmed and inwardly accepted by the patient. Individuation and self-development consciously include suffering and death, and this very insight was part of the existential experience of the critical year of 1944.

Also of significance, finally, is the striking synchronicity of Jung's inner experiences with the dates of world history: the process of his *nekyia* or night sea journey into the depths of the soul reached its provisional goal at the moment when World War I was drawing to its conclusion. And the experience of the heights of the sacred marriage came to Jung when World War II had entered its final stage. This is one more indication that the essentially "internal" process of individuation does not go on in some inner space cut off from the world. Rather, it can only be realized within the larger context of life as it is lived. The interpersonal dimension belongs to it, just as does total participation in the destiny of the peoples and cultures of one's times, and thus in their crises and devastating worldwide catastrophes—no dimension of humanity or the world can be left out!

Profound insights are wont to be paid for in such a way that they deal a perceptible shock to the concrete everyday life. In this case, for example, Jung's convalescence forced him to resign himself to the fact that for a full year he must forgo returning to his beloved tower in Bollingen. And when at last his doctor once again allowed him an "excursion," he did not stay there long. Asked what it had been like this time in Bollingen after so long an absence, he could only answer in astonishment: "It was hell!" "He then explained," Barbara Hannah recounted, "that he had not realized, in the comfortable life at Küsnacht, how little physical effort he could make, but at Bollingen he as reminded of that at every touch and turn. He did not stay very long those Easter holidays, for he realized he would have to change his whole attitude to the place before he could be happy there again. He had always done everything himself there—cut wood, draw water, manage his sailing boat, and so on—and of course for several years after such a bad heart attack he could do none of these things for himself. It was not the primitive life he minded; right to the end he steadfastly refused his friends' entreaties to have at least one room with modern conveniences. It was the helplessness of seeing jobs that needed doing and not being able to do them."[2] There was certainly no lack of practical advice and active help—Franz Jung, his only son, was after all an architect, and eventually did his bit as well, as soon as his father consented to a partial "modernization" of the tower. In the decade and a half that remained to him Jung made use of his tower no less than before, as a spot for concentrated work and a place for individual relaxation. For:

> After the illness a fruitful period of work began for me. A good many of my principal works were written only then. The insight I had had, or the vision of the end of all things, gave me the courage to undertake new formulations. I no longer attempted to put across my own opinion, but surrendered myself to the current of my thoughts. Thus one problem after the other revealed itself to me and took shape.[3]

For the scarcely recuperated Jung, a chapter in itself was represented by the great flood of letters that commenced with the war's end. The daughter of his old friend Hans Schmid, Marie-Jeanne, who had a gift for languages and had been trained as a secretary, helped him to keep the daily workload under control and set up a filing system. Until about 1925 Jung's sister Gertrud, who died in 1935, had attended to the most pressing office work, and then Emma Jung and her daughter Marianne had helped out as secretaries. To be sure, correspondence with friends and colleagues overseas had not come to a complete standstill during the war, but between 1939 and 1945 even the Swiss population had been quite hampered. Because of the war's influence many letters sent were lost, particularly en route to the United States and to and from England.

The numerous communications from abroad showed Jung that not only had he not been forgotten, but interest in him and his work had continued to increase, although not a few authorities, from his own clique as well as the other departments of psychoanalysis, approached Jungian analytical psychology as always with great reservations. And precisely because the objection was continually raised that Jung was too difficult, too pretentious, perhaps even shrouded in "mystical obscurity," he took the trouble to respond to the many inquiries and criticisms with personal letters. Among these were soon found regular epistles, for example in his correspondence with theologians of both denominations, among them the English Dominican Father Victor White, who had thoroughly familiarized himself with Jung's output. In this respect not a few of these reply letters represent valuable aids to the interpretation of his work. They also serve to help establish the philosophical and theological position of Jung the psychologist, who energetically resisted any attempt to classify him as philosopher or theologian.

There was still a rather small circle of friends and students in attendance when Jung resumed his work in the Psychological Club on 9 June 1945. How much events in Germany during the Third Reich and after the collapse of the Hitler regime had preoccupied him was shown by the essay "After the Catastrophe,"[4] which Jung published in the July 1945 issue of the *Neue Schweizer Monatshefte*. It was his first appearance in this forum since his "Wotan" essay of 1936. Jung said to himself that before reconstruction, attention would have to be paid to "clearing up," to careful reflection on what had happened and what needed to happen in the future. In Germany, occupied in four "zones" by the victorious allied powers, the processes of "denazification" had begun. In Nuremberg the main war criminals, as the victors saw them, were on trial. The problems involved in this undertaking have long been known. Jung's approach was a different one. He too spoke of guilt, of the tragic destiny of a "collective psychological guilt" to which the just and the unjust are equally subject. The concept itself was being hotly debated in the time after the war. And precisely because Jung, who had been defamed as a supposed "collaborator" and "anti-Semite," had dared to speak out, the waves rose up once again. General opinion in Germany must also be taken into account, for example the fact that members of the former Confessional Church had also reaped vehement opposition in 1945, when in October, on the advice of the Reformed Church in Germany, they subscribed to the so-called Stuttgart Declaration of Guilt, based on the premise of a collective guilt of the church and Christians in Germany: "Through us endless suffering has been brought down upon many peoples and countries. What we have often testified to our congregations we now declare in the name of the whole church: indeed through long years we have fought in the name of Jesus Christ against the spirit that has found its fearsome expression in the rule of National Socialist power, but it is our fault that we did not confess more courageously, pray more faithfully, believe more cheerfully, or love more keenly."[5]

Men like the later German president Gustav Heinemann, the Bishop of Hanover Hanns Lilje, and Pastor Martin Niemöller, who was interned for years in a concentration camp, numbered among the signatories of this document. So it was small wonder that C. G. Jung's article, published a quarter of a year earlier and thus seemingly unprepared, ran into fierce opposition. He was criticized for having written, among other things:

> If a German recognizes his moral inferiority as collective guilt before the world and makes no attempt to mitigate and explain it away with flimsy arguments, he has a reasonable chance of being taken after a time for a respectable person and thus of being released from the collective guilt at least in the eyes of individuals.[6]

Psychotherapeutically speaking, he said, it was a great advantage if one owned up to one's own guilt. In this sense Germany and all of Europe had a unique opportunity to look to the inner, moral human being, even though the thoroughly difficult outward circumstances of life in 1945–1946 naturally stood in the foreground. Hence with the sensible acceptance of collective guilt a great step forward had been taken, even if it had not yet resulted in the hoped-for healing.

All these statements strengthened the widespread aversion toward Jung. Once again he became the target of vile attacks, even inside Switzerland. Experience shows that partial truths combined with misunderstandings tend to produce a personality profile that scarcely has anything in common anymore with the actual human being concerned—even with all his admitted errors and failings. Some—with Erich Kästner, for example, in the *Neue Zeitung*, published by the American occupation forces in Munich in 1945—demanded that Jung should be willing to declare a clear *mea culpa* of his own. Others, such as Ernst Bloch, who was hardly an adequately competent judge in the case of Jung, degraded him to a "fascistically frothing psychoanalyst."[7] But with this we abandon the ground of any kind of responsible criticism.[8]

In the midst of these confrontations fell Jung's seventieth birthday on 26 July 1945. The possibilities for travel in postwar Europe were still considerably circumscribed, so that there were still hardly any foreign Jungians in Zürich at the time. Hence the birthday celebration took place in decidedly familiar surroundings. Only the round-number birthdays which came later, the seventy-fifth, eightieth, and eighty-fifth, would become public events. To the tea party that gathered in the garden in the afternoon, only students and friends from the nearby vicinity were invited. As Barbara Hannah describes it: "There was a marvelous atmosphere at that party, for we were all so deeply thankful, after the fright of the year before, that he was still with us to celebrate the day. By this time his health had greatly improved; in fact, visitors were inclined to think he seemed as well as before his illness. But his heart was always a cause for anxiety. . . ."[9]

Olga Fröbe-Kapteyn presented the twelfth volume of her famous *Jahrbuch* as a testimonial volume to the jubilarian as her constant and most faithful coworker since the beginning of the annual Eranos conferences. In it she evaluated Jung's intensive collaboration with scholars and professionals from many fields, emphasizing the fruitfulness of the archetypes in analytical psychology. The Bern historian Walter Wili called attention—much as had already been done by the *Festschrift* for Jung's sixtieth birthday—to the dimensions that had been reached by the interdisciplinary dialogue stimulated and furthered by Jung. The authors of the other eight, to some extent comprehensive contributions, all devoted to the idea of the archetype, included the Jesuit Hugo Raliner (Innsbruck), Louis Massignon (Paris), John Layard (Oxford), and Andreas Speiser (Basel).

With Jung's attainment of biblical age, the question occurred to the followers of Jungian psychology of how the work that he had begun could be provided with a secure institutional anchorage and care, or continuation. The ladies of the Psychological Club, especially Jolande Jacobi, envisioned the establishment of a proper institute for the training of psychotherapists along the lines Jung had shown. What did Jung himself think of this? "I can only hope and wish that nobody will become a 'Jungian,'" says his letter to his Dutch colleague J. H. van der Hoop in early 1946:

> I do not advocate any doctrine, you see, but only describe facts and draw certain conclusions which I think are worth discussing. . . . I promulgate no cut-and-dried doctrine, and I perhorresce at "blind adherents." I do not refuse any one the freedom to adjust the facts in his own particular way, for of course I take this liberty myself.[10]

Thus, for example, he said he was fully able to endorse the Freudian perspective and methods, and he was opposed only at the point when doctrinaire biases were equated with reality and truth. Knowing that this was Jung's attitude, and considering that he disliked spectacular events, it was decided to forgo informing him on his birthday of the plan for the founding of a C. G. Jung Institute. In fact when he did hear of it, he indicated his refusal. It is all the more surprising, then, that barely three years later he accepted the project and recommended the establishment of such a center in Zürich, taking into account the fact that meanwhile a large number of English and American men and women were traveling to Zürich in order to acquaint themselves with Jung's work on the spot.

In his speech at the inaugural session of the new C. G. Jung Institute on 24 April 1948, the seventy-three-year-old Jung first cast a look back at the beginnings of his activity. In his review appeared not only the founding figures of modern depth psychology—Freud, Janet, Théodore Flournoy—but also the Orientalists Richard Wilhelm and Heinrich Zimmer, as well as the Hungarian classical scholar and mythographer Karl Kerényi, and further the physicists Pascual Jordan and Wolfgang Pauli, with whose help—supplemented by the parapsychological experiments of the American J. B. Rhine—it had been possible to draw an extended picture of reality that transcended both classical physics and previous depth psychology. From the domain of the "Jung school," which was growing willy-nilly, the speaker named numerous women and men in various fields who had taken up the impulses of analytical psychology and carried them forward.

Among those who had come to prominence in Jungian psychology were C. A. Meier, in connection with the dialogue between psychology and physics and the elaboration of the concept of complementarity, Erich Neumann with regard to the content and scope of the history of the development of human consciousness, Esther Harding in the psychology of women, Frances G. Wickes in child psychology, Hedwig von Beit and Marie-Louise von Franz in the psychological exploration of fairy tales, and Toni Wolff and Jolande Jacobi through introductory, systematic works. Besides a few individual studies Jung also named four theologians, the Protestant Hans Schär and the Catholics W. P. Witcutt, Victor White, and Gebhard Frei, who by the time in question had produced works that complemented Jung's perspectives on the psychology of religion. Jung presented his students and coworkers with a large and by no means complete catalogue of problems. He began with questions of theoretical cognitive and experimental psychology, including both the medical-clinical and psychiatric areas and extending to those of the humanities. In closing, Jung said, "Much will remain to be done. It will not all be accomplished; the individual variation of our coworkers on one hand and the irrationality and unpredictability of any such scientific development on the other will see to that."[11]

But Jung left no doubt that in any event quality work would have to be done if the undertaking was to remain alive. This was in tune with the concern of one who was leaving behind a life's work which, though by no means closed, had already shown itself to be many-layered and demanding. Jung may have suspected that there was great danger that a student of his could become a Jungian just the same, sticking to the present position and swearing by the master's words, instead of using the proven methods to deepen and expand the field of research. And in fact Nietzsche's recommendation applies with regard to Jung: "One ill repays one's teacher by remaining forever only his student."[12]

As far as the name of the new organization was concerned, Jung originally had in mind a functional designation such as "Institute for Analytical Psychology" or "Institution for Complex Psychology." He long resisted having not only to be known as a private person, but also to serve as the designation for an "objective thing." But in the end he allowed himself to be persuaded that the use of his name would be much more meaningful than any other nomenclature for the psychology he had founded.

Thus the C. G. Jung Institute could begin. Organizationally it developed from the Psychological Club that had existed since 1916. The available starting capital amounted to 100,000 Swiss francs, coming primarily from the contributions of American investors. The club had the requisite space at its disposal in its house along the Gemeindestrasse in Zurich. The management of the new organization was taken over mainly by members of the Psychological Club, under C. G. Jung as president (until early 1950) and a board of trustees. The five-member administrative body was further made up of Jolande Jacobi, who thanks to her strongly extraverted attitude provided great initiative; Carl A. Meier, Jung's successor as professor at the Swiss Technical Institute; Liliane Frey-Rohn; and Kurt Binswanger. Aniela Jaffé acted as secretary. When Jung resigned in 1950, C. A. Meier assumed the chair and Emma Jung followed as his replacement on the board, ensuring that as honorary president Jung would continue to remain in direct contact with current developments in the C. G. Jung Institute.

In order to demonstrate to the outside world too that the new institution was not supported solely by the Jung school in the strict sense, a number of personalities were prepared to play a role as founding members and to act to an extent as lecturers. To this group, for example, belonged the physicist Wolfgang Pauli, the classicist Karl Kerényi, who was known from the Eranos conferences and his close collaboration with Jung, the Catholic theologian and philosopher Gebhard Frei, and the English Dominican and friend of Jung's Victor White.

Barbara Hannah, who was such a close friend of the Jung family, wondered if it was right to burden Emma Jung, who was already getting on in years herself in 1950, with such duties as those of a member of the board, particularly as she had been busy for years with a large book project, a psychological investigation of the theme of the Grail. "On the one hand, it developed a side of her that she had lived very little before; on the other hand, it took her away from breaking any more new ground in her studies on the Grail. . . . The curatorium [i.e., the board] at that time was very dynamic, and emotional differences of opinion often arose. Emma . . . spent a lot of energy trying to reconcile different points of view. She was certainly an irreplaceable value to the curatorium itself, and also to the institute."[13]

To return to the time before the founding of the C. G. Jung Institute: In his letters from the years after the war Jung repeatedly lamented that he was now forced to do without traveling. The general difficulties to which the formerly warring nations and neutral countries alike were subject were added to, in Jung's case, by his large workload and the "deluge" of letters, all of which had to be mastered with considerably reduced strength. His practice, which was admittedly also considerably reduced, and the compilation of his books, including *On the Roots of Consciousness* and his contributions to the study of symbolism in *Aion*, demanded a concentration which often enough had to be interrupted. One such occasion was the visit to Switzerland in 1946, the first year after the war, of Winston Churchill, British prime minister from 1940 to 1945. "He was enthusiastically received by the Swiss, who looked upon him as the saviour of Europe. There were cheering crowds wherever he drove and several official receptions," Barbara Hannah reported. Jung, moreover, had been bound to Churchill in a remarkable way, for whenever the English politician came near the borders of Switzerland, Jung had a dream about him—only after the fact would he learn from the newspaper that the latter had in fact been there and passed by. Jung explained this by saying that he thought Churchhill, who was about the same age, represented the extraverted element to his own emphatically introverted nature. During the official events that took place in Bern and Zürich between mid-August and mid-September 1946, it fell to Jung to accompany the illustrious guest as table and conversation partner. To the rector of the University of Zürich, Ernst Anderes, he described the meeting with the English politician as "one of the most interesting experiences" of his life.[14] But the social ceremony cannot have meant pure joy to him. Evidently Jung had some trouble finding a medium between the talkativeness Churchill expected and a careful consideration for the needs of a convalescent. Much more relaxed, though, was his dialogue with Churchill's daughter Mary, who brought with her some familiarity with Jung's work. If only from this, a much more pleasant role emerged for Jung.

An especially welcome visit—likewise in August—was that of Father Victor White, if only because the two men had been prepared for each other for a long time by a lively correspondence on the psychology of religion.

A fresh coronary embolism in November once again confronted the patient with death. After his recovery, he wrote to his "Father White"—before long he addressed him familiarly as "Dear Victor"—on 18 December 1946: "The *aspectus mortis* [face of death] is a mighty lonely thing, when you are so stripped of everything in the presence of God. One's wholeness is tested mercilessly." Am amazing dream appeared, which seemed to be the happy outcome of this test of wholeness: high up in the sky was a bluish, diamondlike star, reflected in a round, quiet pool—heaven above, heaven below. Jung's comment was:

> The *imago Dei* [likeness of God] in the darkness of the earth, this is myself. . . . I am no more a black and endless sea of misery and suffering but a certain amount thereof contained in a divine vessel. . . . It seems to me as it I am ready to die, although it looks to me as if some powerful thoughts are still flickering like lightnings in a summer night. Yet they are not mine, they belong to God, as everything else which bears mentioning.[15]

No doubt it did Jung good to have found in Victor White someone to whom he could write something so intimate and by whom he was certain of being understood, whereas otherwise, as a doctor and scholar, he had always to present himself as a scientist, who was required to bring to his empirical observations the highest degree of neutrality and dispassionate objectivity. This relationship had its limits, to be sure, as would soon become evident. These limits appeared, for example, where Jung was compelled to advocate his own distinctive view of good and evil, whereas the English clergyman hewed to the standpoint of Catholic dogma. Thus Jung rejected the notion of evil as an opposite which excluded good (*privatio boni*);[16] for him evil was not an absence of good, but an energy and a driving power that stood diametrically opposed to good and through which alone good attained its full potency as such—a view that had run up against ecclesiastical opposition since the days of Augustine. Thus it was evident that difficulties were inevitable even in his friendly relationship with Victor White. In his foreword to White's study on the psychology of religion, *God and the Unconscious* (1952), Jung once again publicly declared his indebtedness to his frank and unreserved cooperation with the Catholic theologian:

> It is now many years since I expressed a desire for co-operation with a theologian, but I little knew—or even

> dreamt—how or to what extent my wish was to be fulfilled. . . . In the fifty years of pioneer work that now lie behind me I have experienced criticism, just and unjust, in such abundance that I can appreciate any attempt at positive co-operation. Criticism from this quarter is constructive and therefore welcome.[17]

After the studies of the Protestant Hans Schär[18] and the Jesuit Josef Goldbrunner,[19] this was now the third work by a theologian to concern itself extensively with C. G. Jung's psychology of religion and to seek a bridge between theology and depth psychology. This began a development that led to a continuing practical dialogue between the two disciplines.

Another decade and a half had been granted the pioneer in order to bring in the harvest of his lifetime in the form of further important books and to stand by his students with advice and help. But again and again it was evident what strict limits were placed on his health. In the spring of 1947 Jung reported to his old family doctor Jakob Stahel (1872–1950) what his daily routine was like: "Two hours of scientific work in the morning, and after noon a rest and a visit. Every day now I go walking twice for about three quarters of an hour. This is starting to go a little better, although not brilliantly yet."[20] Great patience was called for, coupled with a strict working discipline. And as far as smoking was concerned, cigars or the beloved pipe that was always at hand, it was only with great effort that he managed to limit himself to a responsible moderation. Besides, he said, basically his susceptibility really had nothing to do with smoking. Rather it was the great tension between the demands his patients made on him and the heavy toll exacted from him by his scientific work. Consequently it is in this perspective that we should understand his comments on 17 April 1947 to the Jungian Eleanor Bertine in New York:

> My illness was due chiefly to the terrible conflict between practical work with patients and my creative scientific work. In my illness I found that there was a mountain of thoughts which I should get into shape and of which I

> hadn't known that they existed. I'm now trying to catch up with my unconscious fertility.[21]

With this the writer intimated how much his creative potential was taxed by analytic work. He left unmentioned the other fact that it was only the concrete association with other people, the activity that took up so much of the analyst's time and physical strength, that provided the researcher with the authority for what he did. Only his psychotherapeutic practice and experience brought about the indispensable link with reality without which Jung's work would evaporate into a psychomythology. In fact it is astonishing to see what a great wealth of personally experienced actual examples Jung was able to draw upon for his documentary and illustrative material, whenever he had to shed light in speaking and writing on definite human problems.

The pioneer of psychic research was filled with satisfaction when he got evidence that the work he had begun was being carried on and further developed by his students in all corners of the globe, be it in America or Palestine. He was convinced: "The world needs it badly. It seems to come to a general showdown, when the question will be settled whether the actually existing man is conscious enough to cope with his own demons or not." Jung did not appear to be very optimistic when he wrote these lines on 8 July 1947 to Esther Harding in New York, who together with Eleanor Bertine had been advocating analytical psychology there for many years and had been close to Jung as a friend and colleague since the twenties. For he added: "For the time being it seems to be a losing fight. It would not be the first time that darkness has fallen upon a whole civilization. . . ."[22] A light-bearer of the eminence of a Meister Eckhart, he said, had been buried and forgotten for more than six hundred years. His pessimistic-sounding prognosis resulted from the interim personal balance he struck at the age of seventy-two. To be sure, he was feeling "more or less all right again," yet he regarded life as somehow provisional. Sometimes he felt as if he were doing the things of his daily life for the last time.

> It has a somewhat peculiar ring. For untold years it has happened for the first time that I could not plant my potatoes and my corn anymore and weed has overgrown my piece of black earth, as if its owner were no more. Things and exterior life slip past me and leave me in a world of unworldly thought and in a time measured by centuries.

Does this not mean that the No. 2 of his personality now held sway over the No. 1 still more strongly than before, to the point where the Jung who was so skillfull with handiwork, the gardener and builder, was abandoning—for a time at least—the duties and joys of his everyday life?

In fact, works from the Jungian school multiplied. Jung, in the summer of 1947, had just finished working through Esther Harding's voluminous manuscript *Psychic Energy*, which he praised in his foreword as a comprehensive orientation to the problems of medical psychotherapy: "Dr. Harding's text is one of those books which I would unconditionally recommend to my patients when greater spiritual independence is called for."[23] Aniela Jaffé, his coworker who was to become the secretary of the C. G. Jung Institute, had just "written an excellent work on E.T.A. Hoffmann,"[24] Jung informed Erich Neumann in Tel Aviv. Neumann himself was working on one of his major works, *The Origins and History of Consciousness*. Jung became acquainted with it in manuscript and was full of praise for it. On reading the manuscript of this work, extensive in both content and form, it became clear to him how great the disadvantages were of being a pioneer, and that it was only the second generation, to which Neumann belonged, who could venture on and even attempt to solve tasks which necessarily remained closed to the one who paved the way for a new line of research.[25] Experience shows that works by independent "students" which extend and surpass the familiar positions of the master generally do stir up unease among the orthodox "model pupils." Erich Neumann, too, provided an example of this, especially with his minor work *Depth Psychology and a New Ethic* (1949). Even the manuscript already seemed to cause a stir—but for whom? In the Jung Institute people wondered whether a controversial text that diverged from the traditional beaten path of ethics ought to be published along with other publications of the Jung school, out of regard for the university and the church! Jung himself confessed how strong an impression the brilliantly written and in many respects provocative study had made on him. But he was afraid of its effect "like that of a bombshell. . . . Here we shall get some poison gas in our noses and some knocking on our heads. . . . I am not quarrelsome, but I am pugnacious by nature, and therefore I cannot conceal from you my secret amusement." Nevertheless, he said, as president of the Institute at the time he would—if need be—have to act as captain of the fire brigade. And finally an underhanded compliment to Neumann: "Your writings will be a *petra scandali* [stumbling-stone], but also the strongest impetus to future developments. For that I am profoundly thankful to you."[26]

Jung's extensive introduction to the English edition of Neumann's book went into the problem in such a way as to emphasize the author's daring, acuity, passion, and powers of intellectual penetration, and praised the study as the first noteworthy attempt to formulate and bring under discussion the ethical questions that had been raised by the discovery of the unconscious. Nonetheless, Jung left no doubt that the "new ethic" postulated by Neumann ultimately meant (only) a development and differentiation within, and based on, the "old ethic." Hence it was restricted "to those cases where the attempt is made by people in today's circumstances, under pressure from inevitably colliding responsibilities, to bring the unconscious into a responsible relationship to consciousness. . . ."[27] That he did not stand uncompromisingly behind Neumann, for all that, Jung gave his assurance in a detailed letter to Jürg Fierz, editor of the Zürich *Weltwoche*, after Christian-oriented readers especially feared that Neumann was trying to invalidate the traditional Christian ethics. From them in particular Jung appealed for understanding of the situation of the author, a Jew living quite isolated in Palestine, who belonged to a people who had been sacrificed to a most vicious crime. Otherwise, though, the teacher stood behind his pupil on all essential questions. His only objection was:

> The only mistake that Neumann commits here is a tactical one: he says aloud, incautiously, what has after all always been true. . . . I cannot even be sympathetic if it troubles these so-called Christians. They have richly deserved it. People are always talking about Christian morality, and I would just once like to see the one who really follows it! Not even the faintest understanding is shown toward Neumann, to say nothing of brotherly love. I could only wish for Christians nowadays to see just once that what they are following is not Christianity at all, but a god-awful legalistic religion from which its founder himself tried to free them. . . .[28]

Thus Jung put himself into the line of fire. This did not cause the mountain of manuscripts in his study to diminish, for there was still a number of further works by his students for the master to provide in the years after the war with introductions and hence moral support. Among these, for example, were a psychological interpretation of *The Dream of Poliphilo* (*Hypnerotomachia Poliphili*) by Linda Fierz-David (1946), Esther Harding's *Women's Mysteries* (1948), Gerhard Adler's *Studies in Analytical Psychology* (1949), A. Inge Allenby's religious-psychological study on the origins of monotheism (1950), Jolande Jacobi's English edition of her Paracelsus anthology, as well as other works for which Jung's judgment, and if possible his endorsement, were hoped for.[29] Lastly to be mentioned is the series of books which, under the title *Studies from the C. G. Jung Institute*, documented the advances made by the members of the recently founded place of research and training. The first publications under these auspices included studies by C. A. Meier, Hans Schär, Marie-Louise von Franz, Wolfgang Pauli, the former theologian of the Eastern Church

Gerhard P. Zacharias, and also anthologies on knowledge, anxiety, and evil. Emma Jung's work *The Grail Legend* was part of this series. Thus provision was made for thematic diversity and wealth of interconnections from the beginning:

> Psychology, you see, moves according to its nature among disciplines, for the psyche is the mother of all sciences and arts. Whoever wishes to paint her picture must bring together many colors on his palette. In order to do justice to its subject matter, psychology must support itself on many auxiliary sciences, on whose results it depends for its own prosperity.

So Jung said in his introduction to C. A. Meier's *Ancient Incubation and Modern Psychotherapy*, the volume which inaugurated the studies from the C. G. Jung Institute.[30] This dictum could stand as a motto for all the interdisciplinary works that together received their impetus from analytical psychology.

22

The Codex Jung

The great theme of early Christian Gnosis, which had occupied Jung intensely at the decisive turning point of his middle life,[1] before he came to concentrate on the development of alchemy for psychotherapy, was to return to his field of view again late in his life, and in a surprising way. At first the motive for this was an external one.

Early in 1948 it became generally known that several original Gnostic manuscripts in the Coptic language had been found some three years earlier not far from Nag Hammadi in upper Egypt, near the ancient Khenoboskion about one hundred kilometers north of the temple ruins of Luxor.[2] For science, especially for Gnostic scholarship, this news was a sensation comparable to that which the roughly simultaneous unearthing of the Dead Sea Qumran texts had represented for Old and New Testament studies. The significance of this find was all the greater, and the interest of Gnostic specialists all the stronger, since up to that time knowledge of this ancient "universal religion" and early Christian spiritual movement had had to based largely on quotations from ecclesiastical heretic-hunters and opponents of Gnosis. Hence there was now a legitimate hope of being able to verify the reliability of those quotations and deepen the knowledge of the Gnostic tradition in general. The scope of the texts, discovered in a large jar, was also considerable. There were thirteen volumes, or codices, with fifty-three separate texts of varying content, in all 1153 preserved pages of manuscript. The texts, translated into Coptic from Greek, in all probability dated from the second half of the fourth century. Forty-one of the manuscripts had previously been completely unknown.

From the decades-long and extremely eventful history of the acquisition, scientific development, and publication of this unique find, on which an extensive specialist literature[3] has come into being in the meantime, the following details are of interest with regard to C. G. Jung: The first codex, containing five texts, first came into the possession of the Belgian antiquarian Albert Eid. He allowed the scholars Jean Doresse and Togo Mina to examine the individual texts, which included the *Evangelium Veritatis* or "Gospel of Truth," so called after its opening words. This was not a new gospel text, however, but a sermonlike treatise from the world of Gnostic ideas. The remaining texts were an apocryphal letter of Saint James, a treatise on the resurrection, also called the "Letter to Rheginos," a three-part tractatus on heaven, creation, and man, and finally an ostensible prayer of the Apostle Paul.

In the winter of 1947–48, thus relatively early, the 144-page opus was offered for sale for twelve thousand dollars to the Bollingen Foundation in New York, but this institution which supported the work of Jung declined. Because of his fear that the Codex—to say nothing of the fate of the remaining twelve codices—might be withheld from science for an indefinite time, a young Gymnasium teacher, the Dutch church historian and Gnosis expert Gilles Quispel, later professor of early church history at Utrecht, stepped in as intermediary. He was acquainted with Jung from the Eranos conferences. In the newly founded Jung Institute in Zürich in 1951 he characterized Gnosticism as a universal religion and gave a provisional outline of the Nag Hammadi Codices (NHC), which were only very gradually becoming accessible.[4] Protracted negotiations with the owner of Codex I in Brussels, with the Egyptian government, the Coptic Museum in Cairo, and a buyer or investor still to be obtained were necessary. Quispel's lectures in Zürich were undoubtedly of great interest to Jung's circle. And matters did not stop there. It turned out that the last owner had died in the meantime, and the new whereabouts of the Codex had to be ascertained. Hence Quispel strove intently to secure the valuable fragment for science as quickly as possible. Despite the first failure he had hopes in the Bollingen fund in the United States, which otherwise had a reputation for open-handedness. From the detailed account which Quispel gave of the further course of events, it becomes apparent that at the time most people were still somewhat in the dark about the exact contents and value of the Codex he was trying to acquire:

"Considering this, I contacted Dr. C. G. Jung in Zürich, who most willingly sent several letters to members of the Bollingen board of directors in which he underscored the significance of the Codex and recommended its purchase by the institution. Meanwhile I had learned that the manuscript contained four (!) texts, one of which was entitled "The Gospel of Truth." Not much more was known of it beyond this title. All of our lively efforts were based on the assumption that this "Gospel of Truth" might be identical with the "Evangelium Veritatis," which the church father Irenaeus had informed us was in use among the students of the Gnostic Valentinus in A.D. 180.

"Finally in August 1950, after all these inquiries on behalf of the Bollingen Institute, I was able to determine in Paris that the Codex was being kept in a safe deposit box in Brussels. On 19 July 1951 Dr. C. A. Meier succeeded in finding out the address of the new owner and the price he was asking. In August 1951 it was agreed in Ascona that the Bollingen Foundation would furnish the amount necessary for the purchase, and I was commissioned to determine whether the manuscript was genuine or faked and if it was worth the price. Its examination by experts took place in 1952 in St. Idesbald (Coxyde) . . . . Suddenly the owner requested a postponement, and there were disquieting signals that other interests had appeared which, if they had not already offered a higher sum, were also carrying on negotiations on it. At the same time the Bollingen Foundation placed various understandable conditions on how the purchase money was to be used; but at this moment of urgent haste no agreement could be reached on this. It seemed as if all the efforts of four years were in vain and our endeavors had run aground.

"At this critical instant Dr. C. A. Meier, acting with great enterprise, rendered a great service to science. He discussed the situation with George H. Page of Canton Wallis, who proved to be a modern-day Maecenas and raised the sum necessary for the acquisition. The upshot was that on 10 May 1952 I was able to acquire the Codex in Brussels for the C. G. Jung Institute. . . ."[5] The purchase price came to thirty-five thousand Swiss francs. Approximately a year and a half passed before the new acquisition by the C. G. Jung Institute became publicly known. This in any case was the agreement between Quispel and Henri-Charles Puech, the Paris religious historian. On 15 November 1953, at a small party in the guild hall in Ründen, the manuscript was presented to Jung. "It was a disproportionate affair and neither my doing, nor liking. But I was manouevred into saying in the end a few words about the relation between Gnosticism and psychology," Jung informed his English friend Victor White, since even the *Times* had issued a news item on the subject.[6] This somewhat cold-sounding statement by the one who was honored with the Codex gives the impression that Jung underestimated the actual value of the manuscripts, but this is by no means the case. What is certain is that at this time Jung knew of only four of the actual five texts, and of these four he was familiar with only one, the "Gospel of Truth," which was to be sure the most significant. Still in the same year, Quispel was to find in Cairo some hitherto missing pages belonging to the Codex Jung among among the manuscript holdings acquired by another party in the meantime.

In the address in which he thanked all those who had made the purchase possible and set it in motion, Jung went into the religious-psychological meaning of the Gnostic texts. Consequently he saw in the *Evangelium Veritatis* one of the "many interpretive phenomena which sought to assimilate the exotic and difficult contents of the Christian revelation to the level of the Hellenistic and Egyptian spiritual world of the time."[7] By such interpretive phenomena Jung understood those distinctive reactions that were called forth from the human psyche of a certain time or age when the figure and the message of Christ met the heathen world of Greco-Roman antiquity. These are reflected, for example, in the use of certain symbols, be it that of the fish, the lion, the serpent, or the savior who transmits liberating knowledge (Gnosis) to mankind to bring light into the darkness of the unconscious. As the unconscious is activated by a phenomenon like that of Jesus Christ, it answers with archetypal images, showing in this way how deeply the epiphany of Christ has penetrated the human psyche. Very much more is involved, then, than simply a "theology" that satisfies rational needs without being able to effect the transformation and conversion (*metanoia*) demanded in the New Testament. Jung felt that the Gnostic explanation to the phenomenon of Christ and its attempt to offer enlightenment through Gnosis had not been very successful. On the other hand the church relatively early, from about the mid-second century on, had defended itself against the "universal religion of Gnosis" by uncompromisingly combating the Gnostics as dangerous heretics.[8] And yet despite suppression down to modern times this gnostic interpretive phenomenon has been maintained, and thanks to many metamorphoses of its outward appearance Gnosis has survived. Just as the Kabbalah allowed the revival of a primitive gnosis in Judaism, so the hermetic nature-philosophy of alchemy historically represents an interpretive manifestation analogous to early Christian Gnosis. Jung concluded:

> Because comparison with their earlier historical stages is very important for the interpretation of the modern phenomena, the discovery of authentic Gnostic texts is of the greatest interest to our line of research in particular, the

> more so as the latter is of not only a theoretical but also a practical nature.[9]

With this Jung quite consciously placed himself and his analytical and archetypal psychology within the tradition of genuine Gnosis. However misleading such a statement might be, taken out of context—by it is understood a spiritual vitality in which the fundamental powers of the spiritual world, the archetypes, prove to be effective—Jung and those who worked according to his method had nothing to fear from this designation.[10]

23

The Signs of Age: Creativity and Growth

Carl Gustav Jung, the "wise old man" of Küsnacht, the "magician" of the Bollingen tower, was approaching the last decade of his life. Soon he would be seventy-five. "He himself is very little changed," remarked Esther Harding in her diary in June 1948, after she and Eleanor Bertine were able to visit him at his home in Küsnacht again for the first time after the war. But the aging Jung would stand for no well-intentioned flattery. His tall figure was slightly stooped; his features were harder, and his white hair had thinned. "My head is growing feathers," he joked about himself. Alberto Moravia, at that time a correspondent for a Milan newspaper, had a different recollection of Jung. What stuck in his mind was the Swiss man's powerfully affecting facial expression. Not a few times had the elderly Jung been likened to a Swiss peasant. And he looked like one, too, especially when housekeeping around his Bollingen tower or making his daily rounds, puffing thoughtfully on his pipe, with a rude staff in his hand. The Italian writer had been impressed by his bright ruddy cheeks and above all his penetrating eyes. And as for his sporty woolen clothing, it had a rather plain appearance, but in an unmistakably "Faustian atmosphere."[1]

He was seen still differently by someone like Aniela Jaffé,

who had known Jung for almost twenty years when in 1955 she became the secretary and collaborator of his last years, and thus was around him nearly every day. What came to her mind more than anything was his physical delicateness, the elderly man's almost fragile appearance, which was for the most part overlooked "because it paled beside a feeling of power that radiated from him; no one who met him could help being impressed by it. It was not the power of severity, Jung was too benevolent, too kindly, and even in his old age too devoted to people, and his sense of humor too pronounced for that. Nor was it the power of erudition or a rich and differentiated intellect; his respect for any true knowledge and ability on the part of others was too great for that—no one was more eager to learn than he was. Jung's strength had but little to do with what is commonly called authority. What was so impressively felt in him sprang from the superiority of one who had had a life-and-death struggle with his creative genius and had conquered it, but who was marked by the fight. Such a strength is profoundly human. . . ."[2]

Jung was able to celebrate his seventy-fifth birthday during a period of several years of creative activity in which the whole variety and multidimensionality of analytical psychology once again became visible. In 1950, as volume 7 of the *Psychological Essays*, he published *The Structure of the Unconscious*. The book contained, among other things, the text of his earlier Eranos lecture of 1933, "A Study in the Process of Individuation,"[3] although in a thoroughly revised and considerably enlarged form. Here Jung showed not only how the process of individuation or maturation of the psyche can turn out and what revealing historical parallels—for example from the work of Jakob Böhme—can be drawn to it, but also the dangerous tendencies that must be avoided if one is not to risk the loss of psychic equilibrium through an inundation (inflation) by the contents of the unconscious. It is clear furthermore that individuation or self-realization, as Jung repeatedly described it, can never be gone through more than partially. No one can say he has completed the process in its entirety, particularly as the acceptance of one's own death, as the "last trial" of life, is an inevitable component of this self-development. That which reveals itself in dreams, in visions, and in fateful experiences can at best be understood as sign-posts and milestones along a way that cannot be surveyed by the ego-consciousness.

It is characteristic of the variety of Jung's creative output in these years that the various aspects of his late work were discussed in conversations with students, visitors, interviewers, and not least with numerous correspondents. While he worked on books like *Aion* or *Answer to Job* or *Mysterium Coniunctionis*, he had to take a stand on such widely divergent questions as those of religious experience, parapsychology, alchemy, the relationship of physics and psyche, the burning questions of present and future. Nineteen fifty was the year in which Pius XII proclaimed the dogma of the Assumption of Mary, thus granting expression to the value of womanhood in a way that seemed extremely meaningful to the depth psychologist, and one whose importance he was compelled to give adequate attention in his later work.[4] On the other hand, for some time the so-called UFO phenomena had been seen in the heavens, which—as is psychologically noteworthy—stirred the imaginations of countless contemporaries. More than ever, basic questions of present and future belonged to the psychologist's field of endeavor.

Typical of Jung's nature, as always, was his need to make his inner experience and the psychological insights he had gained manifest in external work as well. The output of his late years especially illustrates how much the research and work that had found objective, universal form in analytical psychology also always symbolized Jung's own process, his own individuation. The stage for these events, above all, was Bollingen. Only now did Jung go into why he had had to build his tower in such a peculiar way, creating as it were the container for his own self-development. In the *Memories* he set forth his explanation:

ollingen. (*Top, left*) The first tower, built in 1923. (*Top, right*) The tower in its nal form (1956). (*Bottom, left*) The elderly Jung at the woodpile. (*Bottom, ght*) The stone next to the tower, "a manifestation of the occupant."

> It might also be said that I built it in a kind of dream. Only afterward did I see how all the parts fitted together and that a meaningful form had resulted: a symbol of psychic wholeness.
>
> At Bollingen I am in the midst of my true life, I am most deeply myself. Here I am, as it were, the "age-old son of the mother."[5]

And with Jung the word "symbol" is always used in its full sense—that is, concretely, to mean the joining together (Greek *symballein*) of the mental and spiritual with the natural and material.[6] Its meaning is not to be sought "behind" things; rather it is in, with, and among things that that which could not be expressed in another, more precise way is embodied in typical form. Hence for Jung—in contrast to Freud—the symbol is much more than a mere (one-dimensional) sign, and more than an allegory that remains on the rational surface. Because this is so, in 1950 Jung began to express what the tower meant to him in symbolic form in its turn—one symbol by means of another. Alongside the tower, the vessel of his self-development, he created a kind of "monument" of stone, that is to say a moment of meditative realization through which the observer could grasp for all time the process of maturation. Thus it became an object of meditation, and by no means simply a memorial meant to recall something past. There was a remarkable story connected with the laying of this stone, which Jung told as follows:

> I needed stones for building the enclosing wall for the so-called garden, and ordered them from the quarry near Bollingen. I was standing by when the mason gave all the measurements to the owner of the quarry, who wrote them down in his notebook. When the stones arrived by ship and were unloaded, it turned out that the cornerstone had altogether the wrong measurements; instead of a triangular stone, a square block had been sent: a perfect cube of much larger dimensions than had been ordered, about twenty inches thick. The mason was furious and told the barge men to take it right back with them.

> But when I saw the stone, I said, "No, that is my stone. I must have it!" For I had seen at once that it suited me perfectly and that I wanted to do something with it. Only I did not yet know what.[7]

It is typical of Jung, this wish that is not controlled by any external knowledge but receives its direction and definition from an intuitive impulse. Spontaneously, a Latin verse from the alchemist Arnaldus de Villanova (died 1313) occurred to him, and thus he had found the text that was to fill one side of the cube. In English the Latin passage reads:

> Here stands the mean, uncomely stone,
> 'Tis very cheap in price!
> The more it is despised by fools,
> The more loved by the wise.

The very source of this dictum makes it clear that this refers to none other than the "philosophers' stone." At the same time, the connection between the stone and self-realization is obvious. And as far as the further elaboration of the rough stone was concerned, this likewise followed in the main an intuitive course. In the middle of its front side Jung "recognized" a small circle; that is, he saw it in his mind's eye. The circle seemed to stand out from the surface of the stone as if on its own, and soon something appeared within it, the figure of a little man such as Jung had once fashioned as a child and treated as a confidant. He carried a lantern in his left hand and pointed the way with his right; on his cloak the sign of Mercury was clearly visible, the union of sun and moon, the quintessence of wholeness. Jung himself described him as a kind of Kabir or the Telesphoros of Asklepios, figures from the ancient mysteries. While he was working on this side, from the center outward, more inscriptions occurred to him, with which he covered the remaining space on the front side, divided into four parts. This time it was a Greek text: ". . .this is Telesphoros, who roams through the dark regions of this cosmos and glows like a star out of the depths. He points the way to the gates of the sun and to the land of dreams." And in fact the right hand of the little man in the small circle did point to the sun, the sign of Jupiter in his left, when Venus and the moon were in opposition, identifying the land of dreams. After the third side of the stone, facing the lake, had also been arrayed in alchemistic texts, it only remained for the stone-carver and tower-dweller of Bollingen to fulfill a kind of duty as chronicler. Thus one finds today, under Arnaldus de Villanova's maxim, the words in Latin: "In remembrance of his seventy-fifth birthday C. G. Jung made and placed this here as a thanks offering, in the year 1950."[8]

And what of the side turned away from the observer, the one concealed by shrubbery? Jung left it unworked, of course, although he had actually "considered" it. He asked the recorder of his memoirs:

> Do you know what I wanted to chisel into the back face of the stone? "*Le cri de Merlin!*" For what the stone expressed reminded me of Merlin's life in the forest, after he had vanished from the world. Men still hear his cries, so the legend runs, but they cannot understand or interpret them.[9]

A very meaningful remark, when one considers on the one hand the role Merlin played in the medieval Grail tradition, and on the other the fact that Jung's placing and shaping of this stone had to do with himself and his own process of transformation and integration. According to the legend Merlin, the great sorcerer, bard, and medicine man or shaman of Celtic mythology, was begotten by the devil himself, but his mother was a pure virgin. And instead of displaying his father's tendencies, he opened himself to the powers of healing and himself became a champion of healing, especially in the vicinity of the Holy Grail.[10] And precisely here lay the extraordinary part of his essential nature, for he combined within himself the primal opposites of light and darkness, heathen and Christian. That which had more and more torn the Christian tradition asunder was united, more or less completely, in Merlin. The fact that the (not fully formed) Grail figure stood in immediate proximity to alchemistic symbolism on the

Bollingen stone does not seem strange; indeed the mysterious Grail itself, the *lapis exillis*, was conceived of as a stone vessel which harbored the healing elixir, tangible to men.

Jung himself of course, as we have seen, had been reminded of the Grail mystery in an extremely impressive way through a dream he had had while visiting India early in 1938. And there was still another aspect that indicates the archetypal significance of Merlin for Jung. Marie-Louise von Franz pointed out[11] how shocked Jung was when many years after the building of his Bollingen tower, his refuge away from the world, he became better acquainted with the Merlin tradition, with which he had had but little familiarity up to then. According to the tradition Merlin had retreated to the solitude of the forest in order to escape from the troubled world, the world of King Arthur and the Round Table. According to Breton legends he had disappeared into a kind of rock tomb, a "tower" (!). Hence people also spoke of a "stone of Merlin," set up far away from all the turmoil of the world of men. If *esplumoir* refers to the designation for Merlin's refuge in a cage in which falcons molted, thus going through a transformation, this too is a striking parallel to Jung's undertaking in Bollingen, an individually fashioned quest for the Grail. (Further possibilities for interpretation, which Marie-Louise von Franz spoke of later, can be dispensed with here.)

One thing is indisputable: like the tower, the laying of this stone, as well as the various bas-reliefs Jung had chiseled from the rough stone blocks of his tower, in the end had to do only with himself. They were manifestations, illustrations of his own process. His works in the bluish-green sandstone he found around Bollingen are also not be be measured by esthetic standards. When an American sculptor put several questions to him concerning his works in Bollingen, he made it clear to him how little what he had created there could be comprehended by the rules of that art. In his letter of 1 September 1952, Jung answered:

> I'm no artist. I only try to get things into stone of which I think it is important that they appear in hard matter and stay on for a reasonably long time. Or I try to give form to something that seems to be in the stone and makes me restless. It is nothing for show, it's only to make these troublesome things steady and durable. There is not much of form in it, chiefly inscriptions and you would learn nothing from it.[12]

With this he retreated, politely but definitely aloof, into his own "tower."

If this and similar moments give rise to a picture of C. G. Jung as a magus, one must nevertheless make it clear what dimension of his personality one is speaking of when placing him in the domain of the aloof and esoteric or magical and shamanistic. This applies only to the normally hidden personality No. 2, the inner man who needed such a refuge as a place, as well as a spiritual attitude, if he was to be equal to his life's mission. For all that, the physician and scholar, teacher and author, moved with great matter-of-factness on the social parquet. That the same Carl Gustav Jung was able to switch from the one sphere to the other without falling victim to that sickness which he had described as a young psychiatrist and which he had come to know to a certain extent as a threat up to his middle life—schizophrenia—was characteristic of him. He demanded of his critics a sensibility commensurate with this fact.

24

Answer to Job

On the whole there are three publications which stand out from the work of C. G. Jung's later years. These had to do partly with the subject of self-development, represented in alchemical symbolism as the *Mysterium Coniunctionis.* This two-volume work, supplemented by a third volume of texts, arranged and with commentary by Marie-Louise von Franz, can be considered the real work of Jung's old age. Its author had begun it during the war years, before he had reached his seventieth year. Thematically the separate volume *The Practice of Psychotherapy,* which had appeared earlier, also belonged in this context. Being concerned over and over in this late period with the questions of "Present and Future" (1957), in 1958 Jung published "Flying Saucers: A Modern Myth"—"flying saucers" or UFOs being seen in the skies had been the subject of widespread debate for some time. Among other things, there was heated controversy over the question of whether they were earthly missiles of a potential enemy power or flying machines of some "extraterrestrials" that had to be reckoned with.

But the object of a much more specialized, theological debate was to be Jung's *Answer to Job*, a work that with elemental impact raised as no other had done fundamental questions of the image of God, as well as those of human existence in contrast to the transcendental, and the problem of good and evil. *Answer to Job* thus stands out from the long series of all the rest of his books in that here the writer is not a researcher concerned with the scientific demonstration of facts. The floor went rather to one who was profoundly agitated, who in his challenging, almost violent confrontation with the image of the God of the Old Testament, Yahweh, felt compelled to write down from the heart everything that had formed an indelible part of his life for decades. At bottom it had been present for Jung even in the visionary inner perceptions of his early childhood imagination, in which he had felt a powerful dark side in God himself, or more exactly in the image of God. One thinks also, for example, of his experience before the Basel cathedral and the liberating effect that the dropping a great mass of dung on the "house of God" had produced in Carl Gustav as a student!

One contributing factor in the writing was an illness which had a productive function. In the spring of 1951 Jung was repeatedly bedridden, as his liver was giving him trouble. Then, amid fevered states which gave the impression that his whole physical and mental structure was, as it were, collapsing, the patient was seized by the idea of the Book of Job. The book "came to him," as he once explained in a letter to his French friend and Eranos colleague Henry Corbin. The inspired character of the event is unmistakable, albeit clearly different from the earlier "Septem Sermones ad Mortuos." And although Jung by his own admission was not an auditory type—one fixated on hearing sounds internally and externally—he perceived what pressed in upon him, and was to be turned into language through him, as a "great music," like something by Bach or Handel. "I felt as if I were listening to a great composition, or rather a concert. The whole thing was an adventure that befell me, and I hurried to write it down."[1] That it was not a scientific book was already shown by the jacket copy for the first edition in 1952. Rather it was a "personal confrontation with the world of traditional Christian ideas," spurred by the dogma of Mary advanced shortly before by Pius XII. Nor did he speak at all as a theologist, but—as always—as a doctor, who could not escape the many religious questions of his practice and above all his entire personal experience. Added to this were the great contemporary events of the just-ended world war, with its flash floods of deceit, injustice, subjugation, and mass murder, which had shocked all humanity. Thus there was reason enough to ask, "What does a kind and almighty God have to say to this?" Fundamentally, he said, this question, posed thousands and millions of times, was long overdue. Between the lines was an unstated warning: no one expected dogmatic orthodoxy or the attempt at repeated theodicy—that is, an additional justification of God in whatever form—from a rationally thinking or even ecclesiastically committed theologian!

The very fact that a man of the mentality of a C. G. Jung took up his pen to free himself of the violent emotions that the Book of Job produced in him deserves notice. This text, assigned in Luther's Bible to the so-called instructional books, and in Buber's interpretation to the body of "scriptural works," is unquestionably among the great religious poetical works of world literature.

And apparently there is more than one Job tradition in the biblical sense. Job may reflect an explosion that has been renewed from time to time: Martin Luther acknowledged how much effort the book cost him from the linguistic point of view alone. Philosophers of the prominence of Johann Georg Hamann were mightily attracted to it. Probably best known is the relation of the Book of Job to the "Prelude in Heaven" of Goethe's *Faust*, with its curious dialogue between God and Satan, as if they were two gamblers betting on the genuineness of Job's devotion. The fascination which the biblical Job—admittedly or not—has exerted on modern people since Kierkegaard is easily demonstrated. The Danish Socrates made several attempts to get closer to him in his book *Recapitulation*: "If I had not had Job! It is impossible to describe or to shade exactly the meaning and the manifold significance he has for me. I read him not as one reads any other book, with the eye, rather I read the book as it were in my heart, and with the eye of the heart I read it, understand the particulars in the most distinct way as if in clairvoyance. . . ."[2]

For the existential philosopher Karl Jaspers, who was in Kierkegaard's philosophical tradition, it was the ambiguity of the relationship of God to man and man to God that caused unease. The Marxist philosopher Ernst Bloch, an atheist of Jewish extraction, could not and would not escape the bewilderment of the sufferer confronted with the avenging god Yahweh, considerable as the misinterpretations could and must be which Bloch bestowed on this book of the Bible.[3]

Thus Jung's Job theme did not come out of the blue, although he could not have been motivated by the contexts of those named. How could he have been? But contemporaneity and "simultaneity" (Kierkegaard) marked out the intellectual field from which Jung cannot be disengaged. Other, more immediate contemporaries belonged here as well. There was Jung's in many respects dissimilar countryman, the theologian Karl Barth, who in four exegetical essays in his monumental *Church Dogmatics* contrasted Job with the crucified Christ and his work.[4] That the theologian expected no substantial explanatory help of the psychologist requires no special proof. But at least marginally Barth attested that Jung had written "in human terms a very moving document—and incidentally one extremely revealing of the psychology of the professional psychologist!"[5]

Almost simultaneously with Jung and in his immediate vicinity, in Zürich, a Jewish woman was recording her own Job-experience, an experience vibrating with Jobiads, the numerous and inextinguishable; this was Margarete Susman. She had drawn upon Job as the book of the destiny of the Jewish people, seeking to obtain from Job a ray of light on an uncertain path.[6]

It is only in historical context, against the background of these interpretations of Job, but above all in clear contrast to them, that the contours of the Jungian picture of Job stand out. For where others wished to lay open the Old Testament book, to "bring it closer" to themselves and hence to people of today,

Jung's aim was from the first a different one, at any rate not one of theology or literary criticism, but rather antitheological. That it would consequently be a "hard nut" for the unprepared, he freely admitted. Those who found in it too much sarcasm, irony, and "suchlike rubbish," Jung advised, could simply let it alone and not bother with it.[7] Or in positive terms, as in a letter from November 1955: "The book does not pretend to be anything but the voice or question of a single individual who hopes or expects to meet with thoughtfulness in the public."[8] Thus it is a thoroughly personal and intimate book, by one deeply troubled and moved, and thus the strict opposite of a scientifically argued biblical commentary.

Jung read the text quite consciously without the aid of critical apparatus, so as not to arouse the slightest impression of wishing to be swayed by prior theological exegesis. Jung's provocation was preceded by that of the unknown biblical author who wrote some centuries before the common era. Job, a blameless man who lives according to the law and the religious order, becomes the victim of an experiment, nay a wager, between God and Satan—in itself already rather a lot to ask of the poor Bible reader! The question is how much Job's piety and devotion to God are really worth. Would he still remain faithful to God if he lost all he had, his sons and daughters, plagued with leprosy, staring death in the face? The crushing blows of fate are compounded by the disheartening, nagging remonstrances of his own wife and his know-it-all friends. Heated debates are followed finally by the confrontation between Job and God/Yahweh. Faced with the omnipotence of the Creator, the tormented human becomes aware that he is a created being and subject to death—and he survives. But what of the image of God that is uncovered here? What of the "righteousness" of Yahweh? Does this not reveal a contradiction in Yahweh with which the suffering human being, awakening to consciousness, must come to terms? Questions upon questions!

With good reason, attention has sometimes been drawn to what Tenzler called the "fundamentally interlocking nature of

Jung's personal and scientific conception of God."[9] Only from this point of view is his attitude toward religious reality and the problem of Job understandable. Of course it is also true that Jung viewed his own experience and perception in the light of other testimony from religious and intellectual history, in comparison for example with those by whom the contradictory and antagonistic in God had been taken into account. Thus it was not simply a wish to emphasize the admittedly violent face of contemporary history—the state of humanity since Auschwitz and Hiroshima—as the only point of the Book of Job, as seems to be so in other authors, for example Margarete Susman.

Asked about the genesis of his *Answer to Job*, Jung pointed out that he had been concerned for many years with the central problem involved in it, that of the antagonism of Christ and Antichrist. In his previous book *Aion* (1951),[10] which shed deep light on the symbolism of the age of Christ, the Age of Pisces, those questions had still remained unsettled—a further impetus to take up these problems from a new approach. Jung had long felt that the results of psychology contradicted the ecclesiastical doctrine which saw evil as an absence of good (*privatio boni*).

> Psychological experience shows that whatever we call "good" is balanced by an equally substantial "bad" or "evil." If "evil" is a *me on*—nonexistent—then whatever there is must needs be "good."[11]

So Jung said, pointing to developments in the history of dogma. According to dogma, neither good nor evil could have its origin in man, since in Job 1:6 the so-called Evil One (Satan) turns out to be virtually one of the sons of God. The text reads: "Now there was a day when the sons of God came to present themselves before the Lord, and Satan came also among them." Satan, then, as Christ was later, a son of God! Whereas Clement of Rome (first century C.E.), whom Jung often cited in *Aion*, spoke of God's ruling the world with a right and a left hand—that is, with Christ and with Satan—

this originally monotheistic Christianity would seem to have become dualistic; the part of the one God that is personified in Satan is split off to become the evil that opposes God. Hence in his letter of November 1955, which was published as a preface to his book on Job, Jung wrote:

> If Christianity claims to be a monotheism, it becomes unavoidable to assume the opposites as being contained in God. But then we are confronted with a major religious problem: the problem of Job. It is the aim of my booklet to point out its historical evolution since the time of Job down through the centuries to the most recent symbolic phenomena like the *Assumptio Mariae*, etc.[12]

But naturally this was not meant to imply that the author intended merely to collect and comment upon historical evidence, as had been done for example even in his study of medieval natural philosophy.

> All this pointed to a *complexio oppositorum* and thus recalled again the story of Job to my mind: Job who expected help from God against God. This most peculiar fact presupposes a similar conception of the opposites. . . .
>
> For several years I hesitated. . . , because I was quite conscious of the probable consequences and knew what a storm would be raised. But I was gripped by the urgency and difficulty of the problem and was unable to throw this off. Therefore I found myself obliged to deal with the whole problem and did so in the form of describing a personal experience, carried by subjective emotions. I deliberately chose this form because I wanted to avoid the impression that I had any idea of announcing an "eternal truth."[13]

Jung read the Bible, and the Book of Job with it, as "utterances of the soul." Though this might appear at first sight to be a psychologization of sacred texts, which seems to drag down their revealed contents from the transcendent, pneumatic level to that of the "merely" psychic, this notion turns out to be unfounded. For on the one hand Jung expressly did not speak as a theologian or prophet of a revelation claiming final validity, and on the other hand "soul" is not identical with the ego of everyday consciousness. What was meant was rather that depth and that immeasurable total range of spiritual reality where—out of reach of human discretion and feasibility—archetypes are at work. What is imparted, often along with great shocks (as a *mysterium tremendum*), is archetypal images and influences. They appear on the horizon of human experience. And only that which "clicks" there, that which becomes clear and is attested to by people, as the recipients of such experiences, in definite situations in their lives, is subject to psychological observation.[14] Holy Scripture, or "God's word in the words of man," is nothing other than such "documents of the soul," which bear the signatures of those who received them even in their diction and their metaphysical language. Any other "immediate revelation" which would dispense with passing through an organ of human perception would be imperceptible, and thus also neither certifiable nor understandable. And is it not so that only the incarnation of God can bring the "wholly other" into existence? For this reason, here as in many other places, Jung had to stress emphatically that he neither desired nor was able to make any kind of statements about God, but only about *images* or *conceptions* of God, as they took place in people in this way. Thus the human soul, the locus of the theophany, is always "only" the vessel of an ultimately inexhaustible content that is beyond the reach of the ego (cf. 2 Cor. 4:6ff). Thus there are numinous factors which shape the human intellect as well as the emotional life in all its depth and scope. For this reason alone Jung could make no use at all of a dissociated objectivity. He could not leave himself "outside," but had to include himself, with all his emotions, when reading so demanding a book as that of the biblical Job. Therefore he repeatedly remarked:

> I write not as a scholar (which I am not), but as a layman and a doctor who has been privileged to look deep into the spiritual lives of many people. What I express is of course pri-

> marily my own opinion, but I know that I also speak in the name of many who have fared as I have.[15]

These statements of Jung's, which call to mind his point of departure and his procedure, for example his way of reading the Bible, demanded to be taken into account. And precisely because not a few of his critics evidently had not read his Preface or had not taken it seriously, Jung's advice on this point was well founded.

The author pointed out how full of contradictions and practically overflowing with emotions is the picture which the Old Testament draws of Yahweh: the Creator is the angry one, burning with passion, the reckless destroyer of everything that is opposed to God. Hence Jung's summation: "A state of affairs constituted in such a way can only be described as amoral."[16] This "divine darkness" is revealed in the Book of Job through Yahweh's allowing the man to be groundlessly hounded out of the land of Uz. On the other hand, in his suffering Job recognizes the injustice of God, and above all that in answer to his love and faith this God finds himself opposed to the people of his covenant (Job 16:19ff). Nevertheless the tormented Job sticks to him: "I know that my Redeemer liveth"! (19:25). Evil exists together with good—in Yahweh. In the clear knowledge of this contradiction Job hopes in Yahweh (the Redeemer) against Yahweh (the Terrible). To the extent that Job bases his hope on such a realization, he gains insight into Yahweh's double nature. This realization on the part of his creation reacts upon the creator, and hence Jung sees the real reason for God's becoming man, that is for the incarnation of Christ, in his confrontation with Job.

> . . .God becomes man. This means nothing less than the transformation of God which overturns the world. It means more or less what the creation did in its time, namely an objectivization of God.[17]

Here, in the life and suffering of Christ, the other son of God (in contrast to Satan), comes the real answer to Job. The problem that starts with and through Job, which is expressed in the image of God and reflected in Job's fate, finds its solution through the "Redeemer." For Jung, God becomes conscious of himself in Christ; the son appeases the wrath of his father—a situation that is nowhere more impressively and universally expressed than in the theosophy of Jakob Böhme.[18] Further, the example of Böhme is significant because it illustrates how this process, radiating from the inner dynamics of the divine to the whole of cosmology, could become a spontaneous experience for a man who with no knowledge of tradition or depth psychology was driven to this staggering inner perception.

For Jung the incarnation, the humanization, of God was by no means ended with Christ, but only begun. There was a progressive "approximation of the believer to the status of the son of God" wherever the Holy Spirit pitched his tent among men.

> The ongoing, immediate influence of the Holy Spirit on those who are called to be God's children means *de facto* an ever-widening incarnation. Christ, the son begotten by God, is the first-born, who is followed by a great number of posthumous sisters and brothers.[19]

Trains of thought such as this should not cause us to forget that Jung continued to speak as a psychologist, who had in mind solely the humanization, or individuation, of man, even when speaking of the coming to consciousness of God. It is the human being who must attain the goal of life, the meaning of life, his wholeness or Self. It is a completeness which should not be confused with moral or religious and holy perfection. The integration of man has always been described and longed for as a *hierosgamos* or sacred marriage, for example in such forms as the marriage of the Lamb. It involves not only—as in Jung's psychotherapy—the integration of the shadow as the sum of the dark, mostly denied and unconscious side of one's nature, but above all also the elevation of the feminine, the "equalization" of women. This equality refers not merely to full social recognition of women, but rather is equivalent to a metaphysical and spiritual anchoring of women. That is to say, if the traditional image of God in the Old and New Testaments carried explicitly patriarchal traits, and if the whole of Western civilization for two millennia has borne the stamp of this, then great attention must be paid to a process that makes, or could make, allowance for the need for the integration of human beings after the elevation of the feminine.

Because the announcement on 1 November 1950 of the dogma of the bodily ascension of Mary immediately preceded the composition of *Answer to Job*, and the debate among the various theological and ecclesiastical-ecumenical viewpoints had stirred up great waves at that time, Jung went into this in detail. His experiences in the field of religious psychology, and in particular the psychology of religion or the contents of religion, had encouraged him to take a positive stance toward this recent Marian dogma. His esteem for it could hardly have been greater. In the dogma of the Assumption of Mary he saw "the most important religious event since the Reformation."[20] The method of papal argumentation, he said, which had in the past been compelled (and able!) to do without biblical substantiation, was he said extremely plausible to the psychological mind. Moreover the logical consistency of the papal declaration was unsurpassed, whereas Protestantism remained "a religion of men" because it did without this metaphysical anchoring of women. But:

> The feminine demands just as personal a representation as the masculine. . . . Just as the person of Christ cannot be replaced by an organization, so neither can the bride by the Church. . . .[21]

Jung's sarcasms, his way of evaluating the figures of God in the Old and New Testaments, are unquestionably a chapter in themselves. Thus the psychologist claimed to get rid of his aversions by falsely attributing "an unholy fantasy" to the apocalyptist John. The Christ of the apocalypse "behaves rather like an ill-tempered, power-conscious 'boss.'. . ." The psychological critic of John's revelation strung together a whole series of contradictions and reproaches.

Jung, it seems, did not feel particularly comfortable with himself after the manuscript had been written and a few friends set eyes on it. A number of theologians appeared to be shocked, and even Emma Jung had misgivings, while younger people were favorably impressed. To Aniela Jaffé he wrote from Bollingen on 29 May 1951 that he had still not fully digested this "*tour de force* of the unconscious."[22] He spoke of an "aftershock" that still made him uneasy himself. On another occasion Jung admitted that he had really not yet found the right way to present what he had had to say in *Answer to Job* in order to be rightly understood. Early in 1952, to the Reformed theologian Walter Uhsadel of Hamburg, he advertised his book on Job, then in press, as a "polemic." And though Jung had expressed concern already months before its appearance, for example in a letter of 30 August 1951,[23] that he had stirred up an "inferno," a scant year later his astonishment was great. It "causes the weirdest misunderstandings," reads a letter of 28 July 1952.[24] To Upton Sinclair he complained: "People mostly don't understand my empirical standpoint." But was it only his empirical standpoint, after all? Should not the very personal confession found in a letter of 28 July 1952, to an Israeli woman living in Tel Aviv, be taken at least as seriously? This read: "I am always seeking quiet. I am a bundle of opposites and can only stand myself when I observe myself as an objective phenomenon." And after his capacity for physical effort, at the age of seventy-seven, had perceptibly diminished, he was almost afraid of new inspirations that would exact too high a degree of work from him. And of course over and over there were, as also in the Job book, "inspirations" that insinuated themselves with an almost compelling power which overwhelmed the recipient, which he was thus hardly able to withstand. Thus all these letters show something of Jung's psychic predicament and his thoroughly personal suffering through what the majority of his critics took as simply an intellectual provocation.

This resulted in an extremely lively debate between Jung and his theological critics, or those who argued on behalf of the faithful, although Jung had not really been writing for them. Because he did not count himself among the fortunate possessors of the truths of faith, but knew very well the suffering of the unbelieving yet still religious seeker, *Answer to Job* was ultimately written only for those people who like Job suffered on account of God. More notably, this took place at the time when Rudolf Bultmann's theory of demythologization was being no less controversially debated.[25] For a generation of theologians at least, this was to carry the day through a cross-section of creeds and nations, while Jung's religious-psychological and therapeutic contribution was downgraded to a marginal phenomenon as an attempt at a remythologization of Christianity.

At this period of his life the circle of those who were beginning to understand Jung's intention was understandably small. There were only a few, such as the Swiss theologian Hans Schär, to whom he could acknowledge soon after the publication of *Answer to Job* that he had discharged the difficult task of editing it in "very objective fashion." Jung felt compensated for "a thousand misunderstandings" by the pleasing letter he had already had from Erich Neumann in Tel Aviv in December of 1951. For his student Neumann, Jung's book on Job was the finest and most profound of all that the master had written, insofar as one could call it a "book." The Jewish analyst wrote: "It is a book that moves me deeply. . . . In a certain sense it is a debate with God, like that of Abraham when he pleaded with God over the ruin of Sodom. It is particularly—for me personally—also a book against God, who allowed six million of 'his' people to be slain, for of course Job is really also Israel, and I mean this not in a 'petty' sense, as I know full well that we are only the paradigm for all of humanity, in whose name you speak, protest, and console. And precisely the conscious one-sidedness, and indeed often incorrectness of what you say, is for me an inner proof of the necessity and justness of your attack—which is of course no attack, as I know very well. . . ."[26] Could the unorthodox nontheologian Jung be supposed to have understood the inner situation, that of the Jews before God, better than the many Christian theologians, from the theologians in his own family down to those for whom a Reformed parson's offspring had become a traitor to God?

Finally, that friendship could change abruptly to hostility, sparked by Jung's Job-apology, is shown by the example of the Englishman Victor White. After his first reading of it, the Dominican father still acted delighted and gratefully excited. Soon he began to have second thoughts, the misgivings of one who suddenly realized that agreement with psychological insights could lead to conflict with Church dogma. He began publicly to defame Jung's work, to insinuate that his friend was naive and poorly informed on theological matters. It is quite remarkable that statements of this kind came directly from Victor White, for, as Laurens van der Post commented, "if anyone were in a position to know the extent of Jung's theological knowledge, research, and interest in religion, and his grasp of its history and implications for life past and present, it was Victor White. Yet despite this, Jung, up to the end, respected what had brought him and White together and understood Victor White's situation, committed as he was to a priority of prescribed faith"[27]—as were many others with and after him! Finally, for the present the official records in the case of Job and Jung cannot be closed, if one considers how closely the two disciplines, theology and depth psychology, referred to each other in intensive collaboration in *Answer to Job*.[28] The problem is not historical, but more and more existential, particularly as the suffering of Job does not cease; it multiplies a millionfold. Not only is this comment found in the letter Jung wrote to a Protestant theologian in 1951; the author also pointed this out:

> It seems to me that it is only the person who seeks to realize

his humanity who does God's will, not the one who takes flight before the sad fact "man." . . . To become human seems to me to be the intention of God in us. . . . God has obviously not chosen to be his sons those who hang on to him as a father, but those who have found the courage to stand on their own feet.

Sarcasm is the means by which one conceals injured feelings from oneself, from which it can be gathered how much the knowledge of God has wounded me, and how much I would have preferred to remain as a child in the fatherly protection and avoid the problem of the opposites. It is probably even harder to free oneself from good than from evil. But without sin there is no breaking away from the good father. . . . One way or another certain questions must be openly asked and answered. I took it as my duty to encourage this.[29]

25

Mysterium Coniunctionis

Since C. G. Jung had come into contact with alchemy in the course of the twenties, he had been like a wanderer in the high mountains. After a diligent search for materials in preparation and after a laborious ascent, he had climbed—menaced by steep precipices—peak after peak. Roping down ahead of schedule was out of the question. The danger of going astray in the labyrinthine heights was increased still more by the longing for new vistas, the intoxication of the mountain air. Carl Gustav Jung, the enthusiastic mountain climber, could no longer extricate himself from the world of alchemistic symbolism, to withdraw from the secret path of the soul which Heraclitus said cannot be measured by steps. So it is understandable that what had been somewhat tentatively put forward at first only to a small audience, for example in the Psychological Club or at the Eranos conferences (from 1933), and then developed in the weighty volume *Psychology and Alchemy* (1944), did not let the explorer rest. His "investigations into the separation and combination of the psychic opposites in alchemy" were to accompany him to the last days of his life. Hence in his *Memories*:

> Since my aim was to demonstrate the full extent to which my psychology corresponded to alchemy—or vice versa—I wanted to discover, side by side with the religious

questions, what special problems of psychotherapy were treated in the work of the alchemists.[1]

One of the central ideas in this effort was that of the *coniunctio*, the unification whose parallelism to the processes of integration on the path of individuation invited such studies—with the goal in both cases being to come closer to the secret of the unification of the opposites, the *mysterium coniunctionis*, and in this coming nearer to gain insights on the path of one's own individuation which go beyond mere intellectual knowledge to the existential nature of transformation and maturation. To this extent it corresponded to early Christian Gnosticism, the object of Jung's earlier researches, because "Gnosis" was also not aimed at intellectual information, but at a thoroughgoing change in the person, his awakening to a new, higher life, which is not damaged by earthly death.

As far as his field of endeavor as a whole was concerned, Jung occasionally stated that it had always been painful to him that in depth psychology it was inherently necessary to deal with so many fields of culture that it could nowhere lead to a completeness of scientific specialization, particularly in the case of the pioneer who first had to locate and explore the hitherto disparate areas. Alchemy, he said, was such a field, which it seemed profitable to him to go into. And Marie-Louise von Franz, who accompanied him in this as a coworker, remarks on this point: "The alchemistic tradition enabled him to connect the experiences and insights he had acquired through his direct, personal 'descent into the unconscious' with an objectively existing parallel material and to represent it in this way. This also made possible a connection with his insights into the historical roots of European intellectual development."[2]

As Jung was writing the Foreword to *Mysterium Coniunctionis* in October 1954, he cited a 1941 essay by Karl Kerényi on the Aegean festival in Goethe's *Faust*. This essay,[3] he said, had prompted him more than ten years ago to tackle his last great work, this very *Mysterium Coniunctionis*. He must have read it in manuscript, because as early as 18 January of that year he had mentioned to the author his great interest in the subject. He confessed to the "remarkable mood" this text had put him in. It was above all the figure of Goethe's Homunculus, he said, that fascinated him. But this was not enough: Jung's further comment that he would have to "mull over" Kerényi's essay for a while suggests a meditative approach in which what has been read once is returned to over and over again after being enriched time after time from the unconscious, especially if one or more nights intervene in which one has slept on the problem. Jung aptly spoke in his letter of an "incubation," a process such as was gone through in one of the ancient places of the healing mysteries, for example Epidaurus: after one had called upon the god himself in the *abaton* or healing room, there was a chance of meeting in sleep and dreams Asklepios, the god of healing, in order to be cured by him.[4] Then Jung expressed the faint hope in regard to this work: "Perhaps I will manage to arrange my psychological material in a form that fits it better."[5]

Some eight weeks after this letter he returned to the subject. He let it be known that he had already been thinking over the whole subject "for years," admittedly without having come to a satisfactory result. Naturally it was clear to him as an authority on alchemy that what had been called up was the central concept of the alchemical *coniunctio*, which was intimately bound up with the production of the Faustian Homunculus. Thus Jung wrote to Kerényi:

> The Aegean Festival is one aspect of this problem, whereas the problem itself extends infinitely further: on one hand along the line of the *hierosgamos* to Gnosis and Christian mythology and on into Indian Tantrism, and on the other via the Homunculus into the psychology of alchemy.[6]

Furthermore—he admitted here—Jung had been entertaining "for some time now" the plan of looking into this fascinating motif of the *coniunctio*, and so Kerényi's encouragement was welcome. Ideally he would have liked to get straight to work, but then the Paracelsus anniversary intervened in 1941, to which he—the self-styled nonspecialist—was expected to contribute some "Paracelsica." But his absorption in the work of the great Hohenheimer could not have been very much of a distraction, for his considerable influence on the alchemy of his time is well known. Thus the researcher was on familiar ground. In fact his efforts led into work on the subject of the *coniunctio*, for it soon became clear to Jung that a mere psychological commentary on Kerényi's essay would not be sufficient. The size of the subject, the difficulty of the problems involved, and the wealth of the material to be considered explain why Jung spent more than a decade working on *Mysterium Coniunctionis*. It should also be remembered that his heart attack in 1944 considerably reduced his efficiency and the pace of his work.

If his previous work consisted in opening up the side field of alchemy, as he did in *Psychology and Alchemy*, it was now time to go deeper. Thematically, his study on "The Psychology of the Transference," which appeared a little later (1946),[7] also belonged here. It might have been surprising that it was not only personal taste or mere theoretical interest that prompted the author to build a bridge between alchemy and psychology. He was guided, as he remarked expressly, by practical necessity. This arose from the concrete opposition of therapist and client, in which the "transference" arose as an autonomous influence of the unconscious, for example in the form of the projection of the ideas and feelings of one on the other, and thus not only from patient onto analyst. Thus it is a process of relationship between two people.[8] Jung had compared the process with the mixing of two different chemical elements or substances. If a "bond" is produced, both are "altered." It can only be noted incidentally that the original Freudian concept of transference is unlike that of Jung.

Obviously, the transference phenomenon and its psychological elucidation in "Psychology of the Transference" already led into the problem of opposites and already made familiar the process of both chemical and psychological unification. Therefore Jung's introductory statement there was:

> The fact that the very idea of mystical marriage was to play such an important role in alchemy is not surprising, inasmuch as the expression usually used for it, *coniunctio*, refers primarily to what is today called chemical combination, and what brings together the elements to be combined is today known as "affinity"; but earlier various designations were used which all expressed human and in particular erotic relationships, such as *nuptiae* [wedding], *matrimonium* and *coniugium* [marriage], *amicitia* [friendship], *attractio* [attraction], and *adulatio* [flirtation]. . . . The more anthropomorphic and theriomorphic these terms prove to be, the more obvious becomes the role of playful fantasy and with it the unconscious. . . .[9]

Clearly *coniunctio* represents an archetypal image of the development of the human intellect, which expresses sometimes as sacred marriage, sometimes as mystical or chemical wedding,[10] the deepest longing of mankind, be it more erotic or—with no contradiction—more religious or even more technical and chemical in emphasis. It is always the combination of what has been separated, by means of which the individual is raised to a higher state, that of wholeness or selfhood. The outward process—be it a technical operation or a religious act—becomes the symbolic expression of an inward state, and even more: of a *mysterium* that encompasses the dimensions of both inner and outer and provides a hint of the *unus mundus*, the reality of a unified world.

It was to this that the author of the *Mysterium Coniunctionis* directed his readers' attention, after discussing in the introductory chapters of Volume 1 the individual components of the *coniunctio*, the paradox-filled alchemical tradition and the diverse manifestations of the opposites, and then presenting in Volume 2 the paired entities of Rex and Regina (King and Queen) and Adam and Eve as personifications of the process of unification and transformation. The wide scope of the subject and the great difficulty in mastering it lay not least in the fact that it considered not the material domain alone, nor solely that of psychic experience. Across both of these extended conflicting tension-fields, such as heavenly versus earthly, as well as spiritual versus physical and material, to limit ourselves to these original pairs of opposites. Arranging these two (or similar) pairs of opposites—as has often happened in iconography—perpendicular to each other results in the *quaternio*, a four-sided figure representing totality: above and below, right and left. Draw a circle around this cross, and we have the basic structure of a wholeness-symbolizing mandala, as it has been practically ubiquitous in Christian and non-Christian tradition, in both East and West.

Though the objection has repeatedly been made against Jung that whatever he touched turned into a psychic phenomenon, his later work in particular shows how much importance he placed in the nonpsychic, or more precisely in that which lay beyond psyche and material, which embraced and thus united *both* domains of existence. The already mentioned results of his researches into synchronicity, which should be included with his alchemy and *coniunctio* studies, showed how much it was empirical observations and not speculation that moved him, as a psychologist, to incorporate the material aspect. Synchronicity, as is well known, comes into play wherever there is a connection between an inner (psychic) event—be it a dream, a spontaneous thought, an idea—and an external fact, a "coincidence" that has the same meaning for the individual who experiences it. To walk barefoot over broken glass in a dream and the next day emerge uninjured from a dangerous situation, for example, points in this direction. A further characteristic is that the familiar principle of cause and effect seems to be suspended here, for which reason Jung conceived of synchronicity as an "acausal connecting principle." It is striking indeed that extremely analogous parallel phenomena are known in microphysics, which is why a dialogue between physics and psychology, and with parapsychology as well, has appeared promising at this point.

Thus over and over it was empirical indications which induced Jung to adopt the designation *unus mundus*, the original, one, unified world. It was a concept of medieval nature philosophy which corresponded in turn to the *agnosia* of the Gnostics and was equivalent to a primeval unconsciousness. Jung believed that the alchemistic nature-philosophers had anticipated the concept of the collective unconscious. But this brings us to the question of where this uniform arrangement of the universal—in the strict sense—*unus mundus* comes from. And clearly there is no more fitting sign to illustrate what is meant than the symbol, universal in its turn, of the mandala (Sanskrit, "circle"), for:

> The mandala symbolizes through its central point the ultimate oneness of all the archetypes as well as the diversity of the world of appearances, and hence forms the empirical correlate to the metaphysical notion of an *unus mundus*. The alchemistic correlate is the *lapis philosophorum* and its synonyms, particularly the microcosm.[11]

If the symbolism of the mandala is the psychological correlate to the alchemistic *unus mundus*, then the synchronicity which Jung described is its parapsychological analogue.

Jung continually pointed out the degree to which the alchemist's experimentation was also determined by the meditative element, so that one could speak of a psychological correlate to the practical *opus* of the experimenter. Yet the purely intellectual *unio* does not yet constitute the wise man, nor the work. Likewise the mental effort does not yet represent the peak or end point of the *opus alchymicum*, but only the first phase of the procedure.

> The second stage is reached by the joining of the *unio mentalis*, that is the oneness of mind and soul, with the body. But the completion of the *mysterium coniunctionis* can only be expected when the oneness of mind, soul, and body has been joined with the *unus mundus* of the beginning. This

Mandala by C. G. Jung.

> third stage of the conjunction became the object of metaphorical representation in the style of an *assumptio* and coronation of Mary, wherein the mother of God represents the body. The *assumptio* is really a wedding festival, the Christian version of the *hierosgamos*, whose original incestual character played a great role among the alchemists.[12]

Thus there are elements, states, and aspects of the *coniunctio* which, because of the variety of their reciprocal relationships, their wealth of images, and the multidimensionality of their symbols—so far at any rate—are difficult to grasp. And any attempt, as it were, to take into custody that which exceeds the rationality of the ego-consciousness, even for example in the service of the "proof of God," resembles the questionable demands aimed at quantifying the qualitative and making it measurable, definable, and manipulable. Such attempts are by their very nature doomed to failure. One need not be a confirmed pessimist to admit this.

What nevertheless becomes clear from Jung's studies, and what is rather suspected than conclusively proved from the aforementioned reasoning, is the transcendental background of a "reality of oneness." By this is understood the common background against which microphysics and depth psychology operate. This is

> as much physical as psychic, and hence neither, but rather of a third, neutral nature which can be grasped at best allusively, as it is essentially transcendental.[13]

And further:

> The transcendental psychophysical background is equivalent to a "potential world," insofar as in it all those conditions are at hand which determine the form of empirical phenomena.[14]

With this are opened, as the Paracelsist Gerhard Dorn so often quoted by Jung expressed it, "windows on eternity." The horizons are widened with the widening of human consciousness that is always implicit in our discussion of the *coniunctio*. Therefore the alchemist and the depth psychologist arriving at an adequate experience are not far from all those who have achieved a qualitative extrasensory, or rather spiritual experience, be it in the style of Zen, through the *samādhi*-experience, or in a Western method of meditation better suited to the conscious disposition and mental structure of Western people. When Jung came to speak of meditation and contemplation in the second volume of his work on the *coniunctio*, he was admittedly skeptical of their value to the West. What he said in the early fifties was to be sure not entirely superseded by the "mystical movement" and the psychohygienic or meditative self-realization boom that arose later, but serious interest in methods of spiritual instruction had grown considerably in the meantime. Jung's high regard for self-knowledge, which included the precincts of the unconscious, on the whole most likely underscored the significance of meditative efforts.

What insights Jung had to pass on to his time are obvious, insights which he first related to himself. He told himself, for example: if I know that the nature of reality lies in the infinite, the unconditional, the eternal, then things lose their power to fascinate. Their thingness becomes transparent. And when we understand that in this life we are already linked with the *unus mundus* and thus with that infinity and eternity, our desires change along with our attitude. Our "priorities" are adjusted. This opens up a completely new view of life and a new relationship to our fellow men and the whole world around us. For, as Jung wrote a few years after finishing *Mysterium Coniunctionis*:

> In the final analysis, we count for something only because of the essential we embody, and if we do not embody that, life is wasted. In our relationships to other men, too, the crucial question is whether an element of boundlessness is expressed in the relationship.
>
> The feeling for the infinite, however, can be attained

> only if we are bounded to the utmost. The greatest limitation for man is the "self"; it is manifested in the experience: "I am *only* that!" Only consciousness of our narrow confinement in the self forms the link to the limitlessness of the unconscious. In such awareness we experience ourselves concurrently as limited and eternal, as both the one and the other. In knowing ourselves to be unique in our personal combination—that is, ultimately limited—we possess also the capacity for becoming conscious of the infinite. But only then!
>
> In an era which has concentrated exclusively upon extension of living space and increase of rational knowledge at all costs, it is a supreme challenge to ask man to become conscious of his uniqueness and his limitation.[16]

Needless to say, these lines from C. G. Jung's late years tallied with his manifold, deeply plumbed experience. One of the most drastic of Jung's late experiences was undoubtedly his heart attack in the spring of 1944. In the year in which *Psychology and Alchemy* appeared, this event was part of the process which the author of the *coniunctio* book had to undergo. Hence it was no coincidence that Jung came to know from his own "intuition," when near death, what the sacred marriage, the leitmotif of the entire work, ultimately meant!

Other events which pointed up the finiteness but also the uniqueness of human existence came in the time of the elaboration and composition of this late work, giving him, as it were, additional existential draft. In the spring of 1953, totally unexpectedly, literally from one day to the next, Toni Wolff died. Considering how close she had been to the explorer of the archetypal world and how she had been able to inspire his production from the unconscious, this loss was a heavy one. To his friends Jung admitted that not only had he not reckoned with her death, as she was thirteen years his junior, but that conspicuously, despite their intimate relationship, there had been no hints whatsoever of Toni's death. Barbara Hannah, who was equally close to both of them, recounted the great shock that Jung's health suffered during those weeks:

> . . .his tachycardia returned, he kept an unusually high pulse for several weeks, and was not well enough to go to the funeral. Outwardly he kept extremely calm, so that both his wife and his secretary told me they thought he had overcome the shock after a few days, but from my notes for April, 1953, I see that he said himself that his pulse was still between 80 and 120; moreover, this trouble continued for some time. . . .
>
> Although it took Jung a long time to overcome the shock physically, he was able much sooner to find a psychological attitude to Toni's death and to accept the pain it gave him.[17]

Thus it is hardly possible to comprehend the writings that belong to his late work without reading with them the fate-runes of their author which lie hidden, as it were, between the lines of these books.

Jung was able to keep himself clear of any overestimation of what he had set down in *Mysterium Coniunctionis*. For despite the daunting abundance of what the author had won in the way of knowledge and insight in connection with alchemy and psychology, he was fully aware of the fragmentary and incomplete character of his research results in this area. Long after he had finished the work, to which as a third volume Marie-Louise von Franz added an equally weighty volume of text and commentary on the medieval alchemical text *Aurora Consurgens*,[18] he recalled the fate of some of the alchemists. It spoke well for their honesty that after years of continuing toil they were able to produce neither gold nor the highly praised philosophers' stone, and openly admitted this. To these men, "failures" in the popular sense, Jung compared himself. He too had in the end been unable to solve the riddle of the *mysterium coniunctionis*. In a letter of 15 October 1957 he wrote, at the age of eighty-two:

> On the contrary I am darkly aware of things lurking in the background of the problem—things too big for our horizons. . . . To deal with the *coniunctio* in human words is a disconcerting task, since you are forced to express and formulate a process taking place "in Mercurio" and not on the

level of human thought and human language, i.e., not within the sphere of discriminating consciousness. . . . The "way" is not an upward-going straight line, f.i. from earth to heaven or from matter to spirit, but rather a *circumambulatio* of and an approximation to the Centrum. We are not liberated by leaving something behind but only be fulfilling our task as *mixta composita*, i.e., human beings between the opposites.[19]

26

A Modern Myth

That a doctor and psychotherapist could not stop with merely pointing out the psychosomatic conditions of the individual is nowhere clearer in Jung's output than in his late work. Strictly speaking, analogous motifs emerged in visions and dreams around the middle of his life, when for example immediately before World War I Jung saw Central Europe inundated with blood, or the continent covered by an ice age, while he was charged with distilling a healing medicine for others. And although he did not remain entirely free of the illusions of his time during the early years of National Socialism, he did at least pay attention to the rumors of "Wotan" and the raging of the "blond beast," as the masses of the intelligentsia in university and church were not yet able to be clearly aware of the depth and the scope of what was happening. In any case his notes before the First World War and during the thirties can be taken as a depth psychologist's contribution to the diagnosis of his time, even if the actors and especially their sacrifice might sometimes have required a more precise and urgent presentation of their psychic predicament.

After the catastrophe had run its course in 1945, the Swiss doctor was not satisfied with the then lengthy and much-debated "mastery of the past," not even from the viewpoint of a "neutral" who had been little affected by the events, but turned his attention anew to present and future. (There is no need to refute Ernst Bloch's ignorant imputation that Jung of all people reduced "the libido and its unconscious contents entirely to the primitive."[1] No one familiar with the theory and practice of analytical psychology is in any doubt about the leading role it assigns to prospective, future-oriented factors in the psychic life.) So the question was to interpret the phenomena of the time as symptoms for deeper-lying states of affairs, and in view of more far-reaching processes. The psychotherapist became the interpreter of an age, or more precisely, referring to the premillennial years, he became the diagnostician of a change in consciousness.

Jung was conscious of the hazards involved if he commented from his own point of view on the contemporary phenomenon of "things seen in the skies," to shed light on processes in the field of the human psyche. In the Preface to his article on UFOs, "A Modern Myth," he noted:

> Of course I know that as in the past my voice is much too weak to reach the ears of the many. It is not arrogance which drives me, but my conscience as a doctor that counsels me to fulfill my duty in order to warn those few to whom I can make myself heard that events are in store for mankind which signal the end of an eon.[2]

Jung had nothing to add to the popular rumors of a possible end of the world. Rather he referred to the ancient idea of the Platonic year, in which the earth's axis revolves around an imaginary point in the course of more than 25,000 years. This means that at intervals of some 2100 years a shift in the vernal equinox takes place. Where the equinox in the third and fourth millennia of the pre-Christian era stood in the sign of Taurus, and until around the turn of the millennium in the sign of Aries, the Christian era began with a shift to the constellation of Pisces. Around the year 2000 C.E.—at best only approximate and not entirely consistent dates can be given—comes the transition to the age of Aquarius, the water-carrier.[3] Even if one does not wish to adhere to this ancient time-reckoning, astonishingly it does signal a change that applies primarily to human and humanistic consciousness. And it is in this context that Jung's statements are to be seen, as he continued:

> There are, it would seem, alterations in the constellation of the psychic dominants, the archetypes, the "gods," which cause or accompany long-term transformations of the collective psyche. This transformation began within historical tradition and left its traces, first in the passing of the age of Taurus into that of Aries, then from Aries to Pisces, the beginning of which coincides with the rise of Christianity. Now we are approaching the great change to be expected with the entering of the vernal equinox into Aquarius.[4]

Discussion of this line of thinking is not without its problems. Jung knew only too well that he was risking the reputation as a scientist, which he had fought hard for and had occasionally been called into question, since "astrologers" of doubtful shadiness had also been taking up this topic. His resolve stood firm to deal with such questions nonetheless; he gave explicit assurances that this did not happen lightly. "I am, to be honest, troubled by the lot of those who have been unprepared for the events and surprised by them and surrendered unsuspectingly to their incomprehensibility." There was also an external impulse to write this book on UFOs; it came from his son-in-law, the architect Walther Niehus, the husband of Marianne Jung, who died only four years after her father in 1965. The book is dedicated to Niehus.

As far as the so-called UFOs were concerned, a flood of literature had been produced at various intellectual levels: eyewitness accounts of single and multiple observers and attempts to assign the phenomena seen in the sky to human experience and ultimately arrive at plausible explanations. As for the explanation itself, the door was open to speculations of every kind. In many cases the problems began already with the process of observation. Over and over it was said how difficult it was, if not impossible, to get a clear idea of these unidentified flying objects, because they did not behave like solid bodies, although in many respects they gave this impression. Rather, they appeared weightless and fleeting, like thoughts. These characteristics matched the supposition that they were intelligently controlled by a quasi-human pilot.

Jung had expressed his opinion in this sense four years before the book appeared, in an article he published—at the urging of the science journalist Georg Gerster—in the Zürcher *Weltwoche* of 9 July 1954. While sightings of UFOs were known from all over the world, Jung for his part had to say that he himself had never seen any such thing. Nevertheless the fact remained:

> Something is being seen. What is seen may be in individual cases a subjective, in the case of several or even many simultaneous observers a collective vision (or rather hallucination). Much like a rumor, such a psychic phenomenon would have a compensatory significance; it would be a spontaneous response from the unconscious to the present conscious state, or to anxiety over the apparently hopeless world political situation, which at any time may lead to a universal catastrophe.[5]

In times of distress and uncertainty, men's gaze turns for help toward the heavens. It is from there that signs are expected. Jung pointed out in particular the round shape of the UFOs, and thus the mandalalike structure of these flying bodies. At the same time he advised against any speculation, feeling rather that the scientific institutions and governmental or military agencies which had access to the results of more precise investigations should make their information available to the public.

What had become increasingly probable to him—besides a possible psycho-physical basis—was "an essentially momentous psychic component," inasmuch as objects such as UFOs represent call upon conscious *and* unconscious fantasy. Jung expressly declined to give an opinion on the possible physical reality of UFOs. But on the other hand he admitted that even with sound-minded observers with all their faculties, things can be perceived that do not exist. One prerequisite for this—Jung spoke of a "visionary rumor"—was an unusual emotion, in contrast to the ordinary rumor, for whose propagation and development the curiosity and sensationalism present everywhere are sufficient. "But its elevation to the status of vision and hallucination stems from a stronger agitation and therefore a deeper source."[6]

This deeper source—actually it is a far-reaching underground spring—undoubtedly stands for the world of the archetypes. For just as Jung, at the time of the menacing unleashing of National Socialism, had seen in the march step of the brown-shirted columns, the verbiage of the Nazi officials, and the mass applause of (nearly) an entire people the workings of the storm god Wotan as the manifestation of a powerful archetype, so it was here too. For the circular and spherical shape which the UFOs as a rule were said to have indicates a symbol of wholeness or the Self. With regard to skeptical contemporaries, the overwhelming majority of whom look for the perilous and the hopeful alike rather in external factors, the phenomenon of UFOs should demand attention. Of course, he said, it was essentially a question of withdrawing the projections—like any—that were directed toward the heavens, that is of taking into consideration the possibility of a symbolic significance for people at the moment of crossing the threshold of consciousness. But for Jung such a projection was still no foregone conclusion. Rather he once recommended (in late 1957) that a competent psychiatrist should investigate the conscious and unconscious mentality of UFO witnesses in order to determine whether UFOs were to be traced to the projection of unconscious contents. Projection or not, Jung occasionally pointed out that every new experience had two points of view, one the fact as such, and the other the way in which it is understood.[7] Obviously, as a psychiatrist he was primarily concerned with the question of understanding, of witnessing and reacting.

As his secretary Aniela Jaffé reported, even in the last years of his life Jung established a special UFO archive, in which he collected books, professional journals, and newspaper clippings with sightings from all over the world, as well as letters, dream accounts, and his own notes on the problem.[8] Some of this material was included in "Flying Saucers: A Modern Myth." On the whole, the author was able to state, on the basis of present-day and notable historical evidence, "that the unconscious makes use of certain fantasy elements in presenting its contents which can be compared with the UFO phenomenon."[9]

Notwithstanding his main interest in the psychic side of the phenomenon, Jung did not cease to take into account also the arguments of those who devoted themselves mainly or exclusively to the investigation of the possible technical aspects of UFOs. He had familiarized himself regarding radar observations through the physicist Max Knoll, professor of electronics at Princeton University. There was a certain amount of collaboration between Jung and the Aerial Phenomena Research Organization (APRO) in the United States, which named the psychologist an honorary member regardless of his differing approach. In the summer of 1959 Charles A. Lindbergh (1902–1974), accompanied by his wife Anne and the German-American publisher Kurt Wolff, was Jung's guest in Bollingen. The elderly host was informed of the official research in the United States, but made Lindbergh clearly aware that a whole multitude of things were happening around the world of which the famous aviator and the aviation experts had no idea.[10]

Technical data and attempts at physical explanation are just insufficient to do justice to phenomena which in times of crisis stir the emotions so strongly and incite them to the most unusual, fantastic conceptions. And though it was not possible for Jung to solve the UFO problem with ultimate certainty, his contributions and reflections were aimed at making known the one-sidedness of a strictly technical view of the world. These were the years in which mankind was about to prepare for the first moon landing—another fact whose effect on the psychic disposition of a great part of humankind is not to be underestimated. Jung also spoke from this perspective in his *Memories*:

> There is the general feeling, to be sure, that we have reached a significant turning point in the ages, but people imagine that the great change has to do with nuclear fission and fusion, or with space rockets. What is concurrently taking place in the human psyche is usually overlooked.[11]

The decisive factor in this context is what is meant here by the human psyche. For only a psychology which reckons with the dimensions and the workings of the unconscious is able to develop the necessary sensitivity to extraordinary phenomena of the time. For example, where previous psychology had typically traced the accomplishment of psychologically induced symptoms at best to suggestive, or autosuggestive, tendencies, Jung's archetypal psychology made reference to factors in the collective unconscious, which he had explored in the course of decades and documented by means of a remarkable wealth of empirical material. Their collective character was underscored by the very fact that UFOs could appear everywhere. As "spontaneously appearing circular images of unity, which represent a synthesis of the opposites within the psyche," they seemed to indicate an instance of psychic compensation. Indeed, such a compensation is called for by a world marked by powerful divisions, in West and East, in North and South, in "blocs" and systems, in the exploitation and destruction of the planet. . . .

Such a statement by the depth psychologist is certainly not the last word on the subject, especially if one takes seriously Jung's intimations of the end of an era and the onset of a new age, and if—and here lies the crucial point—one wishes to be sure of the spiritual significance of what is seen as signs in the heavens.[12]

27

Late in Life

> I observe myself in the stillness of Bollingen, with the experience of almost eight decades now, and have to admit that I have found no plain answer to myself. I am in doubt about myself as ever, the more so the more I try to say something definite. It is even as though through familiarity with oneself one became still more alienated![1]

On the threshold of his eightieth year—strictly speaking at the time of this letter he was a quarter of a year shy of seventy-nine—this confession of C. G. Jung the man seems far too skeptical, if not despairing. Doubtless it is more than the sheer resignation of an old man who sees the thread of his life running out. Even this short epistolary note can only be rightly understood in the larger context of his life and work. And the context of his life shows that this was a man who had had a practically overwhelming wealth of insights and experiences, quite apart from his scientific results as a psychological researcher. And because these experiences—"like a fiery stream of basalt"—had come to him from the sources of the archetypes, their recipient was alone. The circle of those who referred to comparable inner events, dreams, and visions or at least could understand them was very small, and so all the greater was the danger of being overwhelmed by the impressive and powerful images, for example in such a way that the recipient of such visions identifies with these images, thus losing his psychic equilibrium. So far as we know, Jung was threatened by this only at the time of his middle life, when he had to withstand his intense confrontation with the unconscious. The mild understatement that he, the "wise old man of Bollingen," whence the above lines were written, was in doubt about himself, thus lacks self-awareness and ought to be taken rather as a kind of protective statement. By declining a summary of his successes, justified in itself, and abstaining from all superlatives, he showed how clearly—now more than ever—he was able to distinguish between the everyday ego of the old, tired, and increasingly inefficient C. G. Jung and the personality that had grown up on the path of self-discovery that he really was.

Another time, a good year later, he characterized his fundamental situation at the moment with the words:

> My name enjoys an existence quasi-independent of myself. My real self is actually chopping wood in Bollingen and cooking the meals, trying to forget the trial of an eightieth birthday.[2]

How lucky he was to have the Bollingen tower as a refuge! For unquestionably there were trials which disturbed the rhythm of his daily life now that he had become famous. Almost every day the postman delivered a bundle of letters from all over the world to 228 Seestrasse. These needed answering. And Jung favored even unknown questioners and seekers of advice with appropriate answers. Even when Aniela Jaffé, his part-time secretary since 1955, lent a hand with the writing and organizing, the correspondence absorbed much of his strength. "Jung's correspondence was terribly extensive and therefore often the cause of complaints and grumblings," she recalled. "It was obvious that the letters tired him out. But they held an important place in his life. When his libido no longer flowed into the form of scientific works, the letters took the place of the manuscripts and became the receptacle for his creative thoughts. Thus their number continually grew in his later years. But above all they formed a link to the world, and that reconciled him, living in the introverted, withdrawn way he did, with all the trouble and effort they caused him. He needed the letters, he had to admit; and if out of misplaced consideration I forwarded too little mail on his vacations, I earned an appropriate reprimand."[3]

Disregarding for the moment the ever-growing number of students and friends who continually knocked at Jung's door, there was also an inexhaustible stream of other visitors by whom he could not escape being overrun, especially when they were writers and journalists expecting a more or less in-depth interview. Among these, some of them already mentioned, were Alberto Moravia, the scholar of comparative religion Mircea Eliade for *Le Combat* of Paris, Charles Baudouin several times, Frederick Sands for the London *Daily Mail*, Stephen Black and John Freeman for the BBC, Gordon Young for the *Sunday Times* of London, Georges Duplain for the *Gazette de Lausanne*, and of course journalists from the larger German-language newspapers in Switzerland. In view of these well-intentioned, work-furthering "surprise attacks," it was more a protective gesture that was thought up by Medard Boss, president of the International Congress of Psychotherapy. For the Congress which gathered in July 1954 and its hundred or so participants, he organized a chartered cruise on Lake Zürich, arranging it so that the power boat appeared near the house in Küsnacht at a convenient hour in the afternoon and made its presence known by blowing its horn and ringing its bell, so that Jung could return the waves and cheers of his many foreign colleagues from his balcony. The American author Claire Myers Owens, who was visiting Jung at the time, shared the incident with her readers.[4]

C. G. Jung's birthdays had for some time no longer been exclusively family occasions, but took on the character of more public, which is to say more fatiguing events, particularly as the guest of honor did not relish being at the center of large spectacles. His eightieth birthday on 26 July 1955 formed a great and festive occasion. The organizers took care

Jung on his eighty-fifth birthday with his children, grandchildren, and great-grandchildren, 26 July 1960.

to arrange the day's events so that the jubilarian could cope with the whole thing: the official birthday ceremony was preceded by the private party in his home in Küsnacht. Even so, about forty relatives were gathered for this, including his five children and most of his nineteen grandchildren. His first great-grandchildren also made an appearance. The English physician E. A. Bennet, who was Jung's house guest at the time, was declared an honorary member of the family on this day, a turbulent one for Jung and his wife. Ruth Bailey, Jung's companion on the trip to East Africa, had been part of the clan for some time as a long-time family friend. The Psychological Club staged a large afternoon celebration in Zürich. For the wider circle of his students, the members of the C. G. Jung Institute in Zürich set up two more celebrations, one in the morning for all those who had shown an interest in C. G. Jung, and a separate, so to speak high-level official one, with representatives of various Jungian groups, including those from overseas, this one for invited guests only. For both of these the comfortable Dolder Grand Hotel, situated high above Zürich, served as the venue, and the guest of honor was present at both. Despite the great number of those who appeared, there was the pleasant atmosphere of an informal human gathering, as one would hardly have expected from its public character. Jung stayed an unusually long time, even though he still had a strenuous day ahead of him. But the official evening event was different. To be sure, Jung appeared happy to have the specially bound prepublication copy of his *Mysterium Coniunctionis* in hand, as well as the weighty two-volume *Festschrift: Studien zur Analytischen Psychologie C. G. Jungs*. But it was not lost on careful observers that his relaxed mood of that morning had vanished and that he endured the festive words of greeting only with forced politeness. His speedy departure was probably excused with consideration for the day's fatigue. But when Barbara Hannah sought Jung out in Bollingen a few days later, she learned from him how the guest of honor himself had felt about the great discrepancy between the two events: in the morning it was the large crowd of those who wanted to be near Jung for the sake of the subject itself, of whom he said that it was *they* who would carry on his work. In the evening, in contrast, it was the strict regulation ruled by the institution.[5] Jung was anything but fond of high words and sterile ceremony.

Part of the record of honor and esteem was a special number of the professional psychological journal *Psyche*. The Swiss Technical Institute in Zürich, where Jung had taught for many years, granted him the degree of Doctor of Science *honoris causa*—a comparatively late appreciation of his merits. But the text of the document bestowing the honor briefly and yet comprehensively characterized what was owed to Jung. Thus his honorary promotion in Zürich was:

> To the rediscoverer of the wholeness and polarity of the human psyche and its tendency toward unity;
> The diagnostician of the phenomena of human crises in the age of science and technology;
> The interpreter of primitive symbolism and the process of individuation in mankind.

But abroad too the honoree was being commemorated, in London, New York, San Francisco, Calcutta—everywhere the Jungian school was establishing a foothold. A number of journalists did more, introducing to their readers probably the best-known psychologist living at the time. Among these were Michael Schabad, who interviewed Jung for the Basler *National-Zeitung*. An astonishing part of this conversation, in which Jung was asked about a number of important moments in his life, is certainly a reference to various intellectual kinships. Jung's affinity with Goethe, the author of *Faust* as well as his *Farbenlehre* on color theory, and the spiritual uncoverer of the "primitive plants," was well known, as was that with William James, whom he had been able to know personally. But against this, he astounded his interviewer from Basel by declaring as one of his intellectual kin Rabbi Ber, the Maggid of Mezeritch, one of the great charismatic leading figures of eastern Jewish Chasidism in the eighteenth century.[6] This student of the founder of Chasidism, the Baal Shem Tov (Israel ben Eliezer), he said, had been an impressive personality. With this Jung may have had in mind, among other things, his gift for "teaching" through small everyday matters, as in this traditional saying handed down by Rabbi Ber: "I did not go the the Maggid of Mezeritch to learn Torah from him, but to watch how he tied his shoelaces."[7] Thus one could say, analogously, in order to know C. G. Jung in his totality, it was not enough to study his books, nor to do analytic work with him in his study in Küsnacht; one had to accompany him to Bollingen and be there as he cultivated his cornfield, worked on his stone, felled trees, chopped firewood, and cooked his food.

Also during July, Stephen Black was in Küsnacht with his television team to interview Jung for the BBC.[8] They sat on the terrace in front of the house, Emma Jung at her husband's side. Once again the images from the decisive stages of his life were discussed: his absorption in the world of the unconscious, the encounter with Freud and Adler, down to some practical questions of psychotherapeutic work, which Jung had to admit cost much time and money and engrossed people completely, for it involved a process of education and healing and hence was not to be made light of. And as far as Jung's physiognomy was concerned, which the BBC reporter wished to put across to the radio audience in a second broadcast, Stephen Black was inclined to compare the octogenarian with a typical Swiss peasant. Amused, Jung agreed: "Well, I think you are not just beside the mark. That is what I have often been called."[9]

And Emma Jung? At the moment she was an attentive listener. She did not take part in the conversation. One could tell by looking at her that she had overcome a serious illness not long ago. In the spring she had had to undergo surgery. And because her recovery dragged on for some time, Ruth Bailey had come from England to take over the management of the household. It had been agreed that in the future Ruth would look after things in the Jung home no matter who the surviving spouse was. On the eightieth birthday Emma Jung, now seventy-three, was able to fully enjoy the festivities. She even felt strong enough to spend some time with her husband in the Bollingen tower. But the state of good health which lasted for both of them into the fall came to a sudden end for Emma; early in November she once again became gravely ill. A short stay in the hospital showed that the original medical prognosis of a few more years of life, admittedly expressed with great reservation, was in error. Emma Jung died on 27 November 1955.

Jung was deeply stricken, evidently much more so than by Toni Wolff's death two years before. "In all my eighty years," Barbara Hannah attested, "I have never seen a marriage for which I felt such a spontaneous and profound respect. Emma Jung was a most remarkable woman, a sensation type who compensated and completed her husband in many respects."[10] This judgment was confirmed by many who knew Emma and Carl Gustav well. Aniela Jaffé referred to Emma Jung's presidency of several years in the Psychological Club and her activity as a teaching analyst and in the C. G. Jung Institute, adding: "Emma Jung's life was one of uncommon richness and was one of fulfillment, because her faithfulness to her own nature coincided with her faithfulness to her husband and her profound understanding of his life's work."[11] It was not granted to her to complete her major work on the mystery of the Grail. Marie-Louise von Franz brought the book to a conclusion, and it was possible for it to appear during Jung's lifetime, in 1960. Laurens van der Post had a vivid memory of Emma Jung as both lecturer and hostess: "She was an immensely sensitive, shy, solicitous, circumspect, and introverted spirit. . . . Yet she was as dauntless as she was enduring and delivered her meaning with great precision, erudition, and understanding."[12]

It need not be particularly stressed that what the Englishman had to say caught only a small segment of the total personality of C. G. Jung's wife, when we consider how even as a young woman, with astonishing personal maturity, Emma Jung had stood up to Sigmund Freud for her Carl, and how she had endured and helped to smooth over the considerable tensions with which the family was burdened by other women, and especially Jung's relationship to Toni Wolff. Writing to his friend Erich Neumann in Tel Aviv on 15 December 1955, the widower gave voice to his great shock at losing Emma: "The shock I underwent is so great that I can neither concentrate nor recover my ability to express myself." And then he reported a kind of enlightenment, a "great illumination" which had suddenly taken him by surprise two days before Emma's death, affording him like a flash of lightning a glimpse into the secret of life that was embodied in this woman and had influenced his life to such a great extent. "I can only think that the illumination came from my wife, who was then mostly in a coma, and that the tremendous lighting up and release of this insight worked back upon her and was one reason that she could die such a painless and regal death."[13]

Now the stillness, "the audible silence," was around him. He could not and would not have it removed, for this feeling of nearness beyond death and the grave also had a special message for him which was not to be dulled or suppressed. But it was a great help that Jung's children, especially his daughters, looked after their father and regularly visited him by turns. As had been agreed while Emma was still alive, Ruth Bailey moved from England to Küsnacht and cared for C. G. Jung during the last five and a half years of his life. It was important to him to have about him a helper and companion who would in no way be forced by the charge to neglect her own family, as would have been the case with his children.

By the end of the fateful year of 1955 the rich harvest of his life had for the most part been brought in. *Mysterium Coniunctionis*, Jung's major work, was finished, and the first part had just been published. For various reasons, however, the ever-busy Jung could not retire. For one thing, he was continually haunted by thoughts about the future. There were still books to be written, such as that on the UFO phenomena we have already discussed. His life and work as a whole still called for suitable documentation, partly in the form of an edition of his collected works which had to be prepared, partly in the shape of the personal review of his life which his students and friends hoped for from him—the *Memories, Dreams, Reflections* which would at least shed light on the important stages of his inner path, thereby allowing something to emerge of the in many ways still enigmatic psychologist from Küsnacht. As for the edition of his works, the German edition, arranged by his long-time Zürich publishers Max and Albert Rascher, was preceded by the English-language *Collected Works*. Thanks to large contributions by American friends it had appeared from as early as 1953 under the auspices of the Bollingen Series in New York.

Among Jung's activities in these last years we should also not forget the work that was most essential for him. In order to cope with the loss of his wife in his own way, he retreated to Bollingen for a time in the winter of 1955–56: "The close of her life, the end, and what it made me realize, wrenched me violently out of myself. It cost me a great deal to regain my footing, and contact with stone helped me," he recounted in 1957.[14]

Among the carvings he produced in Bollingen in the severe winter of 1955–56 were three stone tablets. On these, which were placed in the open courtyard, he inscribed the names of his paternal ancestors. His family colors also came into their own, as the master of the house painted the ceiling with motifs from the family coats of arms of the Jungs and the Rauschenbachs. On this point Jung noted that his family had originally borne on its arms a phoenix, the motif that illustrated youthfulness and rejuvenation. His grandfather, C. G. Jung the elder, the enthusiastic Freemason and Grand Master of the Swiss lodge, had changed the family arms, however, ostensibly out of resistance against his father. The grandson mentioned this revision in order to point out the historical connection with his own life and thought. In the *Memories* we read on this point:

> In keeping with this revision of my grandfather's my coat of arms no longer contains the original phoenix. Instead there is a cross azure in chief dexter and in base sinister a blue bunch of grapes in a field d'or; separating these is an estoile d'or in a fess azure. The symbolism of these arms is Masonic, or Rosicrucian. Just as cross and rose represent the Rosicrucian problem of opposites ("*per crucem ad rosam*"), that is, the Christian and Dionysian elements, so cross and grapes are symbols of the heavenly and the chthonic spirit. The uniting symbol is the gold star, the *aurum philosophorum*.[15]

Although the heraldic animal of the phoenix represented an essentially spiritual message, there is also no question that Jung was fully able to affirm the Masonic and Rosicrucian symbolism—no doubt because it symbolized the goals and methods of his own work.

It should be remembered that Jung had obeyed the impulse to build the tower in the year of his mother's death (1923), thus introducing the first phase of construction on the newly acquired real estate in Bollingen. Further building stages followed in approximately four-year cycles. After Emma Jung's death he felt a new urge to further construction, recognizing that he should become what he was by nature. After no changes had been made in the buildings for some twenty years, Jung discovered "suddenly" that the whole thing was still lacking an essential part, namely the completion of the central section between the two tower structures to left and right. In this so far only partially executed center section Jung saw the architectural counterpart to his ego. Therefore something now had to happen to it:

> So, in that same year, I added an upper story to this section, which represents myself, or my ego-personality. Earlier, I would not have been able to do this; I would have regarded it as presumptuous self-emphasis. Now it signified an extension of consciousness achieved in old age. With that the building was complete.[16]

With this, then, the keystone was set on an edifice which was not to be judged from the architectural or merely practical standpoint, but which the builder explained as a "place of maturation," in which, and through which, he had lived through the stages of his own individuation. By carving the stone and building the tower, he meant at the same time to fulfill "an impersonal karma" of his family, as if tasks had been assigned to him from out of the past which he had to carry out. This can be sensed, not by a person who pays homage to some vague inwardness, but only by one who is both conscious of his duty to history and aware of his obligation to deal with the things of this world, to live with them and if need be to transform them. It goes without saying that what Jung did in Bollingen should therefore not be mistaken for the restless puttering of an old man. Those who were better acquainted with his inherent life could occasionally be informed in letters of the "advances" in his work; thus to Aniela Jaffé on 18 March 1957, where the enumeration of the highlights is no doubt typical of him:

> I have finished painting the ceiling in Bollingen and done more work on my inscription and—last but not least—rebricked the springs and cooked some good meals and found and bought some excellent wine. All this has rested me and cured me of various irritations. But I don't wish to speak of that. . . .[17]

Furthermore he forgot and even neglected the correspondence, which seemed to have no end and was also important to him in itself. But now—more than before—he gave priority to his life and work in the timelessness of Bollingen. About three weeks in Küsnacht and then a week in Bollingen, that was approximately the rhythm, and naturally Bollingen had long been his obligatory vacation spot. An occasional excursion to Ticino then represented more the exception than the rule. His regained health also still permitted him, as an octogenarian, his only sport of sailing on his beloved Lake Zürich. For obvious reasons he now had to give up mountain climbing and hiking for good. A certain compensation for this and for his great trips abroad of earlier days was automobile trips through Switzerland, as a rule day trips sometimes to Austria or nearby northern Italy, especially when Fowler McCormick's large and comfortable car was available. The guide of Jung's journey to the Pueblos and during his Indian trip now arranged it so that he could spend some time in Switzerland every year. As Ruth Bailey, their fellow traveler in East Africa, was always with the party, these day trips through Switzerland once again reunited the three companions of earlier decades—the Swiss, the Englishman, and the American.

The suggestion of some kind of biography or autobiography was also considered in the fifties. Jung himself had never made an attempt at such a record on his own, for one thing because as an experienced psychologist he knew only too well how good or bad the historical reliability of so-called memoirs was; on the other hand because external occurrences and facts had never seemed particularly memorable to him. What counted for him was only the inner experiences, the stages along the path of the development and maturation of the personality, for which that which can be dated represents only an external framework.[18]

In the summer of 1956 the German-American publisher Kurt Wolff was in Switzerland. At an Eranos conference in Ascona he made the proposal of bringing out a biography of C. G. Jung. Wolff was among a number of those publishing personalities, such as Samuel Fischer, Anton Kippenberg of Insel Verlag, Eugen Diederichs, Reinhard Piper, and a few others, who had given German literature its profile during the first half of the twentieth century. In 1908–1909 Kurt Wolff had joined forces with the young Ernst Rowohlt to provide expressionist poetry with attention from the publishing world. After his emigration to the United States in 1941 he had met Paul and Mary Mellon. These two generous friends of Jung's and benefactors of the Bollingen Foundation in New York engaged Kurt Wolff as their publisher, on the recommendation of Jung's friend Heinrich Zimmer.[19] That his

Jung in his study with his last secretary, Aniela Jaffé, who recorded his *Memories, Dreams, Reflections.*

friends in Zürich immediately seized upon the proposal, particularly since C. G. Jung's advanced age left no room for hesitation, goes without saying. Agreement was also quickly reached on who was to take on the role of biographer, or rather stenographer. Jolande Jacobi, who was active in the Psychological Club and the Institute in Zürich, nominated Aniela Jaffé, and it was settled. Jung himself had first to be won over to the project, and his considerable reluctance to lay himself and his life open to all the world was well known.

After long hesitation he was ready. The weekly sessions began in the spring of 1957. One afternoon a week was set aside for them—very little in the face of the size of the task, but in view of the elderly man's still relatively immense workload, an afternoon a week was rather a lot. The essays "The Undiscovered Self (Present and Future)" (1957), "Flying Saucers: A Modern Myth" (1958), and "A Psychological View of Conscience" (1958) still had to be written and published in these years, as well as the work on the two collected editions in Zürich and New York/London, whose translation into English by R.F.C. Hull continually raised practical problems. In short, the work did not go away, and the planned book of reminiscences represented a new and heavy demand on C. G. Jung.

After Jung had been won over and the biographer engaged, the publisher gave a more precise idea of what he had in mind. Certainly not least out of publishing considerations, he wanted not a biography *of* Jung, but an autobiography *by* Jung, and in order to achieve greater immediacy he should speak himself, but Jung insisted that his "so-called autobiography" should by no means appear under his name. As late as April 1960 he attested explicitly to his son-in-law Walther Niehus that he regarded this book not as his undertaking but as a book that Mrs. Jaffé had written: "I regard the pieces in it written by myself as a contribution to the work of Mrs. Jaffé. The book should appear under her name and not mine, as it does not represent an autobiography written by me."[20] Eventually agreement was reached on a formula of author- and editorship, which took account of the actual division of roles. That it is Jung himself speaking through long stretches of the book is not to be doubted. It was especially the memories of his childhood that attained an astonishing vitality and luminosity for the elderly man. What had once seemed to be only the individual experience of a small Swiss village boy now revealed its significance for the work of the depth psychologist. Without the initial imaginations and dreams of long ago, the accomplishments of this life are hardly understandable. True, Jung had recounted some autobiographical material in his seminar in Zürich in 1925, but only now did the overall scope of these inner experiences become clear. So he was happy to see the impression his "autobiographical sketch" left in his friends. Much had had to remain hidden until now, Jung wrote to Jolande Jacobi in the last year of his life:

> It had to remain hidden because it could not have borne the brutalities of the outside world. But now I have grown so old that I can give up my grip on the world, and the discordant cries die away in the distance.[21]

What had been produced was—in the strict sense of the word—a thoroughly esoteric book, for it documented not external biography and contemporary history, but that which had been perceived "within" as a knowledge-deepening and life-transforming strength.[22]

As important as Jung held the development of the inner person to be and as much as he was filled with concern for the well-being of the individual, as this is expressed in his "Undiscovered Self (Present and Future)," to his advanced age he followed attentively the spectacular events of world history. After Nikita Khruschev, at the twentieth congress of the Soviet Communist party, had publicly condemned the misuse of power during the previous Stalin era, and reformist powers had become stronger in Hungary under Imre Nagy, in October 1958 the Hungarian popular rebellion broke out. Soviet troops put down the uprising in a violent fashion. Jung made no secret of his sympathies, as in two short commentaries he described the bloody suppression of the Hungarian people by the Russian army as "a detestable, beastly crime which should be condemned out of hand." He lamented the "piteous helplessness" of those who had to content themselves with the role of Good Samaritans, unable to stop the Soviet tanks. Self-criticism was not lacking: "In the worldwide moral outcry of the masses one hardly heard the voice of one's own conscience, remembering the evil deeds of the Machiavellianism, short-sightedness, and stupidity of the West, without which the events in Hungary would not have been possible. In Europe lies the hearth of the deadly sickness."[23]

He leveled similar criticism at those responsible for the Suez crisis in the same year, in which Great Britain and France allowed themselves to be provoked into an act of war. "The latter is to be lamented as a reversion to outdated and barbaric political methods." Asked in the spring of 1959, at the age of almost seventy-nine, why he had not raised his voice against other outrages of world politics, for example in the face of the Chinese occupation of Tibet, he admitted that he could offer no rational reason as an excuse for himself. Actually in these matters too, he said, he tended to wait for an impulse from within. Moreover:

> The world situation has reached the stage where even the most stirring words no longer mean anything. What matters more now, it seems to me, is for each of us to be sure of his own attitude. . . . Talk has become much too cheap. Being is harder, and therefore easily replaced by words.[24]

As a doctor his duty lay primarily in diagnosis and—so far as was possible for him on a case-by-case basis—therapy. He concluded his essay "The Undiscovered Self" by confronting mission and responsibility with each other once again:

> It may be permitted a doctor who during a long life has concerned himself with the motives and consequences of psychic disturbances to give his opinion on the questions raised by the present world situation in all the modesty that

> has been imposed on him as an individual. Indeed I am neither encouraged by too great an optimism nor inspired by high ideals, but merely troubled about the fate, the weal and woe of the individual person, that infinitesimal unit on which a world depends, the individual entity in whom—if we rightly understand the Christian message—even God seeks his end.[25]

Erich Neumann criticized his teacher for having spoken on the whole too pessimistically in this text. Jung replied that by "dear God" he had not been able to say anything better on this question, and so the solution would have to be left to fate. Making speculations of any kind on things that did not manifest themselves in some way, for example from the unconscious, was not Jung's concern. Finally, in his old age he was, as he said of himself, "a very busy man," who was virtually inundated with work of all kinds and who hence at times lost his perspective, as appears from several letters in which he apologizes for belated answers. It became ever more difficult for Jung to answer all those who knocked on his "door to the world" in Küsnacht, seeking to converse with the famous man. It even happened once that unannounced guests rang the alarm bell at 228 Seestrasse and then had to be sent away by the lady of the house. When the psychotherapist Gustav Schmaltz, working in Frankfurt, expressed the wish to come right away to Bollingen to confer with him for several days, Jung had to explain politely but definitely how necessary solitude was to him if life was to remain worth living. Often speaking became such a trial to him, he told his colleague, that he had to interject several days of silence in order to "recover from the futility of words." Furthermore, he said, at over eighty-two, he already "had his marching orders," on a great adventure about which he did not want to say much. And in this situation he could not bear having to be a constant companion with anyone for even a few days, not even his closest relations. But he was willing to be available to his colleague from Frankfurt in Küsnacht one afternoon for about two hours.[26]

The letters of his later years, in large part preserved and sometimes rather detailed, show that Jung by no means considered withdrawing into complete silence. Rather these witnesses attest how highly he valued the exchange of views in letters. His correspondents' topics were manifold. In the foreground, of course, always stood basic questions of psychotherapy and isolated subjects of Jungian psychology, whether the doctrine of archetypes, Jung's typology and its relation to Ernest Kretschmer's *Physique and Character*, or practical questions, such as how a carcinoma could originate and be healed on psychic grounds. One letter-writer wanted to know how psyche related to physis, like number to reality. Here as in other cases Jung was able to point out how long he had already been grappling with such questions. Therefore there were occasional references to his writings in which he had expressed his views in more detail.

The German edition of *The Collected Works* began appearing in 1958. The projected eighteen-volume edition opened with Volume 16, which discussed elements of the practice of psychotherapy. For Jung this meant as a rule that here, too, abundant historical material was to be displayed and drawn upon as an aid to interpretation. Thus he wrote in the Introduction to this volume:

> The varieties of psychic behavior are indeed of an eminently historical nature. Not only must the psychotherapist acquaint himself with the personal biography of his patient, but also with the intellectual presuppositions of his nearer and further intellectual milieu, where the influences of tradition and *Weltanschauung* come into play and often play a decisive role. No psychotherapist who is earnestly concerned with the understanding of the whole person is spared the necessity of coming to terms with the symbolism of the language of dreams.[27]

Such statements are met with at every turn in Jung's letters, which as a rule represent replies to other letters. Thus for example the English journalist Melvin J. Lasky, editor of the newspaper *Der Monat* published (at that time) in Berlin, inquired about the psychological aspects in the legend of the Pied Piper of Hamlin, which turned out to be not an incidental theme but a motif with many revealing social-psychological connections. An American questioner asked about personal survival after death and about various phenomena generally referred to as "miracles." Jung knew of certain *post-mortem* phenomena which, on the basis of his long experience, he was not prepared to attribute to subjective illusions. But who was he himself, after all? To what denomination was he to be assigned? Had he himself not called into being a Jungian creed, a "Jungian church"? Such things he definitely rejected as mere defamation. But if one still wanted to affix a religious label to him, the parson's son who belonged to none of the recognized religious communities, one might class him with a kind of "left-wing Protestantism":

> I am definitely inside Christianity and, as far as I am capable of judging about myself, on the direct line of historical development. . . . If the Reformation is a heresy, I am certainly a heretic too.[28]

The elderly C. G. Jung's stance toward Sigmund Freud is interesting. When a doctor from Würzburg asked him about the significance of Freud's Jewish descent for the origin, content, and reception of psychoanalysis, he rejected the so-called racial theory and similar speculations as "highly unsatisfactory bases" for a proper judgment, noting:

> In spite of the astonishing lack of appreciation I incurred on the part of Freud, I cannot fail to recognize his significance as a cultural critic and pioneer in the realm of psychology, even considering my own resentment. A correct assessment of Freud's efforts reaches into areas that concern not only the Jews but all European people, areas which I have tried to shed light on in my works. Without Freudian "psychoanalysis" I would have entirely lacked the key.[29]

With this Jung modified his statements of the turbulent thirties, in which he had expressly declared himself a student not of Freud but of Eugen Bleuler.

It goes almost without saying that the debate over Jung's books, for example the controversial *Answer to Job*, and his work as a whole was continued in the letters. Martin Buber—already in the early 1950s—had spoken up and called him a "monologuist" who was not at all concerned with the concrete relationship between God and man, but rather with a style of Gnosticism, and in whom the quality of genuine dialogue was lacking—a charge that had been brought earlier by Jung's erstwhile student Hans Trüb and was reflected in various inquiries by several correspondents.

Finally, there were theological and religious and spiritual subjects which by and large demanded detailed and lengthy responses, up to and including discussion of questions on Eastern spirituality, the *I Ching*, Zen, and yogic practices. Many times Jung had to remind his readers of his cognitive-theoretical self-restriction as a psychologist, for not a few overlooked the fact that assertions about God, for example, always referred only to the *image* of God, whereas the "background" of all being could be best be supposed, but never rationally defined. What he wrote to an American theologian at the end of his life can be taken as a practical statement: "I was the first to emphasize the enormous role religion plays in the individuation process, as I was the first to raise the question of the relation between psychotherapy and religion in its practical aspects."[30] It is another matter why people sought to dismiss Jung sometimes as atheist or materialist, sometimes as Gnostic or mystic. As to what the question was for him ultimately, he wrote a little earlier to one of the few theologians who offered him understanding, the Catholic Josef Rudin:

> . . .I have long been keenly interested in building a bridge—or at least trying to do so—between the two disciplines which accept practical responsibility for the *cura animarum*: theology on the one hand and medical psychol-

> ogy on the other. Different as their *points de départ* may be, they do both meet in the empirical psyche of the human individual. . . . We are both convinced that our endangered time needs psychological enlightenment, and that someone has to make a beginning, though cannot do it alone. . . .[31]

As was shown already in Jung's lifetime, this beginning influenced many areas of culture and perception. And this very fact is echoed over and over in the letters.

Whereas only a few even of the colleagues of his own "school" managed to speak with the master in Küsnacht at least for a short hour, even in his last years Jung made himself available for a number of interviews. When Georges Duplain, a writer from French-speaking Switzerland, once expressed his amazement at this, Jung admitted that he was actually surprised himself. Doubtless he was aware that this was a chance to go beyond the relatively narrow circle of the Jungian school and get his message across to those who were interested. This would also explain the swift and positive reaction with which he replied to an inquiry from the United States. On 2 April 1957 Richard I. Evans, professor of psychology at the University of Houston, asked if he would be willing to speak in a series of films which were being planned as informational materials for first-semester students. Jung recognized immediately what a good opportunity this offered him to present his work, in four hour-long filmed interviews, for later disseminators. Only ten days later his acceptance reached America. In August of the same year the photos could be taken in Küsnacht, and the actual interview took place on the premises of the Swiss Institute of Technology in Zürich. Evans and his crew, including a reporter from *Time* magazine, were much taken with the brilliant and original Swiss, although they had first to come to grips with his spontaneity and probably also the Jungian subject matter. For as soon as he had greeted them in his garden in Küsnacht, Jung confronted his visitors with the question: "Why do you American psychologists hate me so much?" One can only imagine the peculiar, partly amused and partly roguish twinkle in his eye!

Still less was there an inner distance to overcome. Already at tea the talkative host showed himself for what he was. Richard Evans was struck by his excellent English with its curious Swiss-German accent: "And the dynamism of his nature, his power of expression and his colorful manner of speaking, was very impressive. During our conversations it became clear to me that in C. G. Jung we had found a man who not only had much to offer intellectually, but who would also be able to give an extraordinarily apt account of himself in the spontaneous give and take of the interview."[32] In *Time*, and then in the Houston *Post* of 16 September 1957, one read what effect the Swiss professor had had on his American guest:

"The old gentleman with the white hair and the knowingly flashing eyes leaned back in his armchair and thoughtfully smoked his pipe. Seeming not to notice the microphone around his neck and the camera lens pointed at him, C. G. Jung spoke through the cloud of smoke that wreathed his head. His voice was loud and powerful. . . . 'The world,' said Jung, 'hangs by a thin thread, and that thread is the human soul. . . . It is not the reality of the hydrogen bomb that we need to fear, but what man will do with it. If certain people in Moscow lose their nerve, then the world will be plunged into fire and flames. As never before the world depends on the soul of man.' This, the old wise man explains, is why the exploration and understanding of the human soul is more important than ever. . . . Gently guided by his interviewer Richard Evans, Jung wandered through the whole wide realm of his convictions and theories of the psyche. . . . Jung's presentation was as incomparable as it was fascinating. It was the first time he had ever been in front of a television camera, the first time he had spoken to American listeners since his lectures on "Psychology and Religion" at Yale in 1938, and apart from a few lectures in Zürich, it was his only public appearance in ten years. . . . Jung scintillated and joked, the whole thing seemed to give him the greatest enjoyment. . . . In the studio his eyes sparkled behind his steel-rimmed spectacles, and his bristly white mustache moved when he laughed. . . ."[33] And Jung's laugh spoke for itself!

When George Duplain interviewed C. G. Jung two years later for the *Gazette de Lausanne*, he too met with an outgoing interlocutor. Jung, who particularly toward the end of his life complained that no one understood him, above all his own profession, spoke highly of the reporter:

> Ordinarily my books are treated rather superficially by the press, and little attempt is made to get at their deeper meaning. This is true not only of the daily papers but also of scientific journals. George Duplain goes way beyond this sort of reporting. . . .
>
> In taking the trouble to write such a thoughtful report, Georges Duplain has done a service not only to the interested public but to our psychological knowledge in general.[34]

This referred to the ideas behind "Flying Saucers: A Modern Myth." Asked about the onset of the age of Aquarius, Jung pointed out that such questions arose for the most part out of pure ignorance of the historical tradition.[35] Hardly anyone had read Plato, for instance, and he was among the few who had come very close to the truth. But the notion of the great world year and the world months which go on for more than two thousand years went directly back to what Plato had said. Here too Jung remained an empiricist; that is, he did not derive his own view from old traditions but observed, for example, the transformations that would be seen in the domain of symbols, transformations which pointed to the end of the (Christian) age of Pisces. Among the phenomena of this transition Jung included the greater openness to the unconscious per se, an increasing attention to the expressiveness of dreams, a sensitivity to integration, for example the interrelatedness of physical and psychic reality, and especially a growing desire for self-knowledge, for consciousness, although such needs were at first still to be seen in relatively few contemporaries. The tendency, though, was not to be overlooked. A too one-sidedly rational and too top-heavy and academic way of confronting the world hinders the sense of wholeness that is necessary if people are to find the meaning of their lives.

An interview which was to acquaint a particularly wide-ranging public with Jung's person and way of thinking involved the BBC reporter and deputy editor of the *New Statesman*, John Freeman, who recorded it in Küsnacht in March 1959. It was first broadcast in October and afterward ran repeatedly as a film. The interview contained the remarkable passage in which the reporter swung from Jung's childhood experiences and religious upbringing in the Jung family's parsonage to the present, posing the direct question whether he believed in God now. "Now?" Jung replied, and paused for a moment like a subject in one of his association experiments on the hot seat. Then he admitted that it was really quite a difficult question. And to the surprise of his listeners he added very definitely: "I *know.* I don't need to believe. I know."[36] Instead of going deeper into this point, Freeman went on to other, according to his opinion more "topical" questions, for example on the uncertain future and its manifold possibilities for the destruction of humankind and the whole planet. To the question of whether there would ever be a third world war Jung was unable to give a clear answer, because there was so little clear-cut articulation in the unconscious of his contemporaries. As long as consciousness was not aware of any danger, the unconscious spoke a much clearer language. But what was needed, he said, was a careful observation of the human psyche, because it is man, and the nature of man, from which all perils ultimately arise. And man is unconscious of this unassailable fact in an alarming way—psychology notwithstanding!

Finally the Freeman interview led to the question of death. According to Jung, psychologically speaking, it is, with birth, an equally integral component of life. From this point of view death represents a kind of gate. Whoever does not *want* to go through it shirks life itself; by his denial of death he makes his life meaningless. But how should an old person behave toward death? Jung's advice was clear: having treated innumerable old people and having been concerned himself for years with mastering his own age, for him there was only one way—to live from day to day and look ahead, inevitable as the end my be. Those who do not do this, robbing themselves of their confidence in life in the face of death, look backward, grow stiff, and die while they are still alive.

Further requests for interviews came to Jung, who had meanwhile reached eighty-five. He was even prepared to grant some of these wishes, for example to the *Sunday Times* reporter Gordon Young and to Georg Gerster, an earlier conversation partner, for Swiss Radio. On the other hand he was tired of debating with those who had either not read his books thoroughly or constantly mistook his psychological statements for philosophical or theological ones, thus repeating old misconceptions. On account of his declining physical capacity he had to insist, when the BBC in London requested another interview, that a few precautionary measures would have to be conceded if another broadcast was to take place. Hence Jung was very clear:

> I am sick of talking to people who do not even know the psychological ABC's. There are so many people who either designate themselves as my pupils or aver that they know my "system" that I am always a bit scared when I have to meet an unknown person. I trust you are aware of this serious question. The whole interview depends on it.

And with critical reference to the interview with Richard Evans, he noted further:

> A few years ago [Houston] University got an interview out of me to which they sent a professor of psychology who was completely ignorant and to whom one could not talk intelligently. I had then been still strong enough to push

> him aside and give a free talk about some basic aspects. I could not do that anymore.[37]

C. G. Jung had reached his eighty-fifth year. In order not to burden him unduly, marked as he was by the physical difficulty of old age yet mentally as spry as ever, with the obligatory festivities, the individual events in his honor were spaced out over several weeks. So as to be up to it, Jung stayed for some time in the early summer in Bollingen. As early as four weeks before the twenty-seventh of July, the Psychological Club under the presidency of Cornelia Brunner began with an obviously quite successful fete in the Dolder Hotel in Zürich. The great zest with which the guest of honor gave himself to the occasion was evident from his participation and gratitude. So he was happily surprised at the presence of Elsie Attenhofer, a Swiss cabaret artist whose work he had admired for many years. On his birthday itself congratulatory messages reached Küsnacht from all over the work, which needed to be replied to in their turn. "I have to reconcile myself with some effort to the role of recipient in which I have found myself, so to speak, for fifteen years now,"[38] he wrote to the club's president. A well-filled cask of wine he had gotten, among other things, from the friends of the Psychological Club he seemed to intend using as a kind of "remedy." The appreciative words on his life's work which came from the Swiss ambassador in Vienna he could only answer with candid thanks; such a thing was "a tune not very often heard in the beloved fatherland." An eloquent comment; not a few of the remarks of his last years were in the same vein. This view, not without resignation, was expressed in statements like:

> For decades I have been not understood or misunderstood, although in the beginning I took great pains with regard to "communication and logical persuasion." But on account of the novelty of my subject and of my thoughts I ran up everywhere, so to speak, against an impenetrable wall.[39]

Jung was reminded of his countryman from Basel Johann

Jakob Bachofen, the author of the *Mother Right*, he too an "anachronism." And so Jung consoled himself with being "ahead of his time"—a ray of hope in the gloom of a mood of resignation.

Another recognition, unusual in its own way, came to Jung on the occasion of his eighty-fifth birthday. The little village of Küsnacht named him, after he had lived there for more than half a century, an honorary citizen, even though—as tradition would have required—he had not been born in Canton Zürich. Hence Jung's amazement was great, particularly as he had once been heard to say jokingly that he had "not been guilty of the slightest political merit." To fulfill his duty as a citizen, participating in the innumerable referenda and thereby taking joint responsibility for public policy, is for the genuine Swiss no merit but a social matter of fact. His international fame, decorated with several honorary doctorates, was all the more to be valued when the inhabitants of his own village fully accepted him as one of their own. Therefore he gladly took part in the banquet which the Community Council, headed by its president Eduard Guggenbühl, set up for him in the Sun Hotel in Küsnacht.

But one thing could not be denied: "Jung's eighty-fifth birthday was much more of a strain than his eightieth had been, and it soon became sadly evident that he was indeed five years older. Nevertheless, he went through it all without showing that it was tiring him so much," Barbara Hannah recalled.[40] It was this overfatigue that forced him, for a short time at least, to leave Küsnacht. Whereas usually only Bollingen was considered a place of recreation, he decided this time, together with his friend Fowler McCormick and his housekeeper Ruth Bailey, to visit a little hotel in Onnens, situated amid beautiful scenery in western Switzerland. He had felt at ease there in the past when it was necessary to tune out for a while and yet still have the amenities of a well-cared-for house. But as soon as they set out he began to feel seriously unwell, and he became gravely ill. The doctor summoned to the hotel feared that the patient would die soon. As soon as he was able to travel, Jung consented to his children's and his friends' wish that he return to Küsnacht. Dreams appeared which seemed to suggest that the end was near: Bollingen emerged, but it was "the other Bollingen," a home surrounded in an unearthly radiance; and then a "mother wolverine," teaching her young to dive and swim on a wide stretch of water.

But the end indicated by the dreams did not come, although—or precisely because—the patient accepted it and was ready to start. Though seriously ill, he underwent an improvement that was surprising to all concerned, even recovering his ability to work and creative powers for a few more months. This time he abandoned his custom of going to Bollingen or taking a recreational trip to Ticino, and remained in Küsnacht. In the few hours he was able to use for mental work the old man summoned all his strength—one last time. There was another book to be produced. And so it came about:

When John Freeman had undertaken the above-mentioned mission to film a television interview for the BBC in the spring of 1959, the program had been a remarkable success. One of the innumerable viewers had been Wolfgang Foges, managing director of the firm of Aldus Books in London. As a former resident of Vienna who had lived near Sigmund Freud and been interested in the development of depth psychology, he formed the impression that Jungian psychology deserved a popularization similar to that of Freud's psychoanalysis, whose public appeal was undeniable. And because the amiable contact between Jung and his interviewer was not lost on Foges, he sought to enlist the latter as mediator for his planned book. What he had in mind was a presentation of analytical psychology that would be as universally understandable as possible. "I jumped at the idea and set off once more to Zürich," John Freeman described his mission, "determined that I could convince Jung of the value and importance of such a work. Jung listened to me in his garden for two hours almost without interruption—and then said no. He said it in the nicest possible way, but with great firmness; he had never in the past tried to popularize his work, and he wasn't sure that he could successfully do so now; anyway, he was old and rather tired and not keen to take on such a long commitment. . . ."[41]

Anyone who knew Jung knew that his decisions were taken after thorough deliberation and were as a rule unalterable. And as Foges, for his part, held to his purpose, his recent suggestion seemed doomed to failure. But things turned out differently. Not only did positive reactions multiply to the interview broadcast by the BBC, but there was also a dream: instead of debating with professional people in his study, Jung saw himself standing in an open place before a great crowd, who listened with rapt attention and—the deciding factor, and the reason why it meant so much to him—Jung was understood by the multitude. Hence when Aldus books renewed its proposal, Jung revised his earlier decision and was prepared to collaborate in the writing of a comprehensive book enhanced by interesting illustrative material. What emerged was the volume *Man and His Symbols*, introduced by John Freeman and with contributions by Joseph L. Henderson, Marie-Louise von Franz, Aniela Jaffé, and Jolande Jacobi. Jung himself contributed the essay "Approaching the Unconscious," a work which he himself originally wrote in English and which thus achieved a high degree of general intelligibility. In this last book Jung was concerned with much more than simply a popular introduction to the world of his experience and his psychology. It was above all the richly documented experience of a doctor who had in view the destiny of the individual as well as that of imperiled humankind. As neither the traditional religions nor philosophical systems were able to point a way through the crisis, Jung directed attention in this final article to the individual, who had always stood at the center of his search for knowledge and his therapy, saying:

> The change must indeed begin with an individual; it might be any one of us. Nobody can afford to look round and to

> wait for somebody else to do what he is loath to do himself.[42]

And this "self-conduct," always representing action with an eye toward the Self and self-becoming, thus remained Jung's preoccupation to the close of his life. It was also granted him to finish this last work written by his own hand, down to some changes and additions, before he himself came to an end.

At any rate, his physical powers soon declined perceptibly. Of course, he still received a few visitors and even still made short excursions. On their last trip together on 6 May, exactly a month before his death, as Barbara Hannah recounted from her own experience, Jung however dispensed with the short walk that had hitherto been customary. "He also did not feel like talking, though he seemed anxious to see his favorite roads again; and we drove longer than usual. One strange thing happened on this last drive: we met and were held up *three* times by weddings."[43]

This information on the three wedding processions they came across reveals an important motif, that of the "marriage of death," the final union of the inner opposites at the close of this life, as it is known to religious tradition, myth, and poetry—"Death calls us to a marriage" (Novalis). Jung, who was beginning to lose his attachment to the earthly Bollingen because his gaze was already directed toward the "other Bollingen," may have thought of the experience he had had decades ago when his mother died. Not until a fairly short time ago had he recorded this incident for his memoirs: he had been in Ticino at the time when Emilie Jung-Preiswerk died quite unexpectedly in Küsnacht. The night before, he had a frightening dream, with chaotic goings-on in a primitive place with gigantic boulders in surroundings like a primeval forest. But all in all this deathly terrifying dream had said to him

> that the soul of my mother was taken into that greater territory of the self which lies beyond the segment of Christian morality, taken into that wholeness of nature and spirit in which conflicts and contradictions are resolved.

I went home immediately, and while I rode in the night train I had a feeling of great grief, but in my heart of hearts I could not be mournful, and this for a strange reason: during the entire journey I continually heard dance music, laughter, and jollity, as though a wedding were being celebrated. This contrasted violently with the devastating impression the dream had made on me.

Jung had no illusions about the fearful brutality of death, whether it be the physical or the accompanying psychic event. Yet this was not its only aspect. For him there was another point of view, from which death represented a joyous event:

In the light of eternity it is a wedding, a *mysterium coniunctionis*. The soul attains, as it were, its missing half, it achieves wholeness.[44]

Here Jung himself recalled the joyful element of the dancing girls on Greek sarcophagi and the funeral wedding of the great kabbalist Rabbi Simon bar Yochai.

One of the very few visitors—apart from family, relations, and most intimate friends—to whom Jung was available for conversation to his last years was the Chilean author Miguel Serrano, who was in the diplomatic service and who gave detailed accounts of his encounters with Hermann Hesse and Carl Gustav Jung. Serrano had been his country's representative in India for years and was familiar with Eastern spirituality and tradition. During a trip to the Antarctic he had had Jung's book *The Relations between the Ego and the Unconscious* in his luggage. "There, surrounded by gigantic icebergs, amid the thunderous din of masses of ice breaking off and plunging into the sea, in an atmosphere of gleaming light and burning cold, I studied Jung's work. In almost complete isolation I began to search for something that could bridge the gap which separated the ego of modern man from his unconscious."[45] The outer experience was joined—in compensation—by an inner one, and the reporter wondered which was more meaningful to him: the journey to the eternal ice or Jung's book, which—like analytical psychology in general—pointed out to him a modern path of initiation. Then his first meeting in person with C. G. Jung: "Aside from his inherent vitality, one felt above all his great kindness, together with a certain irony, if not sarcasm. But what impressed me most was the air of distance and mystery that surrounded him. I also recognized that this kindly man possessed a demonic side besides, which could burst forth unexpectedly when a spark set it alight. His gaze was penetrating and searching; it seemed as though he was looking out over his spectacles—and perhaps also beyond his own time."[46] The Chilean visitor noted what had also struck others who had compared the mature man with pictures from his youth, namely the dissimilarity between then and now in the face of this man who had had to go through a drastic transformation, which was visible even in his physiognomy and clearly could not be explained as merely the result of age. This could be noted as early as Jung's fifties and sixties.

After this first encounter in a hotel in Locarno in 1959, there were other meetings, down in fact to the last one on 10 May 1961, barely a month before Jung's death. Like the letters exchanged between the two men, their conversations also concentrated on the central subject of esoterism, which Jung in his late work had termed the *mysterium coniunctionis*, the sacred marriage, whether it involved its mystical or its magical aspect, for example in Tantrism. This great theme was taken up in Serrano's prose poem "The Visits of the Queen of Sheba,"[47] to which Jung contributed one of his last forewords. How right Ruth Bailey was, then, when she told Serrano on the Chilean guest's last visit: "There must be a close affinity between you and Jung. He is always so happy to see you. Even today he is waiting for your visit with interest." With a smile and a roguish, knowing wink the host remarked: "Yes, that's so. The spirit attracts the spirit. Only the right ones come. We are guided by the unconscious, for the unconscious knows."[48] Serrano, then, was a "right one" for him, while highly esteemed colleagues and friends of Jung's had knocked at his door in vain for months.

After weeks of illness, a stroke, and days of weakness and confinement to bed, on this afternoon of 10 May 1961 C. G. Jung seemed revivified. Even now he still had his mental alertness and brilliance. They spoke of experiences on the fringe, near death. From Serrano's notes, Jung said:

> Today nobody listens anymore to what lies behind the words. . ., to the Ideas that underlie them. Indeed, my work consists above all in giving new names to these Ideas and realities. Let's take for example the word "unconscious." I have just finished reading a book by a Chinese Zen Buddhist. I felt as if we were talking about one and the same thing and were simply using different words for it. The use of the word "unconscious" is not the decisive thing; what counts is the Idea that lies behind this word.[49]

Jung by no means read only Eastern literature in these last weeks, although the unprepared visitor might have been surprised to find in this old man, sitting by the window wrapped in a ceremonial Japanese robe, a doctor who had again and again drawn his visitors' attention to the real essence of Western man, the experience of Christ. On a small table next to Jung lay a copy of *Le phénomène humain* by Pierre Teilhard de Chardin. This great nature philosopher and mystic, a French Jesuit unappreciated during his lifetime, was only really discovered in the sixties—and only for a short time, as it turned out. Jung was one of his readers. Asked whether he had studied it yet, Jung answered, "Yes, and it is a wonderful book."

But was it a matter of books, then, of systems of thought and therapeutic methods? Serrano intimated how he saw the master in Küsnacht, as one who had reconnected the people of this century with the occult and the spiritual. Again, he let Jung speak for himself:

> I have tried above all to make plain to Christians what the Savior really is and what the resurrection means. In our day no one seems to know or remember this anymore; but the Idea still survives in their dreams. . . .[50]

The moment of parting had come. Guest and host knew there was not enough strength for more; Jung's daughter and son-in-law were at the door waiting for their father. Miguel Serrano had written down many thoughts that united the two men. But one thought, one image, one dream had made an indelible impression on him. It came from a previous meeting, when Jung was speaking as if to himself:

> Once there was a flower, a stone, a crystal, a queen, a king, a palace, a lover and his beloved, somewhere, a long, long time ago, on an island in the middle of the ocean, five thousand years ago. . . . Such a thing is love, the mystical flower of the soul. That is the center of the Self. . . .

Then he went on, as if in a dream: "Nobody understands what I mean. Only a poet could sense it."

Serrano said, "But you are really a poet yourself! . . . And this woman, is she still alive?"

As if emerging from mythical pasts and returning to the historical dimension, Jung answered, letting the other have the clue to the riddle (to the extent it was necessary at all): "She died eight years ago. . . . I am very old. . . ."[51]

Whether this date was accurate and was based on an exact reference in their conversation, or whether these words, spoken in 1959, referred to Toni Wolff who had died six years earlier in 1953 may never be known. But if this were so, it would emphasize once more that the intimate relationship between her and Jung was much more than a friendship between two people—at which the overrighteous may take offense.

ung toward the end of his life, at the door of his house in Küsnacht.

28

Under the Sign of Wholeness: The End

C. G. Jung's end lay immediately ahead—only a few weeks and days of further declining strength. For some months he knew and even occasionally said that he "had his marching orders," as he put it. One more time he had himself taken out for a drive in his own auto, as it was necessary to say goodbye to the world and the things around him. The earthly Bollingen had already drawn far into the distance. Now and then he looked out across the lake from the balcony of his house in Küsnacht, and the last days played themselves out between his bedroom and his study on the second floor. On 17 May an embolism occurred, a blood clot in the brain. The few visitors who still appeared noticed a slight impairment of his speech. Ruth Bailey, who was now near him day and night, recalled: "It happened during breakfast. . . . After a few days he recovered, and talking tired him less. Only he could no longer read well, so mostly I read to him. Then came the thirtieth of May: After another peaceful and happy previous day, while we were drinking tea at the window of his study, he had a second stroke. That was the last time he was in that room; from then on he stayed only in his bedroom."[1]

"Do the people know that I am dying?" he asked once, as though he wanted to be sure that his distant friends were informed of his departure from the earth. But there are more impressive tidings than external information, as Jung knew. Above all, he could not be restrained as those closest to him may have intended. Visions and meaningful dreams and daydreams preceded him, as he had already started out on his last walk. Eight days before his death he told Marie-Louise von Franz of a vision in which he had seen the destruction of a large part of the earth—"Thank God, not all of it," he added—a hopeful look into the gloom of his premonitions.

Ruth Bailey shared some of their last conversations with Miguel Serrano. In a letter of 16 June, ten days after Jung's death, she wrote: "During the last two days he lived in a faraway world and saw wonderful and magnificent things there, of that I am sure. He smiled often and was happy. When we sat on the terrace for the last time, he spoke of an enchanting dream he had had; he said: 'Now I know the truth down to a very little bit that is still missing. When I know this too, then I will have died.' Then later he had another dream which he told me about in the night. He saw a huge, round boulder standing on a high pedestal. At the foot of the stone was engraved the inscription: 'This shall be a sign unto you of wholeness and oneness.'" And Ruth Bailey added the personal note: "Throughout that whole day I must have known that he had now left me. Probably I knew it inside, but repressed it. And that was good; I would hardly have been able to do what needed to be done for him. All I could do was watch over him day and night. . . ."[2]

The dream Ruth Bailey reported contained a few other motifs; in one Jung saw many pots on the right side of a square place, in another the dreamer observed trees with fibrous roots growing around this place. Among the roots shone golden threads. These dream elements, suggesting the image of wholeness, pointed to connections with ancient mysteries, the symbols of germinating seed, that is, rebirth. In ancient Egypt people spoke of the dismembered pieces of the god Osiris which were kept in pots and of whose resurrection they were certain. Adonis, the god of resurrection, was honored by sowing fast-growing seeds in boxes, thereby representing the coming of new life. The Gospel of John has the grain of wheat that falls on the earth, dies, and for that very reason "bringeth forth much fruit" (John 12:24). Barbara Hannah recalled how Jung sometimes applied the image of the pot when taking on a student or a patient. He would say for instance, "Oh, I thought he or she was a good pot, and therefore I would invest in it."[3] Hence there was no doubt that the image and likeness of roots played an important role in Jung's conceptual world and hence naturally represented a means of expression in his dreams. Thus in his memoirs we find the passage referring to the rhizome:

> Life has always seemed to me like a plant that lives on its rhizome. Its true life is invisible, hidden in the rhizome. The part that appears above ground lasts only a single summer. Then it withers away—an ephemeral apparition. When we think of the unending growth and decay of life and civilizations, we cannot escape the impression of absolute nullity. Yet I have never lost a sense of something that lives and endures underneath the eternal flux. What we see is the blossom, which passes. The rhizome remains.[4]

Thus it was the witness to an imperishable world who was confirmed one last time, by the productions of his unconscious (to the extent they were verifiable), in what had determined him and his activity, however the one scarred by weakness and at times haunted by despair, the earthly ego of person No. 1, might be overcome by thoughts of futility and ignorance.

On the afternoon of 6 June 1961, at about four in the afternoon, it was over. Jung died in the bosom of his family in his home in Küsnacht. The "burning demon" of his will to live, as he had once called it eight years earlier, escaped. A very last tribute to him might have been the last words he said to Ruth Bailey the night before: "Let's have a really good wine tonight." He had always liked a good red wine and drunk it with gusto.

It later turned out that not a few of Jung's closest friends had been "aware" of his passing. Laurens van der Post, for example, who was on a voyage from Africa to Europe, one afternoon witnessed a sudden vision which he described thus:

> I suddenly had a vision of myself in a deep, dark valley in avalanche country, among steep, snow-covered mountains. I was filled with a foreknowledge of imminent disaster. I knew that even raising my voice in the world of this vision could bring down the bulging avalanches upon me. Suddenly, at the far end of the valley, on one Matterhorn peak of my vision, still caught in the light of the sun, Jung appeared. He stood there briefly, as I had seen him some weeks before at the gate at the end of the garden of his house, then waved his hand at me and called out, "I'll be seeing you." And then he vanished down the far side of the mountain.
>
> Instantly I fell asleep and slept for some eighteen hours. I woke next morning just as the sun was rising, and pushed aside the curtains of the porthole of my cabin. I saw a great, white lone albatross gliding by it, the sun on fire on its wings. As it glided by it turned its head and looked straight at me. I had done that voyage some fifty times and such a thing had never happened to me, and I had a feeling that the day before me was going to be utterly unlike any other day I had ever experienced. I had hardly got back into bed when my steward appeared with a tray of tea and fruit, as he always did, and handed me the ship's radio news. I opened it casually. The first item I saw was the announcement that Jung had died the previous afternoon at his home in Zürich. Taking into consideration the time and the latitude and longitude of the ship's position, it was clear that my dream, or vision, had come to me at the moment of his death.[5]

Similar synchronistic phenomena were common, and on the day Jung died there was a definite increase in them. Soon after his death a strong thunderstorm came up. Lightning struck a tall poplar tree on the edge of the lake in his garden and tore a great hole in its trunk, so that afterward the ground was littered with small pieces of bark. Barbara Hannah recalled how shortly before the moment of his death she had been fetching her car and found that the relatively fresh battery had run down. When Ruth Bailey telephoned her about a half hour later with the news, Miss Hannah was better able to comprehend the motiveless connections of this "coincidence."

Such acausal phenomena, in all their unusualness, were something as natural for Jung as life itself, or dreaming. He too was aware that today more than ever an expansion of view and consciousness is necessary, if the "miraculous" is not to be split off from the supposedly normal. He had expressed it simply some months before his death, in a letter of 10 August 1960:

> It is quite possible that we look at the world from the wrong side and that we might find the right answer by changing our point of view and looking at it from the other side, that is, not from outside, but from inside.[6]

This statement on the required turning from without to within, however, cannot be taken as absolute. Jung also knew and respected the dimension of the between. Hence it is surely no coincidence that two days after this letter, in regard to the early death of his English friend Victor White, he recorded the following sentence:

> The living mystery of life is always hidden between Two, and it is the true mystery which cannot be betrayed by words and depleted by arguments.[7]

And Gerhard Adler, the co-editor of *The Collected Works* as well as later the letters of C. G. Jung, who had once emigrated to England—he too was among the last to visit the departing Jung—reported of his final meeting: "He sat in his library and seemed to be deeply absorbed in himself. It was clearly perceptible that his attention was directed entirely to the inner realm of psychic images. Then he noticed me, and in a trice his expression changed. He turned toward me, and the place of his deep introversion was taken by a cordial and lively relatedness. The two aspects—concentration on the inner world and immediate openness to other people—imparted a memorable picture of the wholeness of this man."[8]

After the funeral service, the so-called "send-off" in the village church in Küsnacht, Carl Gustav Jung was buried in the Küsnacht cemetery. The rectangular gravestone, the height of a man, bore the arms of the Jung family, and beneath this the names of father, mother, sister Gertrud, Emma Jung-Rauschenbach, and C. G. Jung. The top and bottom borders repeated once more the motto he had chosen for his house:

> *Vocatus atque non vocatus deus aderit.*
> Called or not called, the god will be there.

The right and left sides contained a saying from the great resurrection chapter of the First Epistle to the Corinthians (1 Cor. 15:47):

> *Primus homo de terra terrenus*
> *Secundus homo de caelo caelestis.*
>
> The first man is of the earth and is earthly,
> the second man is of heaven and is heavenly.

Burial place of the Jung family in the Küsnacht churchyard. (Photograph taken in the 1960s.)

Essays

Western Consciousness and Eastern Spirituality

During C. G. Jung's lifetime and after his death, the reproach was voiced from various quarters that the Swiss depth psychologist had not only encouraged interest in Eastern religiosity, but strengthened syncretistic tendencies toward the blending of religions in modern people. The well-known Dutch theologian Willem A. Visser't Hooft, for many years general secretary of the Ecumenical Council of the church, described C. G. Jung's school as "the strongest force" on which such a fundamental syncretistic mood was based. Although Visser't Hooft did not declare Jung's efforts in the psychology of religion to be unfounded in principle, he did draw the conclusion: "In any case Jung's psychology contributed directly or indirectly to the creation of a religious eclecticism in which the most diverse religious conceptions are assembled without any possibility of real spiritual judgment."[1]

These words from the Dutch Protestant were preceded by a

statement of Jung's in 1936, in which he objected to the "bankruptcy" of Protestantism, splintered as it was into hundreds of denominations, which "syncretistic outgrowths and . . . the importation on a mass scale of exotic religious systems" had at least alleviated. The picture that had arisen, he said, was approximately equivalent to the Hellenistic syncretism of the third and fourth centuries.[2] Nonetheless, it cannot be entirely denied that Jung did in fact sometimes omit certain possible distinctions, for example in this very essay on "Yoga and the West," where he mentioned in the same breath such hardly comparable movements as Christian Science, the Theosophy of Helena Petrovna Blavatsky and Annie Besant, and Rudolf Steiner's anthroposophy. For all that, though, against sweeping suppositions it must be maintained that on the one hand Jung wished to be understood as neither a religious historian nor propagandist for Oriental religiosity, and on the other his psychological statements must not be mistaken for theological or philosophical ones. Hence in Jung's case the usual ecclesiastical argument falls short.

There is no lack of investigations of comparative cultural morphology that make it reasonable to distinguish between Eastern (Asiatic) and Western (European and American) culture, and indeed "on clearly demonstrable structural principles," according to William S. Haas. Differing conceptions of time and reality and differences in philosophical thinking on both sides have been presented and examined often enough. This would probably be agreed to by Jean Gebser, who stresses that the concept of "opposition," which arises from Western rationality, is by itself insufficient to characterize the comparison of the two intellectual and cultural hemispheres. "The view that West and East are opposites is false. . . . West and East are complements. Compared with the dualistic, divisive character of opposites, that of complements is of a polar, unifying nature. The opposite is a concept, the complement a constellation. . . . Thinking that is nothing but rational and oppositional leads to division, and in the long run to death. If in contrast one consciously moves in the field of polar tension of complementarity, the possibility of a harmonious wholeness appears."[3]

The central premise of Jean Gebser's assertion is based on insights of Jung's. It should at least be noted that beyond this there were further noteworthy parallels in the work of Rudolf Steiner, who undertook to elaborate this theme long before either of them.[4] Above all there are two polar pairs of Jungian psychology which are involved here: conscious and unconscious, and the extraverted and introverted attitude types. The one factor from time to time requires a certain reconciliation to and harmonization with the other, and only thus does wholeness come within sight. In other words, the encounter of East and West has to do with the individuation process of humankind, with that great task of the present and future whose depth and full scope have hardly been considered up to now! To be sure, Rudyard Kipling's verse from 1889—"Oh East is East and West is West, and never the twain shall meet"—has become a household saying, but the assurance has long lost its validity, even though until now this "meeting" has occurred primarily in the economic and technical sector, and large parts of Asia have been inundated by Western rationality. Conversely, Eastern spirituality, from which the westernized Chinese, Japanese, and Indian is largely estranged, has come to the West. Jung pointed out the danger that traditional religious notions can perish from the lack of understanding of their "guardians": "The same thing could happen to us as in China, where for example a Chinese philosopher like Hu-shih is ashamed to know anything about the *I Ching*, and where the profound significance of the concept of the Tao has been lost, and in its place people worship electric locomotives and airplanes."[5]

In the context of his coming to grips with a publication by Arthur Koestler, Jung, at the age of eighty-five, expressed his view of the Eastern and Western approaches to reality, shedding light on the intellectual stance peculiar to Western people, determined by *ratio* and extraversion:

> Rationality is only one aspect of the world and does not cover the whole field of experience. Psychic events are not caused merely from without and mental contents are not mere derivatives of sense-perceptions. There is an irrational mental life within, a so-called "spiritual life," of which almost nobody knows or wants to know except a few "mystics." This "life within" is generally considered nonsense and therefore something to be eliminated—curiously enough in the East as well as in the West. Yet it is the origin and the still-flowing source of Yoga, Zen, and many other spiritual endeavours, not only in the East but in the West too.[6]

Thus C. G. Jung recognized, on the one hand, the need of the intellect-ruled Western mentality to be supplemented; he knew that East and West each represented half of the one spiritual universe and that each of these standpoints, though they were at variance with each other, had its psychological justification. But on the other hand Jung made no bones about his rootedness in the Western tradition, which bore the stamp of Christianity, and which made it seem impossible to him to accept untested or simply imitate the arrangements by European people of the Eastern spirit, which he also admired.

Before dealing with Jung's numerous statements on general and specific problems of the spiritual life of the East—the pertinent works are assembled in Volume 11 of *The Collected Works: Psychology and Religion: West and East*—it should be asked what significance he attributed to this area. In the preface to the second edition of his commentary on the Chinese text *The Secret of the Golden Flower*, edited by Richard Wilhelm, Jung commented on misinterpretations like those mentioned at the outset, which many readers of the book might make. It had often been found, he said, that people thought that the aim of its publication was to put a method of finding salvation into the hands of the Western public. "Such people have then tried—failing completely to understand anything I said in my commentary—to imitate the 'methods' of the Chinese text. Let us hope there were only a few of these representatives of the spiritual nadir."[7]

Jung saw the second misconception in the notion that he had in his commentary been describing to a certain extent his own special psychotherapeutic methods, which consequently were supposed to consist in his suggesting Eastern ideas to his patients as possible healthy goals. Such a notion, he said, was wrong and based on the still widespread assertion that psychology was an invention for a specific purpose and not an empirical science, as he had always represented it.

Jung also refuted these misunderstandings in other contexts. Characteristic of his attitude toward the East, for example, is the commemorative address he gave in Munich on 10 May 1930, on the death of Richard Wilhelm. There he demanded, for the understanding of Eastern spiritual culture, the overcoming of the prevailing prejudice along with a simultaneous opening up to foreign mentality. By this he meant an "understanding openness, beyond any Christian resentment, beyond any European arrogance." Then:

> A mere sensation or a new thrill is of no use to the European mind. We must rather learn to earn in order to possess. What the East has to give us should be merely a help to us in a work which we still have to do. What good is the wisdom of the Upanishads to us, and the insights of Chinese yoga, if we abandon our own foundations like outworn mistakes, to settle thievishly on foreign shores like homeless pirates?[8]

The speaker was no less clear in pointing out the need to expand the European concept of science, emphasizing that those who wished to experience the living wisdom of China must first begin with themselves, with the self-knowledge that stems from European tradition, for "our way begins with the reality of Europe, and not with yoga exercises that are supposed to blind us to our own reality." Jung foresaw—even in 1930—that "the Spirit of the East is really *ante portas*!" And he already saw two possibilities in the approaching confrontation between East and West. A healing power could by all means be concealed in it, but so could "a dangerous infection." Consequently the diagnostician left it to his client's judgment to make what he could of these possibilities. In the meantime, after more than half a century corresponding experiences could be attained—positive as well as negative.

Some five years after this address in Munich, in February 1936, Jung published in English in the Calcutta journal *Prabuddha Bharata* the already-mentioned article "Yoga and the West." If his studies together with Richard Wilhelm had earlier prompted him to delve into the nature of East Asian tradition, this small treatise showed how he evaluated the Indian system of mental and physical education as a Western psychologist. No doubt the studies on Kundalini Yoga he had carried out with the Indologist Wilhelm J. Hauer made themselves felt here. Jung looked first at the developments that had introduced Westerners to the conflict between faith and knowledge, between religious revelation and rational deduction. Jung found a

> lack of direction [which] borders on psychic anarchy. . . . Through his historical development, the European has become so far removed from his roots that his mind was finally split into faith and knowledge, in the same way that every psychological exaggeration breaks up into its inherent opposites.[9]

With this statement the author did not fail to appreciate that aspects of the history of consciousness could be won from this route which Erich Neumann had placed under his lens.[10] Jung's finding—which, significantly, he published in an Indian journal—was:

> The split in the Western mind therefore makes it impossible at the outset for the intentions of yoga to be realized in any adequate way. . . . The Indian . . . not only knows his own nature, but he knows also how much he himself is nature. The European, on the other hand, has a science of nature and knows astonishingly little of his own nature, the nature within him.[11]

This is reminiscent of his demand for a picture of man that embraced all of reality, consciousness as well as unconscious. Further, the psychologist looked at the differing psychic disposition which is something quite other in Eastern people. Therefore his advice was to study yoga carefully after all, which did not mean, however, to practice it at all costs. The question of practicing an Oriental course of training was indeed one that could not be taken seriously enough. Jung's thought culminated in the provocative forecast: "In the course of the centuries the West will produce its own yoga, and it will be on the basis laid down by Christianity."[12] Even this statement should probably be taken with a grain of salt, if confusion is to be avoided with what has occasionally come into circulation as "yoga for Christians" or "yoga for the West." Clearly more was intended than simply a pragmatic evaluation of Eastern practices for Western people. So it remains to ask what such a yoga might look like, that would be suited to Westerners, their specific human burden, their particular state of consciousness, and would—in contrast to Eastern yoga—be oriented to the experience of Christ.

In speaking of such a path of initiation and the search for spiritual knowledge which corresponds to the modern state of consciousness as well as continuing the tradition of an esoteric Christianity, one cannot ignore the mention of anthroposophy. Rudolf Steiner presented his "anthroposophically oriented spiritual science" primarily as a "way of knowledge, which might guide the spiritual in man's nature to the spiritual in the cosmos."[13] Compared with the humanistic and scientific disciplines, it was an "enlargement" of the view of natural science. This amounts to an overcoming of the one-sidedness whose correction concerned C. G. Jung in his own way, although there can be no question of a direct contact or even ideological connection. Jung did not pursue the thought of a Western "yoga" path any further. Anthroposophy was just as suspect to him as was its founder. "I have already read a few books by Steiner and must confess that I have not found anything in them that would be of any use to me at all," Jung wrote in 1935.[14] And a quarter century later the old man told a pair of English visitors, partly in earnest and partly in jest, that he would have preferred to have Steiner locked up.[15] Of course it is not out of the question that Jung referred less to Steiner than to his uncritical disciples. Thus the letter from 1935 reads:

> I have also become acquainted with very many anthroposophists and theosophists and have always found to my regret that these people imagine all kinds of things and assert all kinds of things for which they are incapable of producing any proof at all.[16]

And Jung cannot have been entirely uninformed. His cousin Ernst Fiechter (1875–1948), the architect of his home in Küsnacht, was an anthroposophist, a student of Steiner himself, and toward the end of his life he was a priest in the service of the (anthroposophical) Community of Christ.[17] In family relationships the subject of anthroposophy cannot have been excluded.

Jung's misgivings regarding a path of spiritual knowledge were undoubtedly of a fundamental nature and not at all directed against any particular method, be it an Eastern or a Western discipline. As can be gathered from one of the late letters to Melvin J. Lasky, the experienced depth psychologist saw the problem where people sought to bypass spiritual originality and spontaneity by means of a practice of one kind or another. But naturally, primal spiritual experience cannot be manufactured at will. As can be observed, the number of those who travel the path consistently is small, while the mass of adherents devote themselves to the mere recitation of the sayings of the master:

> [One seeks,] through the application of a method, to attain the effect of the primordial experience, namely, a kind of spiritual transformation. The depth and intensity of the original emotion become a passionate longing, an enduring effort that may last for hundreds of years, to restore the original situation. Curiously enough, one does not realize

> that this was a state of spontaneous, natural emotion, or *ekstasis*, and thus the complete opposite of a methodically construed imitation.[18]

Great as Jung's skepticism was, he had to concede in all honesty that a patient and careful effort did have a definite psychic influence, positively as well as negatively. Thus, for instance, people eagerly pursued Zen and yoga—instead of concerning themselves with the irrational life within themselves—and preferred to consider only that which lies within reach on the surface. But the secret longing for wholeness remains. The state of affairs remains that the West is too much cut off from the unconscious and the East tends to identify itself with it completely. An encounter of East and West is especially not without danger when Eastern magical methods are adopted without control, when the necessary safeguard that is always called for in the face of the unconscious is dispensed with. Otherwise it is all too easy for a kind of inflation to take place, an inundation from the unconscious for which the ego is no match. For, as Jung continued in a letter he wrote to Australia in December 1960:

> These Eastern methods don't enrich consciousness and they don't increase our real knowledge and our self-criticism, and that is the thing we need, namely a consciousness with a wider horizon and a better understanding. That at least is what I am trying to do for the patient: to make him independent and conscious of the influences of the unconscious.[19]

Thus Jung's relationship to the subject of a process of initiation was rather a broken one. This does not exclude the possibility that analytical psychotherapy can lead to insights which benefit spiritual development. The path of individuation and the process of initiation correspond to one another. This is shown by the confrontation and collation with the anthroposophical way of knowledge[20] and also by undertakings such as Count Karlfried Dürckheim's "initiative therapy."[21] Jung himself did not feel called upon to be a renewer of culture or founder of a science of initiation. But a psychologist with his innate far-sightedness would have found an investigation into the ways of spiritual training practiced in the West desirable. One wonders whether this suggestion—beyond an interpretation of the *Exercitia Spiritualia* of Ignatius and the alchemistic process—was ever made to him.

It remains to establish that C. G. Jung did indeed compose psychological commentaries on texts from the area of Eastern religions and philosophies, and wrote detailed forewords to the books of D. T. Suzuki and Heinrich Zimmer, as well as the *I Ching*. But anyone who wishes to go further into his call for a Western "yoga" finds himself continually faced with skeptical statements. At decisive moments—such as on his journey to India—Jung's own unconscious directed him to the center of Western esoterism, the search for the Holy Grail. And it is left to the readers of Jung's works to take up the abundantly scattered references to Gnostic elements, Rosicrucianism, and the mystical path and make them bear fruit for themselves and their own inner way within the context of his interpretation of alchemy. Here lies a treasure that has as yet hardly been raised, a treasure for both religious and spiritual seekers.[22]

C. G. Jung in Dialogue and Dispute

Considering that C. G. Jung belonged to the introverted attitude type and that consequently his manifold and often extraordinary inner experiences were bound to have provided special meaning, his great readiness for conversation and meetings, and also for confrontation and debate, might be surprising. Those who are haunted by experiences that go far beyond the "average" threaten many times to become isolated. Not seldom do the words "No one understands me" come to their lips—a complaint that the old man did in fact voice often.

Undeniably, experiences which may be called—in the strict sense of the word—esoteric, "inner" things, not only cannot be imparted to others at will, but can only be understood—so far at least—by those few who have attained similar inner perceptions and insights. The "reality of the soul," as Jung learned to see it, consists in the fact that it cannot be adequately described by the categories of the inside, or the depths. The dimension of the inter-(personal) always comes into play, especially in Jung's primary field of endeavor, psychotherapy. Here the decisive factor is that, and how, the person faces his fellow human beings, for "analysis is a dialogue demanding two partners. Analyst and patient sit facing one another, eye to eye; the doctor has something to say, but so has the patient."[1] Important as the method of "treatment" is in itself, compared with the relationship of analyst and analysand its significance is nevertheless secondary. It is so because the relationship between two people is built and worked out not only on the conscious level. On the one hand each of the two is in contact with his own unconscious, but on the other hand the unconscious of one acts upon and reacts to the unconscious of the other—a process of relationship which can at best be only very incompletely brought into the open, and at worst hardly at all.

It is self-evident that the encounter with the patient, or client, has great significance for the psychotherapist. Jung acknowledged how much he had learned from them not only for his research but also for the process of his own self-knowledge:

> My patients brought me so close to the reality of human life that I could not help learning essential things from them. Encounters with people of so many different psychological levels have been for me incomparably more important than fragmentary conversations with celebrities. The finest and most significant conversations of my life were anonymous.[2]

Naturally this is called for by the doctor's obligation to confidentiality, but also by the mystery of togetherness which escapes transcription.

As far as the confrontation with certain "celebrities" goes, however, Jung—himself a famous person early on—did not avoid such meetings, as is shown by his multifarious cooperation with congresses of all kinds and in certain social circles such as Count Hermann Keyserling's "School of Wisdom" in Darmstadt and even more Olga Fröbe-Kapteyn's Eranos conferences in Ascona. But it is also documented by his work, in which opinions on prominent contemporaries are found, and not least by the wealth of correspondence which continued to the last months of his life. Most interesting and instructive are Jung's statements representing his insights and research results against other points of view.

One might have thought that dialogue, genuine conversation, would have a particularly good chance between two dia-logicians, not in the sense that one simply agrees with or "gives in" to the other, but more that of careful listening and a readiness to take seriously the "immense otherness of the other," as Buber said. If one tries to test this by example and turns, for example, to Jung's encounter with the dialogue thinker Martin Buber, the attempt comes off as a bitter disappointment. Buber, only three years younger than Jung, had himself gone through a phase of inner (mystical) experience as a young man, before he was able to make the step from mysticism to dialogue and thus to the "I and Thou," the dimension of the interhuman.[3] After this turnabout was completed, Buber reacted with extreme sensitivity when he saw the interpersonal falling prey to an apersonal, "mystical" inwardness. In his book *The Eclipse of God* (English edition 1952, German 1953), Buber considered the relation of religion and philosophy, illustrating it with examples of a number of historical positions from Spinoza to his contemporaries Sartre, Heidegger, and Jung. To encounter the reality of religious belief, for Buber, meant "to live devoted to the believed, unconditionally affirmed, absolute essence. In all great philosophy, in contrast, it appears that rational truth means to make the absolute its object, from which every other object must derive."[4] Hence, he said, religion was based on a true I-Thou relationship, whereas the philosophical act led to a view of unity, an I-It experience. "The existent, to man, is either opposite or object. The nature of man is built upon this duality in his relationship to the existent—opposition and observation."[5] What he had said of the basic attitude of philosophy Buber transferred to that of the psychological view. With this the difference between him and Jung was obvious, because for Jung religion was always also "a living connection to the psychic processes that are not dependent on consciousness, but take place in the obscurity of the psychic background." And God—called by Buber the "most loaded of all human words"—was usually conceived of by Jung as "autonomous psychic content." Buber was anxious to declare that in this way the being or nature of God, God's Thou-ness, was denied or at least missed. On the basis of numerous indications offered by the Jungian conceptual framework (for example Self and Self-becoming), and by means of numerous references to the basic writings of analytical psychology, Buber arrived at the conclusion that what was involved here was Gnostic ideas without exception, and that meant ideas which contradicted in principle the Judeo-Christian belief in God. For Buber the case was clear: whoever chose the path of Gnosis as Jung had and granted only the "reality of the soul" missed the "eternal Thou" and added to the "eclipse of God in our time"—a weighty charge.

C. G. Jung took up the challenge. A debate lasting some years was set in motion, in which—even before the writing of Buber's *Eclipse of God*—a number of younger contemporaries engaged who felt themselves obliged as much to Jung as to Buber, among them Hans Trüb and Arie Sborowitz.[6] Jung would even have been prepared to abandon the label "Gnostic" that had been hung on him without further ado, had it not been a nasty swear word in the mouth of a theologian. However, the fact that Buber proceeded from ideas that had been raised continually in theological circles compelled the affected party to oppose him. It was the erroneous assumption of this critics, which Jung had corrected time and again, that he spoke of a being or nature of God, when in fact as a psychologist he admitted only experience as his sole basis for knowledge. Thus Jung wrote in one of his replies:

> It should not be overlooked that I deal with those psychic phenomena which prove empirically to be the bases of metaphysical concepts, and that when I say, for example, "God," I can refer to nothing other than demonstrable psychic patterns which are indeed shockingly real. . . . It is certainly not the task of an empirical science to determine the extent to which such psychic contents are influenced and determined by the presence of a metaphysical Godhead. . . . I do not doubt his [Buber's] conviction of his living relationship to a divine Thou, but I am, as always, of the opinion that this relationship first of all goes to an autono-

> mous psychic content which is defined one way by him and otherwise by the Pope.[7]

Moreover Jung was afraid that Buber, out of understandable ignorance of psychiatric experience, failed to comprehend what he really meant by "reality of the soul" and the process of individuation.

Buber, like the one he had called into question, likewise could not fend off a certain irritation when he complained of an alleged "transgression of the boundaries" on the part of psychology: "We want to get out of this ingenious ambiguity once and for all!" Correspondingly unambiguous, then, was the judgment handed down in the same context on the incompetence of psychology on the truth-content of belief in God, as if Jung had ever had such an assertion in mind. Hence, in his reply to a retort of Jung's, Buber wrote: "Psychology, which treats of the mysteries without understanding the attitude of faith to the mystery, is the modern manifestation of Gnosis. Gnosis is to be understood as not only a purely historical but an all-human category. It . . . is the real adversary of the reality of faith. . . ."[8] Buber's surprisingly harsh judgment implies the accusation that C. G. Jung, as the witness and mediator of present-day religious experience, was to be made jointly responsible for the eclipse of God. For even in one of the first chapters of Buber's book of that title we find the sentence: "Whoever is unwilling to endure the effective reality of transcendence, our opposite, as such collaborates on the human side in the eclipse."[9] But was such an unwillingness present in the psychologist? All the same, the dialogue between these two intellectual founding figures of the century was doomed to failure from its inception. Jung could not remember there ever having been any "personal friction" between the two opponents, "and I do not think that Buber has ever been impolite to me. The only trouble with him is that he does not understand what I am talking about," reads a letter to an American inquirer from 1952.[10]

This rather casual note should of course not be taken as a

minimization, as if this controversy were solely a theoretical misunderstanding that would not allow two old men to reconcile themselves. For even the empiricist Jung was enough of a *homo religiosus* to be concerned with the troubling question of the experience of God and its theological, or psychological, interpretation down to the last months of his life, with explicit reference to Buber.[11]

Scarcely less problematic turned out to be the relationship between Jung and many of his contemporaries who had been schooled in depth psychology. As a rule these critics began by taking for granted Jung's extraordinary contributions in the investigation of the life of the human psyche, but then drew attention to the far-reaching consequences made necessary by a critical coming to terms with analytical psychology. So, in this respect, Baron V. E. von Gebsattel pointed to the danger of a style of psychologism (which Jung himself denounced!), when in Jung, or rather the Zürich school, in the sense of Buber's criticism the "inner God" was placed ahead of the personal God of biblical faith, for example. The image of man which underlies Jungian psychology, he said, might involve archetypal factors which were constellated by inner experiences, but the authority that could make the decision vis-à-vis the unconscious was lacking. Gebsattel reduced his apprehension to the quite simple denominator: "If this is not psychologism, then one might just as well call an elephant a daisy and claim to be a botanist."[12] That such statements do little to promote useful dialogue is obvious, even when they are repeated by other prominent colleagues such as Viktor E. Frankl, for example,[13] or varied as by Medard Boss.

With Erich Fromm, who had openly voiced his aversion to Jung since the mid-thirties, as with Paul J. Stern after him, Jung rose to the status of "prophet of the unconscious." But as such—as Fromm attempted to portray him—he had not proclaimed prophetic wisdom but rather, and this with regard to the tension-filled thirties, produced only the "naive assertions of a reactionary romantic," or perhaps a ruthless opportunist. To be sure, Fromm also did not hesitate to attribute all sorts of contributions and advances, beyond Freud, to his unliked colleague from Zürich. But his contempt could hardly have been more appalling when he wished—subliminally!—to make Jung jointly responsible for the contemporary intellectual crisis of modern people: "The majority, of course, still cling to religious conceptions, but for most these conceptions have become empty formulas, and no longer the expression of a reality to which they feel tied. Under these circumstances Jung's lack of commitment and authenticity is fascinating to many who find themselves in the same situation. With his blend of outmoded superstition, indeterminate heathen idol worship, and vague talk about God, and with the allegation that he is building a bridge between religion and psychology, Jung has presented exactly the right mix to an age which possesses but little faith and judgment."[14] With this he nearly attained Ernst Bloch's level of Jung-defamation. With some bewilderment Rainer Funk, in his carefully edited edition of Fromm's works, noted how surprised many readers continually were at the sharp, not to say shameful statements on the part of the great Jewish social philosopher. Funk suspected some "very personal reservations. One cause of these might also be the fact that Jung had been able to attract many—and above all wealthy—people with his psychology in the United States. . . ."[15]

From being a critic of Freud, Fromm quickly became his apologist, concluding: "Although psychoanalysis has much to thank him [Jung] for, essentially he disregarded the central core of it, the search for truth and the deliverance from illusions, and replaced it with a seductive spirituality and a brilliant obscurantism." Indeed, he said, for Freud there was at least still the category of truth; Jung equated God with the unconscious. The problem of truth, or truthfulness, did not exist for him at all. How particular Fromm himself was about the truth can be read a few lines further on, where he purported to unveil Jung's past at the time of the Third Reich: "Jung praised the Nazis as long as they were winning, and when they lost the war he turned away not only from the Nazis but the whole German people. In his personal conduct he displayed a lack of conscience and veracity."[16] This could only have been written by one ignorant of the facts.

While these statements were written when the accused could no longer defend himself (!), Fromm's criticism that Jung's concept of truth was "untenable" was an old one. It was found in the lectures which Fromm presented at Yale University in 1949[17]—the same Terry Lectures to which Jung had been invited twelve years earlier. In a brief statement Jung had published on another occasion (London, 1958), he recalled that it lay outside the reach of people to make absolute assertions, although it was ethically imperative to be fully responsible for one's own subjective truth.

> Every human judgment, however great one's subjective conviction might be, is subject to error, especially judgments which deal with transcendental subjects. Fromm's philosophy, I am afraid, has not yet gotten past the level of the twentieth century; but man's drive to power and his hubris are so great that he believes in an absolutely valid judgment. No scientifically thinking man with a sense of intellectual responsibility can afford such arrogance. These are the reasons why I insist on the criterium of existence, in the domain of science as well as in that of religion, and on immediate and original experience. Facts are facts and contain no falsehood. It is our judgment that brings in the element of deception.[18]

Jung evinced a peculiar delight in expressing opinions on matters of art. And he made no secret of how much he revered the recognized masters of "classical" music, poetry, and pictorial art. The productions of the moderns were much more problematic for him. To the Welsh painter Ceri Richards, who to his surprise had presented him with a painting in 1958, the seventy-eight-year-old Jung confessed that he had no relation whatever to modern art, unless he understood a picture. And by understanding he meant, for example, when a picture could be grasped "as a confession of the secret of our time."

Generally, he said, it was apparently the duty of modern artists "to show the world in its obscurity." Jung only regretted that artists mostly did not know themselves what they were doing. Unquestionably, here too it was not the art or literary critic speaking, but the doctor and psychologist, in the strict sense of the psychology of the archetypes, which did not inquire after some possible neurotic personal limitations on the part of the artist concerned, as could be expected of psychoanalysis. For Jung the secret of creativity was altogether "a transcendental problem which psychology cannot answer, but only describe." In an essay on "Psychology and Literature" from the year 1930, in which Jung expressed himself on this subject,[19] he did admit that the personal psychology of a writer, and thus any creative person, could if need be be followed into the roots and the furthest branches of his work. But the nature of a work of art consisted not in the personal characteristics, rather—and this is where the archetypal dimension came into play—in the fact

> that it rises far beyond the personal, speaking from and for the spirit and the heart of humanity. . . . Every creative person is a duality or a synthesis of paradoxical qualities. On the one hand he is human and personal, but on the other an impersonal, creative process. . . . Art is innate in him as a driving force which takes hold of him and makes him its instrument. . . . As a person he may have moods and wishes and his own aims, but as an artist he is "human" in a higher sense, he is a collective person, a carrier and former of the unconsciously active psyche of humanity.[20]

In concrete terms, it was not a person with the biography of a Goethe who created *Faust*, "but the psychic components of *Faust* made Goethe. And what is *Faust*? *Faust* is a symbol, not a mere semiotic reference to or allegory for something long known, but the expression of something deeply alive at work in the German psyche, which must have helped Goethe to be born."[21]

Among the writers with whom Jung was directly or indirectly connected relatively early was Hermann Hesse. Struggling with a number of personal problems and psychosomatic complaints, the author spent a convalescent stay in the Sonnmatt sanatorium near Lucerne in 1916 and placed himself in the psychotherapeutic care of Dr. Josef B. Lang, a student of Jung's. Through Lang he became better acquainted with Jung's work, beginning with *Symbols of Transformation*. Hesse's reading of Jung continued for some years, about as long as work in depth psychology continued to interest him. Beyond this there were meetings between the Zürich psychotherapist and the writer, who lived in Montagnola. Jung recognized that Hesse had adopted and elaborated on his thoughts in some of his books, first in *Demian* (1919), and also in *Siddhartha* as well as *Steppenwolf*. In particular, it was the man who is searching for his true ego and aspiring to self-realization whose fate the novelist dramatized. Considering that Hesse was working on the *Demian* material as Jung was still occupied with his own confrontation with the unconscious, but the writer let himself be guided by the psychologist, it is striking that the latter, as one of the first readers of *Demian*, wrote to Hesse on 3 December 1919: "Your book affected me like the light from a lighthouse in a stormy night."[22] Who, then, had shown the light to whom? Hesse commented in retrospect: "I have always had respect for Jung, but his writings have not had as much of an impression on me as those of Freud."[23] A respect, cooled somewhat by distance, which was displayed until his old age in Hesse's critical reviews, but also revealed itself in greetings and signs of a certain friendship. Hesse remembered having a nice impression when he had read at the Club in Zürich and had a few sessions of therapy with Jung in the early twenties; "only at that time I began to realize that for the analysts a genuine relationship to art is unattainable; they all lack the organ for it."[24] Yet the psychologist could not pass over the artist's productions with indifference. The following episode may be typical of the style and the difficulty of a dialogue between the two. In the autumn of 1936, Hesse had sent to Küsnacht a copy of "The

Dream of Josef Knecht," a short poem, which later found inclusion in *The Glass Bead Game*. Jung expressed his thanks to Hesse for sending it and seemed "deeply impressed by the beauty of its form and content," but immediately added the curious psychologist's question as to whether it was an actual dream and who the dreamer had been. The poet, he said, however, need not answer. And apparently he did not, for no reply from Hermann Hesse exists. And that itself is an answer.

A number of other authors, particularly English-speaking ones, became connected with Jung. Among the first of these was H. G. Wells, whom Jung called his friend as early as the twenties and whose biographer Vincent Brome identified as practically a "Jungian."[25] His novel *Christina Alberta's Father* contained almost word-for-word descriptions of the Jungian anima concept. In the first volume of his trilogy *The World of William Clissold*, which appeared in London in 1926, was a long section in which Jung appears, characterized in a sympathetic manner, discussing with a small audience questions of the development of consciousness and spirituality after a reading in the Queen's Hall.[26] In the 18 November 1928 edition of the *Neue Zürcher Zeitung* one could read a letter from Wells to the editor, in which he wrote concerning Jung: "It would be inadmissible for me to judge him as a man of science and philosophy; this should be left to his colleagues. But as a writer concerned with all the questions of the human soul and the development of human society, I consider Dr. Jung's thoughts, writings, and experimental results . . . a bright light in my darkness and a gold mine for reflection."

After World War II the English author and dramatist J. B. Priestley was also among the numerous visitors who came to Küsnacht and interviewed Jung, who confirmed how much he had enjoyed some of the writer's novels and plays. Jung called Priestley's 1946 BBC presentation *Description of a Visit to Carl Jung* "a masterpiece." The positive contact continued, for some years later Jung still appeared to be deeply impressed when he got hold of an article from Priestley's pen praising his output, which he found confirmed Priestley's understanding of his work. So his letter of 8 November 1954 read:

> You as a writer are in a position to appreciate what it means to an isolated individual like myself to hear one friendly human voice among the stupid and malevolent noises rising from the scribbler-infested jungle. . . . Your succour comes at a time when it is badly needed. . . ."[27]

Finally, Jung's lifeline crossed early with that of James Joyce. During the First World War the still rather unknown later author of *Ulysses* (which appeared in Paris in 1922) stayed in Zürich; in fact he was supported by the same Edith Rockefeller McCormick (1872–1932) who was close to Jung and vigorously promoted his Psychological Club and thus Jung's work. He himself only met the Irish writer personally much later, when the latter consulted him on account of his mentally disturbed daughter Lucia. Jung arrived at the conclusion that his mentally ill daughter was her father's real *femme inspiratrice*; that is, that his unconscious psyche (anima) had been extensively identified with her, whereas Joyce himself was afflicted with a latent psychosis by this very fact.

> His "psychological" style is definitely schizophrenic, with the difference, however, that the ordinary patient cannot help talking and thinking in such a way, while Joyce willed it and moreover developed it with all his creative forces. Which incidentally explains why he himself did not go over the border. But his daughter did, because she was no genius like her father, but merely a victim of her disease.[28]

It is obvious that in the case of Joyce and many other modern authors or artists a gray area must be dealt with if one wishes to incorporate considerations of depth psychology, especially when one reads *Ulysses*, which makes considerable demands on reader and translator from the point of view of its language alone. When Jung wrote to the author, again living in Zürich, in 1932, he confessed that he had been brooding for almost three years on this book, which was so monstrous in its own way. It had presented the world, he said, with disturbing psychological problems, and even given him, the psychologist repeatedly called on for advice, "no end of trouble." He had learned a great deal from it, but what he had to say about it was not without a note of contradiction, for especially here condemnation and admiration lay very close together for Jung. Hence he confessed: "I shall probably never be quite sure whether I did enjoy it, because it meant too much grinding of nerves and of grey matter. I also don't know whether you will enjoy what I have written about *Ulysses*," Jung wrote to Joyce, referring to his essay, the monologue "Ulysses,"

> because I couldn't help telling the world how much I was bored, how I grumbled, how I cursed and how I admired. The 40 pages of non-stop run in the end is a string of veritable psychological peaches. I suppose the devil's grandmother knows so much about the real psychology of a woman, I didn't. . . .
>
> At all events you may gather from my article what *Ulysses* has done to a supposedly balanced psychologist.[29]

As we learn from Joyce's biographer Richard Ellmann, the writer, who was famous for this sort of thing, showed Jung's letter around proudly as evidence of his now certified psychological perspicacity. His wife, Nora, who would know, countered the supposed knowledge of women which Jung had confirmed in her husband with the pithy statement: "He [Joyce] doesn't understand a thing about women. . . ." This is what can happen to one person of insight when another one ratifies his power of penetration!

As for Jung's monologue on *Ulysses*, in 1927 Daniel Brody, director of the Rhein Company in Zürich, published a German edition of Joyce's book. Apparently it was also he who had asked Jung for a psychological interpretation.[30] The only version known today[31] is one that was clearly revised later and published in 1932 in the *Europäische Revue* in Berlin, and then included in *Wirklichkeit der Seele* (1934), and is the only detailed piece of literary criticism we have from Jung's pen. As a psychotherapist who could not stop doing therapy whatever he did, and as a psychiatrist who stood by his "professional bias," Jung warned his reader. Anyone who expected, in contrast, that he would offhandedly explain *Ulysses* in particular, and modern art in general, as a product of schizophrenia missed the mark. Still, he said, there was a certain analogous relationship, in that for example the schizophrenic showed "seemingly the same tendency" to alienate reality from himself, or conversely himself from reality. And generally speaking:

> In modern artists it is not individual illness that produces this tendency, but the spirit of his time. He responds not to an individual impulse but to a collective flow, which, it is true, has its source not directly in consciousness, but rather in the collective unconscious of the modern psyche. Because it is a collective manifestation, it also affects the various areas identically, painting as well as literature, sculpture as well as architecture.[32]

Jung thought it indicative that Vincent van Gogh, one of the spiritual fathers of modern art, had actually been mentally ill. In any case, in this context, seen from the archetypal, collective point of view, Joyce's *Ulysses* was "a *document humain* of our time, and more: he is a mystery." The psychologist from Küsnacht called to him:

> O Ulysses, thou art a veritable prayer-book for the white-skinned man whose faith is in objects and who is accursed by objects! Thou art an *exercitium*, an *askesis*, an agonizing ritual, a magical procedure, eighteen alchemical retorts arrayed one behind the next, wherein with acids, poisonous vapors, coldness, and heat, the Homunculus of a new world consciousness is distilled! Thou sayest nothing and betrayest nothing, O Ulysses, but thou workest. . . .[33]

No less effective was the pictorial art of a Pablo Picasso. Jung had also devoted a shorter essay to him in 1932. The essayist was able to persuade himself of the great Spaniard's power of magical attraction when a Picasso exhibition consisting of 460 pieces was staged at the Zürich art gallery in September and October of that year. This time too the psychologist, who worked as a painter and sculptor himself, had not picked up his pen of his own accord, but was approached by the *Neue Zürcher Zeitung*. And because Joyce embodied, as it were, the "literary brother" of pictorial artists of the rank of a Picasso, Jung transferred to him the analogous relationship he asserted there, inasmuch as it involved perceptions and creations which received their decisive impulse from the deep regions of the human psyche, and hence did not stem from arbitrary make-believe. Here, as always, he was contradicted. Occasionally Jung had to confront his critics, who found his articles on Joyce and Picasso too negative. But the elderly Jung rejected the suggestion that he undertake a similar analysis of, say, Klee or Kokoschka. He would have kept on being contradicted. Those born later would do well to realize that several generations had passed since that relatively early experience, and the factor that had once been particularly disquieting had lost its explosive effect. The general consciousness had caught up.

Jung's interpretation contained no devaluation, in that he saw the creative artist in the context of mystery and initiation, with its passages through catharsis and nekyia. Therefore he was able to write of Picasso, for example:

> In view of Picasso's bewildering diversity one hardly dares suggest it; I would rather say what I have found in my material. The nekyia is not an aimless, purely destructive, titanic crash, but a meaningful *katabasis eis antron*, a descent into the cave of initiation and secret knowledge. The journey through the history of the soul of humankind has as its goal the restoration of the person as a whole. . . .[34]

Among the large group of those with whom Jung exchanged views in various fields was the English art historian and writer Sir Herbert Read, like Jung himself often a lecturer at Eranos. A chapter in his book *The Art of Art*

Criticism[35] is devoted to Jung and was published as a special offprint by Rascher Verlag on the occasion of Jung's eighty-fifth birthday.[36] The elderly honoree attested to the author's courage and honesty, "two qualities the absence of which in my critics hitherto has hindered every form of understanding. Your blessed words are the rays of a new sun over a dark sluggish swamp in which I felt buried," Jung opened his vote of thanks of 2 September 1960. And then again the lamentation found so often in his late letters:

> I often thought of Meister Eckhart, who was entombed for 600 years. I asked myself time and again why there are no men in our epoch who could see at least what I was wrestling with. I think it is not mere vanity and desire for recognition on my part, but a genuine concern for my fellow-beings. . . . I see the suffering of mankind in the individual's predicament and vice versa. . . .
>
> After 60 solid years of field-work I may be supposed to know at least something about my job. But even the most incompetent ass knew better and I received no encouragement. On the contrary I was misunderstood or completely ignored. Under those circumstances I even grew afraid to increase the chaos of opinion by adding considerations which could not be understood.[37]

Was total lack of understanding and refused dialogue the answer to one who was willing for it?

Then, as far as Joyce and Picasso were concerned, the depth psychologist characterized them both as "masters of the fragmentation of aesthetic contents and accumulators of ingenious shards." He saw at work the strength which led to dissolution. In both cases, he said, they were pandering to the morbidity of their time. Ruthless strength in Picasso; negative aspects in modern art per se—such was Jung's pessimistic summary at the age of eighty-five. Herbert Read responded carefully to Jung's views in his reply of 19 October 1960. He confirmed the fragmentation process he had referred to as being manifested in contemporary artistic production, but rejected the notion of a willful destructiveness. "The motive [of the artist]," Read explained, "has always been (since the beginning of the century) to destroy the conscious image of perfection (the classical ideal of objectivity) in order to release new forces from the unconscious. This 'turning inwards' . . . is precisely a longing to be put in touch with the Dream, that is to say (as you say) the future. But in the attempt the artist has his 'dark and unrecognizable urges,' and they have overwhelmed him. He struggles like a man overwhelmed by a flood. He clutches at fragments, at driftwood and floating rubbish of all kinds. But he has to release this flood in order to get nearer to the Dream. My defence of modern art has always been based on this realization: that art must die in order to live, that new sources of life must be tapped under the crust of tradition."[38] Read referred to the transitional character of the entire era, as Jung himself had repeatedly confirmed it, and adduced Simone Weil, in whom we find the dictum: "The essence of created things lies in their transitional nature. They are intermediate terms leading from one to the next, without end. They are connecting links on the way to God, and we must come to know them as such."

All in all, C. G. Jung's talent for dialogue, despite its size, was probably impaired here and there; it was always conditioned by the point of view of depth psychology, be it in opening up new perspectives or marking off extrapsychological viewpoints.

Herbert Read concluded his account of his meeting with Jung in his garden in Küsnacht—which probably took place in the early fifties—thus: "In the course of our long conversation we had gone into the garden, and now Jung sat in the cool shade of a tree, more than ever like a Chinese sage. We listened to the plashing of oars in the water and the sound of distant voices, and fell into silence, in which we became aware that here too a meaningful coincidence held sway. It seemed as though the earth, sky, and water had also been listening, and the oneness of the impression was the oneness of complete sympathy, the *sympatheia* which according to the Stoic doctrine draws together all elements in peace and harmony."[39]

Prolegomena to a History of Jung's Influence

"I stand isolated between the faculties and must depend on someone else to seriously concern himself with this line of research, which up until now has happened only in a very few cases."[1] This sober statement, not without bitterness, by Jung at the age of eighty-five agrees with those extremely pessimistic remarks in which the founder of analytical psychology complained of how little he was read and how seldom—so far at least—understood, and that he had had to resign himself "to being posthumous." The reference to Meister Eckhart, who had had to wait six centuries, was cold comfort. The prospects of the young psychiatrist at the Burghölzli in Zürich and the designated "crown prince" of Sigmund Freud had once seemed extremely optimistic, considering his acceptance in the United States (from 1909) and the first, to be sure still tentative reception of the specifically Jungian expressions of research and therapeutic methods in depth psychology. But to the extent to which Jung was able to expand the horizon of his knowledge to the transpersonal and collective unconscious and the world of archetypal reality, the intellectual—and even more, spiritual—demands on his audience also increased. So long as one pursues a relatively conscious or ego-centered psychology, the possibility of easier calculability and verifiability is offered, and *ratio* is assured of a relatively high tribute. One can point, as happens in classical psychoanalysis, to the personal unconscious with its mechanisms of defense and repression, or to traumatic experiences in one's own past, and thus to actual events that one has undergone as a suffering person, whose burden one carries. All this is indisputable, and this makes "science" possible. It becomes very much more difficult when the horizons are widened and deepened.

Quite new demands arise the moment one "digs deeper," and incorporates the experiences of humanity, those factors which have normally been recorded in the spiritual and religious traditions of humankind. This much more complex way of looking at things requires an outstanding extension of the conscious horizon. One must take the step from the everyday, dissociated, divided ego to the Self which represents a spiritual and psychic completeness or wholeness. It is important not only to interpret this Self, but to walk the path toward self-development, or individuation. The human being can no longer remain what he is, but must—out of fateful necessity—become what *his essential nature* makes him. Thus a psychology oriented to the self-becoming of man no longer remains bound to the past with its early traumatic impressions and its instinctive fate, but opens a vista on the dimension of the future. Hence such a "therapy" means not the removal of troublesome symptoms in order to make the person simply "functional" or conform to the existing norms of the community. To psycho-analysis is added psycho-synthesis; wholeness comes into the picture, not at the expense of the ego, but in the extension of the ego and the inclusion of the Thou—personal, social, and humanistic. For true self-becoming is not brought about apart from reality as it is lived and to be lived; rather the world of one's fellow humans and things represents—as we have seen—the indispensable transit stations of individuation. All this explains why Jung's analytical psychology is more "difficult" than many another therapeutic practice, and certainly more taxing, for it lays claims upon the whole person. But because of this it is also quite literally more promising.

Hence the Jungian way need not shrink from comparison with a path of spiritual knowledge along which processes of initiation are passed through. So it is understandable that Count Karlfried Dürckheim, for example, in the essential points of his Initiation Therapy, not only referred to Jung but shared in his discoveries.[2] But such paths of knowledge must not only be known about; they must also be traveled.

Undoubtedly, this points to Jung's innermost concern, individuation as a path to self-development, which is not only to be considered from the therapeutic standpoint but has to do with the maturation of the personality and the discovery of meaning, and thus reaches deep into the spiritual and religious. What had once begun in the field of psychiatric and psychotherapeutic activity found its full expansion into cultural and religious life. At first Jung's activity naturally affected his patients and students. Not a few of them became his collaborators, after experiencing in themselves the effectiveness of his "treatment." Concepts like "complex" and "archetype," "extraversion" and "introversion"—along with a number of others—found entry into common parlance, even though Jung's typology fell into the critical crossfire just as the doctrine of the archetypes or his introduction of the term "collective unconscious."

If the objection was occasionally raised that Jung's psychology was more a psychomythology, if it was even equated with a religious-psychological worldview or substitute religion, its relationship to praxis must not be forgotten. The methodical foundations Jung provided should be remembered, beginning with the association test, which attracted great notice in the professional world in his early period; through the method of active imagination, by which the contents of the unconscious can be activated; down to the style of dream interpretation with its subject and object levels; that is, it turned out to be important and practicable to distinguish clearly whether the images and figures in a dream are to be connected with the subject himself or whether other, external objects are meant. Jung's methods of painting or artistic representation from the unconscious were adopted or modified by other therapists. In group therapy—as is little known—Alcoholics Anonymous received a decisive impulse from Jung. Since the origins, influence, and further development of analytical or complex psychology have been presented by others—for example, Gustav R. Heyer, Henry F. Ellenberger, Carl A. Meier, Hans Dieckmann, and Eberhard Jung[3]—a general overview may be justifiable here.

As a line of psychological research and method of therapy, the work of C. G. Jung has taken its place in the cultural canon, so that in many respects it has gone beyond itself and forms a bridge to other disciplines. This corresponds to the need of all those who endeavor to overcome the one-sidedness of a purely natural-scientific and technically oriented style of knowledge, working to avoid alternatives that are unproductive because they exclude other perspectives, be they nature versus spirit, conscious versus unconscious, Western thought versus Eastern spirituality. Jung's intensive concern with symbols, myths, and archetypes—seemingly unusual at first sight—provided aids to understanding not only for the grasp of psychic phenomena. Above all they made available building blocks and "catalysts" with whose help seemingly disparate groups of problems and fields of endeavor could be reached. In the forum of the Eranos conferences which have taken place for over half a century, interdisciplinary conversation (as discussed above) was and is preserved in an exemplary way, when natural scientists of various specializations, mythographers, religious scholars, anthropologists, and not least theologians entered the dialogue. Under the rubric of a scarcely less grandly conceived "synopsis"—not synthesis!—the International Community of Physicians and Ministers (today the International Society for Depth Psychology) has been active from Stuttgart since 1949. Here every year adherents of the various schools of depth psychology come together to talk with theologians as well as members of related occupations. Its founder, the physician and psychotherapist Wilhelm Bitter, took pains from its inception to see that the side of Jungian psychology remained represented. Much like the above-mentioned Eranos *Yearbook*, the annual conference reports give a glimpse into the work carried on there.[4]

A considerable share of the fruitfulness of depth psychology and the dialogue with it undoubtedly falls to the theology of the various denominations (Protestant, Roman Catholic, Greek Orthodox), to the extent they are in a position to transcend all-too-narrow confessional and denominational bounds.[5] It is astonishing and at the same time moving to follow by means of the two volumes of letters the passion with which C. G. Jung wrestled with the theologians for years, whether expounding upon his position and defending himself against dogmatic shortsightedness or stressing the long-neglected factor of religious experience. Shortly before his death he still appeared delighted to receive from John A. Sanford of the Trinity Episcopal Church in Los Angeles a copy of a sermon which spoke from the heart to him and his experience. In his reply of 10 March 1961 Jung wrote:

> It is a historical event, as you are—so far as my knowledge goes—the first one who has called the attention of the Christian congregation to the fact that the Voice of God can still be heard. . . .
>
> The understanding of dreams should indeed be taken seriously by the Church, since the *cura animarum* is one of its duties, which has been sadly neglected by the Protestants. . . .
>
> The pilgrim's way is spiked with thorns everywhere, even if he is a good Christian, or just therefore.[6]

One might also think of how fruitful an effect Jung's understanding of symbols, his doctrine of the archetypes, had on theologians of the rank of Paul Tillich,[7] whether because the experience of Self corresponded to that of God, or because quite new approaches to biblical exegesis were opened up by archetypal psychology.[8]

Thus Jung's resigned assertion about his supposed isolation

is very much less justified at the threshold of the third millennium than it was at the end of his life. Still, statements like those found in "The Undiscovered Self: Present and Future," one of his last major works, are nonetheless worth pondering in this connection:

> Just as man, as a social being, cannot live in the long run without being connected with the community, so too the individual finds the real justification for his existence, and his own spiritual as well as moral autonomy, nowhere but in an extramundane principle that is capable of relativizing the overpowering influence of external factors. The individual who is not anchored in God can offer no resistance, on the strength of his own resources, to the physical and moral sway of the world. For this man needs the evidence of his own inner, transcendent experience. . . .[9]

And elsewhere in the same text:

> I am convinced that it is not Christianity, but the conception and interpretation of it hitherto, that is antiquated in the face of the circumstances of today's world. The Christian symbol is a living being that carries the seeds of further development within itself. It can continue to develop, and it depends only on whether we can decide to meditate once again, somewhat more thoroughly, on the Christian premises. . . .[10]

BIBLIOGRAPHY

Jung's literary work consists of individual titles, anthologies and readers, lectures, and *The Collected Works of C. G. Jung*, vols. 1–19 (Bollingen Series No. 20, Princeton University, 1953–1979). In addition there is the autobiographical *Memories, Dreams, Reflections* (rev. ed., Pantheon Books, 1973) and *C. G. Jung: Letters*, edited by Gerhard Adler and Aniela Jaffé, vols. 1 (1906–1950) and 2 (1951–1961), published by Princeton University Press (Bollingen Series No. 45). These and other works are given in volume 19 of *The Collected Works*, "Bibliography."

THE COLLECTED WORKS OF C. G. JUNG

1. *Psychiatric Studies*

On the Psychology and Pathology of So-Called Occult Phenomena
On Hysterical Misreading
Cryptomnesia
On Manic Mood Disorder
A Case of Hysterical Stupor in a Prisoner in Detention
On Simulated Insanity
A Medical Opinion on a Case of Simulated Insanity
A Third and Final Opinion of Two Contradictory Psychiatric Diagnoses
On the Psychological Diagnosis of Facts

2. *Experimental Researches*

STUDIES IN WORD ASSOCIATION (1904–1907, 1910)
The Associations of Normal Subjects (by Jung and F. Riklin)
An Analysis of the Associations of an Epileptic
The Reaction-Time Ratio in the Association Experiment
Experimental Observations on the Faculty of Memory
Psychoanalysis and Association Experiments
The Psychological Diagnosis of Evidence
Association, Dream, and Hysterical Symptom

The Psychopathological Significance of the Association Experiment
Disturbances in Reproduction in the Association Experiment
The Association Method
The Family Constellation
PSYCHOPHYSICAL RESEARCHES (1907–1908)
On the Psychophysical Relations of the Association Experiment
Psychophysical Investigations with the Galvanometer and Pneumograph in Normal and Insane Individuals (by F. Peterson and Jung)
Further Investigations on the Galvanic Phenomenon and Respiration in Normal and Insane Individuals (by C. Ricksher and Jung)
Appendix: Statistical Details of Enlistment; New Aspects of Criminal Psychology; The Psychological Methods of Investigation Used in the Psychiatric Clinic of the University of Zurich; On the Doctrine of Complexes; On the Psychological Diagnosis of Evidence

3. *The Psychogenesis of Mental Disease*
The Psychology of Dementia Praecox
The Content of the Psychoses
On Psychological Understanding
A Criticism of Bleuler's Theory of Schizophrenic Negativism
On the Importance of the Unconscious in Psychopathology
On the Problem of Psychogenesis in Mental Disease
Mental Disease and the Psyche
On the Psychogenesis of Schizophrenia
Recent Thoughts on Schizophrenia
Schizophrenia

4. *Freud and Psychoanalysis*
Freud's Theory of Hysteria: A Reply of Aschaffenburg
The Freudian Theory of Hysteria
The Analysis of Dreams
A Contribution to the Psychology of Rumour
On the Significance of Number Dreams
Morton Prince, *Mechanism and Interpretation of Dreams:* A Critical Review
On the Criticism of Psychoanalysis
Concerning Psychoanalysis

The Theory of Psychoanalysis
General Aspects of Psychoanalysis
Psychoanalysis and Neurosis
Some Crucial Points in Psychoanalysis: The Jung-Loÿ Correspondence
Prefaces to *Collected Papers on Analytical Psychology*
The Significance of the Father in the Destiny of the Individual
Introduction to Kranefeldt's *Secret Ways of the Mind*
Freud and Jung: Contrasts

5. *Symbols of Transformation*
Appendix: The Miller Fantasies

6. *Psychological Types*
Appendix: Four Papers on Psychological Typology

7. *Two Essays on Analytical Psychology*
On the Psychology of the Unconscious
The Relations between the Ego and the Unconscious
Appendices:
New Paths in Psychology
The Structure of the Unconscious

8. *The Structure and Dynamics of the Psyche*
On Psychic Energy
The Transcendent Function
A Review of the Complex Theory
The Significance of Constitution and Heredity in Psychology
Psychological Factors Determining Human Behaviour
Instinct and the Unconscious
The Structure of the Psyche
On the Nature of the Psyche
General Aspects of Dream Psychology
On the Nature of Dreams
The Psychological Foundations of Belief in Spirits
Spirit and Life
Basic Postulates of Analytical Psychology
Analytical Psychology and *Weltanschauung*
The Real and the Surreal
The Stages of Life

The Soul and Death
Synchronicity: An Acausal Connecting Principle
Appendix: On Synchronicity

9. Part I: *The Archetypes and the Collective Unconscious*
Archetypes of the Collective Unconscious
The Concept of the Collective Unconscious
Concerning the Archetypes, with Special Reference to the Anima Concept
Psychological Aspects of the Mother Archetype
Concerning Rebirth
The Psychology of the Child Archetype
The Psychological Aspects of the Kore
The Phenomenology of the Spirit in Fairytales
On the Psychology of the Trickster-Figure
Conscious, Unconscious, and Individuation
A Study in the Process of Individuation
Concerning Mandala Symbolism
Appendix: Mandalas

Part II, *Aion: Researches into the Phenomenology of the Self*

10. *Civilization in Transition*
The Role of the Unconscious
Mind and Earth
Archaic Man
The Spiritual Problem of Modern Man
The Love Problem of a Student
Woman in Europe
The Meaning of Psychology for Modern Man
The State of Psychotherapy Today
Wotan
After the Catastrophe
The Fight with the Shadow
Epilogue to *Essays on Contemporary Events*
The Undiscovered Self (Present and Future)
Flying Saucers: A Modern Myth
A Psychological View of Conscience
Good and Evil in Analytical Psychology
Introduction to Wolff's *Studies in Jungian Psychology*

The Swiss Line in the European Spectrum
Reviews of Keyserling's *America Set Free* and *La Révolution Mondiale*
Complications of American Psychology
The Dreamlike World of India
What India Can Teach Us
Appendix: Documents

11. *Psychology and Religion: West and East*

WESTERN RELIGION
Psychology and Religion (The Terry Lectures)
A Psychological Approach to the Dogma of the Trinity
Transformation Symbolism in the Mass
Forewords to White's *God and the Unconscious* and Werblowsky's *Lucifer and Prometheus*
Brother Klaus
Psychotherapists or the Clergy
Psychoanalysis and the Cure of Souls
Answer to Job

EASTERN RELIGION
Psychological Commentaries on *The Tibetan Book of the Great Liberation* and *The Tibetan Book of the Dead*
Yoga and the West
Foreword to Suzuki's *Introduction to Zen Buddhism*
The Psychology of Eastern Meditation
The Holy Men of India: Introduction to Zimmer's *Der Weg zum Selbst*
Foreword to the *I Ching*

12. *Psychology and Alchemy*

Introduction to the Religious and Psychological Problems of Alchemy
Individual Dream Symbolism in Relation to Alchemy
Religious Ideas in Alchemy
Epilogue

13. *Alchemical Studies*

Commentary on *The Secret of the Golden Flower*
The Visions of Zosimos
Paracelsus as a Spiritual Phenomenon
The Spirit Mercurius
The Philosophical Tree

14. *Mysterium Coniunctionis: An Inquiry into the Separation and Synthesis of Psychic Opposites in Alchemy*

15. *The Spirit in Man, Art, and Literature*
Paracelsus
Paracelsus the Physician
Sigmund Freud in His Historical Setting
In Memory of Sigmund Freud
Richard Wilhelm: In Memoriam
On the Relation of Analytical Psychology to Poetry
Psychology and Literature
Ulysses: A Monologue
Picasso

16. *The Practice of Psychotherapy*
GENERAL PROBLEMS OF PSYCHOTHERAPY
Principles of Practical Psychotherapy
What Is Psychotherapy?
Some Aspects of Modern Psychotherapy
The Aims of Psychotherapy
Problems of Modern Psychotherapy
Psychotherapy and a Philosophy of Life
Medicine and Psychotherapy
Psychotherapy Today
Fundamental Questions of Psychotherapy
SPECIFIC PROBLEMS OF PSYCHOTHERAPY
The Therapeutic Value of Abreaction
The Practical Use of Dream-Analysis
Psychology of the Transference
Appendix: The Realities of Practical Psychotherapy

17. *The Development of Personality*
Psychic Conflicts in a Child
Introduction to Wickes's *Analyse der Kinderseele*
Child Development and Education
Analytical Psychology and Education: Three Lectures
The Gifted Child
The Significance of the Unconscious in Individual Education
The Development of Personality

Marriage as a Psychological Relationship

18. Parts I and II: *The Symbolic Life*

Miscellaneous Writings, including Forewords, Epilogues, Reviews, Letters, Addresses, and occasional supplements to Volumes 1–17

19. *Complete Bibliography of C. G. Jung's Writings*

The published writings of C. G. Jung including translations
The Collected Works
The Seminars of C. G. Jung

20. *General Index to "The Collected Works"*

CHRONOLOGY

1875	Carl Gustav Jung is born in Kesswil, Canton Thurgau, on 26 July, the son of the Reformed Protestant parson Johann Paul Achilles Jung (1842–1896) and his wife, Emilie Preiswerk (1848–1923).
1876	The family moves to Laufen on the Rhine Falls near Schaffhausen.
1879	Move to Kleinhüningen near Basel.
1884	Birth of sister Gertrud (d. 1935).
1886	Jung enters the Gymnasium in Basel.
1895–1900	Studies in science and medicine at Basel University; state examinations 1900.
1895–1899	Spiritistic sessions with his cousin, the medium Helene Preiswerk.
1900	Decision to specialize in psychiatry; in December assistant at the Burghölzli psychiatric clinic in Zürich under Professor Eugen Bleuler. Certification to practice medicine in all Swiss cantons.
1902	Dissertation: *On the Psychology and Pathology of So-Called Occult Phenomena.*
1902/03	Winter semester with Pierre Janet at the Salpetrière in Paris.
1903	14 February: Marriage to Emma Rauschenbach, Schaffhausen (five children: Agathe Niehus, Gret Baumann, Franz Jung-Merker, Marianne Niehus, Helene Hoerni).
1903/05	Volunteer doctor at Burghölzli. Experimental works including *Studies in Word Association*; discovery of the feeling-toned complexes.
1905/09	Senior doctor at the Burghölzli.
1905/13	Lecturer on the medical faculty of Zürich University.
1906	Public advocacy of Freud's psychoanalysis. Beginning of correspondence with Freud.
1907	February: first meeting with Freud in Vienna. "The Psychology of Dementia Praecox."

1909	Departure from the clinic as a result of personal differences with Bleuler and overwork; beginning of private practice in his newly built home in Küsnacht near Zürich. September: Guest lecturer with Freud and Ferenczi at Clark University in Worcester, Mass.; honorary degree. Editor of the *Jahrbuch für psychologische and psychopathologische Forschungen*, published by Freud and Bleuler. Book edition of *Studies in Word Association*.
1910	March: Nuremberg Congress founds the "International Psychoanalytic Association," with Jung as president (to 1914). *Wandlungen und Symbole der Libido.* September: Lectures at Fordham University in New York; Jung accentuates his views diverging from Freud's; honorary doctorate.
1913	August: In lectures to the Psycho-Medical Society in London, Jung designates his style of research "analytical psychology." September: Munich Congress of the International Psychoanalytic Association reelects Jung as president. October: Steps down as editor of the *Jahrbuch*.
1914	20 April: Resignation as president. July: Secession, with the Zürich branch, from the International Psychoanalytic Association.
1916	"Septem Sermones ad Mortuos," text from his confrontation with the unconscious. "The Transcendent Function"; first mention of the method of active imagination. "The Structure of the Unconscious." Founding of the Psychological Club in Zürich.
1917/18	Medical Corps doctor and commandant of an English internment camp at Châteaux-d'Oex.
1918–c. 1926	Studies of Gnostic writings.
1921	*Psychological Types*.
1923	Death of his mother. Beginning of construction of the tower on land acquired on upper Lake Zürich in 1922; last wing completed in 1955.
1924/25	Study trip to the Pueblo Indians in North America.
1925/26	Study trip to the Elgonyi of Mount Elgon, East Africa.

1928 “The Relations between the Ego and the Unconscious.” “On Psychic Energy.”
Beginning of alchemical studies, at first in collaboration with Richard Wilhelm.

1929 Commentary on *The Secret of the Golden Flower*, translated by Richard Wilhelm.

1930 Vice-president of the General Medical Society for Psychotherapy, with president Ernst Kretschmer.

1930/34 “Interpretation of Visions,” English seminar in the Zürich Psychological Club.

1931 *Seelenprobleme der Gegenwart.*

1932 Prize for Literature, City of Zürich.

1933 After Kretschmer’s resignation, provisional president of the General Medical Society for Psychotherapy until its reconstitution in 1934.
Beginning of lectures at Swiss Technological Institute in Zürich.
August: Beginning of the Eranos conferences, with “A Study in the Process of Individuation.”

1934 May: Founding and presidency of the International Society for Medical Psychotherapy in Bad Nauheim; editor of the *Zentralblatt fur Psychotherapie und ihre Grenzgebiete* (until 1939).
August: Second Eranos paper, “Archetypes of the Collective Unconscious”; *Wirklichkeit der Seele.*

1934/39 “Psychological Aspects of Nietzsche’s Zarathustra,” English seminar at the Psychological Club in Zürich.

1935 Named titular professor at the Swiss Technological Institute, Zürich.
Tavistock Lectures in London on “Analytical Psychology, Its Theory and Practice.”
On his sixtieth birthday: “Die kulturelle Bedeutung der Komplexen Psychologie.”
Psychological commentary on *The Tibetan Book of the Dead.*

1936 Lecture on “Psychological Factors Determining Human Behavior,” given at the Tercentenary Conference at Harvard University; honorary doctorate.
August: Eranos paper “Religious Ideas in Alchemy.”

1937 Terry Lectures at Yale University on “Psychology and Religion.”

1937/38 Invited by the British Indian government in India; honorary doctorates at the Universities of Calcutta, Benares, and Allahabad.

1938 Medical Congress for Psychotherapy at Oxford; honorary doctorate at Oxford University.

1939 Honorary member of the Royal Society of Medicine in London.

1940 *Psychology and Religion*, book edition of the Terry Lectures.
August: Eranos paper "A Psychological Approach to the Dogma of the Trinity."

1941 With Karl Kerényi, *Essays on a Science of Mythology*.
Lectures in Basel and Einsiedeln on the 400th anniversary of Paracelsus' death.

1942 *Paracelsica. Zwei Vorlesungen.*
Resignation as titular professor at the Swiss Technological Institute in Zürich.

1943 15 October: Named Professor in ordinary of psychology at Basel University.

1944 Abandonment of university teaching duties after heart attack.
Psychology and Alchemy.

1945 Honorary doctorate at Geneva University on his seventieth birthday.
Festschrift in Eranos *Jahrbuch, Zur Idee des Archetypischen.*

1946 *Psychologie und Erziehung.*
Aufsätze zu Zeitgeschichte.
"The Psychology of the Transference."

1948 Founding of the C. G. Jung Institute in Zürich.
Symbolik des Geistes.
Über psychische Energetik und das Wesen der Träume.

1950 *Gestaltungen des Unbewussten.*
On his seventy-fifth birthday, Eranos *Jahrbuch, Aus der Welt der Urbilder.*

1951 *Aion*; researches in historical symbolism.
August: Jung's last Eranos lecture, "On Synchronicity" (enlarged in 1952 under the title "Synchronicity: An Acausal Connecting Principle").

1952 *Symbols of Transformation* (revised and expanded version of *Wandlungen und Symbole der Libido* of 1912).
Answer to Job.
Renewed serious illness.

1953ff	Jung's *Collected Works* appear in the Bollingen Series, New York.
1954	*Von den Wurzeln des Bewusstseins. Studien über den Archetypus.*
1955	Honorary doctorate at Swiss Technological Institute, on his eightieth birthday.
	Festschrift by students and friends, *Studien zur Analytischen Psychologie C. G. Jungs.*
	Mysterium Coniunctionis, Vol. 1.
	Psychological commentary on *The Tibetan Book of the Great Liberation.*
	27 November: Death of Emma Jung.
1956	*Mysterium Coniunctionis*, Vol. 2.
1957	Beginning of work on *Memories, Dreams, Reflections*, with Aniela Jaffé.
	"The Undiscovered Self."
1958	"Flying Saucers: A Modern Myth."
	"A Psychological View of Conscience."
	First volume of *The Collected Works* in German, Vol. 16: *Praxis der Psychotherapie.*
1959	"Good and Evil in Analytical Psychology."
1960	Named honorary citizen of Küsnacht on his eighty-fifth birthday.
1961	"Approaching the Unconscious," Jung's last introduction to Analytical Psychology, written in English, in *Man and His Symbols* (1964).
	6 June: After a short illness Jung dies in his home in Küsnacht.
	9 June: Burial in the Küsnacht cemetery.

NOTES

Abbreviations of works frequently cited:

CW	*The Collected Works of C. G. Jung.* New York 1953–1967; Princeton, N.J., 1967–1978.
GW	*Die gesammelten Werke von C. G. Jung.* Zürich, 1958–1970.
Br I–III	C. G. Jung: *Briefe*, ed. Aniela Jaffé in collaboration with Gerhard Adler. Olten-Freiburg, 1972–1973.
M	*Memories, Dreams, Reflections*, by C. G. Jung. Recorded and edited by Aniela Jaffé. Trans. Richard and Clara Winston. New York: Vintage Books, 1965.
F/J	*Sigmund Freud/C. G. Jung: Briefwechsel*, ed. William McGuire and Wolfgang Sauerländer. Frankfurt, 1974.
Letters	*C. G. Jung: Letters.* Princeton, N.J., 1975.

1. *"I Am on My Road and I Carry My Burden"*

1. Br III, 194f.
2. See Aniela Jaffé's Introduction in M v–xiv.
3. M vii–viii.
4. To Gustav Steiner on 30 December 1957, Br III, 145.
5. It is entirely appropriate that the transpersonal psychology that has developed only since the seventies relies in essential points on C. G. Jung; cf. Erhardt Hanefeld in the Foreword to Roberto Assagioli, *Handbuch der Psychosynthesis* (Freiburg, 1978).
6. Herakleitos of Ephesus, Fragment 45, in Hermann Diels, *Die Fragmente der Vorsokratiker*, Rowohlts Klassiker der Literatur und der Wissenschaft 10 (Hamburg, 1957), p. 26.
7. See my essay at the end of this volume, "C. G. Jung in Dialogue and Dispute."
8. Viktor von Weizsäcker, *Natur und Geist* (Munich, 1964), p. 111.
9. Marie-Louise von Franz, *C. G. Jung: Sein Mythos in unserer Zeit* (Frauenfeld-Suttgart, 1972), p. 16ff.
10. Count Hermann Keyserling, quoted in Gustav R. Heyer, "C. G. Jung: Ein Lebensbild," in *Aus meiner Werkstatt* (Munich, 1966), p. 167.

11. J. H. Schultz, *Psychotherapie* (Stuttgart, 1952), p. 172.
12. C. G. Jung in R. J. Evans, *Gespräche mit C. G. Jung* (Zürich, 1967), p. 84.
13. G. Gilli, "C. G. Jung in seiner Handscrift," in *Die kulturelle Bedeutung der Komplexen Psychologie* (Berlin, 1924), p. 511ff.
14. Gustav R. Heyer, "C. G. Jung: ein Lebensbild," p. 166.
15. Ibid., p. 171ff.
16. Letters I, 46.

2. *Origins and Genealogy*

1. Jung's horoscope, supplied, with detailed commentary, by Jung's daughter Gret Baumann, is based on a time of birth of 7:32 P.M. *Spring* (New York, 1975), p. 36ff.
2. M 7.
3. Letter of 25 February 1958 to Karl Schmid, Br III, 158.
4. That Jung may not always have felt quite so strongly rooted in the Swiss people appears from an essay in the *Neue Schweizer Rundschau* 24, no. 6 (Zürich, 1928). Under the heading "The Significance of the Swiss Line in the European Spectrum"—it was a review of Count Keyserling's *Spektrum Europas*—Jung stressed that he did not think of himself as a "model Swiss." Rather, he said, he was "Swiss only on the mother's side for approximately 500 years," but on his father's side "only for 106 years." GW X, 522.
5. Br III, 159.
6. *Symbole der Wandlung*, GW V, 13.
7. Cf. "Von den Archetypen des kollektiven Unbewussten," GW IX, I, 33.
8. *Symbole der Wandlung*, GW V, 13f.
9. Aniela Jaffé in *Erinnerungen, Träume, Gedanken von C. G. Jung* (Zürich, 1962), p. 399ff.
10. Gustav Steiner, *Erinnerungen an C. G. Jung: Zur Entstehung der Autobiographie* (Basler Stadtbuch, 1965), pp. 117–163; cf. H. F. Ellenberger, *Die Entdeckung des Unbewusssten* (Bern, 1973), II, p. 891.
11. Ernst Jung, *Aus den Tagebüchern meines Vaters* (i.e., C. G. Jung the Elder) (Winterthur, 1910).
12. *Erinnerungen, Träume, Gedanken*, pp. 399ff.; for a critique of these statements of C. G. Jung's see Stefanie Zumstein-Preiswerk, *C. G. Jungs Medium* (Munich, 1975), p. 117.
13. Discrepancies had already been pointed out; cf. Johannes Tenzler, *Selbsterfahrung und Gotteserfahrung: Die Persönlichkeit C. G. Jungs und ihr zentraler Niederschlag in seiner Komplexen Psychologie* (Munich-Paderborn, 1975), p. 35. Cf. also Jung's letter of 30 December 1959 to his cousin Ernst Jung, Br III, 227ff.

14. Wilhelm His, *Gedenkschrift zur Eröffnung des Vesaliums*, quoted in Albert Oeri, "Ein Paar Jugenderinnerungen," in *Die kulturelle Bedeutung der Komplexen Psychologie* (Berlin, 1935), p. 526.
15. *Erinnerungen, Träume, Gedanken*, p. 404.
16. Cf. H. F. Ellenberger, *Die Entdeckung des Unbewussten*, vol. II, p. 885.
17. M 91–92.
18. "The Swiss Line in the European Spectrum," CW 10, 481–482.
19. *Erinnerungen, Träume, Gedanken*, p. 405ff.
20. Albert Oeri, op. cit., p. 526.
21. M 48–49.
22. Br III, 354.
23. "The Significance of the Father in the Destiny of the Individual," CW 4, pp. 301–323.
24. Letter of 18 August 1936; Br I, 277.
25. H. Ellenberger, vol. 2, p. 885.
26. Stefanie Zumstein-Preiswerk, *C. G. Jungs Medium*, p. 114.
27. E. A. Bennet, *C. G. Jung: Einblick in Leben und Werk* (Zürich, 1964), p. 23.
28. M 93.

3. *"Possession of a Secret"*

1. M 41–42.
2. M 7.
3. Ibid.
4. M 9–10.
5. M 11–12.
6. M 13.
7. Marie-Louise von Franz, *C. G. Jung*, p. 26. See also the psychiatrist Thorkil Vanggaard's monograph *Phallos: Symbol und Kult in Europa* (Munich, 1971), which was written more as a contribution to sexual research and does not consider the Jungian viewpoint.
8. Hippolytus of Rome, quoted in Hans Leisegang, *Die Gnosis*, 3rd ed. (Stuttgart, 1941), p. 122ff.
9. M 211.
10. *Mysterium Coniunctionis*, CW 14.
11. *Psychology and Alchemy*, CW 12.
12. M.-L. von Franz, op. cit., p. 33.
13. Gerhard Wehr, *Friedrich Nietzsche: Der Seelenerrater als Wegbereiter der Tiefenpsychologie*, Fermenta cognitionis 12 (Freiburg, 1982).
14. Nietzsche, *Fröhliche Wissenschaft*, aphorism 343: "Was es mit unserer Heiterkeit auf sich hat." in *Werke in drei Bänden*, ed. Karl Schlechta, vol. 2, p. 206.

15. Th. Vanggaard, *Phallos*, p. 182.
16. M 15.
17. Albert Oeri, op. cit., p. 524ff.
18. M 17–18.
19. M 19.
20. Ibid.
21. Ibid.
22. Uwe Peters, *Wörterbuch der Tiefenpsychologie* (Munich, 1978), p. 101.
23. Antony Barton, *Freud, Jung und Rogers* (Stuttgart, 1979), p. 90.
24. M 18.
25. M 19.
26. M 21.
27. Ibid.
28. Johannes Tenzler, *Selbstfindung und Gotteserfahrung*, pp. 56–57.
29. *Symbole der Wandlung*, GW V, 426.
30. M 32–33.
31. Jean Paul, quoted in J. Tenzler, op. cit. p. 58.
32. Cf. V. H. von Gebsattel, "Numinose Ersterlebnisse," in *Das Bild des Menschen in der Wissenschaft*, ed. W. J. Revers (Schweinfuhrt, 1964), pp. 313–328.
33. M 24.
34. M 27–28.
35. M 31.
36. M 31–32.
37. M 32.
38. A facsimile of the report is in Aniela Jaffé (ed.), *C. G. Jung: Bild und Wort* (Olten-Freiburg, 1977), p. 19.

4. *Two Personalities*

1. M 34.
2. M 87.
3. M 39–40.
4. M 42–43.
5. M 62.
6. M 40.
7. M 93.
8. Br II, 495. For more detail on this connection, see Gerhard Wehr, *Stichwort Damaskuserlebnis: Der Weg zu Christus nach C. G. Jung* (Stuttgart, 1982).
9. "Die Bedeutung des Vaters für das Schicksal des Einzelnen" (1909); GW IV, 363f.

10. Barbara Hannah, *Jung: His Life and Work, A Biographical Memoir* (New York, 1976), p. 51.
11. Cf. Br II, 278.
12. Cf. Br III, 22.
13. "Die psychologischen Aspekte des Mutter-Archetypus" (1938/1954), GW IX, Teil I, p. 101.
14. M 50.
15. M 52.
16. M 75.
17. M 72–73.

5. *Studies in Basel*

1. Br II, 216ff.; 295; Br III, 25. Cf. also Philipp Wolff-Windegg, "C. G. Jung, Bachofen, Burckhardt und Basel," in *Spring* (1976), pp. 137–147.
2. Letters 2, pp. 621–622.
3. M 86.
4. Gustav Steiner, quoted in H. F. Ellenberger, op. cit., vol. 2, p. 891.
5. M 95.
6. Albert Oeri, "Ein Paar Jugenderinnerungen," in *Die kulturelle Bedeutung der Komplexen Psychologie* (Berlin, 1935), p. 524ff.
7. Ibid. Cf. also Aniela Jaffé, *C. G. Jung: Bild und Wort*, pp. 23–24.
8. M 99.
9. Ernst Benz, *Franz Anton Mesmer und die philosophischen Grundlagen des animalischen Magnetismus* (Wiesbaden, 1977). Gerhard Wehr, *Louis Claude de Saint-Martin: Das Abenteuer des "Unbekannten Philosophen" auf der Suche nach dem Geist*, Fermenta cognitionis 9 (Freiburg, 1980).
10. Alfons Rosenberg, *Der Christ und die Erde: Oberlin und der Aufbruch zur Gemeinschaft der Liebe* (Olten-Freiburg, 1953). John W. Kurtz, *Johann Friedrich Oberlin: Sein Leben und Wirken* (Metzingen, 1983).
11. Ernst Benz, *Emanuel Swedenborg: Naturforscher und Seher* (Munich, 1948).
12. M 99.
13. Excerpts from Jung's youthful diaries in A. Jaffé, *C. G. Jung: Bild und Wort*, p. 27.
14. Ibid., p. 25.
15. M 108–109.
16. M 110.

6. *Experiments in Parapsychology*

1. "Ein moderner Mythus" (1958); GW X, 429.
2. M 105.
3. Ibid.
4. Jung carefully preserved the four fragments of this knife, keeping them in the safe in his study. On the first day of her service as his secretary in 1955, Aniela Jaffé caught sight of these ominous shards. Cf. A. Jaffé, *From the Life and Work of C. G. Jung* (New York, 1971), p. 123.
5. The exact dates differ. To judge from Jung's accounts he could have come into contact with the medium in late summer of 1898. A. Jaffé assumes an earlier date. Helly Preiswerk would then have been only fourteen years old. Consequently the two psi-phenomena would not have taken place until later. Cf. Stefanie Zumstein-Preiswerk, *C. G. Jungs Medium*, p. 17ff.
6. Ernst Jung, *Aus dem Tagebuch meines Vaters* (Winterthur, 1910), quoted in Stefanie Zumstein-Preiswerk, op. cit. 114–115.
7. *Zur Psychologie und Pathologie sogenannter okkulter Phänomene* (1902); GW I, 19–20.
8. Stefanie Zumstein-Preiswerk, op. cit. 56.
9. GW I, 19ff.
10. Stefanie Zumstein-Preiswerk, op. cit. 82.
11. GW I, 43ff.
12. Justinus Kerner, *Die Seherin von Prevorst* (1829) (Stuttgart, 1958), pp. 117ff, 165ff.
13. M 107.
14. Gustav Steiner, *Erinnerungen an C. G. Jung: Aud der Studentenzeit* (Basler Stadtbuch 1965), p. 159.
15. GW I, 92.
16. GW I, 98.

7. *Psychiatrist at Burghölzli*

1. H. F. Ellenberger, *Die Entdeckung des Unbewussten* (Bern, 1973), vol. 1, p. 7.
2. M 111.
3. Auguste Henri Forel, *Rückblick auf mein Leben* (Zürich, 1935).
4. H. F. Ellenberger, op. cit. vol. 2, p. 893.
5. Hans H. Walser, "Psychoanalyse in der Schweiz," in *Die Psychologie des 20. Jahrhunderts* (Zürich, 1977), vol. 2, pp. 1195–96.
6. N 113–114.
7. Br I, 161–162.
8. Br II, 197. On Bleuler and his work, see also Helmut Kindler, "Die Schule Bleuler," in *Die Psychologie des 20. Jahrhunderts*, vol. 10, p. 24ff.

9. Both articles, among others, are found in CW 3.
10. M 127.
11. H. F. Ellenberger, vol. 1, p. 449.
12. Ibid., p. 449ff.; see also *Die Psychologie des 20. Jahrhunderts*, vol. 1: "Die europäische Tradition," p. 687ff.
13. H. F. Ellenberger, vol. 2, p. 944.
14. Here too, to be sure, there are contradictory opinions, according to which Jung was constrained to great austerity in Paris as well.
15. Stefanie Zumstein-Preiswerk, *C. G. Jungs Medium*, pp. 101–102.
16. The relevant texts are found in CW 2. For an introduction see C. A. Meier, *Die Empirie des Unbewussten: Lehrbuch der Komplexen Psychologie C. G. Jungs*, vol. 1 (Zürich, 1968).

8. *The Encounter with Emma Rauschenbach*

1. For a systematic introduction see especially C. A. Meier, *Die Bedeutung des Traumes* (*Lehrbuch der Komplexen Psychologie C. G. Jungs*, vol. 2) (Olten-Freiburg, 1972).
2. M 8–9.
3. Jung paid great attention to the Swiss saint; see "Brother Klaus," CW 11, pp. 316–323. Cf. also Marie-Louise von Franz, *Die Visionen des Nikolaus von Flüe* (Zürich, 1959; 2nd, expanded ed. 1980).
4. M 80.
5. *Erinnerungen, Träume, Gedanken*, p. 406.
6. Sigmund Freud, quoted in Theodor Reik, *Hören mit dem dritten Ohr: Die innere Erfahrung eines Psychoanalytikers* (Hamburg, 1976), pp. 15–16.
7. A. Jaffé, *C. G. Jung, Bild und Wort*, p. 132.
8. Letters 2, p. 611.
9. A. Jaffé, op. cit., p. 132.
10. Emma Jung, *Animus und Anima* (Zürich, 1967).
11. GW II, 208.
12. Sabina Spielrein, *Über den psychologischen Inhalt eines Falles von Schizophrenie* (Vienna, 1911). Toni Wolff, *Studien zu C. G. Jungs Psychologie* (Zürich, 1959).

9. *Sigmund Freud*

1. M 149.
2. "Sigmund Freud" (1939); GW XV, 53ff.
3. M 147, no. 2.
4. M 147.
5. Ronald W. Clark, *Sigmund Freud* (Frankfurt am Main, 1981), p. 165.
6. S. Freud, *Briefe 1873–1939*, 2nd, expanded ed. (Frankfurt, 1960), p. 86.

7. On Freud's correspondence with Bleuler, among others, see Martin Grotjan, in *Die Psychologie des 20. Jahrhunderts*, vol. 2, p. 46ff.
8. GW III, 3–4.
9. Cf. F/J 342.
10. Jung to Freud on 10 October 1907, F/J 101.
11. In contrast, cf. the editorial comment in William McGuire (ed.), *The Freud/Jung Letters* (Princeton, 1974), p. xvi; F/J p. xv.
12. "Die Hysterielehre Freuds," GW IV, p. 9.
13. M 148–149.
14. Br I, 39.
15. F/J 5.
16. F/J 241.
17. F/J 19.
18. Joachim Kaiser, in *Süddeutsche Zeitung*, 7/8 Sept. 1974.
19. Martin Grotjahn, in *Die Psychologie des 20. Jahrhunderts*, vol. 2, p. 49.
20. Emma Jung in F/J, pp. 504–505.
21. M 149.
22. F/J 14.
23. M 149.
24. Jung seems to be in error in giving the year as 1910, as no meeting with Freud in Vienna is known to have happened in that year. It must refer to his second visit to Vienna from 25 to 30 March 1909; cf. F/J 239.
25. M 150.
26. Joachim Scharfenberg, *S. Freud und seine Religionskritik als Herausforderung für den christlichen Glauben* (Göttingen, 1968). Albert Plé, *Freud und die Religion* (Vienna, 1969). Heinz Zahrnt (ed.), *Jesus und Freud* (Munich, 1972).
27. M 151.
28. S. Freud/Karl Abraham, *Briefe 1907–1926* (Frankfurt, 1965), pp. 61–62.
29. M 155–156.
30. M 361.
31. F/J 239–240.
32. *La Psicosintesi*, 1910. Cf. Roberto G. Assagioli, *Handbuch der Psychosynthese: Angewandte Transpersonale Psychologie* (Freiburg, 1978).
33. F/J 240.
34. M 361–362.
35. F/J 103.
36. Br I, 23.
37. Ernest Jones, quoted in R. W. Clark, *S. Freud*, p. 286.
38. F/J 140.
39. F/J 156–157.

40. F/J 160.
41. S. Freud, "Zur Geschichte der psychoanalytischen Bewegung" (1914), in *Selbstdarstellung: Schriften zur Geschichte der Psychoanalyse* (Frankfurt, 1971), pp. 162–163.
42. Ulrike May, "Psychoanalyse in den USA," in *Die Psychologie des 20 Jahrhunderts*, vol. 2, p. 1219ff.
43. William James, *The Varieties of Religious Experience* (1901–1902).
44. Ernest Jones, quoted in R. W. Clark, *S. Freud*, p. 297.
45. M 158.
46. Ibid.
47. M 161.
48. Ibid.
49. Freidrich Creuzer, *Symbolik und Mythologie der alten Völker.* Leipzig-Darmstadt, 1810–1823.
50. R. W. Clark, *S. Freud*, p. 302ff.
51. Quotations from Jung in A. Jaffé, *C. G. Jung, Bild und Wort*, p. 51.
52. A. Jaffé, op. cit. p. 52.
53. M 365.
54. M 366.
55. Letters 1, p. 531.
56. "Psychic Conflicts in a Child," CW 17, pp. 1–35.
57. Cf. F/J 235.
58. M 367.
59. S. Freud, *Selbstdarstellung*, op. cit. p. 80.
60. *Erinnerungen, Träume, Gedanken*, p. 366.
61. Ernest Jones, *Sigmund Freud: Leben und Werk* (Bern, 1978), vol. 2, p. 81.
62. M 368.
63. M 369.

10. *The Inevitable Break*

1. F/J 283.
2. F/J 280; 286; 292.
3. Freud/Pfister, *Briefe 1909–1939* (Frankfurt, 1963), p. 33.
4. Correspondence between Freud and Ferenczi, 3 April 1910, quoted in E. Jones, vol. 2, p. 93.
5. F/J 360.
6. *Eine Mithrasliturgie, erläutert von Albrecht Dieterich* (Heidelberg, 1903; Königsberg, 1909).
7. *The Standard Edition of the Complete Psychological Works of Sigmund Freud*, vol. 11 (1910).

8. F/J 365.
9. F/J 396.
10. *Symbole der Wandlung*, GW V, 501.
11. F/J 469.
12. F/J 364.
13. F/J 418.
14. F/J 425.
15. *Symbols of Transformation*, p. xxvi.
16. F/J 465.
17. M 364.
18. M 363.
19. S. Freud, *Gesammelte Werke* IX and Fischer *Taschenbuch*, p. 147.
20. F/J 508.
21. Freud's letter of 29 October 1910 quoted in E. Jones, vol. 2, p. 172.
22. The photo of the Congress can be seen, among other places, in A. Jaffé (ed.), *C. G. Jung*, pp. 54–55, and a portion of it in the present volume.
23. S. Freud/Karl Abraham, *Briefe 1907–1926* (Frankfurt, 1965), p. 118.
24. Lou Andreas-Salomé, *In der Schule bei Freud: Tagebuch eines Jahres 1912/13* (Munich, 1965).
25. Ibid., p. 15.
26. F/J 499.
27. F/J 505.
28. M 150.
29. F/J 515.
30. "The Freudian Theory of Hysteria," CW 4, pp. 10–24.
31. F/J 239–240.
32. F/J 233.
33. F/J 254–255.
34. The diary and correspondence between Sabina Spielrein and C. G. Jung and S. Freud were discovered in 1977 in the Palais Wilson in Geneva, earlier seat of the psychological institute of Geneva University. Documentation and interpretation, originally in Italian, exists in the following editions: Aldo Carotenuto and Carlo Trombetta, *Diario di una segretta simetria, Sabina Spielrein tra Jung e Freud* (Roma, 1980); Sabina Spielrein, *Entre Freud et Jung: Dosier d'ecouvert par Aldo Carotenuto et Carlo Trombetta* (Paris, 1981); Aldo Carotenuto, *A Secret Symmetry: Sabina Spielrein between Jung and Freud* (New York, 1982).
35. Cf. Marianne Niehus-Jung's information in Br I, 12.
36. Emma Jung, "Ein Beitrag zum Problem des Animus," in C. G. Jung, *Wirklichkeit der Seele* (Zürich, 1934).
37. Cf. "Archetypes of the Collective Unconscious," CW 9, i, pp. 3–41.

38. Bruno Bettelheim, in New York *Review of Books*, 30 June 1983, reviewed by G. Bliersbach in *Psychologie heute*, November 1983, with a letter from Gerhard Wehr December 1983.
39. F/J 497.
40. F/J 522.
41. For a detailed description of this campaign see H. F. Ellenberger, *Die Entdeckung des Unbewussten*, vol. 2, pp. 1086–1094.
42. F/J 556.
43. On the history of the formation of this concept cf. Liliane Frey-Rohn, *Von Freud zu Jung* (Zürich, 1969), p. 216ff.
44. "Zur Psychoanalyse" (1912); GW IV, 105.
45. GW IV, p. 110. In the Foreword to the second edition (1954), Jung referred to the Fordham lectures as a milestone on the long road to scientific efforts toward depth psychology. Ibid. p. 111.
46. Text in William McGuire and R. F. C. Hull (eds.), *C. G. Jung Speaking: Interviews and Encounters* (Princeton, 1977), pp. 11–24.
47. F/J 571.
48. F/J 572.
49. F/J 578–579.
50. M 157.
51. F/J 579.
52. F/J 580.
53. Freud/Karl Abraham, *Briefe*, p. 130.
54. F/J 600.
55. M 287–288.
56. "General Aspects of Psychoanalysis," CW 4, pp. 229–242.
57. "On the Psychology of the Unconscious," in C. G. Jung, *Two Essays on Analytical Psychology* (New York, 1956), p. 91.
58. F/J 30–31.
59. F/J 266. Cf. Roberto G. Assagioli, *Psychosynthesis* (New York, 1965).
60. Cf. "Psychoanalysis and Neurosis," CW 4, pp. 243–251.
61. CW 6.
62. Gross (1877–1920), along with Jung, was one of the few creative students of Freud in the early period of psychoanalysis. Based on a certification by Freud, he became Jung's patient for a time at Burghölzli. Aside from his theoretical efforts in the area of psychopathology, to which Jung repeatedly referred in his early works, Gross was an important figure in the colony of reformers and anarchists on Monte Verità near Ascona as well as in the Swabian artistic and literary scene during the first two decades of this century, especially on account of his erotic and utopian ideals. Detailed accounts are given, among others, by Martin Green, *Else und Friede, die Richthofen-Schwestern* (Munich, 1976), pp. 48–92; Robert Lucas, *Frieda von Richthofen: Ihr Leben mit D. H.*

Lawrence (Munich, 1972); Emanuel Hurwitz, *Otto Gross—Paradiessucher zwischen Freud und Jung* (Frankfurt, 1979); Hurwitz, "Psyche—Sexuelle Revolution und Mythenforschung," in *Monte Verità (Ausstellungskatalog)* (Milan, 1980), pp. 107–116. In Leonhard Frank's novel *Links, wo das Herz ist*, Gross figures as "Dr. Kreutz."

63. "Zur Frage der psychologischen Typen," GW VI, 551.
64. Lou Andreas-Salomé, *In der Schule bei Freud.* pp. 130–31.
65. Cf. Wolfgang Leppmann, *Rilke* (Bern, 1981), pp. 320–321. Uwe Henrik Peters, *Anna Freud* (Munich, 1979), pp. 50–51.
66. Br II, 103.
67. Br III, 110.
68. Freud, *Selbstdarstellung*, p. 195.
69. F/J 612.
70. Freud/Karl Abraham, *Briefe*, pp. 178, 180.
71. Ibid., p. 168.
72. Freud, *Selbstdarstellung*, p. 201.
73. Br I, 50.
74. CW 3, pp. 203–210.
75. M 168.
76. Br II, 151.
77. Quoted in A. Jaffé (ed.), *C. G. Jung: Bild und Wort*, pp. 63–64.
78. Freud to Putnam, quoted in R. Clark, *Freud*, p. 378.
79. Lou Andreas-Salomé, quoted in R. Clark, *Freud*, p. 379.
80. E. A. Bennet, *C. G. Jung: Einblicke in Leben und Werk* (Zürich, 1963), p. 70.
81. Alexander Mitscherlich, "Auch ein bürgerliches Trauerspiel: Der Briefwechsel Sigmund Freuds mit C. G. Jung," in *Frankfurter Allgemeine Zeitung*, 25 May 1974.

12. *The "Night Sea Journey"*

1. M 3.
2. M 176.
3. M 175.
4. Margarete Susman, *Auf gespaltenem Pfad: Festschrift zum 90. Geburtstag* (Darmstadt, 1964), p. 39.
5. M 176.
6. *Symbols of Transformation*, p. xxv.
7. With good reason, Marie-Louise von Franz traces the outlines of this myth in her book on Jung.
8. Marie-Louise von Franz, *C. G. Jung: Sein Mythos in unserer Zeit* (Frauenfeld, 1972), pp. 11–12.
9. M 170.

10. M 157.
11. M 173.
12. M 174–175.
13. M 177.
14. M 189.
15. Walter Shewring (trans.), *The Odyssey* (London, 1980), p. 128.
16. Cf. "Grenzfall," in J. Laplanche and J. B. Pontalis, *Das Vokabular der Psychoanalyse* (Frankfurt, 1972), p. 172.
17. Leo Frobenius, *Das Zeitalter des Sonnengottes* (Berlin, 1904). Cf. Jung's numerous references and citations, e.g., in *Symbols of Transformation.*
18. Gerhard Wehr, *Esoterisches Christentum: Aspekte, Impulse, Konsequenzen* (Stuttgart, 1975).
19. M 192.
20. M 179.
21. M 188.
22. M 180.
23. M 181.
24. On Simon Magus and Helena in heretical Gnosis see Gerhard Wehr, *Auf den Spuren urchristlicher Ketzer* (Schaffhausen, 1983).
25. M 182.
26. Br I, 385.
27. M 235.
28. M 184.
29. Manfred Lurker, *Götter und Symbole der alten Ägypter*, 2nd ed. (Bern and Munich, 1974), p. 96.
30. "Psychologische Typen" (1921), GW VI, 511.
31. "General Aspects of Dream Psychology," CW 8, pp. 237–280.
32. Paul J. Stern, *C. G. Jung: Prophet des Unbewussten* (Munich, 1977), p. 139ff. The author, so informative in many other regards, unfortunately neglects to name his sources, and so his presentation nearly amounts to gossip in precisely the noteworthy passages.
33. Toni Wolff, "Strukturformen der weiblichen Psyche," in *Studien zu C. G. Jungs Psychologie* p. 269ff.
34. Ibid., p. 275.
35. Barbara Hannah, *C. G. Jung*, p. 117.
36. Ibid., pp. 118–119.
37. Jung in a letter of 18 June 1958: "It is unfortunately true that when you are wife and mother you can hardly be the hetaira too, just as it is the secret suffering of the hetaira that she is not a mother. There are women who are not meant to bear physical children, but they are those that give rebirth to a man in a spiritual sense, which is a highly important function" (Letters 2, p. 455).

38. B. Hannah, op. cit. pp. 119–120.
39. Ibid., p. 120.
40. Facsimiles are contained in A. Jaffé, *C. G. Jung*, p. 67ff.
41. M 188.
42. A. N. Ammann, *Aktive Imagination: Darstellung der Methode* (Olten and Freiburg, 1978).
43. M 190–191.
44. Complete text in M 378–390.
45. Kurt Rudolph, *Die Gnosis* (Göttingen, 1977), p. 380ff.
46. Gerhard Wehr, *Auf den Spuren urchristlicher Ketzer*, pp. 110ff., 216ff.
47. M 379.
48. M 384.
49. M 192.
50. M 195–196.
51. *Erinnerungen, Träume, Gedanken*, p. 203.
52. M 199.

13. *The Work*

1. "Vorreden zu den *Collected Papers on Analytical Psychology*" (1916), GW IV, p. 335.
2. M 168.
3. "Psychotherapeutische Zeitfragen—Ein Briefwechsel" (1913/14), GW IV, p. 304.
4. Freud, *Three Essays on the Theory of Sexuality*, 1905.
5. Liliane Frey-Rohn, *Von Freud zu Jung*, pp. 114–115.
6. CW 7, pp. 3–117.
7. Jung, *Two Essays*, pp. 13–14.
8. Ibid., p. 16.
9. M 200–201.
10. Cf. Willem Cornelis van Unnik, *Evangelien aus dem Nilsand* (Frankfurt, 1960). For studies on the Nag-Hammadi finds see *Gnosis: Festschrift für Hans Jonas* (Göttingen, 1978).
11. M 201.
12. Gerhard Wehr, "Heilige Hochzeit" (unpublished manuscript).
13. "The Structure of the Unconscious," CW 7, p. 290. Here Jung used the term "individuation" to refer to a "seemingly irrational process of development" whose product was individuality.
14. Jung, *Two Essays*, p. 182.
15. "The Transcendent Function," CW 2, pp. 67–91.
16. Jung, *Two Essays*, p. 90.

17. Hermann Rorschach, *Psychodiagnostik: Methodik und Ergebnisse eines wahrnehmungsdiagnostischen Experiments* (Bern, 1921).
18. Ernst Kretschmer, *Physique and Character* (Berlin, 1921).
19. Foreword to 7th edition, 1937, in GW VI, p. xi.
20. Jung, *Two Essays*, 54.
21. M 222.
22. GW VI, pp. 439–440.
23. Ibid., pp. 444–445.
24. Br I, 121.
25. Br I, 241.
26. "The Relations between the Ego and the Unconscious," CW 7, pp. 121–241.
27. "On Psychic Energy," CW 8, pp. 3–66.
28. "Theoretische Überlegungen zum Wesen des Psychischen" (1946), GW VIII, 228.

14. *Traveling and Tower-Building*

1. Lao-tse, *Tao Te Ching*, trans. D. C. Lau (New York, 1963), p. 108.
2. A. Jaffé, *Aus C. G. Jungs Welt* (Zürich, 1979), p. 17.
3. M 367.
4. M 246–247.
5. Br I, 57.
6. Hannah, *C. G. Jung*, p. 140.
7. M 371–372.
8. M 238.
9. Hannah, *C. G. Jung*, p. 142.
10. M 240.
11. M 244.
12. M 225.
13. Ibid.
14. M 225–226.
15. Br I, 218.
16. Laurens van der Post, *C. G. Jung: Der Mensch und seine Geschichte* (Berlin, 1977), p. 79.
17. M 249.
18. M 248.
19. M 251.
20. M 252.
21. M 252–253.
22. Letters 2, p. 596.

23. Letters 1, pp. 101–102.
24. Both texts in CW 10, pp. 29–49 and 50–73.
25. GW X, p. 92.
26. GW X, p. 64.
27. *[Analytical Psychology.] Notes on the Seminar in Analytical Psychology...* Comp. by Cary F. de Angulo and rev. by C. G. Jung. Arranged by members of the class. Cf. CW 19, p. 209.
28. A typescript and notes by Esther Harding are in existence; cf. CW 19, p. 209.
29. Cf. Jung's psychological Foreword to the *I Ching*, CW 11, pp. 589–608.
30. M 253–254.
31. Br I, 64–65.
32. William McGuire and R. F. C. Hull (eds.), *C. G. Jung Speaking*, pp. 32–37.
33. M 254.
34. M 261.
35. M 265.
36. M 269.
37. M 264.
38. Laurens van der Post, *C. G. Jung*, p. 80.
39. Ibid., p. 83.
40. M 272.
41. M 273.
42. M 274.
43. Hannah, *C. G. Jung*, p. 180.

15. *The Encounter with Alchemy*

1. M 200.
2. Alexander von Bernus, *Alchymie und Heilkunst* (Nürnberg, 1948), pp. 95–96.
3. Mircea Eliade, *Schmiede und Alchemisten* (Stuttgart o.J., 1960), p. 12ff.
4. Gerhard Wehr, *Esoterisches Christentum* (Stuttgart, 1975), pp. 211ff., 216ff. Wehr, *Jakob Böhme: Der Geisteslehrer und Seelenführer* (Freiburg, 1979) (Fermenta cognitionis 4).
5. Herbert Silberer, *Problems of Mysticism and Its Symbolism* (New York, 1917). Further preanalytic works are Ethan Allan Hitchcock, *Remarks upon Alchemy and the Alchemists* (Boston, 1857), and Hitchcock, *Swedenborg, a Hermetic: Being a Sequel to Remarks upon Alchemy and Alchemists* (New York, 1958).
6. Marie-Louise von Franz, "Psyche und Materie in Alchemie und moderner Psychologie," in *Der unwahrscheinliche Jung: Beiträge zum 100. Geburtstag* (Zürich, 1975), p. 42ff.
7. M 202.

8. M 203.
9. Wehr, *Esoterisches Christentum*, p. 192ff.
10. "Psychologie und Alchemy" (1944), GW XII, p. 47.
11. "The Psychology of the Transference," CW 16, pp. 163–321.
12. Marie-Louise von Franz, *C. G. Jung*, p. 292ff.
13. Pascual Jordan, quoted in Br I, 231.
14. "Vorrede zu *Das Geheimnis der goldenen Blüte*," GW XIII, p. 13.
15. CW 8, pp. 417–519.
16. M 205–206.
17. M 206.
18. Complete text in *Die Bruderschaft der Rosenkreuzer*, ed. Gerhard Wehr (Cologne, 1984).
19. Gerhard Wehr, *Christian Rosenkreuz* (Freiburg, 1980) (Fermenta cognitionis 10).
20. CW 12.
21. "The Vision of Zosimos," CW 13, pp. 57–108.
22. GW XII, pp. 487–488.
23. M 205.
24. M 209.
25. "Psychologie und Alchemie," GW XII, pp. 395–491.

16. *Eranos*

1. Alfons Rosenberg, "Eranos—Der Geist am Wasser," in *Flugblätter für Freunde: Aus der Werkstatt von Alfons Rosenberg* (Zürich, 1977), leaflet 80.
2. *Eranos Jahrbuch* 1933. Edited by Olga Fröbe-Kapteyn (Zürich, 1934), pp. 5–6.
3. *Monte Verità: Berg der Wahrheit*, ed. Harald Szeemann (Mailand, 1980).
4. Robert Landmann, *Ascona-Monte Verità: Auf der Suche nach dem Paradies* (Zürich, 1973), p. 316ff.
5. Cf. Ernesto Buonaiuti, *Die exkommunizierte Kirche*, ed. Ernst Benz (Zürich, 1966).
6. *Eranos Jahrbuch* 1933, p. 231ff.
7. "A Study in the Process of Individuation," CW 9, i, pp. 290–354.
8. Alfons Rosenberg, *Eranos—Der Geist am Wasser*, p. 2.
9. *Eranos Jahrbuch* 1933, p. 201.
10. Ibid., p. 203.
11. *Eranos Jahrbuch* 1934 (Zürich, 1935).

12. Wilhelm J. Hauer, "Vom totalen Sinn der deutschen Revolution," in *Kommende Gemeinde*, vol. 5, no. 2/3 (July 1933), p. 4.
13. Cf. Prof. Hauer's Yoga seminar, held from 3 to 8 October 1932 in the Psychological Club in Zürich. The internal transcript of the event includes Jung's commentary and answers to questions.
14. Br I, 183.
15. *Eranos Jahrbuch* 1934, p. 7.
16. Ibid. 192–193.
17. Ibid., p. 229; cf. the formulation in GW IX, part 1, pp. 13–52.
18. Quoted in Aniela Jaffé, "Jung und die Eranos-Tagungen," in *Eranos Jahrbuch* 1975 (Leiden-Cologne, 1977), p. 11.
19. Ibid.
20. Mircea Eliade, *Im Mittelpunkt: Bruchstücke eines Tagesbuches* (Vienna, 1973), p. 75.
21. A Jaffé, "Jung und die Eranos-Tagungen."
22. *Aus Gesprächen mit C. G. Jung: Aufgezeichnet von Margret Ostrowski-Sachs*, typescript (Montagnola, 1965), p. 40.
23. Alfons Rosenberg, *Die Welt im Feuer: Wandlungen meines Lebens* (Freiburg, 1983), pp. 146–147.
24. Olga Fröbe-Kapteyn, in *Eranos Jahrbuch*, vol. 18, *Aus der Welt der Urbilder* (Zürich, 1950), pp. 7–8.
25. Adolf Portmann, in *Eranos Jahrbuch* 1961 (Zürich, 1962), p. 8.

17. *The Remarkable Journey to India*

1. C. A. Meier, *Bewusstsein* (*Lehrbuch der Komplexen Psychologie C. G. Jungs*, vol. 3) (Olten-Freiburg, 1975), pp. 79–80.
2. A. N. Ammann, *Aktive Imagination.*
3. Arthur Avalon, *The Serpent Power* (Madras, 1958).
4. Cf. Werner Bohm, *Chakras*, 2nd ed. (Weilbeim, 1966). Carl Friedrich von Weizsäcker and Gopi Krishna, *Die biologische Basis religiöser Erfahrung* (Weilheim, 1971). Gopi Krishna, *Kundalini* (Weilheim, 1968).
5. Cf. n. 453.
6. Letters, 1, pp. 235–236.
7. M 275.
8. "Die träumende Welt Indiens" (1939), GW X, 564.
9. GW X, 566.
10. Cf. the interview at the Basel Psychology Club on 1 November 1958, in *C. G. Jung Speaking*, pp. 370–391.
11. GW X, 572.
12. Ibid., 567.
13. Ibid., 568.

14. M 277.
15. M 278.
16. M 280.
17. M 282–283.
18. "The Holy Men of India," CW 11, pp. 576–586. Heinrich Zimmer, *Der Weg zum Selbst: Lehre und Leben des Sri Ramana Maharishi* (1944) (Düsseldorf, 1974).
19. M 275.
20. "Was Indien uns Lehren kann" (1939), GW X, 580.

18. *Again and Again, the Religious Question*

1. "Ziele der Psychotherapie" (1929), GW XVI, 49.
2. "Psychotherapie und Seelsorge" (1932), GW XI, 362.
3. "Bruder Klaus" (1933), GW XI, 349.
4. GW XVI, 15.
5. M 75.
6. Hannah, *Jung*, p. 239.
7. "Psychologie und Religion," GW XI, 1.
8. Rudolf Otto, *Das Heilige: Über das Irrationale in der Idee des Göttlichen und sein Verhältnis zum Rationalen* (1917), numerous editions (Munich, 1979).
9. "Psychologie und Religion," GW XI, 4.
10. GW XI, 98.
11. Rudolf Bultmann, "Neues Testament und Mythologie" (1948), in *Kerygma und Mythos I*, ed. Hans Werner Bartsch (Hamburg-Bergstedt, 1960).
12. "Über die Archetypen des kollektiven Unbewussten" (1934), GW IX, part i, p. 33.
13. Ulrich Mann, *Theogonische Tage* (Stuttgart, 1970), p. 59.
14. "Psychologie und Religion," GW XI, 97.
15. GW XI, 88–89.
16. Hans Schär, *Religion und Seele in der Psychologie C. G. Jungs* (Zürich, 1956), p. 6.
17. Ibid., p. 13.
18. "Psychologie und Religion," GW XI, 63.
19. *Eranos Jahrbuch* 1940/41 (Zürich, 1942), p. 32ff.
20. Aniela Jaffé, *Der Mythus vom Sinn im Werk von C. G. Jung* (Zürich, 1967), pp. 9–10.
21. Br I, 428ff.
22. Br II, 241.

19. *National Socialism*

1. Quoted in Gerhard Baetze, "Psychoanalyse in Deutschland," in *Die Psychologie des 20. Jahrhunderts*, vol. 2, p. 1179.
2. Freud's letter of 31 July 1933 to Simon Freud, quoted in R. W. Clark, *Sigmund Freud*, p. 549.
3. Marie-Louise von Franz, in the Foreword to Wolodymyr Walter Odaynyk, *C. G. Jung und die Politik* (Stuttgart, 1975), p. 11.
4. Freud, *Massenpsychologie und Ich-Analyse* (Vienna, 1921).
5. Wilhelm Reich, *Maassenpsychologie des Faschismus* (Copenhagen, 1933).
6. "Vom Werden der Persönlichkeit" (1932), GW XVII, 204.
7. Ibid., 201.
8. "Über das Unbewusste" (1918), GW X, 25.
9. "Die Bedeutung der Psychologie für die Gegenwart," GW X, 178.
10. Thomas Mann, "Freud und die Zukunft," lecture presented in Vienna on 8 May 1936, in *S. Freud: Abriss der Psychoanalyse* (Frankfurt, 1953).
11. Erich Neumann, "Freud und das Vaterbild," *Merkur* 8 (1956).
12. Letter of 9 June 1933 to Prof. J. H. Schultz, in Br I, 164.
13. Br I, 180. For this reason H. K. Fierz wrote of the International Society for Medical Psychotherapy, Lausanne, in the *Süddeutsche Zeitung* of Munich on 1 November 1972: "When E. Kretschmer stepped down from the presidency after the seizure of power by Hitler, it was not C. G. Jung but Prof. Göring who became president of that society. Jung, for his part, then founded in 1934, with colleagues from various countries, the International Society for Medical Psychotherapy, which still exists today and of which the undersigned is General Secretary. The aim of this founding was to provide support for German colleagues abroad. The German G.M.S.f.P. became a national group of the International Society, and Jung was president of the International Society, as well as president of the Swiss national group, but not the German one!"
14. "Rundschreiben" (1934), GW X, 595.
15. "Contribution to a Discussion on Psychotherapy," CW 10, pp. 557–558.
16. "Begrüssungsansprache zum 9. Internationalen Ärztlichen Kongress für Psychotherapie in Kopenhagen" (1937), GW X, 613–614.
17. Br I, 174.
18. Br I, 190.
19. "Geleitwort, in *Zentralblatt für Psychotherapie und ihre Grenzgebiete*" (1933), GW X, 581–582.
20. Gustav Bally, "Deutschstämmige Therapie," in *Neue Zürcher Zeitung*, 27 February 1934.
21. GW X, 584.
22. GW X, 587–588.
23. S. Freud/Karl Abraham, *Briefe*, p. 47.

24. Aniela Jaffé, *Aus Leben und Werkstatt von C. G. Jung* (Zürich, 1968), p. 95.
25. CW 10, pp. 157–173.
26. GW X, 191.
27. Wilhelm J Hauer, *Deutsche Gottschau: Grundzüge eines deutschen Glaubens* (Stuttgart, 1934).
28. A. Jaffé, *Aus Leben und Werkstatt von C. G. Jung*, p. 92.
29. the text of the interview, preserved on photograph records, is found in *C. G. Jung Speaking*, pp. 59–66.
30. *Psychological Analysis of Nietzsche's Zarathustra*, part I, lecture 1, 6 June 1934; cf. CW 19, p. 213.
31. "Wotan," CW 10, pp. 179–193.
32. GW X, 206.
33. GW X, 214.
34. GW X, 266.
35. *C. G. Jung Speaking*, p. 128.
36. Ibid., p. 135.
37. Laurens van der Post, *C. J. Jung*, p. 42.
38. Gerhard Wehr, *Der deutsche Jude Martin Buber* (Munich, 1977).
39. A. Jaffé, *Aus Leben und Werkstatt von C. G. Jung*, p. 101.
40. Cf. Leonhard Baker, *Hirt der Verfolgten. Leo Baeick im Dritten Reich* (Stuttgart, 1982).
41. A. Jaffé, *Aus Leben und Werkstatt von C. G. Jung*, p. 104.
42. Ibid.
43. Cf. CW 19, p. 210.
44. The individual articles are referred to here according to their appearance in the respective volumes of the *Collected Works*; see the General Bibliography, CW 19.
45. E. A. Bennet, Foreword to "Über Grundlagen der Analytischen Psychologie," GW XVIII, part 1, pp. 16–17.
46. *Die kulturelle Bedeutung der Komplexen Psychologie*, ed. Psychologischen Club Zürich (Berlin, 1935).
47. Alfons Paquet, in *An der Schwelle: Bericht über die Arbeitswoche des Köngener Kreises in Königsfeld vom 1.–7. Januar 1937, über Grundfragen der Seelenkunde und Seelenführung*, ed. Rudi Daur (Heilbronn, 1937), p. 47.
48. C. G. Jung, quoted in ibid., p. 37.
49. Rudi Daur, ibid., p. 38.
50. "Sigmund Freud als kulturhistorische Erscheinung" (1932), GW XV, 51.
51. "Sigmund Freud" (1939), GW XV, 60–61.

20. *The Second World War*

1. Br I, 355.
2. Barbara Hannah, who had close ties with the Jung family, tells of a telephone call from a federal agency in Bern, according to which Jung was to get to safety immediately, in expectation of an assault by German troops on Switzerland. His name was said to be on a Nazi blacklist, and hence he would be especially endangered in the event of an invasion by the German army (B. Hannah, *Jung*, p. 269). After the swift overthrow of France, the threat of such an event was thought to have been lifted in Switzerland.
3. Letters 1, p. 285.
4. Alfons Rosenberg, *Durchbruch zur Zukunft: Der Mensch im Wassermann-Zeitalter* (Munich, 1958).
5. Cf. C. G. Jung, *Aion: Researches into the Phenomenology of the Self*, CW 9, part 2.
6. *Modern Psychology.* Private printing, part 4, *Process of Individuation: Exercitia Spiritualia of St. Ignatius of Loyola.* Cf. CW 19, p. 212.
7. CW 11.
8. "Rückkehr zum einfachen Leben" (1941), GW XVIII, part 2, 622.
9. CW 15.
10. CW 13.
11. "Paracelsica" (1941), GW XIII, 125–126.
12. *Eranos Jahrbuch* 1942; now in CW 13, pp. 191–200.
13. Letters 1, p. 319.
14. Cf. also A. Jaffé, *Aus Leben und Werkstatt von C. G. Jung*, p. 55ff.
15. Marie-Louise von Franz, Foreword to GW XIV, part 1, p. ix.
16. Barbara Hannah, *Jung*, p. 277.
17. M 289.
18. M 291.
19. M 292.
20. Hannah, *Jung*, p. 278.
21. Gerhard Wehr, "Heilige Hochzeit" (unpublished manuscript).
22. *Der Sohar: Nach dem Urtext*, ed. Ernst Müller (Vienna, 1932), p. 388ff.
23. M 294.
24. Hannah, *Jung*.
25. Br II, 511.
26. Br I, 427.
27. Letters 1, p. 358.
28. Br I, 496.

21. *After the War*

1. Letters 1, p. 376.
2. Hannah, *Jung*, 285.
3. M 297.
4. CW 10, pp. 194–217.
5. *Kirchliches Jahrbuch der Evangelischen Kirche in Deutschland 1945–1948*, Ed. Joachim Beckmann (1950), pp. 26–27.
6. GW X, 223.
7. Ernst Bloch, *Prinzip Hoffnung* (Frankfurt, 1959), p. 65.
8. Jung took a definitive stance toward what had happened, in his "Epilogue to Essays on Contemporary Events," CW 10, pp. 227–243.
9. Hannah, *Jung*, p. 286.
10. Br II, 9.
11. "Rede anlässlich der Gründungssitzung des C. G. Jung-Instituts," GW XVIII, part 2, 509.
12. Friedrich Nietzsche, *Also sprach Zarathustra*, in *Werke in drei Bänden*, ed. Karl Schlechta (Munich, 1966), vol. 2, p. 339.
13. Hannah, *Jung*, pp. 298–299.
14. Letter of 22 September 1946, Br II, 54.
15. Letters 1, pp. 449–450.
16. *Gut und Böse in der Psychotherapie*, ed. Wilhelm Bitter (Stuttgart, 1966). *Das Böse* (Studien aus dem C. G. Jung-Institut 13), Zürich, 1961. M.-L. von Franz, "Psychologische Überlegungen zum Problem des Bösen in der Sicht C. G. Jungs," in Gerhard Zacharias (ed.), *Das Böse* (Munich, 1972), p. 30ff. Irene Beck, *Das Problem des Bösen und seiner Bewältigung: Eine Auseinandersetzung mit der Tiefenpsychologie von C. G. Jung vom Standpunkt der Theologie und Religionspädogogik* (Munich and Basel, 1976).
17. C. G. Jung, "Vorwort zu V. White: *Gott und das Unbewusste*," GW pp. 325–339.
18. Hans Schär, *Religion und Seele in der Psychologie C. G. Jungs* (Zürich, 1946).
19. Josef Goldbrunner, *Individuation: Die Psychologie C. G. Jungs* (Freiburg, 1949).
20. Br II, 66.
21. Letters 1, p. 455.
22. Letters 1, p. 469.
23. C. G. Jung, Foreword to Esther Harding, *Das Geheimnis der Seele: Ursprung und Ziel der psychischen Energie* (Zürich o. J., 1948), p. 10; now in GW XVIII, part 2, p. 503.

24. Aniela Jaffé, *Bilder und Symbole aus E. T. A. Hoffmanns Märchen...*, in *Gestaltungen des Unbewussten* (Zürich, 1950).
25. Erich Neumann, *The Origins and History of Consciousness* (New York, 1954).
26. Br II, 140.
27. GW XVIII, part 2, 663.
28. Br II, 143ff.
29. Jung's forewords are reprinted for the most part in CW 18.
30. C. A. Meier, *Antike Inkubation und moderne Psychotherapie* (Zürich, 1949).

22. *The Codex Jung*

1. Gilles Quispel, "C. G. Jung und die Gnosis," in *Eranos Jahrbuch* 1968 (Zürich, 1969), p. 227ff.
2. On the history of the discovery see Kurt Rudolph, *Die Gnosis: Wesen und Geschichte einer spätantiken Religion* (Göttingen, 1978), p. 40ff.
3. W. C. van Unnik, *Evangelien aus dem Nilsand* (Frankfurt, 1960). Martin Krause, "Die Texte von Nag-Hammadi," in *Gnosis: Festschrift für Hans Jonas* (Göttingen, 1978), pp. 216–243.
4. Gilles Quispel, *Gnosis als Weltreligion* (Zürich, 1951; 2nd, expanded edition, 1972).
5. Gilles Quispel, quoted in W. C. van Unnik, *Evangelien aus dem Nilsand*, pp. 20–21.
6. Letters 2, p. 138.
7. GW XVIII, part 2, p. 890.
8. Gerhard Wehr, *Auf den Spuren urchristlicher Ketzer: Christliche Gnosis und heutiges Bewusstsein* (Schaffhausen, 1983).
9. GW XVIII, part 2, p. 893.
10. Wehr, *Auf den Spuren urchristlicher Ketzer*, pp. 249–263. Wehr, *Stichwort Damaskus-Erlebnis* (Stuttgart, 1982), pp. 162–163.

23. *The Signs of Age*

1. *C. G. Jung Speaking*, pp. 186–189.
2. A. Jaffé, *Aus Leben und Werkstatt von C. G. Jung*, p. 108.
3. Now in CW 9, part 1, pp. 290–354.
4. In the so-called ecumenical debate this aspect has scarcely been made use of. The well-known confessional and denominational arguments have been in the foreground.
5. M 225.
6. Cf. the definition of "Symbol" in *Psychological Types*, CW 6.
7. M 226.
8. M 227–228.

9. M 228.
10. Heinrich Zimmer, "Merlin," in *Abenteuer und Fahrten der Seele* (Düsseldorf, 1977), p. 189ff. Emma Jung and Marie-Louise von Franz, *The Grail Legend* (New York, 1972).
11. M.-L. von Franz, *C. G. Jung*, p. 337ff.
12. Letters 2, p. 83.

24. *Answer to Job*

1. Br II, 332.
2. Søren Kierkegaard, quoted in Walter Strolz, *Schöpfung und Selbstbesinnung* (Zürich, 1973), p. 163, with further documentation.
3. Jaspers takes up the theme of Job especially in *Der philosophische Glaube angesichts der Offenbarung* (Munich, 1962).
4. Karl Barth, *Hiob*, ed. Helmut Gollwitzer (Neukirchen & Vluyn, 1966).
5. Ibid., 31.
6. Margarete Susman, *Das Buch Hiob und das Schicksal des jüdischen Volkes* (Freiburg, 1968).
7. Letters 2, p. 330.
8. Ibid., p. 282.
9. Johannes Tenzler, *Selbstfindung und Gotteserfahrung* (Munich-Paderborn, 1975), pp. 196–215.
10. CW 9, part 2.
11. Letters 2, p. 281.
12. Ibid., p. 282.
13. Ibid.
14. Cf. Jung's introduction to the problems of the psychology of religion in "Psychologie und Alchemie" (1944), GW XII, p. 28: "Psychology concerns itself with the act of seeing, and not with the construction of new religious truths, where after all the already existing doctrines have not yet been appreciated and understood. In religious matters, as is well known, one cannot understand anything that has not been experienced within oneself. Only in inner experience does the relationship of the soul to that which is shown and preached externally reveal itself in the form of a kinship or an analogy. . . ."
15. "Antwort auf Hiob," GW XI, 392.
16. Ibid., 393.
17. Ibid., 431.
18. Jakob Böhme, *Die Morgenröte bricht an: Zeugnisse der Naturfrömmigkeit und der Christuserkenntnis* ed. Gerhard Wehr (Freiburg, 1983). Gerhard Wehr, *Jakob Böhme in Selbstzeugnissen und Bilddokumenten* (Reinbek, 1971).
19. GW XI, 445.
20. GW XI, 498.

21. GW XI, 499.
22. Br II, 223–224.
23. Br II, 228–228.
24. Letters 2, p. 79.
25. See n. 496.
26. Erich Neumann's letter to Jung of 5 December 1951, quoted in Br II, 243.
27. Laurens van der Post, *Jung and the Story of Our Time* (New York, 1975), p. 223.
28. Otto Wolff, "C. G. Jungs Antwort auf Hiob," in *Dialog über den Menschen: Festschrift für Wilhelm Bitter zum 75. Geburtstag* (Stuttgart, 1968). Gert Hummel, *Theologische Anthropologie und die Wirklichkeit der Psyche* (Darmstadt, 1972). Johannes Tenzler, *Selbstfindung und Gotteserfahrung*, pp. 216–317.
29. Letters 2, pp. 28–29.

25. *Mysterium Coniunctionis*

1. M 212.
2. Marie-Louis von Franz, Foreword to *Mysterium Coniunctionis*, GW XIV, part 1, p. ix.
3. Karl Kerényi, *Das Ägäische Fest* (Amsterdam and Leipzig, 1941), now in Kerényi, *Humanistische Seelenforschung* (Munich, 1966), p. 116ff.
4. Cf. C. A. Meier, *Antike Inkubation und moderne Psychotherapie*, pp. 62–63.
5. Br I, 366.
6. Br I, 370.
7. CW 16.
8. Cf. "Principles of Practical Psychotherapy," CW 16, pp. 3–20.
9. "Die Psychologie der Übertragung," GW XVI, pp. 178–179.
10. J. V. Andreae, "Die Chymische Hochzeit Christiani Rosenkreutz Anno 1459," in *Die Bruderschaft der Rosenkreuzer*, ed. Gerhard Wehr (Cologne, 1984).
11. "Mysterium Coniunctionis" (1968), GW XIV, part 2, p. 231.
12. Ibid., 234.
13. Ibid., 232.
14. Ibid., 317–318.
15. Ibid., 270ff.
16. M 325.
17. Hannah, *Jung*, p. 313.
18. New York, 1966.
19. Letters 2, pp. 393–396.

26. *Late in Life*

1. Ernst Bloch, *Das Prinzip Hoffnung*, vol. 1, pp. 61–62.
2. "Ein moderner Mythus" (1958), GW X, 337.
3. Arthur Schult, *Astrosophie als kosmische Signaturenlehre des Menschenbildes* (Bietigheim, 1971), vol. 2, p. 669ff. Alfons Rosenberg, *Durchbruch zur Zukunft: Der Mensch im Wassermann-Zeitalter* (Munich, 1958).
4. "Ein moderner Mythus," GW X, 338.
5. GW XVIII, part 2, 671.
6. GW X, 343.
7. GW XVIII, part 2, 678.
8. A. Jaffé, *Aus Leben und Werkstatt von C. G. Jung*, p. 109.
9. GW X, 443.
10. *C. G. Jung Speaking*, pp. 406–409.
11. M 334.
12. Emil Bock, "Zeichen am Himmel: Zu dem Buch von C. G. Jung," in *Die Christengemeinschaft* 1958, pp. 168–172.

27. *Late in Life*

1. Br II, 386.
2. Letters 2, p. 270.
3. A. Jaffé, *Aus Leben und Werkstatt von C. G. Jung*, p. 131.
4. *C. G. Jung Speaking*, pp. 237–238.
5. Hannah, *Jung*, pp. 323–324.
6. Martin Buber, *Die Chassidische Botschaft* (Heidelberg, 1952). Gerhard Wehr, *Der Chassidismus: Mysterium und spirituelle Lebenspraxis* (Freiburg, 1978).
7. Gershom Scholem, *Die jüdische Mystik in ihren Hauptströmungen* (Frankfurt, 1957), p. 377.
8. *C. G. Jung Speaking*, pp. 252–267.
9. E. A. Bennet, *C. G. Jung*, p. 178.
10. Hannah, *Jung*, p. 325.
11. A. Jaffé, *C. G. Jung, Bild und Wort*, p. 134.
12. Laurens van der Post, *Jung and the Story of Our Time*, p. 228.
13. Br II, 525.
14. M 175.
15. M 232.
16. M 225.
17. Br III, 79–80.
18. Cf. his letter to Gustav Steiner of 30 December 1957, Letters 2, pp. 406–407.

19. Kurt Wolff, *Briefwechsel eines Verlegers 1911–1963* (Frankfurt, 1980), p. 1x.
20. Br III, 293–294.
21. Br III, 333.
22. On Jung as esoteric Christ, cf. Gerhard Wehr, *Esoterisches Christentum*, p. 261ff. Wehr, *Stichwort Damaskus-Erlebnis: Der Weg zu Christus nach C. G. Jung* (Stuttgart, 1982).
23. GW XVIII, part 2, 682.
24. Br III, 248.
25. "Gegenwart und Zukunft" (1957), GW X, 336.
26. Br III, 95–96.
27. Foreword to GW XVI.
28. Letters 2, p. 334.
29. Br III, 90.
30. Letters 2, p. 334.
31. Br III, 295.
32. Richard I. Evans, *Gespräche mit C. G. Jung und Äusserungen von Ernest Jones* (Zürich, 1967), pp. 25–26.
33. Ibid., 27–28.
34. *C. G. Jung Speaking*, pp. 410–411.
35. Ibid., 412–414.
36. Ibid., 428.
37. Letters 2, p. 574.
38. Br III, 325.
39. Letter of 16 May 1956; Br III, 25.
40. Hannah, *Jung*, p. 343.
41. John Freeman, Introduction to *Man and His Symbols* (New York, 1964), p. vi.
42. *Man and His Symbols*, p. 91.
43. Hannah, *Jung*, p. 346.
44. M 313–314.
45. Miguel Serrano, *Meine Begegnungen mit C. G. Jung und Hermann Hesse in visionärer Schau* (Zürich, 1968), p. 61.
46. Ibid., 66.
47. Bombay, 1960.
48. Serrano, *Meine Begegnungen*, p. 121.
49. Ibid., 131.
50. Ibid., 132.
51. Ibid., 81.

28. *Under the Sign of Wholeness*

1. Ruth Bailey to Serrano, 16 June 1961, ibid., 136.
2. Ibid.
3. Hannah, *Jung*, p. 347 n. j.
4. M 4.
5. Laurens van der Post, *Jung*, pp. 372–274.
6. Letters 2, p. 580.
7. Letters 2, p. 581.
8. Gerhard Adler, quoted in A. Jaffé, *C. G. Jung, Bild und Wort*, p. 217.

Western Consciousness and Eastern Spirituality

1. Willem Visser't Hooft, *Kein anderer Name: Synkretismus oder christlicher Universalismus* (Basel, 1965), pp. 34–35.
2. "Yoga and the West," CW 10, p. 530.
3. Jean Gebser, *Asienfibel* (Frankfurt, 1962), p. 111; now "Asien lächelt anders," in Gebser, *Gesamtausgabe*, vol. 6, p. 109.
4. Citations and references in Gerhard Wehr, *C. G. Jung und Rudolf Steiner* (Stuttgart, 1972).
5. Br III, 48. Hu-shih, Chinese ambassador to the United States from 1938 to 1942, was one of the innumerable intellectuals who dismissed his country's spiritual tradition as useless nonsense, whereas C. G. Jung was among the first Europeans who—even in the early twenties—concerned themselves seriously with the *I Ching*, thus before Richard Wilhelm's translation of this ancient book of Chinese wisdom into German.
6. Letters 2, p. 600.
7. GW XIII, 14.
8. "Zum Gedächtnis Richard Wilhelms" (1930), GW XV, p. 69.
9. "Yoga and the West," CW 11, pp. 532–534.
10. Neumann, *The Origins and History of Consciousness*
11. "Yoga and the West," CW 11, p. 533.
12. Ibid., 537.
13. Rudolf Steiner, *1. Anthroposophischer Leitsatz*. Gerhard Wehr, *Der innere Weg! Anthroposophische Erkenntnis, geistige Orientierung und meditative Praxis* (Reinbek, 1983). Cf. n. 761.
14. Br I, 261.
15. C. G. Jung, quoted in Katharine Grant Watson, "A Visit to C. G. Jung," in *The Christian Community*, no. 1 (1976), p. 19.
16. It is less a question of evidence than of self-won spiritual experience.
17. Cf. Gerhard Wehr, *Rudolf Steiner: Biographie* (Freiburg, 1982), p. 383.
18. Letters 2, p. 601.
19. Letters 2, p. 613.

20. Cf. nn. 761 and 770.
21. Karlfried Graf Dürckheim (ed.), *Der Zielfreie Weg: Im Kraftfeld Initiatischer Therapie* (Freiburg, 1982); Gisela Schoeller, *Heilung aus dem Ursprung: Praxis der Initiatischen Therapie nach Karlfried Graf Dürckheim und Maria Hippius* (Munich, 1983); Rüdiger Müller, *Wandlung zur Ganzheit: Die Initiatische Therapie nach Karlfried Graf Dürckheim und Maria Hippius* (Freiburg, 1983); Manfred Bergler, "Die Anthropologie des Grafen Karlfried von Dürckheim im Rahmen der Rezeptionsgeschichte des Zen-Buddhismus in Deutschland" (Dissertation, Erlangen-Nürnberg, 1981).
22. Wilhelm Bitter (ed.), *Abendländische Therapie und östliche Weisheit* (Stuttgart, 1968).

C. G. Jung in Dialogue and Debate

1. M 131.
2. M 145.
3. Paul R. Mendes-Flohr, *Von der Mystik zum Dialog: Martin Bubers geistige Entwicklung bis hin zum 'Ich und Du'* (Königstein, 1978).
4. Martin Buber, *Gottesfinsternis* (1952/53), in *Werke I*, p. 525.
5. Ibid., 536.
6. Arie Sborowitz, *Beziehung und Bestimmung: Die Lehren von Martin Buber und C. G. Jung in ihrem Verhältnis zueinander* (Darmstadt, 1955); Hans Trüb, *Heilung aus der Begegnung: Eine Auseinandersetzung mit der Psychologie C. G. Jungs, mit einem Geleitwort von Martin Buber* (Stuttgart, 1962).
7. GW XI, 660.
8. Buber, *Gottesfinsternis—Replik*, in Buber, *Werke I*, p. 602.
9. Ibid., 520.
10. Letters 2, pp. 101–102.
11. Cf. the passages referring to Martin Buber in Letters, 2.
12. V. E. von Gebsattel, *Christentum und Humanismus* (Stuttgart, 1947), p. 36.
13. Viktor E. Frankl, *Der Mensch auf der Suche nach Sinn: Zur Humanisierung der Psychotherapie* (1959; Freiburg, 1972), pp. 44–45.
14. Erich Fromm, "C. G. Jung, Prophet des Unbewussten," in Fromm, *Gesamtausgabe*, vol. 8, p. 130.
15. Rainer Funk, in Fromm, *Gesamtausgabe*, vol. 8, p. 411.
16. Erich Fromm, "Die philosophische Basis der Freudschen Psychoanalyse" (1962), in *Gesamtausgabe*, vol. 8, p. 228.
17. Erich Fromm, "Psychoanalyse und Religion," *Gesamtausgabe* 6, p. 235ff.
18. GW XVIII, part 2, pp. 755–756.
19. "Psychologie und Dichtung" (1930), GW XV, p. 114.
20. Ibid., 116.

21. Ibid., 118.
22. Br III, 385.
23. Hermann Hesse to Emanuel Meier, quoted in Br II, 184.
24. Ibid.
25. Vincent Brome, in *Spring* 1975, p. 62.
26. H. G. Wells, in *Spring* 1975, pp. 56ff.
27. Letters 2, p. 192.
28. Letters 2, p. 266.
29. Letters 1, p. 99.
30. Cf. the editorial comments in GW XV, pp. 146–147.
31. "'Ulysses': A Monologue," CW 15, pp. 109–134.
32. GW XV, 130.
33. Ibid., 145.
34. Ibid., 156.
35. London, 1957.
36. Herbert Read, *C. G. Jung (Zum 85. Geburtstag von Professor Carl Gustav Jung, 26. Juli 1960)* (Zürich, 1960).
37. Letters 2, pp. 586–589.
38. Herbert Read, quoted in Letters 2, p. 591 n. 8.
39. Herbert Read, *C. G. Jung*, p. 29.

Prolegomena to a History of Jung's Influence

1. Br III, 380.
2. Cf. n. 778.
3. Gustav R. Heyer, "Komplexe Psychologie—C. G. Jung," in *Handbuch der Neurosenlehre und Psychotherapie III* (Munich and Berlin, 1959), pp. 285–326. H. F. Ellenberger, *Die Entdeckung des Unbewussten*, vol. 2, pp. 878–994. C. A. Meier, *Experiment und Symbol: Arbeiten zur Komplexen Psychologie C. G. Jungs* (Olten-Freiburg, 1975). *C. G. Jung im Leben und Denken unserer Zeit* (on his hundredth birthday, with articles by C. A. Meier, W. Bernet, M. Fierz, H. Marti, and J. Rudin) (Olten-Freiburg, 1975). Hans Dieckmann and Eberhard Jung, "Weiterentwicklung der Analytischen (Komplexen) Psychologie," in *Die Psychologie des 20. Jahrhunderts*, vol. 3, pp. 853–912 (with refs.). Numerous further works, some with detailed bibliographies, in *Die Psychologie des 20. Jahrhunderts*, especially vols. 3 and 4.
4. The conference reports, originally published by Wilhelm Bitter and including complete texts of the lectures, cover such topics as Anxiety and Guilt (1952), The Problem of the Father (1954), The Transformation of the Person in the Ministry and Psychotherapy (1956), Rehabilitation versus Punishment (1957), Meditation in Religion and Psychotherapy (1958), Magic and Miracles in Medical Science (195), Good and Evil in Psychotherapy (1959), The Crisis and Future of Woman

(1962), Mass Hallucination in History and the Present (1965), Evolution, the Belief in Progress and the Hope of Salvation (1970), Life Crises (1971), the Practice of Dynamic Group Work (1972), etc.

5. *Zeitschrift für Analytische Psychologie*, vol. 7 (1976), no. 3, published a literature survey on Jung and theology, with 442 book titles on this subject area alone.
6. Letters 2, p. 630.
7. Paul Tillich et al., "Religiöser Symbolismus," in Tillich, *Gesammelte Werke*, vol. 5; Tillich, *Systematische Theologie I/III* (Stuttgart, 1956–). Gerhard Wehr, *Paul Tillich in Selbstzeugnissen und Bilddokumenten* (Reinbek, 1979).
8. Gerhard Wehr, *Stichwort Damaskus-Erlebnis: Der Weg zu Christus nach C. G. Jung* (Stuttgart, 1982); Wehr, *Wege zu religiöser Erfahrung: Analytische Psychologie im Dienste der Bibelauslegung* (Darmstadt and Olten-Freiburg, 1974); Maria Kassel, *Biblische Urbilder: Tiefenpsychologische Auslegung nach C. G. Jung* (Munich, 1980); Eugen Drewermann, *Tiefenpsychologie und Exegese*, vol. 1 (Olten-Freiburg, 1984).
9. "Gegenwart und Zukunft" (1957), GW X, 287.
10. GW X, 308.

INDEX OF NAMES

Abraham, Karl, 104, 109, 112, 114, 129, 138, 149, 152, 155–158, 317
Adler, Alfred, 28, 98, 114, 129–131, 137–138, 146–147, 156, 160, 165, 199–201, 422
Adler, Gerhard, 91, 310, 312, 363, 456–457
Adonis, 453–454
Allenby, A. Inge, 363
Allers, Rudolf, 314
Anderes, Ernst, 357
Andreae, J. V., 25
Andreas-Salomé, Lou, 104, 138, 156–157, 160
Angulo, Jaime de, 228
Antoninus Pius, 194
Aquinas, Thomas, 337
Arbraxas, Abrasax, 195
Archimides, 216
Aristotle, 207
Arnaldus de Villanova, 377–378
Aschaffenburg, Gustav, 101–103
Assagioli, Roberto G., 111, 155
Attenhofer, Elsie, 442
Augustine, Saint, 268, 358
Augustinus, 211, 229
Aurobindo Ghose, Sri, 283–284

Baal Shem Tov, 422
Bach, J. S., 382
Bochofen, Johann Jakob, 55, 443
Baeck, Leo, 325–326
Bailey, Ruth, 237–244, 420–428, 443, 448, 452–458
Bakunin, Mikhail Alexandrovich, 263
Bally, Gustav, 315
Barth, Karl, 384
Basilides, 194–195
Baudouin, Charles, 418
Baynes, Helton Godwin (Peter), 218, 234–244, 333
Beckwith, George, 234–244
Beit, Hedwig von, 354
Bennett, E. A., 160, 327, 420

Ber, Maggid of Mezeritch, 421–422
Bergson, Henri, 160
Bernet, Walter, 49
Bernoulli, Rudolf, 267
Bernus, Alexander von, 246
Bertine, Eleanor, 218, 359–360, 371
Besant, Annie, 460
Bettelheim, Bruno, 143
Bezzola, Dumeng, 155
Biano, Ochwiay (Antonio Mirabal, Mountain Lake), 229–232
Biedermann, Aloys Emanuel, 60
Binet, Alfred, 83, 116, 156
Binswanger, Kurt, 355
Binswanger, Ludwig, 99, 104–105, 112, 146
Bitter, Wilhelm, 490
Bjerre, Poul, 138, 155–156
Black, Stephen, 418, 422
Blavatsky, Helena Petrovna, 162, 460
Bleuler, Eugen, 5, 74–75, 78–85, 92, 98–99, 104, 112–115, 137, 158, 436
Bleuler, Manfred, 81
Bloch, Ernst, 5, 352, 383, 410
Böhme, Jakob, 247, 258, 301, 372
Bonhoeffer, Dietrich, 341
Boss, Medard, 418, 474
Breuer, Josef, 82, 97
Brill, Abraham A., 112, 116, 127
Brody, Daniel, 481
Brome, Vincent, 479
Brüel, Oluf, 314
Brunner, Cornelia, 442
Brunton, Paul, 279
Buber, Martin, 216, 263, 267–268, 324, 383, 436, 471–474
Buchner, Ludwig, 119
Bultmann, Rudolf, 297, 393
Buonaiuti, Ernesto, 264
Burckhardt, Jakob, 55, 58, 128

Calvin, John, 44–47
Cammerloher, Moritz Carl von, 267
Carus, Carl Gustav, 61
Chamberlain, Neville, 323, 334
Charcot, Jean-Marie, 82
Charlemagne, 229–230
Churchill, Mary, 357
Churchill, Winston, 357
Cimbal, Walter, 314
Clement of Rome, 386–387

Columbus, 230
Corbin, Henry, 273, 276, 382
Cornelssen, Lucy, 279
Cortez, 230
Creuzer, Friedrich, 120, 128
Crichton-Miller, Hugh, 331
Crookes, William, 62

Daladier, Edouard, 323
Darwin, Charles, 119
Daur, Rudi, 328–329
Deuticke, Franz, 134, 158
Dieckmann, Hans, 489
Diederichs, Eugen, 428
Dieterich, Albrecht, 132
Dionysius the Areopagite, 268
Doresse, Jean, 366
Dorn(cus), Gerhard, 259, 280, 336, 404
Dürckheim, Count Karlfried, 467–468, 488
Dulles, Allen Welsh, 344
Duplain, Georges, 418, 437, 439
Duttweiler, Gottfried, 332

Eckermann, J. P., 1
Eckhart, Meister, 360, 484, 486
Eid, Albert, 366
Eitingon, Max, 158, 304
Eliade, Mircea, 246–247, 273–274, 418
Elijah and Salome, 180–182, 188, 191
Ellenberger, Henry F., 76, 82, 489
Ellmann, Richard, 481
Empedocles, 207
Erasmus of Rotterdam, 93
Evans, Richard J., 7, 437–442

Federn, Paul, 98, 104
Ferenczi, Sandor, 104, 112, 117, 129, 137, 155
Fiechter, Ernst, 92–93, 224, 466
Fierz, Jürg, 362
Fierz-David, Linda, 363
Fischer, Samuel, 428
Flournoy, Théodore, 159, 353
Flüe, Niklaus von (Brother Klaus), 90, 301
Foges, Wolfgang, 444–445
Forel, Auguste Henri, 78
Frankl, Viktor, 474

Franz, Marie-Louise von, 5–6, 26–28, 94, 170, 249, 305–306, 335, 337, 342, 354, 363, 381, 397, 407, 423, 445, 453
Franz Ferdinand, Archduke, 166
Franz-Joseph, Emperor, 98
Freeman, John, 418, 440–445
Frei, Gebhard, 354, 356
Freud, Anna, 157
Freud, Sigmund, 4–5, 28, 50, 79, 82, 84, 91, 96–126, 127–160, 163–175, 199–205, 216, 223, 247, 305–306, 309, 317, 330, 353, 376, 399, 422–423, 435–436, 444, 475, 478, 486
Frey-Rohn, Liliane, 201, 335, 337, 355
Fröbe-Kapteyn, Olga, 262–277, 337, 352, 470
Frobenius, Leo, 177
Fromm, Erich, 474–475
Funk, Rainer, 475

Gandhi, Mohandas, 283–284
Gabsattel, Baron V. E. von, 474
Gebser, Jean, 460–461
Gerhardt, Kurt, 264
Gerster, Georg, 412, 441
Ghose, Sri Aurobindo, 283–284
Gilli, Gertraud, 7–8
Goethe, J. W. von, 1, 4, 14, 43–44, 62, 66, 133–134, 182–185, 191, 208–209, 253, 257, 293–294, 383, 397–399, 421, 477
Goethe, K. A. von, 14
Gogh, Vincent van, 482
Goldbrunner, Josef, 359
Göring, H. M., 311–315
Görres, Joseph, 62
Groddek, Georg, 104
Gross, Otto, 156, 177, 263
Grotjahn, Martin, 104
Guggenbühl, Eduard, 443

Haas, William S., 460
Haeckel, Ernst, 145
Haemmerli-Schindler, Theodor, 339
Hall, Stanley, 115–126
Hamann, Johann Georg, 383
Hamlin, Pied Piper of, 435
Handel, Georg Frederich, 382
Hannah, Barbara, 50, 188–190, 218, 221, 243–244, 294–295, 334–342, 348, 352, 356–359, 407–407, 420–423, 427, 443, 446, 454–456
Harding, Esther, 218, 332, 354, 360–363, 371
Hartmann, Eduard von, 107
Hartmann, Franz, 263

Hattinberg, J. von, 155
Hauer, Jakob Wilhelm, 267, 279, 318, 464
Hauffe, Friederike, 73
Hegel, G. F. W., 296
Heidegger, Martin, 324, 471
Heiler, Friedrich, 264
Heinemann, Gustav, 351
Henderson, Joseph L., 445
Heraclitus, 4, 202, 396
Hermes Trismegistos, 171, 277
Herodotus, 128
Herwig, J. H., 324
Herzl, Theodor, 17
Hesse, Hermann, 263, 274, 447, 478–479
Heydt, Baron von der, 273
Heyer, Gustav Richard, 8, 18, 264–265, 310, 312, 489
Hinkle, Beatrice M., 138
Hippocrates, 207, 339
Hippolytus of Rome, 195
His, Wilhelm, 15–16
Hislop, Francis Daniel, 237
Hitler, Adolph, 304–330, 331–335, 344, 350
Hoch, Dorothee, 50
Hoffmann, E.T.A., 361
Hölderlin, Friedrich, 181
Homer, 126, 174–177
Honegger, Johann Jakob, 128–129, 177
Hoop, J. H. van der, 353
Hull, R.F.C., 430
Humboldt, Alexander von, 15
Hu-shih, 461

Ignatius of Loyola, 34, 468
Ireneus of Lyon, 367
Irminger, H., 302

Jacob, 222
Jacobi, Jolande, 334, 337, 353–355, 363, 430–431, 445
Jaffé, Aniela, 2–3, 13–14, 91–92, 190, 215–217, 245, 272, 274, 301–302, 310, 317, 320, 324–326, 333–337, 355, 361, 371–372, 392, 407, 413–414, 417–418, 423, 430–431, 445
Jahan, Shah, 285
James, William, 116–126, 156, 201, 421
Janet, Pierre, 82–83, 92, 102, 116, 353
Jaspers, Karl, 5, 384
Jean Paul (Richter, J.P.E.). *See* Paul, Jean

Jesus Christ, 24–25, 47–48, 258, 287, 291, 307, 368–369, 384–392, 449, 465
Job, 381–395, 436
John (Gospel), 293, 424
Jones, Ernest, 112–126, 127, 135, 149, 155, 157
Jordan, Pascual, 255, 354
Joyce, James, 480–484
Joyce, Lucia, 480
Joyce, Nora, 481
Julius Caesar, 229
Jung, Agathe (daughter), 92, 123, 129, 192
Jung, Carl (ancestor), 13
Jung, Carl Gustav the Elder (grandfather), 12–17, 43, 55, 63, 70, 72, 78, 91, 425–426
Jung, Eberhard, 489
Jung, Emilie, née Preiswerk (mother), 9, 12, 18–21, 31–38, 44, 47, 51–52, 56–57, 64, 68–71, 77, 87, 225, 446–447, 457
Jung, Emma, née Rauschenbach (wife), 91–95, 109, 122–126, 129, 134–143, 149, 173, 188–190, 218–219, 225, 294, 334, 338, 349, 355–356, 364, 392, 407, 420–426, 457
Jung, Franz (son), 92, 129, 193, 332, 348
Jung, Franz Ignaz (great-grandfather), 13
Jung, Gret (daughter), 92, 129, 192–193
Jung, Helene (daughter), 93
Jung, Johann Paul Achilles (father), 9, 16–21, 31–38, 47–54, 56–58, 78, 293, 457
Jung, Johanna Gertrud (sister), 9, 57, 64, 68–71, 77, 349, 457
Jung, Marianne (daughter), 93, 132, 217–218, 349, 411
Jung, Paul (brother), 9
Jung, Sigismund von (great-grandfather's brother), 15
Jung, Sophie, née Frey (grandmother), 16, 19
Jung-Stilling, Heinrich, 62

Kahane, Max, 98
Kaiser, Joachim, 104
Kant, Immanuel, 61–62
Kästner, Erich, 351–352
Keller, Alwine von, 342–343
Kerényi, Karl, 276, 354, 356, 397–399
Kerner, Justinus, 62
Kestner, Lotte, 14
Keyserling, Count Hermann, 6, 232, 234, 325, 470
Khruschev, Nikita, 431
Kierkegaard, Sören, 383–384
Kipling, Rudyard, 461
Kippenberg, Anton, 428
Kirsch, James, 305

Klee, Paul, 483
Klingsor and Kundry, 181
Knickerbocker, H. R., 322–324, 334
Knoll, Max, 264, 414
Koestler, Arthur, 461
Kokoschka, Adolf, 483
Kraepelin, Emil, 78, 80, 131
Krafft-Ebing, Richard von, 65–67, 76, 98, 107
Krainefeld, W. M., 312
Kretschmer, Ernst, 207, 310, 434
Kuhn, Hans, 236–237, 335

Laban, Rudolf von, 263
Lang, Josef B., 478
Lao-tse, 181, 215, 266
Lasky, Melvin J., 435, 466
Layard, John, 276, 352
Leeuw, Gerardus van der, 276
Leisegang, Hans, 276
Leonardo da Vinci, 132
Lewisohn-Crowley, Alice, 335
Lilje, Hanns, 351
Lindbergh, Charles A. and Anne, 414
Liszt, Franz, 14
Loy, R., 201
Luther, Martin, 60, 211, 383

McCormick, Edith Rockefeller, 228, 480
McCormick, Fowler, 227–228, 234, 279, 428, 443
McCormick, Harold, 129, 228
Maeder, Alphonse, 78–79, 99, 129, 158–159, 169, 200, 311
Mann, Kristine, 343
Mann, Thomas, 309
Mann, Ulrich, 298
Massignon, Louis, 276, 352
May, Ulrike, 115
Meier, Carl A., 278, 331, 354–355, 363–364, 367–368, 489
Mellon, Mary and Paul, 428
Merlin, 378–379
Mesmer, Franz Anton, 62
Mina, Togo, 366
Mirabal, Antonio. *See* Biano, Ochwiay
Mitras, 131–132
Mitscherlich, Alexander, 160
Moravia, Alberto, 371, 418
Mühsam, Erich, 263
Müller, Friedrich von, 64, 66

Mussolini, Benito, 323, 332

Nagy, Imre, 431–321
Neumann, Erich, 274–277, 303, 310, 354, 361–363, 393–394, 424, 433, 464
Niehus, Walther (son-in-law), 411, 430
Niemöller, Martin, 351
Nietzsche, Friedrich, 28–29, 55–56, 64, 72–73, 138, 156, 174, 178, 201, 211, 296, 321–322, 355
Novalis, 446

Oberlin, Friedrich, 62
Oeri, Albert, 17, 29, 41, 58–60, 74, 174, 273
Olcott, Henry Steel, 162
Ophuijsen, J.H.W. van, 149
Origines, 211
Osborne, Arthur, 279
Osiris, 28, 240, 453
Ostrowski-Sachs, Margret, 274–275
Otto, Rudolf, 262, 295–296
Ovid, 183
Owens, Claire Myers, 418

Page, George H., 368
Paquet, Alfons, 328
Paracelsus, 55, 336–337, 399
Passavant, Johann Carl, 62
Paul of Damascus, 301, 366, 457
Paul, Jean, 37, 296
Pauli, Wolfgang, 255–256, 354, 356, 363
Pelagius, 211
Peterson, Frederick W., 112
Pfister, Oskar, 104, 129
Philemon and Baucis, 182–185, 188, 191, 194, 197
Piaget, Jean, 141
Picasso, Pablo, 482–484
Piper, Reinhard, 428
Pius XII, 373, 382
Plato, 13, 51, 344–345, 410–411, 439–440
Pompey, 229
Porkert, Manfred, 264
Porter, George, 228
Portmann, Adolf, 264, 276–277
Post, Laurens van der, 227, 241–242, 323–324, 394, 423, 455
Preiswerk, Celestine (aunt), 71
Preiswerk, Emilie. *See* Jung, Emilie
Preiswerk, Helene (cousin), 70–75, 83

Preiswerk, Rudolf (uncle), 71
Preiswerk, Samuel (maternal grandfather), 17–19, 70–72, 161
Prel, Carl du, 62
Preistley, J. B., 479–480
Puech, Henri-Charles, 368
Putnam, James Jackson, 104, 116–126, 127, 137, 150, 160

Quispel, Gilles, 276, 366–368

Radin, Paul, 276
Rahner, Hugo, 276
Raliner, Hugo, 352
Ramana Maharshi, 279, 289
Rank, Otto, 104, 137
Rascher, Albert and Max, 425, 489
Rauschenbach, Emma. *See* Jung, Emma
Rauschenbach-Schenk, Bertha (mother-in-law), 90–91
Read, Herbert, 483–485
Reich, Wilhelm, 104, 306
Reik, Theodor, 91, 104
Reitler, Rudolf, 98
Reuss, Theodor, 263
Reventlow, Countess Franziska von, 263
Rhine, J. B., 354
Richards, Ceri, 476–477
Ricksher, Charles, 112
Riklin, Franz, 84, 98–99, 149, 155, 169
Rilke, Rainer Maria, 138, 157, 161
Ritschl, Albrecht, 60
Rockefeller, John D., 228
Rohde, Erwin, 128
Rorschach, Hermann, 207
Rosenberg, Alfons, 262, 265, 275
Rosenberg, Alfred, 318
Rosenthal, Hugo, 312
Rouselle, Erwin, 264, 279
Rowohlt, Ernst, 428
Rudin, Josef, 436–437

Sachs, Hanns, 155
Sadger, Isidore, 114
Saint-Martin, Louis-Claude de, 62
Sand, Karl Ludwig, 15
Sands, Frederick, 418
Sanford, John A., 490
Sartre, Jean-Paul, 471
Sborowitz, Arie, 472

Schabad, Michael, 421
Schär, Hans, 299–300, 354, 359, 363, 393
Schärf, Riwka, 337
Schiller, Friedrich von, 156, 211
Schleiermacher, Friedrich Daniel Ernst, 15
Schmaltz, Gustav, 433–434
Schmid, Hans, 349
Schmid, Marie-Jeanne, 349
Schmidt, Karl Ludwig, 276
Scholem, Gershom, 325–326
Schopenhauer, Arthur, 61, 73, 107
Schrödinger, Erwin, 264
Schultz, J. H., 6
Scipio Africanus, 229
Seif, Leonhard, 149
Serrano, Miguel, 231–232, 447–450, 453
Servier, Jean, 264
Siegfried, 179–181
Sigg, Hermann, 218, 220, 234
Silberer, Herbert, 247–248
Simon bar Yochai, 253, 341, 447
Simon Magus of Samaria, 181
Sinclair, Upton, 392
Speiser, Andreas, 276, 301, 352
Spielrein, Sabina, 94–95, 138–143, 180, 186
Spinoza, Baruch, 471
Spitteler, Carl, 209
Stahel, Jakob, 359
Stählin, Wilhelm, 328
Steiner, Gustav, 2, 14, 74
Steiner, Rudolf, 460–461, 465–466
Stekel Wilhelm, 98, 114, 128–131
Stern, Paul J., 187, 474
Strauss-Kloebe, Sigrid, 267
Stuckelberger, Dr., 43
Susman, Margarete, 168, 384, 386
Suzuki, D. T., 468
Swedenborg, Emanuel, 62

Teilhard de Chardin, Pierre, 449
Tenzler, Johannes, 35–36, 385
Tertullian, 211
Tillich, Paul, 490–491
Trüb, Hans, 436, 472

Uhsadel, Walter, 392

Valentinus (Gnostic), 367
Vanggaard, Thorkil, 28–29
Veltheim-Ostrau, Hans-Hesso von, 279
Visser't Hooft, Willem A., 459

Weil, Simone, 485
Weiss, Edoardo, 104
Weizsäcker, Adolf, 320
Weizsäcker, Viktor von, 5
Wells, H. G., 479
Weygandt, Wilhelm, 100
White, Victor, 275, 350, 354–359, 368, 394–395, 456
Wickes, Frances G., 243, 354
Wilhelm, Richard, 198, 234, 255–256, 328, 353, 462–464
Wili, Walter, 352
Wille, Ludwig, 65
Witcutt, W. P., 354
Wolff, Kurt, 2, 414, 428–430
Wolff, Toni (Antonia), 94–95, 138–143, 187–190, 218, 265–266, 327, 334, 354, 406–407, 423–434, 450
Woodroffe, Sir John (Arthur Avalon), 278–279
Wotan, 321–323, 409, 413

Young, Gordon, 418, 441

Zacharias, Gerhard P., 364
Ziegler, Sophie, 13
Zimmer, Heinrich, 198, 264, 279, 286, 289, 328, 353, 428, 468
Zöllner, Johann K., 62
Zosimus of Pnoplis, 258, 294
Zumstein-Preiswerk, Stephanie, 73
Zwingli, Huldreich, 211

SOURCES OF ILLUSTRATIONS

From *Errinerungen, Träume, Gedanken (Memories, Dreams, Reflections)*, ed. Aniela Jaffé (Olten-Freiburg im Breisgau: Walter, 1984): pages 32 (top), 33 (top), 429.

From *C. G. Jung—Bild und Wort: Eine Biographie* (Olten-Freiburg im Breisgau: Walter, 1983): pages 32 (bottom), 33 (bottom), 88, 89, 136, 151, 251, 270, 271, 374 (top), 375, 403, 419, 451.

Foto Mönsted, Zurich: frontispiece.

Verkehrsverein Basel: page 46.

Foto Lothar Nahler, Hillesheim: page 176.

Collection of E. Edinger, Los Angeles: pages 250, 282.

Collection of G. Wehr, Schwarzenbruck: page 457.